Algeria & France

1800–2000

Modern Intellectual and Political History of the Middle East
Mehrzad Boroujerdi, *Series Editor*

OTHER TITLES IN MODERN INTELLECTUAL AND POLITICAL HISTORY OF THE MIDDLE EAST

Britain and the Iranian Constitutional Revolution of 1906–1911: Foreign Policy, Imperialism, and Dissent
MANSOUR BONAKDARIAN

Class and Labor in Iran: Did the Revolution Matter?
FARHAD NOMANI and SOHRAB BEHDAD

Corporatist Ideology in Kemalist Turkey: Progress or Order?
TAHA PARLA and ANDREW DAVISON

Cultural Schizophrenia: Islamic Societies Confronting the West
DARYUSH SHAYEGAN; JOHN HOWE, trans.

Factional Politics in Post-Khomeini Iran
MEHDI MOSLEM

Freedom, Modernity, and Islam: Toward a Creative Synthesis
RICHARD K. KHURI

The Genesis of Young Ottoman Thought: A Study in the Modernization of Turkish Political Ideas
ŞERIF MARDIN

Globalization and the Muslim World: Culture, Religion, and Modernity
BRIGIT SCHAEBLER and LEIF STENBERG, eds.

God and Juggernaut: Iran's Intellectual Encounter with Modernity
FARZIN VAHDAT

In the Path of Hizbullah
AHMAD NIZAR HAMZEH

Iranian Intellectuals and the West: The Tormented Triumph of Nativism
MEHRZAD BOROUJERDI

The Kurds and the State: Evolving National Identity in Iraq, Turkey, and Iran
DENISE NATALI

Mohammad Mosaddeq and the 1953 Coup in Iran
MARK J. GASIOROWSKI and MALCOLM BYRNE, eds.

Mysticism and Dissent: Socioreligious Thought in Qajar Iran
MANGOL BAYAT

Religion, Society, and Modernity in Turkey
ŞERIF MARDIN

The Story of the Daughters of Quchan: Gender and National Memory in Iranian History
AFSANEH NAJMABADI

Algeria & France

1800–2000

Identity • Memory • Nostalgia

Edited by
PATRICIA M. E. LORCIN

Syracuse University Press

First Edition 2006

06 07 08 09 10 11 6 5 4 3 2 1

Cartoon in chapter 11: from *Le Monde,* 31 Aug. 2001.
Reprinted with permission of Pancho.

The paper used in this publication meets the minimum requirements of American National Standard for Information Sciences—Permanence of Paper for Printed Library Materials, ANSI Z39.48–1984.∞™

Library of Congress Cataloging-in-Publication Data

Algeria and France, 1800–2000 : identity, memory,
nostalgia / edited by Patricia M. E. Lorcin.—1st ed.
p. cm.—(Modern intellectual and political history of the Middle East)
Includes bibliographical references and index.
ISBN 0-8156-3074-3 (cloth : alk. paper)
1. Algeria—History—1830–1962—Historiography.
2. Algeria—History—Revolution, 1954–1962—Atrocities.
3. French—Colonization—Algeria. 4. French—Algeria—Attitudes.
5. France—Relations—Algeria. 6. Algeria—Relations—France.
I. Lorcin, Patricia M. E. II. Series.
DT294.A238 2006
965'.03—dc22 2006014518

Manufactured in the United States of America

To the victims of the Algerian War

(1954–1962)

Contents

Some Thoughts by Way of a Preface

HENRI ALLEG

A CONSTELLATION OF RESEARCHERS of high quality—historians, sociologists, literary scholars—focusing their attention on a country that is thousands of kilometers away symbolizes, in my view as an optimist, a future world where communication and international relations will, first and foremost, serve the progress of knowledge and bring together people and nations for the common good. No one will complain of this positive, if rather rare, aspect of "globalization."

It is not the least of Patricia Lorcin's merits to have encouraged such a fruitful encounter on the theme of Algeria—an encounter that elucidates certain hitherto unpublished aspects of a past, long deformed and obscured by colonial historiography, and that sheds new light on questions of language, identity, culture, and the complex, but not always confrontational, relationships between Algeria and France.

Because of the colonial situation, until independence, few Algerians were in a position to tackle these issues. For fear of judicial proceedings or serious sanctions, those who risked doing so always had to ensure that their work conformed to the law and did not cast aspersions on the sacrosanct principle of "French sovereignty." On the French side, with certain brilliant exceptions, few authors dared to challenge the colonial dogma that the majority, for reasons of conviction or personal interest, defended as manifest truths. Government officials in Paris at the time, whether they were of the Right or the Left—and in spite of noble declarations concerning the indefeasible rights of freedom of thought and speech—doggedly persisted in keeping under wraps any ideas they considered to be subversive. Permanent repression, direct or indirect, against all challengers; amnesty laws that forbade the denunciation of those responsible for massacres or torture; hypocritical or overt censorship; sealed archives: these were the customary measures used by the authorities, and they remained in use well after the declaration of Algerian independence.

In March 1962, the Evian Accords put an end to the hostilities, but nearly forty years passed before France recognized the fact that it was a war they had fought and not, as they had obstinately persisted in pretending, a simple military intervention "to maintain order" in part of "their" territory. The war was a tragedy that ruined the lives of 2 million young men, who were catapulted into the *djebel* in French uniform, 25,000 of whom never returned and 350,000 of whom still suffer serious psychological problems. It caused the death of hundreds of thousands of Algerians, the annihilation of thousands of villages, and the systematic use of torture and rape. It provoked political upheavals, which brought France to the brink of civil war. And all this was reduced by official historiography to the consequences of a commonplace "policing operation"!

That stage of thinking is over, as is also, no doubt, the period when military officers and "specialists" of colonial Algeria, recounting "their" war, could calmly and insolently reject everything that diminished or contradicted the comforting legend of humane and benevolent "pacification." But carving out the path of truth is still difficult, as was seen in June 2000, when an Algerian woman published her testimony and denunciation of the torture and rape she had undergone as a prisoner of General Jacques Massu's parachutists half a century earlier; and again in November 2001, when General Paul Aussaresses, deputy to Massu during the "battle of Algiers," appeared in a Parisian court and was prosecuted not for torture and summary executions, of which he was by his own admission guilty, but for the scandalous "apology" he made for his behavior in his books on his service (2001a, 2001b). These two events, which the introduction to this edited volume rightly brings to mind, were a great shock to French public opinion, especially among the young, who have been kept in quasi-total ignorance of the war. Conscious of the approaching presidential elections at the time, Jacques Chirac, the French president, and Lionel Jospin, prime minister, were especially sensitive to the emotions raised by these events and hence intervened publicly. It was not, however, to congratulate themselves for the fact that the truth had at last been articulated and recognized, but to calm the unrest and as quickly as possible to close a case that had been so unfortunately opened and was so politically embarrassing. The mistake—for part of the civilian and military hierarchy at least—was not that these crimes had been committed, but that they had been divulged.

Little by little, "official" France was compelled to admit that the flag it unfurled was not always one of "freedom of the people" and the Rights of Man. Nonetheless, those nostalgic for the false glories of the past still took up the stale arguments of the devotees of a colonial domination that had bestowed "light, progress, and civilization." It was in this vein that shortly after the condemnation of Aussaresses (by a mere fine!), some three hundred generals and superior officers, veterans of the Algerian War, gathered together their memories and their conclusions in a collected volume, entitled *Le livre blanc de l'armée française en Algérie* (2001) in which they justified the torture and assassinations committed under their orders, as well as the methods they had been "obliged" to use against the "rebels" and their accomplices.

This publication is, no doubt, the rearguard action of men who are still embittered by the burning memories of colonial wars they fought and lost and who, rather like the émigré aristocrats returning after the French Revolution, have neither forgotten nor learned anything from their experiences. Their attitude is not unique, but it is not that of the majority either. Even if many French men and women still have difficulty admitting that the behavior of some of their compatriots in Algeria can be compared to that of the Nazis during the occupation, most of them, according to recent polls, believe that going to war to preserve *l'Algérie française* was a major blunder that could have been avoided if the government at the time had had the courage to accept the Algerian people's desire for independence.

As for the *pieds-noirs,* the French settlers, repatriated from Algeria, who in the aftermath of the exodus harbored a virulent resentment against an Algeria that had thrown them out and against a France that had "abandoned" them, they are now far more discreet. Only a minority, under the influence of the chauvinistic and quasi-fascist extreme Right, continues to keep the current of anti-Arab racism alive for its electoral profitability, most especially in times of economic crisis that always favor the emergence of breakaway chauvinists, racists, and xenophobes.

But it is not the general trend of French public opinion—far from it. Young people in particular proved this after the first round of the 2000 presidential elections by coming out massively, and for many in a totally unaccustomed manner, against the presidential bid of Jean-Marie Le Pen, who has often been accused of being a fascist and a racist and who has tried to exploit the legacy of odious colonial prejudices. Encounters with young people of different backgrounds in schools, universities, workplaces, and homes encourage a deeper comprehension of the situation. These young people, all of whom cannot envisage any other future but a French one, include the *beurs,* children and grandchildren of immigrant workers, and the *harkis,* Algerian auxiliaries in the French army. Then, too, there are the children and grandchildren of the *pieds-noirs,* often nostalgic for an Algeria they know only thanks to their parents' reminiscences, but that nonetheless forms part of their identity. The books and television films, written and produced by French and Algerian men and women, dealing with the Algerian past, the Algerian War, the behavior of the French army, the attitudes of judges and magistrates during the war also bear witness that in spite of ever-present obstacles, it is still possible to deal serenely with a common history that has for so long been taboo and whose embers still burn.

In a parallel development, the majority of Algerians today, although proud of their independence and the fierce struggle needed to achieve it, no longer see in France—as was so often the case during the war years—the irreducible and implacable enemy, still as determined as it was during the early years of conquest to deny Algerian existence and rights. As odd as it may seem, the French who returned to Algeria after the war to visit the places where they had been billeted as soldiers, declared almost unanimously that during their stay they had been welcomed everywhere with surprising and extraordinary warmth. It was as if their hosts were ignorant of the atrocities the war had wrought on them—although this was certainly not the case because there was not a single Algerian family that did not pay heavily in regaining the nation's freedom.

The Algerians' open-minded behavior is not the result of a calculated desire to show their visitors that they hope to "turn the page." Its origins are older and deeper. For the most part, it stems from the fact that before and during the war—even when Algerians spoke of the oppressing country as though it were one hostile entity—millions of them were also aware that France was not just a country of exploiters and torturers, but also of people who understood their aspirations and who, some among them at least, even concretely demonstrated this understanding by active solidarity. As a country of writers, philosophers, revolutionaries, political parties, and organizations, France had influenced their own thought and provided some of the ideological and political tools for their struggle for independence. The ambivalent love/hate relationship, discussed from a variety of approaches in the rich contributions to this volume, still exists in the way Algerians view France and their past and present relations with it.

Seventy percent of today's Algerian population is younger than thirty years old. In other words, nearly three-quarters of the population never knew the colonial period and know little about it because neither their parents nor their schools have been able to help them understand the extent of the misery, suffering, and humiliation imposed on their people for more than a century. This ignorance and lack of memory explain in part the scepticism, tinged with bitter irony, with which young Algerians respond to the accounts and commentaries of their elders, who contrast the long and lugubrious "colonial night" with the luminous hope promised but never delivered by independence, thus sorely disappointing them. The young people's condemnation of the men who govern their country is ferocious. The anguish of their present situation does nothing to encourage songs of Hosanna in celebration of a historic victory, whose achievements many delight in denigrating, even though in certain areas, such as education, the progress made in the early years after independence was spectacular.

Algeria has provided education for 80 percent of its children, whereas in the colonial period only 10 percent had places in schools, and those spots were nearly all for boys. In less than twenty years, the number of lycées increased by 100 percent. Algeria today has thirty universities, whereas it had only one in 1962, the last year of the "French presence." Since this date, the number of students has risen from 1,300 to 300,000, and, remarkably, young women constitute 56 percent of the total student body of secondary and higher education. Today, however, the Algerian population, which has tripled in forty years (from 9 million souls in 1962 to 27 million in 2000) without a parallel development of the national infrastructure, focuses on the negative side of things. The unemployment rate is at 30 percent, and more than one thousand companies have gone out of business. The economic situation does not provide much scope for the young, who only see a solution in a hypothetical and hazardous immigration to potential host countries, whose doors are increasingly slamming shut in their faces. An old Algerian sadly told me recently, "If foreign embassies would issue visas and there were enough boats, our country would soon be empty of its youth."

For more than a quarter of a century now, those in power in Algeria have long replied with indifference and repression to this desperate situation, so anger explodes in the streets in often uncontrollable demonstrations. Whatever the reasons given for the discontent—whether poverty and unemployment, the need for improved wages, the desire for a democratic government, corruption and unfair promotion, demands for respect of Berber identity, the suppression or reduction of social rights introduced after independence, the dictates of international economic organization, or a foreign policy focused more clearly on imperialism in its diverse forms—the root cause of their demands does not change. It is the same bitterness and the same revolt in the face of arrogant behavior on the part of those in power. It is the intolerable disdain (the word used by the Arabs, *hogra,* is much stronger) with which the people believe they are regarded by politicians who fail to listen to their grievances and by the regime's parvenus and new millionaires, whose extravagant lifestyle is so insulting. In these elements, the groundwork was thus laid for the emergence and development, under pressure from fanatical elements—not all originating in Algeria—of highly irrational and retrograde ideas. How could a country so rich in human resources find itself in such a situation? How could Algeria, a country with a tradition of tolerance, sink into a nightmare of bloody fundamentalist terror with tens of thousands of victims?

To be sure, the history of the country did not start with its proclamation of independence. In order to understand present-day Algeria and its problem, it is essential to keep alive the memory of what has gone before and to delve further into a past that has remained obscured for so long. It is to this end that the remarkable essays presented in this volume contribute. The reductionist responses of certain observers and political analysts are clearly only the bitter but inevitable sequel to the colonial heritage and the period that preceded it.

In postcolonial Algeria, where social structures have been profoundly modified and continue to be so, the uppermost questions are inevitably different from those of the past, although issues of identity, language, and the place and role of religion remain major preoccupations. Until independence, the main contradiction was one that opposed the colonial power to the crushing majority of the colonized peoples. In an era of "globalization," Algerian men—and increasingly Algerian women, who are regularly making their demands felt for full equal rights—must face other problems, other adversaries, and other challenges, essentially the ones that confront the majority of peoples still living in a state of underdevelopment and poverty. Freed from the yoke of foreign domination, they are free neither from its continued pressure on economic, political, and military levels, nor from the pressure applied by the parasitic strata of their compatriots who enrich themselves by serving as go-betweens.

These newly appeared cleavages are slowly carving out a class-ridden society, the behavior and interest of whose members are varied and contradictory. In the short term, they will obviously lead to social movements, political factions, and crises, whose future power structures cannot yet be distinguished, but they will also certainly open a new chapter in the history of Algeria.

Translated by Patricia M. E. Lorcin

Contributors

Henri Alleg is a writer and journalist. In 1958, he published *La question,* describing his experiences of being tortured by the French paratroopers in Algeria. His book, which was quickly banned in France, brought the issue of torture during the war out into the open and contributed to the backlash that developed in France as the war wore on. He has written books on the United States, the former Soviet Union, and China, as well as numerous articles on human rights and allied issues.

Julia Clancy-Smith is an associate professor of history at the University of Arizona, Tucson. She is the author of *Rebel and Saint: Muslim Notables, Populist Protest, Colonial Encounters (Algeria and Tunisia, 1800–1904);* coeditor of *Domesticating the Empire: Race, Gender, and Family Life in French and Dutch Colonialism;* and editor of *North Africa, Islam, and the Mediterranean World from the Almoravids to the Algerian War,* simultaneously published as a special issue of the *Journal of North African Studies.* She has coedited a special issue on colonial history for *French Historical Studies* and is working on two book-length studies: one devoted to trans-Mediterranean migration to nineteenth-century North Africa, the other to education for Muslim girls in colonial Tunisia and Algeria.

William B. Cohen was a professor of history at Indiana University, where he taught from 1967 until his tragic death in 2002. He was the author of several works, among them *Rulers of Empire, The French Encounter with Africans,* and *Urban Government and the Rise of the French City.* At the time of his death, he was working on a book about the Algerian War and French memory.

Joshua Cole is an associate professor of history at the University of Michigan. He is the author of *The Power of Large Numbers: Population, Politics, and Gender in Nineteenth-Century France.* He is currently writing a book on the legacy of colonial violence in France, Algeria, and Madagascar.

Habiba Deming is an associate professor of French and international studies at William Woods University, Fulton, Missouri. She has written on aspects of feminism and the neocolonial discourse in the Maghrebian novel. At present a visiting scholar at Emory University Law School, she is working on a book about the Algerian intellectual crisis between Islam and secularism.

Richard L. Derderian is an assistant professor in the Department of History at California Lutheran University. His research focuses on ethnic minority cultural expression, memory, and national identity in contemporary France. He is the author of *North Africans in Contemporary France: Becoming Visible* and is currently researching the Vietnamese community in France. He has also published articles in *Contemporary French Civilization, Hommes and Migrations, Asia Europe Journal, Radical History Review,* and *Perpetuating Cities.*

Philip Dine is a college lecturer in French in the Department of French, National University of Ireland, Galway. He is the author of *Images of the Algerian War: French Fiction and Film, 1954–1992* and *French Rugby Football: A Cultural History.* His numerous articles on representations of the French colonial empire cover topics such as decolonization, sport, leisure, and popular culture in France. He is currently working on a history of French colonial sport.

Peter Dunwoodie is a reader in French literature in the Department of English and Comparative Literature, Goldsmiths, University of London. He has published extensively on the twentieth-century novel (in France and the Caribbean) and on preindependence Algerian writing in French. His books include *Une histoire ambivalente: Le dialogue Camus-Dostoïevski, Writing French Algeria,* and, coedited with E. J. Hughes, *Constructing Memories: Camus, Algeria, and le Premier Homme.* He is currently working on a book on francophone Muslim Algerian writers of the interwar period.

Yaël Simpson Fletcher is an independent scholar. Her work explores questions of immigration, race, and national identity in twentieth-century France. She has contributed chapters to four edited books: *Domesticating the Empire: Race, Gender, and Family Life in French and Dutch Colonialism, 1830–1962; Imperial Cities: Landscape, Display, and Identity; Gender, Sexuality, and Colonial Modernities;* and *The Color of Liberty: Histories of Race in France.*

Seth Graebner is an assistant professor of French and of international and area studies at Washington University in St. Louis. His work concentrates on the literature and cultural history of modern France and its former colonies. He is the recipient of a 2001–2002 American Council of Learned Societies Fellowship in International Studies for research at the Library of Congress on his current project about modernity in Paris and the Mediterranean city from 1830 to 1900.

Alec G. Hargreaves is the Ada Belle Winthrop-King Professor of French and the director of the Winthrop-King Institute for Contemporary French and Francophone Studies at Florida State University. A specialist on postcolonial minorities in France, he is the author of numerous publications, including *Voices from the North African Immigrant Community in France: Immigration and Identity in Beur Fiction; Immigration, "Race," and Ethnicity in Contemporary France; Racism, Ethnicity, and Politics in Contemporary Europe,* coedited with Jeremy Leaman; and *Post-colonial Cultures in France,* coedited with Mark McKinney.

Lynne Huffer is professor of women studies at Emory University. She is the author of *Another Colette: The Question of Gendered Writing* and *Maternal Pasts, Feminist Futures: Nostalgia, Ethics, and the Question of Difference.* She also edited a special issue of *Yale French Studies* titled *Another Look, Another Woman: Retranslations of French Feminism.* She is currently working on a project about ethical encounters in literature, ethics, and politics.

Patricia M. E. Lorcin is an associate professor of French history in the global context at the University of Minnesota, Twin Cities. Her publications are on colonial Algeria and include the book *Imperial Identities: Stereotyping Race and Prejudice in Colonial Algeria,* chapters to various edited books, and articles in a number of different journals, such as *Isis, French Historical Studies,* and *Culture, Theory, and Critique.* She is at present working on a book on literary women and empire and is coediting a special issue of *French Historical Studies* on France and Islam.

Jo McCormack is a lecturer in French studies at the University of Technology, Sydney, Australia. His research examines the collective memory of the Algerian War in contemporary France. His articles on the legacy in France of the torture during the Algerian War have appeared in *Modern and Contemporary France* and in the edited volume *Memory and Memorials: The Commemorative Century.* He is currently working on a project concerning social activism and collective memory in France.

David Prochaska is a professor of history at the University of Illinois, Urbana-Champaign, where he specializes in colonial history and postcolonial studies. He is the author of *Making Algeria French: Colonialism in Bône, 1870–1920,* a study of French settler colonialism and colonial urbanism based on local Algerian archives. He has published numerous articles on colonial Algeria and colonial photography.

Mireille Rosello is a professor of comparative literature at the Universiteit van Amsterdam and professor of French and comparative literature at Northwestern University. Her main research and teaching interests are postcolonial literatures, cultures, and theories (especially from the Caribbean and the Maghreb); gender constructions; and visual narratives. Her latest books are *Infiltrating Culture: Power and Identity in Contemporary Women's Writing; Declining the Stereotype: Representation and Ethnicity in French Cultures;* and *Postcolonial Hospitality: The Immigrant as Guest.* She is currently exploring the representation of moments of "felicitous encounters" between France and the Maghreb.

Joshua S. Schreier recently completed his doctoral work at New York University. He taught at Colby College and is now an assistant professor at Vassar College.

Todd Shepard is an assistant professor of history at Temple University. He is the author of *The Invention of Decolonization: The End of French Algeria and the Remaking of France.*

Victoria Thompson is an associate professor of history at Arizona State University. She is the author of *The Virtuous Marketplace: Women and Men, Money and Politics in Paris (1830–1870).* Her chapter in this volume is part of a new project on travel and identity in the nineteenth century.

Introduction

PATRICIA M. E. LORCIN

> The struggle of man against power is the struggle of memory against forgetting.
> —Milan Kundera, *The Book of Laughter and Forgetting*

WHEN MILAN KUNDERA'S "NOVEL" *The Book of Laughter and Forgetting* was published in 1980, the concepts of identity, memory, and nostalgia were only just beginning to emerge as important fields of study in their own right. The book was a harbinger of the interest that soon would be focused on these concepts, producing separate theories for each, yet Kundera reminds us that they are in fact intertwined. As an exile from his native land, Kundera reflects on the way in which personal memory and official memory deviate and how memory can be expunged to create new identities. These themes are central to this volume and provide new insights into Franco-Algerian relations.

Since the publication in 1993 of the first work on Franco-Algerian identities (Hargreaves and Heffernan 1993), interest in the subject has grown steadily. Colonial history, from being peripheral to the history of France, has now moved to the forefront and with it Algeria's importance to French politics, culture, and society. No colony was more important to the process of identity formation in modern France than Algeria. Five million Muslims reside in France today, and most come from North Africa. The question of inclusion and exclusion, so essential to identity politics, is therefore a constant as much in the political setting as in the social or cultural setting. Discourses of inclusion often parallel exclusionary practices, mimicking the practices of colonialism. Although scholarly interest in Franco-Algerian relations is largely focused on national concerns, the work of scholars such as Robert Malley (1996) and Matthew Connally (2002) demonstrates that events in Algeria, as it emerged from the period of French colonization, had global significance. It would therefore seem appropriate to reconsider the question of French and Algerian identities in the light of this growing interest and the emergence of new scholarship.

In the introduction to the 1993 volume, Jean-Robert Henry drew attention to the way in which the Franco-Algerian relationship has shaped the multicultural paradigm and the impact France has had on the Algerian political debate, but was less forthcoming on an Algerian contribution to France's cultural self-image. "Algeria," he declared, "generally plays a less prominent role in the construction of a French sense of cultural identity" (Hargreaves and Heffernan 1993, 7). As the essays in this volume demonstrate, however, Algeria was in many ways as vital to France's sense of itself as was France to Algeria.

Concepts of identity, memory, and nostalgia now form an integral part of the intellectual landscape, especially in the field of cultural or postcolonial studies, but it is nonetheless useful to consider why they are compelling tools of analysis and how they are closely entangled in Franco-Algerian relations. Halbwachs's pioneering study *Les cadres sociaux de la mémoire* ([1925] 1975) demonstrated that individual and social memory are so enmeshed as to make their distinction problematic. Since then, memory and its sites have emerged as an organizing concept in the humanities (Nora 1992; Bal 1999; Radstone 2000). To be sure, memory means different things to different people at different times, and in this respect Mieke Bal's distinctions between background memory, narrative memory, and trauma recall are methodologically helpful (1999, vii-vii). The essays in this volume use these concepts in innovative ways.

Naturally enough, Bal's categories are also implicated in personal and collective identity. Background memories, which imply the socially conditioned reflexive memories of individual experience, help to reshape the identities of migrants and exiles. But such memories are also a component of the gaze of travelers and authors as they contemplate the "other," as Victoria Thompson shows us in this volume. Whereas recent studies of exile, migration, and expatriation have concentrated on the postcolonial condition, Julia Clancy-Smith here demonstrates the importance of the colonial period to migratory reconstructions. Recent work on postcolonial identity and its ramifications has coalesced around Bal's second category, narrative memory. Although the majority of such works have emerged from the disciplines of language and literature, Jo McCormack's essay is a substantiation of the fact that the narratives of history are equally important in reformulating French identity in relation to its colonial past. If memory is an important component in the making of history, so too is countermemory. As Svetlana Boym has indicated, countermemory is not merely a collection of alternative facts and texts; it is also an alternative way of reading them (2001, 62). Joshua Schreier's contribution demonstrates the validity of this observation.

The final category of Bal's threesome, trauma recall, is especially relevant both to Franco-Algerian identities and to their political and social ramifications.

Although trauma recall suggests individual memory recuperation and the way in which it shapes identity, in the Franco-Algerian context it is the collective experience of trauma that left its mark on both nations: the trauma of the colonial experience as well as the trauma of decolonization and beyond. The articles by Mireille Rosello, Joshua Cole, Richard Derderian, and David Prochaska creatively explore these types of trauma. But identity as framed by memory and nostalgia is as much about obliterating as it is about remembering the past. Whether such restructuring is a subconscious reaction to personal trauma or a conscious attempt to perpetrate national or individual myths by erasing aspects of the past that are contentious, it constitutes the politics of memory discourses. Contestation, furthermore, is as much about who is entitled to speak for the past as it is about conflicting accounts of what actually happened (Hodgkin and Radstone 2003, 1). Alec Hargreaves's discussion of the triangular tensions between family histories, on the one hand, and the national histories of France and Algeria, on the other, demonstrates the complexity of such contestation.

If identity, memory, and nostalgia are implicated in the inclusive and exclusionary practices that are the essence of such politics, how is nostalgia different from memory, and in what ways do the articles in this volume elaborate on this distinction? Although nostalgia is usually associated with bittersweet reflections on an irretrievable past, it also has a pathological manifestation, which is a substitute for mourning, a clinging to something lost (Kaplan 1987, 468). In such cases, it is a defense mechanism that surfaces when personal disruption or collective upheaval threaten identity. As Lynne Huffer points out in her essay on Derrida, "nostalgia happens precisely because we cannot go home again." The nostalgic, therefore, is always displaced, an exile from time and space. Second-generation French Algerians, North African immigrants, *pieds-noirs* (French and European settlers in Algeria), and *harkis* (Algerians who fought alongside the French), whatever their station in life, are implicated either directly or indirectly in a nostalgia for a past that might have been even more than they are implicated in a past that actually was. Furthermore, Boym reminds us that nostalgia is not just about the past, for "fantasies of the past determined by the needs of the present have an impact on the realities of the future" (2001, xvi). She suggests that nostalgia can be either reflective or restorative. The former is about individual and cultural memory, as demonstrated in the chapters by Alec Hargreaves, Lynne Huffer, and Mireille Rosello. The latter is linked to a national past and future, as illustrated in the chapters by Richard Derderian and David Prochaska.

Some of the most successful works on memory and its importance to identity have dealt with the violence of war.[1] War brings about a blurring of identity lines, be they of gender, class, or nation, and its aftermath of loss is marked by commemorative efforts on both sides to rearrange the past in justificatory terms of heroism, resistance, or duty.[2] Identity is then realigned in relation to the national territory and its narrative. Violence and trauma are also intrinsic to the colonial experience, and in the same way as war they bring about an initial rearrangement of identities to suit the exigencies of conflict, whether of conquest, occupation, or domination.

The underlying framework that defines France's relationship with Algeria is one of violence, a violence central to the Franco-Algerian colonial experience from its inception in 1830 to its close in 1962. The violence of the colonial period, whether of conquest, settlement, or expropriation, forcibly reshaped collective and individual identities, and in the process memory and nostalgia assumed historical significance. Violence became part of the "system" and was incorporated into the social structure of colonial society in racist discourses and repressive practices. The colony's population, therefore, was marked by this presence, which constantly undermined the possibility of equitable relations between the French and the Algerians. The articles in part one of this volume demonstrate the various ways in which this rearrangement took place. Expatriation and exile, physical or psychological, are also essentials to the colonial (or postcolonial) situation. Memory and nostalgia are therefore built into the system and are used from the outset not for justificatory purposes, but to frame a new social setting.[3] They are defensive mechanisms of survival and self-perpetration. At decolonization, furthermore, the losses cannot be commemorated in the same way because the loss (or gain) involved is of the complete territorial entity. Sublimation or silence, temporary or otherwise, become defense mechanisms in the face of an inability or refusal to come to terms with the past, as can be seen in the chapters by Joshua Cole and Habiba Deming in part two.

The Algerian War of Independence (1954–62), however, was pivotal in shaping modern Franco-Algerian relations. It has been variously dubbed the "savage war of peace," the "war without a name," the "uncivil war": evocative labels that suggest the intensity both of the struggle and of its legacy (Horne [1977]

1. To name but three notable examples: Fussell 1975, Mosse 1990, Rousso [1991] 1994. Of relevance to this volume, Stora 1991, 1999, and Evans 1997.

2. For example, see Judt's discussion of intellectual reconstructions after the Second World War (1992, 45–74). For diverse discussions on the way gender differences become blurred, see Melman 1998 and Higonnet 1987.

3. The memory or nostalgia can be for the metropole or a throwback to a romanticized past. See, for example, Lorcin [1995] 1999a and 2002.

1978; Talbott 1980; Le Sueur 2001). The war is important because, invariably, it is the lens through which this relationship is filtered. It is therefore useful to consider briefly what it was about the war that had this impact. The war's violence in relation to the colonial period was not distinguished so much in its quantitative dimension—although casualties were extremely high—as in its sociopolitical one. The sociopolitical violence of the colonial era was vertical, being restricted largely to conflict between the dominant French and the subordinated Algerians. During the war, however, it was vertical *and* horizontal. In addition to fighting each other, the French and the Algerians had to contend with internecine struggles that bordered on civil war. The French were divided between the supporters of an independent Algeria, on the one hand, and the believers in *l'Algérie française,* on the other, whose extremist faction, the Organisation armée sécrète (OAS), carried out a scorched-earth policy targeting Algerians and pro-independence French alike. The power struggle in the Algerian ranks between the Front de libération nationale (FLN) and its opponents—real and perceived—inflicted more casualties on the Algerians than on the French (Thomas 2000, 86).[4] The FLN used "compliant terror," as Martha Crenshaw Hutchinson (1978, 45) has called it, throughout the war. This quadrangular situation created a multilayered palimpsest of narratives on both sides, made up of mythologies, memories, and internalizations, some of which are only now beginning to surface.

Although the legacy of the war is lived differently by the Algerians and the French, the shared common ground includes the connection between nation and violence. The present-day regimes in both France and Algeria have their roots in the Algerian War of Independence. The Fifth Republic was established as a result of the national crisis in May 1958, created by antigovernmental forces in Algiers and headed by General Raoul Salan. The strengthening of the executive in the Fifth Republic's Constitution was not just a maneuver to counteract the Fourth's instability; it also provided Charles de Gaulle with a stronger hand to resolve the worsening situation in Algeria. In the postwar Algerian state, the FLN has dominated the political arena, refusing to relinquish power. Its short-circuiting of the electoral victory of the Front islamique du salut (FIS) in 1992 engendered a civil war, in all but name, that matched the War of Independence in its savagery.[5]

The connection between violence and national identity is not limited to political legacies, however. Violence as torture or violence as dispossession also form

4. The main targets were members of the Mouvement pour la triomphe des libertés démocratiques (MTLD) and the Mouvement national algérien (MNA). An especially vicious attack was carried out at Melouza in May 1957.

5. One hundred thousand deaths in the period 1992–99 (Stora 1999, 114).

part of the lived experience of both countries, although the legacies to each diverge. The French army used torture systematically on both Algerian rebels and French "dissidents."[6] Dispossession and the violence linked to it, in particular cultural uprooting and subsequent alienation, affected both camps. The *harkis* and the *pieds-noirs* were initially the most striking examples of dispossession and its violence. The purging of the *harkis* and other "dissidents" in Algeria and the rejection in France of the *harki* minority who managed to escape the purge and of the *pieds-noirs* who arrived en masse in the summer of 1962 created situations that were inherently divisive. Confronting these situations was problematic. The postindependence imperative of national unity necessitated their internalization until such a time as their divisiveness would no longer pose a significant threat. Although in France the amnesties of 1962, 1964, 1966, 1968, and 1982 helped to expunge the violence of the war, there was no unifying construction, like the "resistance myth" of the post-Second World War period, to redefine identities fractured by war.[7]

The reconstruction of national identity from the social and political fragmentation caused by the war shaped the way in which the war and the colonial period were remembered—or forgotten. Historical memory, as Rousso ([1991] 1994, 4) and Renan ([1882] 1999) before him have pointed out, is a structuring of forgetfulness. Algeria and France structured their forgetfulness differently. For Algeria, the conclusion of the war was a vindication of the longstanding negation by the French of Algeria's claim to nationhood, a negation that had its roots in the colonial mindset.[8] Algeria's dominant memory, in Rousso's sense of the term, was structured therefore in terms of gain.[9] The divisiveness of the war was thus occluded, only to resurface when the 1992–99 civil war rent the country in two. For France, the relinquishing of Algeria was a political, economic, and psychological loss. Although the various groups experienced this loss in different ways—ranging from relief to bitterness and rage—they all nonetheless experienced it acutely. There was a measure of shame attached to the loss, whether it was shame at hav-

6. Henri Alleg is a case in point. His book *La question* (1958) first introduced the French public to the army's use of torture in Algeria.

7. Robert Gildea defines myth, in this instance, as "a collective construction serving a political purpose, namely to define identity, inculcate solidarity and legitimate actions" (2000, 27).

8. One of the most persistent claims of the French was that Algeria was not and never had been a political entity. Indeed, in occupying and colonizing Algeria, the French claimed they had been moving into a political vacuum (see Thomas 2000, 3). Jean-François Guilhaume (1992) categorizes this approach as one of the founding myths of French Algeria.

9. For Rousso, "dominant" memory is a collective interpretation of the past that may attain official status.

ing indulged in the deplorable experience of colonization and colonial warfare, which dishonored France's humanitarian traditions, or shame at having lost what was perceived to be "rightfully French" and thus at diminishing France's world status. These conflicting sentiments meant that no dominant memory could satisfactorily emerge. Instead, there was silence—a silence resonating with France's inability to forget.

The official silence was broken in June 1999, when for the first time the French government acknowledged that a war had been fought over the decolonization of Algeria. During the period 1954–62, the French had termed their activities "des opérations de securité et de maintien de l'ordre" (security operations and maintenance of order).[10] Once the Evian Peace Accords were signed and Algeria gained its independence, the heavy silence that surrounded the subject precluded more precise categorization. The French reluctance, in this instance, to call a spade a spade or, more precisely, a war a war was emblematic of French inability to formulate a coherent narrative about its Algerian past. The affirmation that the "events" of 1954–62 did indeed constitute a war served as a catalyst for a series of personal reminiscences and avowals that further breeched the guarded silence of the past (Beaugé 2000b, 2000c on Louisette Ighilaghriz and Jacques Massu, respectively; Aussaresses 2001b). If the recent rupturing of the official silence that enveloped the war for the past forty years is an indication of the way in which the forgetfulness was structured, the plurality of memory made such forgetfulness vulnerable to contestation. The war was written out of the "dominant" memory, but its memory could not be effaced from the different groups that had participated in it, however marginally. Recurrent articles in the press and an impressive array of works by scholars and literati attest to this fact.[11] The silence surrounding the war had therefore fissured long before it was officially broken.

The Algerian War overshadows the colonial period in shaping France's postindependence relationship to Algeria and more especially to the Muslims of France, most of whom are of North African origin and who now make up 9 percent of the total population. To be sure, the individual recollections of collective

10. On 10 June 1999, the National Assembly started the debate on the substitution of the name *guerre d'Algérie* for "opérations de maintien de l'ordre en Afrique du Nord" in all legal and legislative texts (see Stora 1999, 130).

11. Assessments of the war have appeared from time to time in the French weeklies. See, for example, the special issues of *L'Express* (November 1979) and *Le nouvel observateur* (February-March 2002). For a more comprehensive list of the historical works on the war, see the bibliographies of the relevant texts cited in the works cited section. For a discussion of the literature on the war, see Dine 1994.

trauma and the imagery of bodily injury used by officials and scholars alike suggest the way in which private and public memories intersect. But the desire for additional time to heal is emblematic of France's difficulty in assuming its role as the country with the highest Muslim population in the European Union. As Josette Alia has pointed out, the importance of "French Islam" is neither acknowledged nor well known in France (2002, 4). This obtuseness is indicative of yet another way that the silence surrounding the war—and indeed the colonial period—is lived.

In *Le transfert d'une mémoire: De "l'Algérie française" au racisme anti-arabe* (The Transfer of Memory: From French Algeria to Anti-Arab Racism) (1999), Benjamin Stora presents a convincing case for the way in which the war has shaped postindependence immigrant politics. In the first round of the 2002 French presidential elections, the success of Jean-Marie Le Pen, whose political platform hinged on anti-immigrant—in particular anti-Maghrebi—policies, would appear to bear Stora out. Following the attacks on the World Trade Center in New York City in September 2001, French concerns with internal security and the possible presence of "terrorists" in their midst have exacerbated tensions between the French and the French-Maghrebi populations and have increased xenophobic anxiety, a factor that contributed to the disillusionment with the incumbent parties. But the Algerian War is also part of the incorporated memory that makes up the sense of self of Algerian immigrants and their children and is thus integral to their daily lives (P. Bernard 2002). It also shapes the way they respond to foreign affairs, as evidenced by their reaction to the Gulf War of 1991, the 1992–99 civil war in Algeria, and the escalation of violence in the occupied territories of Palestine.[12] In an interview on the occasion of a rally protesting events in the West Bank, held in Lyon, the organizer of the event stated that the French of Algerian origin were much affected by what was happening in Palestine because they were descendants of Algerian immigrants whose parents had had similar experiences in Algeria years ago. "Everything we see in the media is very close to what our parents lived through in Algeria" (Spicer 2002). More recently, the war in Iraq has elicited a similar response.

In examining the way in which dispossession—the other violence associated with decolonization—has been memorialized since 1962, one cannot help but be struck by the difference between the experience of the *harkis* and that of the *pieds-noirs*. Although both were virtually ignored by French officialdom in the immediate aftermath of independence and relegated to the limbo of war-related

12. For a discussion of the reaction among Franco-Algerians to the Gulf War and the Algerian civil war, see Stora 1999, 114.

silence, the *pieds-noirs,* unlike the *harkis,* soon started to create a multidimensional narrative of loss. Memory was inscribed in images, in writing, in film: all circumscribed by what Kaplan describes as pathological nostalgia.[13] The high quality of some of this artistic production (Cardinal 1975; Roüan 1992) and the colonial nostalgia much of it evoked reached beyond the confines of the *pied-noir* community resident in France to the wider public. The *harkis,* in contrast, were unable to conjure up this type of sympathy owing to both their pariah status and the fact that most were unable to express themselves in a language and manner that would break through constraining social barriers. As Alec Hargreaves points out in chapter 14, first-generation immigrants often had to wait for their children, educated in the institutions and culture of the metropole, to break the silence for them. The *harkis* were no exception.

Memory and nostalgia, as defined earlier, are of course predicated on notions of individual or collective identity. In the context of this volume, these identities have their moorings in colonial Algeria, which, for better or for worse, shaped the way in which memories would be lived or denied. Although the traumas connected to the war were officially effaced or individually sublimated, the colonial experience remained a constant point of reference. The political, social, and cultural relationships established between the European and non-European populations of Algeria during the colonial period were the basis of both the collective identity of the colony and its individual members. To be sure, these identities were fluid and mutable, responding to *événemential* pressures and political exigencies, but the colonial situation remained central to their formulation. In exile or expatriation, these identities were again mutated, producing the "memory" or "nostalgia" associated with hybridity. In this particular context, I stress that *hybridity, memory,* and *nostalgia* are not mere terms used to describe a particular condition, but historical processes in themselves.

The chapters in this volume are divided into three parts, corresponding to the conceptual terms around which the volume is organized. This is not to suggest that the chapters in a given part are exclusively about one concept; indeed, nearly all of them incorporate more than one concept, and all of them include some aspect of the politics of inclusion and exclusion. As the chapters in part one suggest, Franco-Algerian identity was formulated in a number of ways and for a variety of ends. Julia Clancy-Smith does not use the usual metropole-colony dynamic to de-

13. For examples of memory in images, see Azoulay 1980, Cardinal 1994, and Alzieu 2001; for a few examples from the considerable array of memory in writing, see Cardinal 1975; Hureau 1987; Dessaigne 1964, 1996; and Verdès-Leroux 2001; an example of memory in film is *Outre-mer* made in 1992 by Brigitte Roüan.

velop notions of colonial identity, but highlights the horizontal axis that existed between Algeria and Tunisia to show how new identities developed. Tunisia, she argues, was a site of regeneration for Europeans disillusioned with or anxious about the way colonization was evolving in Algeria. Anxiety in the colonial context is also a theme for Victoria Thompson. She demonstrates that far from reinforcing notions of identity, French writers who ventured into the Casbah perceived their identity to be threatened. The discomfort, disorientation, and confusion they often felt in this alien space disrupted the orderliness of their middle-class sensibilities, calling their identity into question and highlighting its vulnerability. Gender, sexuality, and the body were, of course, signifiers of difference in the colonial context, and Thompson's essay analyzes the relationship between them and colonial power structures. The body in the collective sense of a national entity is also the subject of Philip Dine's chapter on sport in the colony. But, as Dine points out, sport was also a way of signaling the success of colonial integration by turning Algerian athletes into national icons. The next two contributions deal with the intersection of culture and identity. Seth Graebner looks at the "publicists" of Algeria whose writing attempted to carve out a cultural identity of regionalism that reinforced the notion of *Algérie française* while attempting to mark out their autonomy from the metropole. Peter Dunwoodie examines the work of Muslim journalists and novelists writing in the colony during the interwar years. He illustrates the conflicting pressures at work in these authors' writings. Although the emerging Algerian novelists were celebrated and marketed on the basis of conformity to metropolitan norms, their nature as francophones rather than French meant that their works were sites of alternative self-representation that reconfigured the dominant, French-imposed themes and sociocultural issues of the time. Yaël Simpson Fletcher, in the last chapter in this section, analyzes reactions to the September 1954 Orléansville earthquake. The disaster created a unity of response among journalists of both European and non-European origin and, with it, an illusion of "national" solidarity. The illusory nature of this cohesion became evident, however, with the outbreak of the War of Independence on November 1 of the same year, but the importance of the chapter lies in the fact that it suggests that if unity born of catastrophe is to be maintained, it needs to be constantly reinforced.[14]

Part two deals with the way in which the past is remembered as well as the way it has been obscured. Joshua Schreier discusses the relationship of Algerian Jews to the French civilizing mission, which sought to turn the diverse popula-

14. For an understanding of the importance of natural catastrophes in creating national identity, see the work of Christian Pfister (2002).

tions under its control into Frenchmen, and reassesses the way in which this relationship had been previously analyzed. By examining the experiences of both Algerian and French Jews in 1848, Schreier suggests that France's civilizing mission was not merely a colonial phenomenon and, when applied to the Jews, was contested on both sides of the Mediterranean. Many of the chapters in this part touch on the trauma of the Algerian War, but Joshua Cole and Jo McCormack focus specifically on the way the war has been occluded or written out of history in France. Todd Shepard, in contrast, looks at the repatriation of the *pieds-noirs* in the immediate aftermath of war and traces the ways in which the war still serves as a realm of memory. William Cohen's chapter underlines the official fears of *harki* repatriation to France—fears that are reflected today in official attitudes toward North African immigrants. He also examines the impact of inclusionary rhetoric and exclusionary practices, shaded by memory of the war, on the *harkis* and their offspring. He thus highlights generational differences in the way memory is occluded or revisited. Habiba Deming's chapter, the last in this part, looks at the question of language in Algeria and, building on Homi Bhabha's concept of mimicry, shows how memories of the colonial discourses of civilizational and linguistic inferiority have been insidiously internalized and are now being reproduced in the postcolonial setting.

Part three focuses on the memories of the "displaced" and how they have been used to come to terms with the past—a nostalgia that is reflective to be sure, but in the Franco-Algerian situation restorative as well. Imagery and symbolism are central to Mireille Rosello's analysis of Mehdi Lallaoui's novel *La colline aux oliviers* (The Olive Grove) (1995a). The two tokens of historical memory in the novel are the olive tree and a pair of earrings. They are both mnemonic devises and cultural symbols: the olive tree being of great significance in Islam, symbolizing the Prophet, light, and humans; the gazelle-shaped earrings, in this case, a secular multifaceted symbol linking Algeria to France across space and time (gazelles are associated with love in North Africa, and in France *beurettes* are sometimes called gazelles). Nostalgia in Alec Hargreaves's contribution is a generational phenomenon. He argues that whereas certain first-generation migrants—in particular those who experienced the colonial era—are inclined to "muffle" their memories, their children and grandchildren often feel the need to revivify them in order to connect to their ethnic origins and, for some, to understand the alienation to both French and Algerian society that they feel or were made to feel. Second and third generations do not share their parents or grandparent's memories and are therefore obliged to resort to nostalgic explorations to situate themselves in the society their families opted for. The counterpoint to the Algerian migrants' nostalgia is that of the *pieds-noirs*, whose families also left Algeria during the period of decolonization. Lynne Huffer's chapter looks at the predicament of the *pied-noir* intellectual. Nostalgia for Algeria—that is, mourning its loss—remained unarticulated for a quarter of a century before being transformed into an autobiographical construction of the French intellectual self. Like Deming, Huffer considers the importance of language in the re-creation of a postcolonial identity, but whereas Deming is concerned with mimetic memory, Huffer's analysis, like Hargreaves's, revolves around reflective nostalgia. Richard Derderian looks at the cultural production of second-generation Algerians, arguing that it is an essential part of the process of working through the past, a restorative act necessary for successful integration into French society. David Prochaska's chapter, which brings the volume to a close, is a multifaceted exploration of the relevance of the colonial past to France, Algeria, and the United States. Prochaska examines differing reactions to and interpretations of two films, *The Battle of Algiers* and *Bab el-Oued City.* He demonstrates how memory is created and then obliterated, only to resurface at a later date as nostalgia for revolution, violence, or domination.

With the realization of the relevance of colonial questions to mainstream French historiography, the problem of Franco-Algerian relations has grown in importance. These essays reflect the changes in interpretation of that relationship over the past decade and demonstrate the contribution that examining Franco-Algerian relations has made to an understanding of identity, memory, and nostalgia.[15]

15. A note on translations in the volume: the individual authors have done all translations of French-language material in their chapters, except where indicated by specific source citations. Authors clarify the source of translation where necessary.

Part One • Identity Reconsidered

I Migrations, Legal Pluralism, and Identities

Algerian "Expatriates" in Colonial Tunisia

JULIA CLANCY-SMITH

> Hajj Ali ben Cherouf . . . died in Tunis about a month ago. The administrator of Muslim estates, assuming that the deceased was Tunisian, went to the deceased's household . . . but Shaykh Belkassem . . . declared the deceased to be an Algerian.
>
> —French consul to Khayr al-Din, 1873

MOST STUDIES OF IDENTITY in Algerian colonial history employ a colony-metropole perspective that privileges vertical exchanges spanning the Mediterranean from north to south and back again. This approach, however, creates bounded entities—France/Algeria—severed from the Maghreb and its many histories. My contribution proposes another line of inquiry: a horizontal axis to investigate the problematic of identity and physical displacements. It argues that historical processes in French Algeria were deeply influenced by events in precolonial Tunisia (1830–81). One of the most important forces was migration, which assumed a number of guises along a spectrum running from voluntary to involuntary or forced departures. Migration and identity are inextricably linked, although in multifarious ways.

In a seminal article, Malek Chebel distinguished "5 grandes stratégies"—concrete, fictive, ideal, mythic, and complex and argued that political or complex identities, which draw upon the other strategies, become particularly critical in relationship to immigration (quoted in Baduel 1987, 12–14). Subsequent scholarship has examined the problematic of identities for Algeria and France from numerous angles—for example, Lorcin's ([1995] 1999a) study of the interplay between imperial ideology, ethnic categories, and cultural distinctions that produced the Kabyle myth (see also Colonna 1975; Pervillé 1984; Christelow 1985). Other works argue that both French and Algerian identities were forged within the crucible of Algerian migration to the metropole after 1900 (Hargreaves and Heffernan 1993; MacMaster 1997). Aside from Alain Messaoudi's (1996) work, however, relatively few studies have considered the question of identities among Algerians as they unfolded outside of France or Algeria. And even fewer studies have examined identities among Europeans or French nationals who initially had settled in Algeria, but subsequently elected to relocate, whether in the Maghreb or elsewhere. This neglect is largely because, as noted earlier, the problem of identity has generally been conceptualized along a vertical axis of inquiry, Algeria/France.

This chapter explores several kinds of population displacements from Algeria to Tunisia mainly during the period from 1830 to 1881: first, the emigration of Algerian Muslims and Jews; and second, the departures of Europeans. Regarding the former, after 1830 there was a rapidly accelerating human traffic out of Algeria, particularly after large-scale rebellions, such as the 1849 revolt led by Bu Ziyan, the Kabyle resistance of the 1850s, and the Muqrani insurrection of 1871. The outpouring of involuntary migrants, including refugees, from Algeria to Tunisia included defeated rebels, tribal dissidents, Muslim leaders, Algerian Jews, and a motley array of others, such as criminals and vagabonds. In my 1994 study of populist protest in colonial Algeria, I argued that the departure of religious notables and rebels from Algeria after 1830 constituted avoidance protest—dissident behavior combined with strategies for survival. Having escaped France's rule in Algeria, some Algerian Muslims and Jews, once in Tunisia, placed themselves more or less willingly under French diplomatic protection, becoming protégés. For the precolonial Tunisian state, this act engendered intractable jurisdictional problems, directly tied to political and religious identities. Of course, similar patterns of displacement can be observed for nineteenth-century Morocco, which also received Algerian exiles, dissidents, or refugees, as did other parts of the Ottoman Empire, most notably Greater Syria (Kenbib 1996).

As for the Europeans, their decision to immigrate to Tunisia can be interpreted not only as an expression of displeasure with colonial policies, but also in some cases as a search for a new identity. If Algeria had represented the colonial "jewel in the crown," by the fin de siècle some French liberals saw it as a signal failure—a moral lesson in what not to do. For those French and Europeans who left Algeria to reside permanently in Tunisia before 1881, crossing the border brought them into the older Ottoman or Mediterranean system of law, justice, and consular protection. Whereas the beylical (i.e., Tunisian) precolonial system of justice was based mainly on an individual's religious identity, the system of legal pluralism in Tunisia recognized the existence of legitimate, distinct spheres of judicial authority claimed by European diplomatic and commercial establishments in Ottoman lands, although there always existed degrees of intersection between various jurisdictions, Ottoman-Muslim and European (Windler 2002). In sum, population movements out of Algeria from 1830 on created enormously contentious questions of jurisdiction, which produced continual local negotiations, conflict, and compromise over an individual's identity and thus insertion into or exclusion from society.

In *Le creuset français* (translated as *The French Melting-Pot* in 1996), Noiriel demonstrates that by the late nineteenth century "the identity paradigm was undergoing fundamental changes" in metropole France (1988, 67–68). Although Noiriel failed to pay adequate attention to the colonial situation, his insistence on novel practices and procedures for marking the foreign and foreigner in France is critical. In an important recent study, which did not, however, foreground the issue of identity, Benton argues that "colonialism shaped a framework for the politics of legal pluralism, though particular patterns and outcomes varied" (2002, 2). Taking Benton's notion of legal pluralism together with Noiriel's emphasis on new methods for inclusion or exclusion, this chapter examines the *earlier* part of the nineteenth century in terms of changes in the "identity paradigm." It takes pre*colonial* Tunisia as its site of investigation for considering Chebel's notion of complex identity in situations of immigration. It seeks to understand how indeed "particular patterns and outcomes [are] varied" when migration, identity, and legal pluralism are traced along a horizontal or trans-Maghrebi axis instead of on a vertical line linking Algeria only to France.

Algerians: Emigration and Protection in Pre-1881 Tunisia

Algerians (admittedly, the name is somewhat anachronistic) from diverse communities had for centuries moved to adjoining states, whether permanently or temporarily, to pursue trade, commerce, education, or political advancement. In the pre-1830 Tunisian beylik, many Algerians from the impoverished Saharan rim lived and labored under the direction of an *amin* (guild master or chief) recognized by the bey (Marty 1948). For example, the public baths *(hammams)* in Tunis had long been monopolized by the Algerian Mzabites; in 1890, Charles Lallemand counted some thirty-five Mzabite *hammamjis* (bathhouse owners) still organized under an *amin* (1890, 51). In addition, the Tunisian rulers had traditionally relied on Berber Zwawa (Zouaves) tribesmen originally from the Kabylia to serve as troops. Of all the Muslims in the beylik regarded as non-Tunisian, the Algerians had always formed the largest contingent and were distinguished as such in the sources. The French landing in the summer of 1830 would inflate their numbers dramatically.

Most Algerians fled to escape the ceaseless warfare, famine, or want, or to avoid living under infidel rule, as in the case of the Bin 'Azzuz clan from Biskra. Others arrived to improve their social situation, although the various and sundry motivations for departure were not necessarily mutually exclusive. Those of the upper or middle classes came to Tunisia from as far away as Oran, although urban areas of the Constantinois and Algérois sent the most emigrants. Because of their class origins, these families were often integrated into the milieu of wealthy Tunis lineages; indeed, notable families, such as the Bin 'Iz al-Din or the Bin al-Shaykh Ahmad, had come as refugees, amassed fortunes, and married into the highest circles in the beylik (Ben Achour 1989, 160–69; Clancy-Smith 1994). Some emigrants had previously entertained rather cozy relations with the French colonial regime. For example, during the conquest of Constantine city in 1837, 'Usman Bushnaq, an Algerian enrolled in the French spahi corps in Bône, arrived in Tunis, supposedly on temporary military leave for rest and recovery, which the beylik routinely supplied to colonial troops, including high-ranking officers. Once in Tunisia, Bushnaq showed little inclination to regain Algeria or to resume fighting under the French flag, despite the fact that his three-year engagement was not yet up. He petitioned the bey for employment in the ruler's service because "he does not wish to return to Bône" (French consul 1837). Cases like that of Bushnaq were legion throughout the nineteenth century.

In his 1847 report, Lieutenant Prax, a naval officer and amateur ethnographer of Saint Simonian persuasion, did a detailed study of Algerians in Tunisia. He found that Algerian merchants were for the most part subjects of the bey. However, artisans and laborers fell into two different groups in terms of jurisdiction. Whereas many remained under the authority of the bey, "the most numerous were under French protection" (Prax 1847). As noted earlier, one of the anomalies of France's harsh conquest of Algeria was that many Algerian Muslims and Jews became French protégés once they crossed the border into Tunisia. The French consulate in Tunis protected their interests, provided justice, and oversaw matters related to civil status as long as they resided in the beylik. Prax again noted in 1847 that "the Algerian who has a *teskéré* [permit; here a certificate establishing identity based on place of birth] presents himself to the French consulate in Tunis and the chancellery delivers to him a passport which costs 8 francs." Although more research needs to be done in this matter, the development of formal procedures recognizing Algerian expatriates as such in nineteenth-century Tunisia may have been a critical element in complex identity formation.

Prax's account contains valuable information regarding the role of the Algerians' *amin* under the new, post-1830 political and jurisdictional order. When Prax visited Tunis, he observed that "those Algerians under beylical protection are administered by an *amin,* al-Hajj Muhammad of Algiers [who] left Algiers for Tunis in 1840 after waiting 10 years for the French government in Algiers to indemnify him for buildings [belonging to him] destroyed to make way for public works." Moreover, "an Algerian who is a subject of the bey can only return to Algeria with the permission of the *amin* who procures a *teskéré* from the bey allowing the Algerian to return home" (Prax 1847). The beys of the Regency of Tunis had long delivered permits for importing and exporting commodities to and from the country as well as, until 1837, for allowing European women to disembark in port (Clancy-Smith 2000). However, the practice of delivering *teskéré* to Algerians returning to their homeland appears to have been an innovation directly linked to increasing migration into the realm. (Of course, the matter of enforcement must be raised because both the beylical state and the French colonial authorities in this period later lacked the resources to police the borders.)

As more and more Algerians arrived seeking haven in Tunisia, the task of French consular officials there became complicated, for it was not easy to determine who could legitimately establish Algerian status and therefore claim France's protection. Moreover, the beylical government was increasingly exasperated by the presence of Algerians in the country, which created jurisdictional squabbles that sometimes erupted in violence. In 1838, French merchants in Tunis claimed, "200 blows of the bastinado were inflicted upon an Algerian by Tunisian authorities, despite the fact that the Algerian had been issued a *carte de sûreté* by the French consulate" (Chambre de commerce et d'industrie Marseille 1838). French consular authorities periodically attempted to systematize the rules of protection for Algerian expatriates in Tunisia. In 1855, Léon Roches, France's consul general in Tunis, set out regulations stipulating that a census be taken of Algerian Muslims and Jews under French protection. All current protégés as well as those arriving in the future were required to carry a *carte de sûreté* written in Arabic, with the name of the bearer, the place of his birth, and the date of his inscription in the registers of the consulate." It was also decreed that "any Algerians who remain more than three years absent from Algeria or from another piece of French territory will no longer be considered a French subject"—a rule that did not, however, apply to Algerians who had settled in Tunisia before 1855 (French consul 1855–56).

Algerian Jews under French protection in Tunisia often faced reprisals by local religious or beylical officials, particularly during periods of political tension between France and the Tunisian government. In 1851, the French vice-consul in Sfax alerted consular authorities in Tunis about "the violent and arbitrary arrest of an Algerian Jew living in Sfax named Chaloum Botbal; the Qadi of Sfax . . . arrested Botbal and subjected him to corporal punishment as well as detention" (French consul 1851a). Because Chaloum Botbal claimed French protection as an Algerian, this gross violation of agreements between France and Tunisia called for intervention by the bey himself. Not all Algerian Jews were treated in this way; many chose to immigrate to Tunisia because of the extremely anti-Semitic climate among Algerian colons and officials alike, which in 1897, for example, triggered anti-Jewish riots in Algiers and elsewhere. Although the situation of indigenous (i.e., Arab) Jewish Algerians living in Tunisia was theoretically resolved by the Senatus-Consulte of 1865 and by the 1870 Crémieux decree, ambiguities and thus conflicts over identity and jurisdiction remained (Sebag 1991; Fellous 2003).

As Algerians poured into Tunisia by land or sea and as Mediterranean settlers arrived in ever-larger numbers in the country after 1850, conflict and crime soared (Larguèche 1999). Crime, criminal jurisdiction, and punishment proved the most difficult matters to resolve. One of the principal tasks of European consuls in Tunisia was to visit the scene of a crime, interview witnesses, commit oral testimony to writing, frequently in several languages, and hopefully bring the guilty to some sort of rough justice—if guilt could be established. The process often took months, if not years, to complete, mainly because of the number of people under different national jurisdictions involved in any daily fracas or serious offense (Clancy-Smith 2002). One of the most spectacular cases of multinational crime with indeterminate jurisdictions occurred in 1866 in Tunis and involved women's issues as well as a long drawn-out struggle over jurisdictional identity (for this case, see Wood 1866).

A Maltese woman named Grazia, widow of Paolo Sciberras and long-time resident of Tunis, was accused by her two brothers-in-law, Calcedonio and Guiseppe Sciberras, of giving birth to an illegitimate child. They also accused Grazia of murdering the newborn with an accomplice, presumably the baby's father. On 6 August 1866, she was ordered to appear in consular court in Tunis to answer the accusation. The witnesses summoned by the prosecutor were Maria Sciberras, the defendant's sister-in-law, and the two servants of the accused woman, residing in her home. Hajj 'Umar and Hamda Bushnaq were Grazia's male domestics who at one time or another claimed or were thought to be Algerian, thus under French protection. Maria Sciberras and Hamda Bushnaq maintained that the accused, Grazia, had given birth to a "full-grown female child, alive and sucking its thumb" and that Hajj 'Umar was the child's father. Although the infant was born alive, Hamda Bushnaq claimed to have seen Hajj 'Umar carrying away the child, wrapped up in his burnoose (cloak); although Hamda "could not tell whether it was alive or dead, he supposed it was only its corpse that Hajj 'Umar was carrying away."

Hajj 'Umar denied all knowledge of the child's birth and, moreover, claimed to be a subject of the bey—and not of France. Consular officials then sent Hajj 'Umar for trial before Tunisian authorities, who in turn determined that Hajj 'Umar was a French subject because he was an Algerian Muslim; thus, he was delivered up to the French consul. After an inquiry, however, the French consulate ruled that Hajj 'Umar had no legitimate claim to France's protection because he did not appear to be Algerian or, at least, could not furnish solid proof of Algerian origins—that is, he could produce neither a *carte de sûreté* nor a *teskéré*.

Part of the archival record is missing, but apparently the case took a number of bizarre twists and turns, and by 23 August 1866 Hajj 'Umar was confined to the beylical prison—for lack of other alternatives—after Tunisian authorities had decided that he was not Algerian and therefore "not a French protégé." Despite careful detective work by European and Tunisian officials in the vicinity of the crime scene, the corpse of the unfortunate child (if there was one) was never found. The fate of the wayward Grazia remains a mystery as well. Given her thoroughly compromised situation within the close-knit Catholic Maltese community in Tunisia (if indeed the accusations were true), one would assume that flight back to Malta would have been a preferred course of action; another was to seek haven in Algeria, if the large Maltese population there had not heard of her alleged transgressions (Donato 1985; Clancy-Smith 2002). (Here it should be pointed out that the flow of compromised individuals was not always only one way, from Algeria to Tunisia, but also moved in the reverse direction.) Whatever the outcome of this representative case, regulations, such as the French consul Léon Roches's 1855 decree creating procedures for establishing Algerian identity in Tunisia, clearly did not prevent the imbroglio over the murdered baby in the next decade.

Many Algerian Muslims who sought refuge in Tunisia did not present themselves to French consular officials. Formal acknowledgment of protégé status, if it became public, was often interpreted negatively by fellow Tunisian Muslims. However, by refusing or simply not claiming France's protection, Algerian Muslims residing in Tunisia were subject to beylical authority, justice, and taxation—a prospect that many found unappealing. Generally speaking, establishing an Algerian identity to invoke French protection came into play during cases of conflict—over debts, property, or inheritance—and particularly during criminal proceedings. Emblematic of the numerous cases linking control over property with jurisdictional identity is the 1873 incident cited at the beginning of this chapter. Hajj Ali ben Cherouf was originally from the Souf oases close to the Tunisian border. Upon his death in Tunis, an agent from the Bayt al-Mal (administration of Islamic religious endowments), assuming that he was a Tunisian Muslim who had died without heirs, went to his house, probably to lay claim to any properties. But Shaykh Belkassem, an Algerian overseeing property matters for his countrymen in the capital, declared that the deceased not only was from the Souf, but also had heirs back in Algeria. The encounter must have been stormy because Belkassem later alleged that the agent had illegally seized the key to Hajj Ali ben Cherouf's home and refused to return it. Subsequently, the Algerians sought the assistance of the French consul, Vallot, who in turn went to the *qadi* of Tunis as well as the Tunisian prime minister for redress. The affair was eventually settled, according to Vallot, by "un acte de notoriété constatant que feu Hajj Ali était Algérien originaire du Souf. Cet acte porte la signature du Qadi de Tunis et a dès lors une valeur incontestable" (a legal act that showed the late Hajj Ali to be an Algerian from Souf. This act bears the signature of the Muslim judge of Tunis and therefore its value cannot be disputed) (French consul 1873). In other words, several distinct, although overlapping, systems of jurisdiction—consular, beylical, and Islamic—were at work here. Legal pluralism paradoxically served as a matrix for the practice of establishing an Algerian identity, while at the same time offering enterprising individuals the opportunity to manipulate gaps or contradictions in overlapping jurisdictions to their personal advantage.

Evidence of the importance of the Algerian community in Tunisia is furnished by the 1876 "projet de la naturalisation Tunisienne à accorder aux émigrants Algériens" discussed between the Gouvernement général civil de l'Algérie and the minister of the interior in Paris (Gouvernement général civil de l'Algérie 1876). Five years later, the 1881 invasion of Tunisia ended the necessity for this proposed solution to the problems of legal pluralism. Myriad cases of disputed Algerian origins and thus of uncertain status occurred until the 1883 treaty imposed upon the Tunisian bey abolished all consular jurisdictions (Sebag 1998, 312–14). What is significant for our purposes is that Algerian identity as embodied in what Noiriel terms "the card and the code" ([1988] 1996, 90) may have been shaped to no small degree in Tunisia by consular *and* beylical procedures. The carrying of the obligatory *carte de sûreté* by some Algerian expatriates and their constant negotiations with Tunisian and French authorities set them apart from both fellow Algerians not under France's protection and subjects of the bey.

Europeans: Displacements and/in Identities

It was not only Algerians who desired to abandon that benighted country after 1830. Tunisia hosted several discrete, yet related, European in-migrations from the 1820s on (Clancy-Smith 2002). First, subsistence migrants came in ever greater numbers from Mediterranean islands, such as Malta, where unfavorable land-man ratios, high fertility, ecological degradation, and a lack of industrialization created a rural subproletariat. Other peoples arrived from areas experiencing political upheaval—for example, Greeks during the Ottoman-Greek Wars of the 1820s and later Sicilians during Italian unification. In addition, ordinary people from the Mediterranean rim, who had initially sought a better life in French Algeria, departed for the beylik. Yet another, slightly different current brought colonial officials, Catholic missionaries, and others into Tunisia from 1830 until well into the twentieth century.

Many of the immigrants arriving in Algerian and Tunisian ports after 1830 were not only socially marginal, but also politically marginalized because they occupied the edges of the emerging system of European nation-states, while being under the pro forma protection of one or another of the powers with a stake in the central Mediterranean. This marginalization made them especially resistant to pigeonholing, quantifying, counting, and tracking because they relatively frequently switched consular protection and thus legal jurisdiction in a conscious survival strategy. Thus, not only their very social marginality but also the ambivalent nature of national identities rendered these migratory populations largely invisible in colonial and nationalist historical narratives until recently. Many of the Maltese, Sicilians, Sardinians, and others residing permanently in the Maghreb after 1830 would be termed *undocumented* today; their presence there was owing to spontaneous or sub rosa immigration outside of official settlement schemes. Some groups proved especially difficult to survey and thereby to govern. This was the case for the Maltese, whose high rate of return migration to their small islands, located close to the Tunisian coastline, resulted in a constant *va et vient* between North Africa and Malta (Clancy-Smith 1997). Moreover, the large non-French communities of Spanish, Italians, and Maltese in French Algeria were barely tolerated and subject to forced repatriation if deemed undesirable or unlawful (Temine 1987). In many cases, the permeable borders between Algeria and Tunisia permitted those accused of crime or without adequate resources to avoid expulsion simply by moving clandestinely to the neighboring country.[1]

Sea transport on modest vessels piloted by Tunisian captains between small ports, such as Collo, Bône, Tabarka, or Ghar al-Millah, proved difficult to control for both French colonial and beylical authorities; for that very reason, these ships constantly brought people out of Algeria to Tunisia. As late as 1876, the

1. The archival records of the *agences consulaires* in the Archives diplomatiques, Nantes, are replete with references to this strategy: Tunisie, 1er versement, cartons 412–420b, 1849–74.

French consul in Tunis complained that "the governor general of Algeria informs me that Tunisian ships that frequent Collo are never in possession of their ships papers indicating the number or names of the passengers that they transport" (French consul 1876). An accurate census was not undertaken in Tunisia until 1906, so we have no way of calculating the actual number of people who relocated from Algeria or who came and went in Tunisia.

Groups as well as individuals left French Algeria from the early conquest period on. Regarding individual departures, the French consul in Tunis noted in 1836 that a French national also sought a post with the Tunisian state: "Monsieur Baquerie, a physician previously serving the ambulance corps in Algiers as a surgeon, and before that a teacher in the Collège d'Alger, wishes to find employment in the troops of His Highness the Bey. He comes highly recommended with proven certificates of qualification" (Schwebel to Raffo 1836). Thanks to the French consul's energetic, if paradoxical, intervention, Baquerie was hired. Such cases occurred throughout the pre-1881 period, particularly during times of rebellion, famine, disease, and drought in Algeria—and these were legion. Not everyone arriving from Algeria boasted professional credentials, however. In 1851, the French consul in Tunis contacted the Sardinian consulate there regarding a letter from Bône's military commander. A Sardinian convict named Veglio, "who escaped from the mine of 'Ain Teboul [in eastern Algeria near La Calle], where he was doing forced labor in the *atelier de boulet,*" had managed to flee and headed straight for Tunis. The fugitive's itinerary was discovered, however, through an intercepted letter that Veglio wrote to one of his comrades still laboring in the mine, informing him of the successful evasion (French consul 1851c). Happily for Veglio, his whereabouts were never discovered, and he probably disappeared into the capital city's floating population by assuming another identity—which is to say, placing himself under a consular jurisdiction other than that of Sardinia or France.

In addition, decisions made in Algiers and Paris regarding the residence of unwanted Europeans in French Algeria had a direct impact on immigration into the beylik, thereby directly contributing to conflicts over protection, status, and jurisdictional identity in Tunisia. In 1843, a *décret ministerial,* based on an 1841 *arrêté* issued by the governor-general, stated that any Maltese-British subjects sentenced in Algeria for crimes committed in the colony and sentenced to more than a year of prison in France were expressly forbidden to return to Algeria once released from prison, even if there existed a kinship network to facilitate the reintegration of the former felon into society there.[2] Because numerous cases of this

2. Centre des Archives d'Outre-Mer, F 80 586, 17 Sept. 1846.

nature occurred, the 1842 and 1843 regulations may have enhanced Tunisia's attraction as a place for Maltese settlement, especially by individuals whose families remained in Algeria. Exploding Maltese and Sicilian immigration undeniably played a major role in the warm welcome afforded to Catholic missionary orders by the Muslim government of Tunisia.

One of the first dissident groups to leave Algeria for Tunisia in the 1840s, the Order of the Sisters of Saint-Joseph, was attached to the Catholic Church. Organized in 1832 soon after the invasion of Algeria, this female missionary movement was founded by Émilie de Vialar, a granddaughter of the king's personal physician; de Vialar was also associated with the Abbot François Bourgade. A teaching and charitable order inspired by Catholic reform in France, the Sisters of Saint-Joseph created establishments in Algiers, Bône, and Constantine between 1835 and 1839, and later throughout the Mediterranean world and Ottoman Empire. In a sense, they followed in the wake of the French army as it conquered eastern Algeria. Resisting attempts by the bishop of Algiers to control her congregation and its numerous works directly, de Vialar had a falling out with Monseigneur Dupuch soon after his arrival in 1839. Jurisdictional conflicts were at play here as well because confusion over the order's status in canon law meant that it was uncertain to whom the founder owed obedience (Dornier 2000, 399–430; Curtis 2002).

The sisters, who numbered about forty women, were forced to abandon all of their educational and charitable houses by 1842. While still in Algeria, de Vialar had instructed some Tunisian children attending the sisters' school in Bône, which led her to consider Tunis as a new home for the congregation. In August 1840, the French vice-consul in the port of La Goulette noted the arrival from Marseille of "some Sisters of Saint-Joseph who have come here to create a charitable establishment. Madame de Vialar is the mother superior of this establishment. She has with her ten Sisters of St.-Joseph." Two years later, when the order was definitively expelled from Algeria, three more sisters arrived in Tunisia from Bône via ship.[3]

The order's founder even had an audience with Ahmad Bey (reigned 1837–55), who granted the order permission to settle permanently and who generously furnished the sisters with a suitable building to rent. The ruler allowed them to set up girls schools as well as to provide health care to both the European population and the Tunisian population; a novitiate was established in La Marsa, a suburb of Tunis, to train women intending to join the order. In the *madina,* a clinic, subsequently l'Hôpital St. Louis, was opened under the bey's auspices in

3. Tunisie, 1er versement, cartons 409b–410b, Archives diplomatiques, Nantes.

1842. Between 1842 and 1880, houses and educational-charitable establishments were created all along the Tunisian coast from Bizerte to Sfax (Machuel 1885, 1889; Planel 2000, 1:116–18). Taking root in the beylik, this branch of the order came to regard itself as having a Tunisian identity; many of the sisters learned Arabic. According to Curtis, de Vialar saw Tunisia, because of its location, as a perfect base for missionary expansion across the Mediterranean. A letter written by de Vialar found in the Archives des soeurs in Tunis stated that "[a]ll the Christians in Tunisia rejoiced at our arrival, and soon the Tunisian and Jewish populations will feel the same way. The indigenous population says 'they come to do good for all' " (quoted in Dornier 2000, 399; see also Guérin 1895, 58–77; Curtis 2002). In 1854, the French consul, Béclard, observed to the bey's secretary that "[t]he Bey has done a great deal for the Catholics, up to now, and I risk abusing his benevolence if I ask for more favors" (Béclard to Bogo 1854). The Sisters of Saint-Joseph made themselves at home in Tunisia and did not hesitate to contact the beys directly to ask for favors or assistance to carry on their work. Some of the sisters apparently quickly mastered the Islamic system of property holding, particularly for those properties having the status of *habous* or *waqf* (akin to *mortmain*), in order to importune the ruler for habitation rights to buildings, invoking Islamic legal procedures.[4] By the eve of the protectorate, they had been thoroughly integrated into local society and culture and were referred to by the Tunisians with the honorific *ulmi* (my mother) (Dornier 2000, 404).

There are a number of ironies to this story. Tunisia had been overwhelmingly Muslim and Arab for many centuries, and, unlike Egypt, Palestine, or Greater Syria, it did not have an indigenous Christian population, although the country boasted an ancient Jewish community. This fact leads to the question of Ahmad Bey's motives for extending such an enthusiastic reception to the Sisters of Saint-Joseph. From 1837 on, fully aware of the menace that the French colonial regime in Algeria posed to the beylik's independence, the Tunisian prince had embarked on a campaign to modernize his country. He outlawed slavery and the slave trade between 1840 and 1846 and introduced a number of reforms to keep the European powers happy, yet at arm's length politically. Ahmad Bey also lifted the ban on allowing European or Mediterranean women to come into the country without his permission, which may have encouraged more in-migration (Brown 1974; Clancy-Smith 2000). The "Christians" of Tunisia, mentioned by de Vialar in her letter, were mainly newly arrived immigrants, mainly Maltese and Sicilians, who

4. See the correspondence in série H, carton 64, dossiers 755–56, armoire 6, Archives nationales de Tunisie, Tunis.

either had left Algeria for Tunisia or had immigrated directly to Tunisia from overpopulated islands. One of Ahmad Bey's motivations for welcoming the sisters was surely the need for some sort of religious and social *encodement* for the subsistence migrants who jurisdictionally were outside the legal purview of the Tunisian state and Islamic law. In addition, many immigrants in this period were single males, much given to public drunkenness, street brawls, and criminal activities, so the sisters were to carry out a civilizing mission among the European migrant population, including first and foremost in the realms of education and morality of women (Clancy-Smith 2002).

Serving in Tunisia as the sisters' chaplain was the Abbé François Bourgade (1806–66), who, like de Vialar, had been a missionary in Algeria between 1838 and 1840. He too appears to have made himself persona non grata there, however, and left for Tunisia in 1841 to educate European children as well as Tunisian boys. Under his auspices, one of the first boys' school was founded in 1842 and opened to Maltese, French, Italian, and Tunisian pupils. The curriculum reflected the students' diverse ethnic backgrounds; lessons were given in Arabic and Italian as well as in French, Latin, and Greek (Vassel 1909). Bourgade, like Algerians residing in Tunisia, attempted to manipulate his special status there to obtain favors refused him by French authorities in Algeria. Lacking adequate funds to return periodically to France, the abbot habitually importuned French consuls in Tunis for free passage on ships bound for Marseille. By 1851, the consul, having repeatedly been "reprimanded by the French government for giving free boat passages to clerics, especially to the Abb. Bourgade," began turning down the abbot's request for a free ride (French consul 1851b). According to Planel, the Abbot was "one of the most controversial figures in the French community in 19th-century Tunis" (2000, 1:119–20). He appears to have had masonic links or been acquainted with expatriates in Tunisia holding masonic convictions, and they were numerous, the first Masonic lodge having been created in 1837 by Italian immigrants (Camou 2000, 360). Owing to his unconventional beliefs and behavior, Bourgade's papal authorization was revoked in 1858, causing "a huge outcry in the Catholic community" in Tunis (Planel 2000, 1:119). But the protest was to no avail: Bourgade, by then ill, was obliged to leave Tunisia, although he left behind a legacy of religious tolerance and educational innovation, some of which survived him. Bourgade, de Vialar, and other Algerian "expatriates" like them regarded Tunisia as a favorable site where policies that were unpopular or untenable in Algeria could be pursued. In stark contrast to Dupuch and Lavigerie, Émilie de Vialar believed that "the interests of Catholicism [were] furthered by fostering respect for other faiths, particularly Islam" (Curtis 2002).

Both de Vialar and Bourgade viewed their teaching mission in Tunisia in a way that anticipated Louis Machuel's (1848–1922) educational reforms of the late nineteenth and early twentieth centuries.

When the French army invaded Tunisia from eastern Algeria in 1881, France claimed only 708 nationals in the entire country. Although accurate figures for other European communities in Tunisia at the time are difficult to obtain, it is known that at least 9,000 Italians and 6,500 Maltese resided in the Tunis region alone, out of a total population for the capital region of slightly less than 100,000 people (Sebag 1998, 303–4). Uncounted thousands of Algerian expatriates called Tunisia home.

Conclusions and Postscripts

By pursuing a horizontal line of inquiry to trace the departures of Algerians and Europeans for pre-1881 Tunisia, this chapter has attempted to reconnect French Algeria with the histories of the Maghreb. It argues that emigration to precolonial Tunisia brought Algerians into a specific system of legal pluralism that paradoxically helped to define what it meant to be Algerian. Attempts by both the beylical government and the French consulate to impose a stable jurisdictional identity on Algerian émigrés and refugees, however ineffective; the endless debates over who could claim French protection; and the devising of new bureaucratic instruments to document an individual's status may have been key factors in the emergence of the kind of complex identity analyzed by M. Chebel. Moreover, Noiriel's " 'genealogy' of the card and the code" (1988, 90), whose origins he seeks uniquely within metropole France, might have ancestry on the colonial periphery and in the early decades of the nineteenth century.

Although some Algerians married into Tunisian families, gradually assuming a new identity, many others remained distinct by marrying within the Algerian diasporic community in Tunisia, retaining collective memories of Algeria as well as a collective identity for generations. Algerian Muslim families in Tunisia produced leading nationalists, such as ʻAbd al-ʻAziz al-Thaʻalibi, founder of the Destour Party, and Tawfiq al-Madani, whose parents fled the Constantine during the 1871 rebellion, or leading members of the Tunisian Communist Party, such as Gladys Adda, whose father was originally from the Jewish community in Batna. Other Algerians, such as Shaykh ʻAbd al-Hamid Ben Badis, leader of the Reformed Ulema, spent long periods of time in Tunis to acquire an Islamic education at the Zaytuna mosque-university. The important point is that the political activism of this group of exiles far outweighed their actual numbers in Tunisia (Kazdaghli 1993; Clancy-Smith 1994; McDougall 2002, 98–99). Indeed, throughout the nineteenth century, key figures in the formation of an Algerian complex identity were expelled from the country by French authorities and died in distant lands. The most obvious example is the emir 'Abd el-Kadir, who after exile in France went to Damascus in 1855, where he attracted a large, diverse following from the Algerian diasporic community in the Ottoman Empire and Mediterranean world.

If native Algerians residing in Tunisia came to regard Algeria as the "mother country" and *l'Algérie Française* as a *marâtre,* a cruel and unnatural mother, the European settlers viewed or were taught to view France as the *mère-patrie.* However, the colonial regime's steadfast refusal to educate Algerians and the vicious denial of the validity of Arabo-Islamic civilization transformed Algeria into an inverted template for the civilizing mission. Thus, some Europeans came to see Tunisia as a site of regeneration for the empire, a space where the mistakes of Algeria could be rectified by more enlightened colonial policies and practices, especially in the domain of education. Although never questioning the civilizing mission, French or European "expatriates" from French Algeria, such as de Vialar, Bourgade, and later Louis Machuel, partially assimilated to Tunisian culture and assumed a new concrete and ideal identity. The great Arabist and educator Louis Machuel, born in Algiers in 1848, abandoned his homeland in 1883 for Tunis, where he died and was buried in 1922; and he was not alone in making this change (Arnoulet 1991; A. Messaoudi 1996).

After 1881, European emigration from French Algeria to Tunisia meant adapting to a different system of colonial law and culture—owing in part to Tunisia's status as a protectorate and to the presence of a large, autonomous immigrant Italian population in the country, whose different status was governed by the 1896 Franco-Italian convention. Another essential distinction was that the brutal *Code de l'indigénat,* instituted in Algeria from the 1870s on, did not exist in colonial Tunisia. Although colonial officials issued legally discriminatory *décrets* and laws from 1885 on, rendering Tunisians second-class subjects before the law, these actions never approached the institutionalized legal violence suffered by the Algerian population in French Algeria (Bach-Hamba [1918] 1991, 69–78). Nor was naturalization seen as desirable for the majority non-French Mediterranean population. Comparing two adjacent French possessions in North Africa from the perspective of migration, identity, and legal pluralism thus reveals surprising variations in terms of "patterns and outcomes."

2 "I Went Pale with Pleasure"

The Body, Sexuality, and National Identity among French Travelers to Algiers in the Nineteenth Century

VICTORIA THOMPSON

IN 1860, the French writer Ernest Feydeau traveled to the city of Algiers.[1] Like all those who in midcentury visited this recently conquered city, Feydeau made a point of going to what was known as the Moorish district or Casbah. Located on the hillside above the French city, or Marine quarter, the Casbah was in reality a multiethnic quarter, housing both Jews and West Africans as well as Muslim city dwellers known as Moors. It could be reached from the Marine quarter by climbing a steep hill. Inside the Casbah, narrow streets followed curving paths, guiding the traveler through whitewashed buildings with few openings to the exterior. Feydeau, again like most French travelers to Algiers in this period, could not suppress the thrill he felt in visiting the old city and especially in seeing the exterior of its houses. He wrote, "the doors of each house, completely closed, reinforced with huge bronze nails and pierced by peep-holes covered with lattice, have a taciturn air, like the doors of the harem or the prison. I went pale with pleasure" (1862, 10).

This comment links sex, the body, and power in a Foucauldian way that has become familiar to us. In evoking in the same sentence the institution that, according to Foucault (1991), best exemplified the new mechanisms of discipline in nineteenth-century European society, the prison, as well as the institution that for Europeans represented licentious sexuality, the harem, Feydeau's comment seems proof of the close connection between discipline and sexuality, the two pillars, in Foucault's work, upon which bourgeois identity was erected.

Feydeau's pleasure only reinforces this impression. In volume 1 of *The His-*

1. I thank Ellen Furlough for her thorough and insightful reading of this essay. I also thank Patricia Lorcin and the members of the Women's History Reading Group at Arizona State University—in particular Rachel Fuchs, Laurie Manchester, and Hava Tirosh-Samuelson—for their comments on an earlier draft.

tory of Sexuality, Foucault depicts pleasure as a primary conduit for power. He writes of, on the one hand, "[t]he pleasure that comes of exercising a power that questions, monitors, watches, spies, searches out, palpitates, brings to light; and on the other hand, the pleasure that kindles at having to evade this power, flee from it, fool it, or travesty it" (1978, 45). We might ask ourselves what sort of pleasure Feydeau was experiencing, for both appear possible. His voyage through the Casbah seems to be a classic Orientalist gesture. Part of the thrill he experienced in the Casbah arose from his confrontation with a mute and mysterious Other that was best exemplified for him, as for other travelers, by the extreme privacy of housing in the Casbah. The impenetrability of this architecture emphasized the "exteriority" of travelers vis-à-vis the population and the culture they encountered; they described it in terms that were, as Edward Said puts it, "meant to indicate that the Orientalist is outside the Orient, both as an existential and as a moral fact" (1978, 20–21). Feydeau's pleasure could thus be seen as a consequence of exercising the power of description over a subject population.

However, Feydeau also set out on his voyage to Algiers to escape what he felt to be the monotony and struggle of his Parisian existence. "Tired of the uniformity of an existence that is constantly dedicated to work, I wanted to recapture serenity by requiring of myself the contemplation of that which matters" (1862, i). Feydeau's pleasure may thus equally be seen as part of an attempt to "evade" structures of power that in France shaped his identity and existence as a writer. If we can envision what Foucault calls the "perpetual spirals of power and pleasure" (1978, 45), we see that Feydeau occupied a position of one who simultaneously both exercises and evades power.

This status was particularly evident in Algiers because of Algeria's ambiguous status as a territory that both was and was not "French." The uncertainty of Feydeau's relationship to power and the consequent instability of his identity as both a Frenchman and an imperialist was manifested, in his travel account as well as in those of other French travelers, through images of bodily penetrability (including, but not limited to, references to sexual relations), lack of mastery over the body and its senses, and physical and psychic disorientation.

The ways in which French travelers presented their bodies in descriptions of Algiers raise questions concerning the relationship between place, body, and identity, as well as questions concerning the clarity of the distinction between the self and the other. The physical and psychological responses that some travelers experienced in Algiers—responses that included pleasure, but also fear, confusion, and disgust—entailed an engagement with the Other that is not usually recognized as part of an Orientalist attitude or experience. According to Said, the Orient serves either as a sort of space for "private fantasy" for the Western self or as a distanced object of study (1978, 176). In either case, Said implies, the Western self does not engage the Oriental Other in any meaningful way. However, if we shift our focus to moments when the traveler appears—willingly or not—to have lost some measure of mastery over his or her self, a measure of engagement with the Other becomes evident.

This shift of focus also asks us to reconsider our understanding of the exotic in French writing on Algiers. Although Feydeau was fascinated with the exotic side of Algerian life, his attempt to capture it in writing was neither part of a project to justify the conquest of the colony, as Panivong Norindr suggests in relation to Indochina (1996, 3), nor an extended exercise in self-validation, as Said would have it (1978, 170). It comes closer to Chris Bongie's formulation of exoticism as a means of indicating loss (1991, 5). However, whereas Bongie defines the exotic as a means of highlighting a perceived loss of traditional values in European society, the travel accounts examined here instead associate the exotic with a loss of bearings experienced by the French traveler. In these sources, the exotic elicits and frames a moment of extreme disorientation, an instance of being thrust from the familiar into the strange in a way that calls into question previously accepted notions of spatial and social organization. Focusing on the exotic as either part of a process of imposing mastery or as a means by which the French bemoaned the impact of modernization presupposes that the French had a clear notion about their relationship to colonial territories. Yet in the mid-nineteenth century the French role in Algeria was unclear. Furthermore, whereas scholarship usually treats the exotic as a quality associated with the non-French Other, in travel accounts such as that of Feydeau exotic locales and individuals change the way in which French travelers think of themselves and their relation to their environment. The exotic thus marks a moment of uncertainty in the French traveler.

These considerations lead us to reconsider the role Algeria has played in constructing identity for both individual French men and women and for the French nation. Jean-Robert Henry, in his introduction to a volume on French and Algerian identity, argues that "Algeria was one of the most familiar and prominent forms of alterity in relation to which modern France defined herself. During this period, Algeria helped to sustain in the French imagination the distinctions between modernity and tradition, between civilization and the desert" (1993, 3). In taking such a view, Henry characterizes Algeria as a well-defined Other against which French identity was constructed, asserted, and maintained. However, in addition to dismissing any possible engagement with the Other, this view of the role of Algeria in forging French identity also overlooks the degree to which, in the early colonial period, Algeria was an unfamiliar territory whose relation to France was contested and unstable.

The first forty years of the French presence in Algeria were characterized by conflict and uncertainty. The conquest of Algeria began on 14 June 1830, when French military forces landed at Sidi-Ferruch. On 5 July, Algiers was taken, but the military campaign was far from over. From 1830 to 1847, the French struggled with a coalition of resistance forces led by Emir 'Abd el-Kadir. Brutal military tactics associated most closely with Governor-General Thomas-Robert Bugeaud led to the eventual defeat of the emir. However, until 1857 the French faced resistance in Kabylia. In addition, local uprisings occurred in 1849, 1859, 1860, and 1864.

In addition to the continued reality of armed resistance, the French faced uncertainty over how much of Algeria should be brought under French control and how it should be administered. Although the initial conquest of Algiers and some of the coastal regions momentarily satisfied members of the French military who, having served under Napoleon, wanted to recapture a sense of armed glory, the extent of the conquest was disputed almost immediately. In the 1830s, several economists recommended withdrawal from Algeria, arguing that the region would not be profitable, while those governmental and diplomatic circles worried that continued occupation would anger England. In 1834, the annexed coastal cities were put under the direction of the War Ministry. As settlement increased, however, colonists argued for the eventual incorporation of Algeria into France with the same status as any French department. While the governments of the both the Second Republic and Second Empire expressed their determination to retain Algeria, continual debate over and changes of policy concerning the status of French colonists—in relation to both the metropolitan French and the indigenous inhabitants of the colony—rendered the colony's relationship to France uncertain and unstable. It is in this context of uncertainty and contestation that French travel literature must be understood. Although the French were undoubtedly "imperialists" in Algeria, what exactly that meant—for both individual French men and women and for the French nation—was unclear.

A relative ignorance of the territory and people of Algeria contributed to this uncertainty. According to historian Claude Martin, "[in 1830] hardly anyone in France knew Algeria" (1963, 64). Before the conquest of Algiers, visitors to the area were few, largely limited to those with diplomatic or commercial interests, and few accounts of the region were published in France. After 1830, an enormous amount of energy was put into the study of Algeria and its people. Most of this work was done by those who accompanied military expeditions or were associated with the colonial administration. Studies of the indigenous population were linked to questions of who would be most likely to support and who to subvert French rule (Lorcin 1999b, 667). However, continued resistance made it difficult to draw such conclusions with any certainty. The difficulties involved in "fixing" the identity of the native population contributed to a consequent difficulty of "fixing" French identity in the colony.

From the very beginning of their accounts, French travelers associated Algiers with the unknown and the incomprehensible. Théophile Gautier described the thrill of approaching the North African coast. In the morning of the second day at sea, he wrote, "with the help of binoculars, we perceived, very indistinctly on the extreme edge of the horizon . . . the first outlines of the Atlas [mountains]. . . . We were going, in a few hours, to be in another part of the world, in this mysterious Africa, which is however only two days away from France. . . . Our emotion was extreme, and we were not the only ones to feel this way" ([1845] 1973, 177–78).[2] Like Gautier, Feydeau highlighted the unfamiliar in describing his approach to the port of Algiers. He found his first sight of the city jarring and had trouble making sense of it from afar: "Everywhere there are nothing but vertical and horizontal planes colliding, confused, intersecting and crossing over each other in a sort of revolt" (1862, 5).

Upon landing, however, travelers were often surprised by the apparent familiarity of the Marine quarter owing to French renovations. "The neighborhood that extends from the Admiralty to the porte d'Azzoun is as French as any chef-lieu of our venerable *départements,*" wrote X. Marmier (quoted in Piesse 1862, 5). In the Marine quarter, one could find virtually everything a Parisian might require: restaurants with fixed-price menus, cafés, clothing stores and hairdressers, bookstores and newspapers, theaters, and the omnibus (Piesse 1862, 1–5). In stressing the traveler's comfort, authors called on the topography of Paris to describe that of Algiers. For Gautier, the Place du Gouvernement, the central meeting square of the Marine quarter, was "like the lobby of the [*théâtre*] des Italiens or of the Opéra in the open-air . . . it's the [café] Tortoni, the boulevard des Italiens" (1862, 185).

The large-scale renovation of the area around the port was in part an attempt to impose, on a structural as well as a symbolic level, a vision of French authority on a colony and population that was still in the process of being conquered (Çelik 1997). By replicating elements of their own capital in Algiers, the French made a powerful statement about the "naturalness" of their occupation. At the same time, the construction of arcades and shopping districts, of hotels, cafés, and

2. The quotes from Gautier in this chapter are translated from the 1865 text, the first version published in its entirety. However, the sections of concern in this chapter appear to be exact reproductions of the text prepared for publication in 1846. Gautier traveled to Algeria in 1845.

restaurants in which the French would feel comfortable, was designed to increase French tourism to the colony.

Part of the attraction of Algiers, however, lay in its difference from Paris. Travelers such as Charles Desprez argued that this difference constituted an improvement in matters such as architecture. "The rue Bab-Azzoun," he wrote, "is embellished with arcades like the rue Castiglione in Paris. This type of construction, of little profit in our foggy country, is perfectly suited to Algeria's climate. Winter and summer, whether the sun darts or the rain whips, it shelters the passerby but does not blind him" (1860, 12). Although Desprez's views on the unsuitability of French architecture for France were idiosyncratic, his conviction that it better suited the needs of the colony was typical of urban planners and colonial authorities during this period. It was not until the early twentieth century that French architects and urban planners began to incorporate indigenous motifs and structures in their work (Wright 1991).

This mixing of Algerian and French—the Algerian sun and French buildings, Algerian warmth and French pleasures—was a recurrent theme in French travelers' descriptions of Algiers that provides insight into French attitudes toward their colony. The Marine quarter, for all its similarity to France, was just different enough to create a sense of the foreign. Attestations of French superiority in matters such as urban planning are accompanied by passages in which travelers revel in what is not French: the climate, the sight of different sorts of people, and the availability of different sorts of pleasures. In this mixing of the familiar and the foreign, descriptions of Algiers by French travelers differ somewhat from most other travel narratives, where the goal was to escape reminders of home and focus on what was "out of the ordinary" (Urry 1990, 11).

French travelers' descriptions of Algiers both drew upon and altered common conventions of the travel narrative. Influenced by romanticism, nineteenth-century travel narratives tended to emphasize the individual traveler's emotional reactions to the sights and experiences of his or her trip.[3] To do this, the narratives drew on the conventions of the picturesque. In this sense, they differed from scientific accounts of foreign—and especially colonial—territories, wherein the goals were to be objective and to create a sense of distance between the author/reader and the areas described.[4] The travel narrative instead highlighted the traveler's involvement in his or her surroundings by emphasizing the emo-

3. A thorough discussion of the influence of romanticism on travel narratives can be found in Buzard 1993, 110–30.

4. For a discussion of these differences, see Edney 1990, chap. 2.

tions elicited by the voyage. The picturesque was used, according to Linda Nochlin, to elicit pleasing emotions that would "mask conflict with the appearance of tranquility" (1989, 50), but extreme emotional states and discomfort were also described and often linked to the traveler's loss of control over his or her physical movements and reactions.

Over the course of the nineteenth century, Europeans' presumed ability to master foreign territories became a central component of their identity. This ability was often articulated with reference to the body. Thus, control over foreign territory assumed certain characteristics located in and acted out by embodied individuals, such as a sense of direction, the ability to conceive of and move in straight lines, and the capacity for envisioning abstract spatial arrangements (Adas 1989). It also was associated with control over one's own body. According to Alice Conklin, by the late nineteenth century "French imperial ideology consistently identified civilization with one principle more than any other: mastery. Mastery . . . of nature, including the human body, and mastery of what can be called 'social' behavior" (1997, 5–6).

In French travelers' accounts of Algiers, however, the traveler's sense of mastery over the body and emotions is constantly challenged. Many travelers experienced great physical and psychic disorientation in the Casbah in particular. Feydeau, for example, was made dizzy by his walk through the old city:

> The network of winding streets dispersed all around me in complicated turns, like those of a labyrinth. Some of these streets meandered capriciously only to end in miniature squares . . . others proceeded straight forward, as if they had been perfectly aligned, and their wooden coverings were so low that at times I was obliged to bend over to pass underneath them; finally there were isolated houses that were perilously balanced, out in the sun, at the edges of demolished material, and when I turned in front of them, I suddenly saw the sea, like a beautiful slab of steel, climb in front of the sky through a large opening. (1862, 10–11)

The Casbah challenged the French visitor, calling into question his sense of direction and ability to make sense of and navigate foreign territory, qualities intimately linked to European identity in the nineteenth century.[5] Although Feydeau found a certain pleasure in this loss of mastery, other travelers found this difficulty in navigating the native city much more unsettling. The traveler Chanony wrote that in going into the Casbah, "[I had to] cling [to the walls] in order to climb up, with my iron-clad shoes, the slippery pavement of these narrow, twisting, and dark alleyways" (1853, 14). Both Théophile Gautier and Louise Vallory

5. See Adas 1989; Edney 1990; Pyenson 1993.

felt a sense of fear in the old city and were eager to return to the European quarter. Gautier's fear was heightened by the fact that he walked through the Casbah at night, when "[t]he architecture . . . took on . . . the most mysterious and fantastic appearance. . . . To night was added the unknown. We heard nearby strange whispers, guttural laughs, incomprehensible words . . . black figures, squatting in doorways, watched us with white eyes. We stepped on grayish masses that changed position while sighing. We walked as if in a dream, not knowing if we were awake or asleep" ([1845] 1973, 194). Moving through streets whose direction and inhabitants were equally mysterious and hard to fathom, whose sights and sounds were nearly incomprehensible, French travelers revealed their inability to navigate, understand, and describe a foreign territory in their accounts.

The French section of Algiers, or Marine quarter, usually described as more comfortable, familiar, and reassuring, could also become a site of disorientation. This disorientation was owing to encounters not with a different urban landscape, but with a different population. Like many travelers, Gautier found the central square of the city, the Place du Gouvernement, disorienting because of its crowd. He described it as "chaos! A place of confusion! The black cloak of the Parisienne brushes in passing against the white veil of the Moorish woman; the embroidered sleeve of the officer scratches the naked arm of the Negro rubbed with oil; the rags of the Bedouin jostle the frock coat of the elegant Frenchman." Walking into this central square with its "bizarre crowd" produced, Gautier asserted, "a sort of vertigo" ([1845] 1973, 185–86, 183). The French body here is presented as vulnerable and nearly permeable to others who brush, scratch, and jostle it. The resulting psychic disorientation—Gautier's vertigo—indicates a loss of mastery over bodily sensations as well as a challenge to his sense of self.

Gautier made this point even more explicitly in his review of the 1852 salon when he commented upon the paintings of Thédore Chassériau, who had also traveled to Africa. In his review, Gautier again wrote of the "vertigo" produced by a trip to Algeria and asserted that "even . . . the most robust [who travel there] return a little Muslim in their hearts" ([1845] 1973, 91). For Gautier, the Orient in general and Algeria in particular challenged a traveler's sense of "Frenchness" in a dizzying manner.

Physical mastery in the colony has also been understood in sexual and gendered terms. Historians have argued that colonial conquest was frequently described in terms that likened it to, at best, seduction and, at worst, rape.[6] In

6. Several chapters in Clancy-Smith and Gouda 1998 analyze this use of gender in French imperialism. The chapter authored by Julia Clancy-Smith, "Islam, Gender, and Identities in the Making

accounts that used this bodily metaphor to describe the imperialist endeavor, the European was gendered male and the native territory female. This gendering served to emphasize hierarchical distinctions between colonizer and colonized.

The tendency to gender feminine the indigenous inhabitants of Algiers is evident in the earliest French travel accounts to the city. Théophile Gautier, for example, wrote that many young Arab men in Algiers possessed a "rare beauty" and commented that "women who are considered beautiful in Paris would be happy to have such heads on their shoulders" ([1845] 1973, 207, 208). Yet, rather than reinforce hierarchies of difference and power, this gendering seemed to unsettle such hierarchies by raising the specter of male homosexuality. Europeans had long associated North Africa and the Middle East with sex between men (Bleys 1996). If the multiplication of "perversions," as Foucault puts it, was one of the trajectories through which bourgeois identity was formed, then Algeria would seem to present itself as a prime theater for the definition and consolidation of bourgeois identity in the nineteenth century. Indeed, the work of numerous scholars of imperialism has demonstrated the importance of sexuality as an axis around which the differences between European and non-European were articulated.[7] However, whereas the British in India, for example, used homosexuality to distinguish both between British and Indian and among different groups of the Indian population, the French tended to blur the difference between French and Arab in their discussions of this issue in Algeria (Sinha 1995, 19).

The French, who referred to male-male sexual relations as "the Arab vice," believed that such sexual practices were common to the native population of Algeria. Some travelers, such as Alexis de Tocqueville, acknowledged the existence of sexual relations between men in Algeria. In describing his 1841 trip to Algiers, Tocqueville wrote, "Evening, a trip to the Casbah. Old Algiers seemed an immense fox burrow: narrow, dark, smoky. The population, at this hour, seems idle and dissolute. Indigenous cabaret where Moorish public girls sing and people drink wine. Mix of the vices of both civilizations" (2001, 37). Tocqueville does not specify if the French practiced this "vice" while in Algiers, but Edouard Adolphe Duchesne, who wrote a study of prostitution in Algiers, was convinced that they did. For one thing, male sexual partners were widely available to French men, even in the Marine quarter. "In Algiers," he wrote, "it is not only women who practice the shameful trade of prostitution; at every step, in the Place du

---

of French Algeria, 1830–1962," discusses the metaphor of rape. This use of gender has also been widely discussed in studies on British imperialism. See, for example, Lewes 1993, McClintock 1995, Sinha 1995.

7. See Hyam 1990; McClintock 1995; Stoler 1995; Clancy-Smith and Gouda 1998.

Gouvernement itself, and at every street corner, you will meet children, young boys between ten and twelve years of age who will address you with the most tenacious provocations and will make you the most obscene propositions" (1853, 45). Duchesne first attempted to explain male homosexuality in Algeria by reference to aspects of Algerian life that were distinctly not French. For example, he discussed the sequestration of Arab women (which made them less available), the supposed sexual passivity of Arab women (which did not satisfy men's appetites), and the climate (which excited those appetites). However, he finished this list of explanations with one that blurred the line between occidental and Oriental sexual proclivities, writing, "One must also perhaps confess that Arabs let themselves be tempted by the truly remarkable beauty of nearly all the young boys. These beautiful, naked heads are displayed in the streets, the bazaars and the public walkways" (1853, 45). Duchesne's reference to the beauty of young Arab men, a "true" beauty that was recognized by French as well as Arab, moved homosexuality outside of the exclusively Arab sphere in which he sought to place it. The cross-cultural acknowledgment of male beauty implies a cross-cultural sexual desire, an implication that Duchesne made explicit elsewhere. French travelers, he lamented, "to satisfy their tastes for what is new, for what is foreign . . . have especially sought and do still seek out the natives" (1853, 78).

What role did this possibility of new sorts of sexual relations and the pleasures they engendered play in the creation of a European, middle-class, and imperialist identity? What was the relationship between homosexuality and assimilation? In travel accounts during this period, mentions of male-male sexual relations are few, and those of female-female relations nonexistent, making it difficult to answer this question. In this case, it is fruitful to expand our search not only to other forms of sexuality, but to other depictions of the body in general. In *Race and the Education of Desire,* Ann Laura Stoler argues that Foucault's focus on masturbation when discussing infantile sexuality is too narrow, for it excludes a variety of concerns regarding bodily relations between children and servants in both the colonial and domestic context, concerns that were intimately linked to questions of national, class, and, to a lesser degree, gender identity (1995, 145). Likewise, same-sex sexual relations can be placed within a larger context of bodily practices and sensations that called into question French travelers' national identity.

If male-male sexual relations were thought to be the Arab vice, then heterosexual prostitution was widely seen as the French vice. Prostitution was an institution that the French believed their conquest, with its disruption of the indigenous economy and the continued presence of French military personnel and of travelers, made possible. However, although different sexual practices were identified with different nationalities, this distinction was also presented as unstable. The French traveler Louise Vallory commented on this instability in her discussion of female prostitution in Algiers. She argued that prostitution among Moorish women was a result of exposure to a French education. In becoming aware of the differences between what they were taught at school and what they practiced at home, these girls "no longer know what to do, and they attempt [to acquire] liberty through *libertinage*. I was in contact with two Moorish women in transition, if I can use this term, and the life of these poor women was dull, tortured, unhappy like that of all beings who symbolize eras of social transformation" (1863, 42–43). Sexuality here seems to function not as a linchpin for the creation of identity, but rather as a marker of instability—a sign of the loss of identity or the transition from one identity to another. For Duchesne as well, the contact between French and Arab led to a generalized moral dissolution. "If one is forced to recognize the unhappy influence of our conquest on the already loose morals of the indigenous population, one must unfortunately also admit that the excessive lenience of Arab morals in such matters has somewhat affected the Europeans, whose level of morality has sensibly lowered on this point [sexuality] as on so many others" (1853, 84). The French conquest thus led not to a clarification of sexual hierarchies, but rather to a troubling blurring of sexual mores, desires, and practices. In Algiers, then, sexuality—like all embodied experience—did not strengthen identity, but rather functioned as a site of uncertainty.

Let us return now to Feydeau's sense of pleasure. All of the authors experienced some degree of pleasure in their travels. They also, however, experienced a deep sense of discomfort in and with their bodies. Foucault writes that "[t]he power which . . . took charge of sexuality set about contacting bodies, caressing them with its eyes, intensifying areas, electrifying surfaces, dramatizing troubled moments" (1978, 44). These "troubled moments" were pleasurable to the extent that they were part of a perceived adventure. Yet the Orientalist texts in which these moments are recounted do not unproblematically create or affirm, as Said has argued, a coherent sense of identity. According to Said, "European culture gained in strength and identity by setting itself off against the Orient as a sort of surrogate and even underground self" (1978, 3). In some ways and in certain places, these travel accounts do, as Said's comment implies, attribute to an Oriental Other all those characteristics and acts that were to be excluded from French respectability. As we have seen, however, these accounts also call into question the characteristics and qualities associated with French identity.

French travelers linked questions of the body and sexuality to a discussion not only of their own identity, but also of the French role in Algeria. Just as they were troubled by the impact of Algeria and its indigenous population on the French body, so too were they concerned about the implications of converting Algerian bodies into French bodies, as the account by Pauline de Noirfontaine demonstrates. Noirfontaine had recourse to the metaphor of fashion—the outward manifestation of identity through the adornment of the body—to express this idea: "I will suppose that we succeed, toward and against all, to make Algeria a branch [*succursale*] of France, and that in the end we introduce the Arabs to our customs, our fashions, and our tastes. Will they be better dressed when they have exchanged their classic burnoose [hooded cloak] for our romantic *patelots,* their poetic turban for our prosaic cap?" (1856, 302–3).

And although their position of "exteriority" vis-à-vis the body of the Other sometimes served to justify and increase the power of the French, namely by positioning them as experts able to render visible and comprehensible this population recently brought under French control, it was, as we have seen, an imperfect exteriority in that the integrity of the French body was constantly breached by willing or unwilling contact with the body of the Other. Furthermore, as Vallory suggested, this body of the Other contained a self that appeared inaccessible to the French and perhaps also more stable. Thus, Vallory wrote that when vanquished, the Arab "turns inward to the interior self over which the conqueror has no hold, and there he dreams, he loses himself in horizons of freedom, of liberty" (1863, 2). This interiorization can be seen as a gesture of self-defense and defiance. Marc Côte has argued that faced with the "forced opening" of colonial conquest, "Algeria barricaded itself, in its houses and its mothers of families" (1988, 111). Vallory, translating that sense of interiorization into a movement toward the inner self, associated it with the possibility of resistance when she wrote that "the assimilation of the conquered race with the conquering race is far from accomplished" (1863, 2). Her vision of the self-contained native provides a stark contrast to that of the French visitor whose mastery over the self was called into question in Algiers. And although Eugène Fromentin argued that "we will annihilate [the native] rather than force him to abdicate; I repeat, he will disappear before mixing with us" ([1858] 1887, 209), the annihilation of the French self is suggested in these accounts far more often than that of the native.

For Vallory and others, what was at stake in Algeria was the relationship between France and its recently acquired colony and in particular the possible failure of the policy of assimilation. Like many other travelers, Vallory contrasted French and Algerian bodies—their appearance, the way in which they perceived and moved through space, and their relationship to the bodies of others—to interrogate the imperialist project in Algeria. What comes across in these travel accounts is a profound unease with "imperialist" as a category of French identity. Thus, although pleasure and power are certainly linked in these travel accounts, they are not always linked in ways that the work of Foucault would lead us to expect. These narratives tend for the most part to present the French as uncomfortable and unnatural visitors in Algiers, visitors whose identity, as manifested through their bodies, was called into question.

This is not to say that the "troubled moments" experienced by French travelers, pleasurable or not, did not call forth a response meant to increase French power in the colony. Indeed, the cultural and physical violence exerted by the French on the Algerian population suggests that the threat to French identity represented by Algeria may have prompted an excessive response of attempted stabilization. However, as Foucault's model of a spiral implies, the power exerted by the French was one that was shaped by an engagement between self and other, an engagement that transformed the French self in the process.[8]

Lisa Lowe (1991) has argued that Orientalist texts often serve as a means of questioning European identities. Complicated by the author's class and gender, as well as by his or her political views, the Orientalist text becomes a vehicle for articulating conflicts of identity rather than a means by which a coherent identity is solidified. This view of the Orientalist text better describes these travel accounts. Similarly, Stoler (1995) maintains that the colonial experience highlighted the vulnerability of European identity. At the same time, however, Orientalist descriptions of Algiers written by voyagers other than the French do not reveal the same uncertainties. Although British visitors, for example, relate emotional reactions to the sights of the city, they do not express the same degree of discomfort and disorientation indicated in the French accounts. George Wingrove Cooke, a British visitor to Algiers, also found himself lost in the Casbah, but thanks to his unproblematic relationship with the indigenous population, he experienced no discomfort or even inconvenience when lost. "There is an excellent fellow," he wrote, "one Hasan, a water-carrier—who often dogs me about at a respectful and unobtrusive distance, because he has discovered that I have a habit of losing my way in these dim labyrinths, and of giving half a franc to the person who helps me back again into the Rue de la Casbah" (1860, 19). In this passage, Cooke's financial power undergirds a relationship in which the Algerian Other remains at a distance, yet always ready to help. The contrast between this portrayal of the traveler/native relationship and Gautier's experience—in which he found himself,

8. This engagement also transformed the self of the Algerian Other, as Frantz Fanon ([1961] 1963, [1952] 1967) has so powerfully argued.

to his horror, stepping upon sighing, huddled humans in the streets of the Casbah—is striking.[9]

Although the British did not feel the same sorts of disorientation, discomfort, and physical vulnerability that the French did in Algiers, they did describe similar sentiments in early-nineteenth-century accounts of their visits to Paris. British travelers, largely at ease in the Casbah, slipped and slid through the streets of Paris; they felt no strong emotions toward the non-European population of Algiers and yet felt disgust when jostled by the Parisian crowds, even as they were tempted by the charms of la Parisienne (Colston 1822; Grant 1844; Jessop 1928). I would suggest, then, that the disorientation of the body evident in these accounts is linked to a sense of uncertainty concerning what it meant to be "English" or "French," a questioning of which direction to take at a point when multiple paths appeared possible and a questioning linked to a specific place that carried with it specific associations. This was certainly true in colonies such as Algeria, whose relationship to the metropole was unclear, but it could also be true of other destinations whose apparent exoticism carried a particularly significant symbolic weight.

In writing about the way in which travelers see the surroundings they visit, John Urry argues, "There is no single tourist gaze as such. It varies by society, by social group and by historical period. Such gazes are constructed through difference. By this I mean not merely that there is no universal experience which is true for all tourists all the time. Rather the gaze in any historical period is constructed in relationship to its opposite, to non-tourist forms of social experience and consciousness" (1990, 1–2). The same argument can be made for the emotional and physical experiences of travelers whose reactions to their surroundings depended on the potential impact such surroundings might have on their sense of self. Thus, whereas French travelers in Algiers were unsettled by the implications of imperialist conquest, the British in Paris were unsettled by the consequences of democratic revolution.

Although all travel contains a measure of what we now call "culture shock," one that is experienced in part through the body, the unwillingness or inability to suppress a sense of extreme distress and disorientation in travel accounts is significant, for it does not appear in all accounts at all times. When it does, it forces

9. French travelers who voyaged through the British colonies repeatedly remarked with surprise on the unflappable and unchanging character of the British in their own colonies (Monicat 1996, 53). Such observations also suggest British "comfort" with the identity of "imperialist," a comfort not shared by the French.

us to question why, at specific times and in specific places, mastery over the body begins to falter and identity is called into question. It forces us to wonder why, at specific times and in specific places, sexuality appears to play a role in the dissolution of identity rather than in its construction. And, finally, it forces us to dig deeper to understand the formation and use of subjectivity and its relation to national identity among nineteenth-century Europeans both at home and abroad.

3 Shaping the Colonial Body

Sport and Society in Algeria, 1870–1962

PHILIP DINE

ON FIRST CONSIDERATION, sport might appear an unlikely inclusion as a topic in a scholarly history of colonial Algeria. Indeed, a sporting universe of horse races and football matches, of boxing bouts and athletics meets, of swimming galas and rowing regattas might all too easily give the impression of having little, if anything, to do with the harsh realities of colonial rule. For sport, insofar as it has been considered at all by historians of French Algeria, has tended to be subsumed in a composite representation of the social world of the territory's European settlers or *pieds-noirs*. As one British historian of the 1954–62 war of national liberation has put it,

> essentially their life and pleasures were those of the true Mediterranean being: the old women sitting and gossiping on shaded park benches, the men arguing and story-telling over the long-drawn-out *pastis* outside the bistros; the protracted silence of the siesta; then the awakening in the cool of the evening, the games of *boule* in dusty squares, under trees populated with revivified and chattering birds. It was a good life, with not too many cares. For the affluent there was the Algiers Yacht Club, the Golf Club, the Club Anglais and the Club Hippique, and skiing up at Chréa in the winter; for the *petits blancs* of Algiers there was the racecourse at Hussein-Dey and football at the Belcourt stadium. The heavy red wine of Algeria was both plentiful and cheap, and above all there was the beach. (Horne [1977] 1978, 51–52)

However, on closer inspection, sport may be seen to provide a privileged means of access to the dualistic political economy of *Algérie française*—together with its supporting symbolic order—just as it has been amply demonstrated to constitute a crucial mnemonic site or *lieu de mémoire* for France's principal colonial rival, Great Britain.

J. A. Mangan, in a 1992 essay helpfully summarizing much of his own extensive research in this field, characterizes imperial sport as "Britain's Chief Spiritual

Export," stressing its composite role as "Moral Metaphor, Political Symbol and Cultural Bond." He spells out his view of sport's contribution to the life of the British overseas empire as follows: "sport was a significant part of imperial culture, and an important instrument of imperial cultural association and subsequent cultural change, promoting at various times in various localities imperial union, national identity, social reform, recreational development and post-imperial goodwill. These imperial and post-imperial outcomes of sport constitute a missing dimension of the historiography of imperialism" (1992, 4).

Although Mangan's comments obviously relate to the British Empire, where the link between what he terms the "games ethic" and imperialism has been systematically explored, the role of sport in French imperial expansion and colonial consolidation has not on the whole been given the attention that it merits. It is true that there are a number of important exceptions to this general rule (Amar 1987; P. Martin 1991; Deville-Dantu 1992a, 1992b, 1992c, 1992d, 1992e, 1997; Hick 1992; Benoit 1996). Nevertheless, the exploitation of modern sport's administrative, political, and symbolic potential within the French colonial empire, from the later nineteenth century until its terminal collapse in the wake of the Second World War, has not yet been subjected to sustained examination. This "missing dimension of the historiography of imperialism" is thus all the more marked in the French context than it is in the British one.

This said, recent conspicuous French success in international sporting competitions, including in particular the 1998 football (soccer) World Cup, has undoubtedly focused popular and scholarly attention in France on the relationship between ethnicity and issues of citizenship, empowerment, and social inclusion (O'Donnell and Blain 1999; Abdallah 2000; Dine 2000). This broad public interest and the closely associated media and political investment in ethnically diverse French teams (in football, but also in athletics, handball, and other sports) have been discussed in terms of new patterns of identification and identity construction, particularly on the part of disenfranchised urban youth of ethnic minority origin. The ethnic minorities in question tend to be variously constructed in popular, journalistic, and indeed scholarly discourses, but inevitably are characterized as "Arabs," "North Africans," and "Algerians," with the all-embracing and apparently more socially inclusive term *beurs* often preferred. However, little attention has so far been paid to the colonial origins of much that is today celebrated in modern French sport. Yet many clues to the significance of sport in colonial Algeria are all the more tantalizing for being both so very familiar and so very limited.

The best-known example of such sporting trails is, of course, provided by French Algeria's most celebrated artistic and philosophical figure, Albert Camus.

I have drawn attention elsewhere to the paradoxical relationship between Camus and sport (Dine 1996a, 178). The Nobel Prize winner's lyrical descriptions of sea bathing in Algeria are rightly celebrated. His somewhat dismissive description of boxing in Oran may be only slightly less familiar, but is also certainly of importance. Similarly, his own early career as a talented footballer (soccer player) before the crippling onset of tuberculosis is clearly reflected in both *La peste* (1947) and the posthumously published *Le premier homme* (1994b). Indeed, the famous image of the young Camus, crouching in his goalkeeper's kit for a team photograph with the Racing universitaire algérois, was precisely the illustration chosen by the Gallimard publishing house when the latter work finally appeared in 1994. Most famously, perhaps, Camus's comment in a 1959 interview that "All I know most surely about morality and obligations, I owe to football" (quoted in Lenzini 1987, 34) is now to be found emblazoned on English-language T-shirts sold by the thousand. Yet to have said this much about Camus, the celebrated Algerian sportsman, comes close to saying all there is to be said about Camus's own writing on the subject of sport, for the theme is conspicuous by its absence from the greater part of his voluminous literary production. Indeed, it is tempting to compare Camus's relative silence on sport with his complete silence on the Algerian War after 1957. Nor is this comparison either frivolous or arbitrary. The effective mobilization of football by the Algerian Front de libération nationale (FLN) is one of the few areas of French colonial sports history to have received significant attention (Amar 1987, 193–96; Lanfranchi 1994; Lanfranchi and Wahl 1996).

Yet much remains to be said about football in France and Algeria, both then and now, as the clear contrast in the public reception of two highly symbolic international matches in the past ten years makes plain. The decisive victory of the ethnically diverse French team—led by their iconic captain Zinedine Zidane, French born of Algerian Kabyle descent—in the 1998 World Cup final on 12 July 1998 was widely hailed as a triumph of a new, inclusive, and multicultural model of the French nation. However, in the other match, a pitch invasion by young supporters of the Algerian side, from the deprived Parisian *banlieue,* brought to a premature end the historic first and supposedly "friendly" meeting between France and Algeria on 6 October 2001 at the new national stadium built in Paris for the triumphal France 98 World Cup. This unexpected outcome was just as quickly and broadly perceived as an indication that the two nations' troubled colonial past still weighed too heavily to permit "normal" sporting relations between them.

Although there can be little doubt that football represents the primary vector for Franco-Algerian sporting exchanges both during the colonial period and since—indeed, I have sought to address some aspects of this tradition elsewhere

(Dine 1996a, 1996b, 2000)—it is by no means the only one. Consequently, in this chapter I concentrate on other aspects of sport in what was the principal territory of colonial settlement in the French Empire in an attempt to flesh out the celebrated sporting fragments presented by Camus.

As David Prochaska reminds us at the outset of his pioneering analysis of the making of French Algeria, "the most common distinction made between imperialism and colonialism—terms too often used interchangeably in intellectual discourse—is that colonialism entails the presence of settlers while imperialism does not" ([1990] 2004, 7). Indeed, it was precisely the presence of a significant settler population that would mark Algeria out as a uniquely valued, but also uniquely troublesome, part of *la France d'outre-mer.* This was all the more true in the wake of the territory's administrative (and mythic) incorporation into the main body of the republic in 1848, a move ultimately destined to render the process of decolonization as traumatic as it was intractable. Although Prochaska himself does not draw attention to the role of sport in his study of colonial society in Bône (modern Annaba) between 1870 and 1920—with the exception of a passing reference to the playing of *boules* as a familiar marker of French identity ([1990] 2004, 207)—he does suggest an analytical model that might usefully be applied here. In particular, his persuasive statement of the need for "a grammar of perception" ([1990] 2004, 208) might as legitimately be applied to sport as it is applied, to considerable effect, to the study of street names, picture postcards, language (specifically *pataouète,* the French dialect spoken in *pied-noir* Algeria), and literature. Sport, I argue, was similarly instrumental in "the formation of a colonial society recognizably Algerian" and, moreover, of an associated culture "that not only came to exist in objective terms, but that [also] became subjectively aware of its existence" ([1990] 2004, 223). My interest in this chapter is sport's particular contribution to the emergence of this self-aware and self-assertive settler culture in colonial Algeria.

It is no coincidence that 1870 and the catastrophic military defeat with which it is forever associated should be the point of departure not only for the advent of civilian government and large-scale civilian settlement in "French" Algeria, but also for the development of modern sports in the territory, just as it was in metropolitan France. Virtually unknown before the Third Republic, sport in its early days in the belatedly industrializing and urbanizing nation would be characterized by imports from France's principal European competitors, Germany and Great Britain, and by links with the military, on the one hand, and with the education system, on the other. It was the desire for national regeneration, at once physical and moral, and thus for *revanche* that motivated the first wave of French sporting associations—namely, the patriotic gymnastics clubs that sprang up in the wake of defeat in the Franco-Prussian War. The physical exercises in question were based on the training regimes used by the victorious German army and were straightforwardly "conscriptive" in nature, as were the patriotic shooting clubs with which they were often associated, in that they were intended to prepare young men for service in the French army. As Pierre Arnaud states, "it is a particular characteristic of French society to have developed a physical culture on a military base" (1987, 20).

This metropolitan enthusiasm for the gymnastic "defense and illustration of the French race," as it was characterized by a slightly later propagandist of physical exercise as a means of national regeneration (Rozet 1911), had its echoes in Algeria in the period between 1870 and 1914. Daniel Hick (1992) is an invaluable guide to this and later sporting developments in colonial Algeria, and I draw on his account extensively here. According to Hick, twenty patriotic shooting associations were recorded in Algeria in 1891 (with 3,110 members), thirty in 1896 (with 4,520 members), with another four new clubs established by 1908 (1992, 28). By the same token, the militantly republican Union des sociétés de gymnastique de France (USGF), founded in 1873, admitted its first Algerian member association in 1882. Algeria had twenty-six gymnastics clubs, totaling 4,598 individual members, by 1896, when Algiers was chosen for the twenty-second annual gathering of the national federation. Although the president of the republic, Félix Faure, had been expected to attend, following a tradition established in 1889, it was the minister of public instruction, Emile Combes, who officiated as three thousand gymnasts competed over three days on the esplanade at Bab-el-Oued. At the same moment, in what was subsequently to be recognized as a momentous illustration of France's leading role in the development of international sporting competitions, the first modern Olympic Games were inaugurated in Athens by Baron Pierre de Coubertin (Hick 1992, 30–31).

If gymnastics, like the overwhelming majority of sports in the period before the First World War, was exclusively confined to Europeans (and for that matter to white males), it was nevertheless a genuinely popular pursuit that allowed for a wide range of participation. It did not thus constitute a marker of social distinction in the way that some military-based sports had previously done, such as fencing, which opened its first club in Algiers in 1882 (Hick 1992, 15). By the same token, traditional equestrian pursuits may have been practiced only by the privileged few, but horse racing rapidly established itself as a hugely popular spectacle with a much broader European audience. In France, horse racing of a recognizably modern kind had begun with the establishment of the French Jockey Club, the Société d'encouragement, in 1833, and had been significantly developed with local and central government support under the Second Empire

(Dine 1992, 183–86). Intriguingly, the first horse racing in Algeria, at Mostaganem, dates from the July Monarchy, according to Hick (1992, 51). This fact would appear to bear out Prochaska's insight into what we might regard as the "demographic bond" between organized leisure, especially sport, and the early colonial situation. He observes that "the colonial city . . . is a preponderantly male society, and a clustering occurs in the productive age categories between fifteen and fifty. . . . There are accordingly few schools, nurseries, hospitals, and, conversely, an abundance of recreational facilities" ([1990] 2004, 20).

This structural underpinning of early Algerian sporting practices is rendered all the more fascinating by Hick's revelation that the local Arab population was allowed to attend such events from 1847 onward. As one colonial commentator noted at the time, the races thus fulfilled not only economic and military objectives, but also political ones "by drawing towards us the Arab populations, who thus little by little become accustomed to contact with us in circumstances that appeal to them" (quoted in Hick 1992, 51). Central to the appeal of horse racing was, as always, the possibility of economic gain through betting, in this case on the state-run pari-mutuel. This aspect of the sport was duly reflected in the popular sporting press that grew up to provide information for all those considering a stake on events at the major hippodromes at Hussein-Dey, Mustapha, Mascara, and elsewhere. Such titles as *Le sport algérien, L'organe des intérêts hippiques, L'Algérie sportive,* and *L'hippique algérienne et tunisienne,* from the 1890s, give a taste of the atmosphere of the Algerian "turf" at this time. As in the early days of Algerian racing, the indigenous population of the territory was not excluded from this new sporting world. So the program for the autumn race meeting at the Mustapha hippodrome in October 1877 specified that the events would include "four races between Europeans and 'Natives' [*indigènes*] . . . [and] a 'steeple chase for gentlemen' . . . as well as a 'race between Natives for horsemen from leading families' [des cavaliers des grandes tentes]" (quoted in Hick 1992, 53). However, this spirit of inclusiveness was in marked contrast to other nascent colonial sports, in which Algerians' participation was destined to be significantly delayed.

In the enthusiasm for gymnastics born of popular Germanophobia, metropolitan France's first wave of sporting imports was to be followed by a second, this time motivated by aristocratic Anglophilia. From about 1880 onward, the so-called English sports of rugby, football, athletics, and rowing were introduced and then rapidly popularized and democratized as they spread from Paris into the rest of the country. The moving spirit behind the new games was Baron Pierre de Coubertin, the father of the modern Olympic Games and an enthusiastic supporter of the use of sport for colonial ends on the model of France's principal imperial rival, Great Britain. Indeed, it was Coubertin himself who in 1912 would implore French overseas administrators to copy the British in consciously exploiting sport's influence to further the colonial cause ([1912] 1992, 181). Although this program would not occur to any great extent before the Great War, the sporting boom that affected metropolitan France in the postwar period did indeed also have a major impact on Algeria, as regards both sporting practices and, increasingly, sporting spectacles. To the fore in these developments were trans-Saharan motor sport, cycle road racing, and football, all of which I have discussed elsewhere (Dine 1996b). However, also of significance were athletics, as well as two other sports, swimming and boxing, which would become particularly developed in colonial Algeria. The territory's cultural commentators, from the most humble hack journalist to its most celebrated literary son, would consequently depict them as such. In the remainder of this survey, I therefore focus on the various contributions made to the construction of a self-assertive colonial consciousness by the swimming and boxing cultures, as highlighted by Camus, and briefly examine the abiding significance of indigenous Algerian athletics.

Central to the mythology of *Algérie française* was the theme of *le peuple neuf,* an original settler race born of the fusion of the various Mediterranean cultures that had provided Algeria with its European population. This new race was held to be superior not only to the indigenous inhabitants of the territory, but also to the general run of the population of *la mère-patrie* itself. For Camus, who was to emerge as the preeminent literary spokesman of the new *pied-noir* community, a defining component of his compatriots' Mediterranean consciousness was precisely an intimate relationship with the sea itself. It is thus no coincidence that Meursault, the eponymous anti-hero of Camus's *L'etranger,* should in his prison cell dream of finding "deliverance" in sea bathing (1942, 119–20). In the same way, Dr. Rieux, the hero of Camus's *La peste,* escapes from an Oran devastated by the plague by taking a swim in the maternally welcoming sea (1947, 230–32). However, it is in his collections of essays, *Noces* (1939) and *L'eté* ([1954] 1994a), that Camus spells out most clearly his appreciation of the pleasures of sea bathing and its contribution to the construction of the unique worldview of "the child-like people of this land" ([1954] 1994a, 41)—a community that he describes elsewhere as "an entire race, born of the sun and the sea, vital and ripe, which draws its grandeur from its simplicity and, standing upright on the beaches, gives its smile of complicity in return for the dazzling smile of its skies" (1939, 21).

The thriving beach culture that Camus celebrates in the essay "L'eté à Alger" ([1954] 1994a, 35–38) indeed seems to reflect a certain reality as regards the European colony's sporting activities in the interwar years. As Hick points out, the characteristic feature of swimming in Algeria at this time, as in metropolitan

France, was the absence of swimming pools, where modern competitions over precise distances and with accurate time keeping could be conducted. Algiers did not have a swimming pool until 1932, and this pool was still the only one available in 1939 to the two thousand members of the local swimming club. If colonial Algeria had an obvious alternative in the easily accessible beaches, the comparative situation in France itself was particularly poor and had been for some time, with only 20 pools in existence in 1922 as opposed to the 1,362 available in Germany, for instance. In Algiers, Oran, and other European centers, swimming competitions were consequently conducted in the local harbor basin rather than in designated pools (Hick 1992, 33–35). Thus, the popular *bains* famously celebrated by Camus and a host of lesser *pied-noir* commentators, such as those at the Padovani beach on the fringes of Bab-el-Oued, were not swimming baths as normally understood, but rather a variety of facilities for swimmers that had been installed to enhance the natural attractions of the location. However, this lack of swimming pools apparently did not have an overly adverse impact on participation in competitive swimming, as indicated by the existence of specialist weeklies such as the Algiers paper *Crawl,* published in the 1930s and devoted to swimming and its very popular offshoot water polo (Hick 1992, 34).

In fact, the 1930s saw the emergence of Algerian champions in French national competitions, including in particular the great star of the period, Alfred Nakache, the Jewish swimmer from Constantine. Nakache's public success reflected a broadening of sporting participation in the interwar period that took in not only Algeria's Jewish community, but also the indigenous Algerian population. Daniel Hick's list of leading Algerian swimmers at this time thus includes the name Ben Sliman as well as contemporaries of European origin (1992, 33). This increasing openness of colonial Algeria's beach culture to the majority population of the territory—if only in part and always on the European population's terms—has enabled post facto literary apologists for *Algérie française,* such as Gabriel Conesa, to assert what might be termed the ludic inclusiveness of the settler colony. He thus asserts that in colonial Bab-el-Oued, "nationality or race had no more importance than the color of one's swimming trunks, each person feeling Mediterranean first and foremost and as such a member of a single huge family" (1970, 169). I return to the respective social status of Jewish and Arabo-Berber sportsmen later, but at this stage in the discussion it is worth noting that the need for investment in sporting infrastructure, in particular swimming pools, continued to be a preoccupation for the colonial authorities until the very last days of *Algérie française.* Thus, on the eve of the Algerian War, the Gouvernement général reported with pride in its *Exposé de la situation générale de l'Algérie en*

1953 that a heated municipal swimming pool had recently opened in Algiers and that an equivalent facility in Oran was in the process of completion (1954, 636).

However, to observers from metropolitan France, the most striking characteristic of Algerian sport by the 1930s was not the territory's lack of facilities, but rather an ingrained propensity to violence on the part of players and spectators alike. Thus, the correspondent of *Paris-Match* in its edition of 23 September 1930 filed a report entitled "In Algeria, Football and Water Polo = Punch-ups [*Bagarres*]" (Redon 1930, 1). In a 1938 review of Edmond Brua's *Fables Bônoises,* Camus's celebration of "those robust people . . . who make love and go swimming, who cheat and jeer and bluster" (quoted in Prochaska [1990] 2004, 229) does not seem too far removed from this frequently rowdy sporting ambiance. Moreover, an acceptance and even a celebration of casual violence as an acceptably "manly" way of settling scores might also be seen to be a more general characteristic of colonial Algeria, as once again reflected in the production of its literary representatives (Lenzini 1987, 18). Camus's account in *L'etranger* (1942) of Meursault's fistfight with an opponent encountered by chance on a tram is to be set against this background, as, perhaps, is his pivotal encounter with a knife-wielding Arab on the beach. Moreover, such a backdrop goes some way toward explaining the considerable success of the codified celebration of violence offered by the spectacle of boxing in Algeria in the interwar years.

Camus's essay "Le minotaure ou la halte d'Oran," written in 1939 but not published until 1954, contains one of his most significant commentaries on Algerian sport. His account of the boxing matches at the Central Sporting Club in the rue du Fondouk is of interest primarily as a firsthand depiction of colonial sporting life ([1954] 1994a, 88–96). It establishes an ironic tone from the outset with the observation that what is on offer in Oran, a city that Camus describes unflatteringly as combining "all the bad taste of Europe and the Orient," is nothing less than "an evening of pugilistic entertainment for the real connaisseur" ([1954] 1994a, 79). The precisely identified location of the boxing club may itself be of significance here, in that it includes the Arabic term *fondouk,* meaning "inn," which had by this time become a derogatory term used by the *pieds-noirs* to refer to a "native" rabble (Sivan 1979, 31). Camus goes on to stress the mediocre quality of the boxers on that night's bill and the poorly appointed venue before noting that a thousand almost exclusively male—and by implication European—paying spectators had nevertheless been attracted by the formal promise that "blood will flow tonight" ([1954] 1994a, 89). For Camus, the interest of the supporting bout between Amar, "the tough Oran fighter who never gives up" (91), and Pérez, "the Algiers puncher" (91), apparently does not include the boxers' ethnic origin—despite their very suggestive and almost caricatural names: he does not comment on this aspect of the proceedings. Rather, he underlines the fighters' status as civic representatives in a "hundred-year-old" (91) rivalry between their two Mediterranean cities, likened here to medieval Pisa and Florence. In the event, Pérez defeats Amar, to the vocal displeasure of the local fans, before a generalized fight breaks out among the spectators, necessitating police intervention to restore order. The main event then opposes a French naval champion against a local contestant in a brutal and ultimately drawn slogging match that Camus describes as more akin to a *corrida* (unruly ruckus). However, Camus's concluding comments are perhaps most worthy of attention for the light they cast on the particular appropriateness of this most uncompromising of sports in the colonial context, in a passage that is suggestive of Roland Barthes's later explication in "Le monde où l'on catche" in *Mythologies* (1957). Like Barthes two decades later, Camus is inclined to see in the ritualized combat of the ring an allegory of underlying social structures. More particularly, he draws attention to philosophical imperatives that with hindsight appear uniquely adapted to the *pieds-noirs'* worldview:

> The crowd drifting outside, beneath a sky filled with silence and stars, has just been involved in the most exhausting of combats. The crowd keeps quiet, melting away, with no energy left for exegesis. There is good and evil, and this religion is merciless. The congregation of believers is now just a collection of black and white shadows that disappear into the night. For force and violence are solitary gods. They leave nothing to memory. On the contrary, they distribute their miracles by the handful, but in the present. They are worthy of this people with no past that celebrates its communions around a ring. Such rites may be rather difficult, but they simplify everything. Good and evil, the victor and the vanquished: in Corinth, two temples stood side by side, one dedicated to Violence, the other to Necessity. ([1954] 1994a, 95–96)

Thus, the Manichean universe of boxing maps easily onto the dualistic political economy of settler colonialism in Algeria, where "assimilation" and "association" or combinations thereof were always destined to remain little more than the rhetorical gloss on more fundamental dichotomies of knowledge and power. Moreover, the vibrant boxing culture that Camus is obliged to acknowledge in Oran, in spite of his obvious reluctance, hints at the broader significance of boxing in Algeria and indeed in colonial North Africa more widely in the 1930s and subsequently.

Like many historians of boxing, André Rauch has drawn attention to the distinctive attractiveness and accessibility of this sport for otherwise marginalized social groups, in particular immigrants and ethic minorities (1992, 30, 329 n. 243). However, Rauch's history of French boxing reveals the special applicability of this general rule in the Algerian colonial context. As Rauch explains, boxing spread to the principal urban centers of North Africa from metropolitan France after the Great War, although with participation initially restricted to Europeans. Indigenous Algerian competitors would thus not make their appearance until the 1930s. However, the obvious talent of "native" boxers such as Bob Omar, who was to die prematurely, allowed the first international bouts to be staged at the municipal stadium in Algiers. By 1939, Rauch suggests, no less than eleven major boxing clubs existed in Algeria, including le Boxing club de Bab-el-Oued, Alger-la-blanche, and le Boxing club Hussein-Dey, but also, very significantly, L'union sportive musulmane de Maison-Carrée. Boxing matches were regularly staged at a wide variety of venues in the city, from the Salle Barbusse with room for five hundred spectators for amateur bouts, all the way up to the ten-thousand-capacity arenas for major professional bouts at the Stade Municipal and the Stade Saint-Eugène. In Oran, so ironically treated by Camus, bouts were staged at venues that included the Casino Bastrama and the Grand Casino, with room for two thousand and three thousand spectators respectively, and, in the summer, at the fifteen-thousand-capacity Arènes d'Eckmuhl (Rauch 1992, 119, 330–31 n. 251).

The creation of boxing clubs by and for the indigenous population of Algeria in the 1930s was typical of the local expansion of sporting associations at this time. It thus mirrored developments both in other sports—such as football, where the "native" Mouloudia club algérois, founded in 1921, had been one of the earliest such associations and was followed by many more similarly named associations—and in the increasingly self-assertive sphere of Algerian nationalist politics. Moreover, such was the popularity of boxing in North Africa by the 1930s, with Casablanca and Tunis also established as major centers, that boxers from all three of the territories' principal ethnic communities, European, Jewish, and "native," began to make an impact in Paris and farther afield. The names of the leading fighters who traveled to metropolitan France as part of organized boxing tours at this time suggest an element of racial integration that is worthy of note: "Marcel Cerdan, Antoine Abad, El Houssine . . . Mak Perez . . . Kouidri, Pernot, Caïd, Georges Jaïs, Ted Maichi, Germain Perez, Robert Bel-Kheir, Sliman, Attaf, René Pons" (Rauch 1992, 299 n. 31). To this list can be added the names of postwar stars such as Robert Cohen, a Jewish boxer from Bône, who in 1954 became bantamweight champion of the world, although he would be beaten in Paris the following year by the then national featherweight champion Chérif Hamia (Rauch 1992, 400–401 n. 129). Like Cohen and Hamia, Alphonse

Halimi was also a successful North African boxing export in the 1950s. Born in Constantine in Algeria, Halimi became bantamweight champion of the world at the Palais des Sports in Paris on 1 April 1957, losing his title a few months later, only to retake it in November of that year and retain it until 1959 (Rauch 1992, 407–8 n. 197)

Among these boxers, Marcel Cerdan stands out as one of France's most celebrated sportsmen. Born in 1916 in Sidi Bel Abbes, Cerdan moved at an early age to Casablanca, where he would later establish himself as a rising star. He won his first national title in his adopted home city in 1938, when he outpointed Omar Kouidri, and went on to be champion of Europe five times before becoming world middleweight champion when he knocked out the American Tony Zale in 1948. Cerdan was to lose his title the following year to Jake "Raging Bull" La Motta and was killed in a plane crash on his way to the United States for the rematch (Rauch 1992, 364 n. 192). As these dates suggest, Cerdan was at his peak throughout the war years and thus helped to provide French society as a whole with a reassuring image of sporting masculinity at this difficult time (Holt 1981, 146). His case might consequently be compared with that of the Tunisian-born Jewish boxer Victor "Young" Perez, whose experience of the Vichy years was very different.

The apparent visibility and success of Jewish boxers in North Africa may helpfully be considered in terms of Rauch's previously noted comments regarding the historical openness of this particular sport to otherwise marginalized communities, together with David Prochaska's broader description of "stranger" groups in colonial society. Prochaska writes: "Stranger groups . . . occupy intermediate positions in colonial society, but they are set off to a greater extent [than other intermediate groups such as Creoles and "people of color"] from both natives and Europeans by a combination of ethnicity, race, religion, and culture" ([1990] 2004, 18). He characterizes the Jews of North Africa as typifying this social category, their intermediate status being reflected in a tendency "to specialize in specific trades and to deal in specific commodities . . . [indicating] functional occupational specialization along ethnic and racial lines" ([1990] 2004, 18). Boxing in colonial North Africa was apparently one such specialized field in which Jews were able to have an impact and consequently in which they were statistically overrepresented. This conclusion is borne out by the case of Gilbert Benaïm, born in 1905, the eldest of seven sons of an Algiers watchmaker, Elie Benaïm. Refusing to follow his father into the family business, Benaïm turned instead to boxing. After a short and not particularly successful amateur career, he moved into promotion, dividing his time between Paris and Algiers and organizing boxing events in both cities throughout the later 1920s and 1930s. Following the Allied troop landings in North Africa in November 1942, he was made responsible for the organization of military sport, including a weeklong boxing festival in Algiers. He went on to perform a similar role for the Allies in Italy, with Cerdan and other champions appearing on the bill in Naples and Rome, before returning to Paris, where he became the boxing matchmaker for the Palais des Sports well into the 1960s (Rauch 386–87 n. 34).

As previously suggested, the case of Victor "Young" Perez was less happy. Born to Jewish parents in Tunis in 1911, Perez soon moved to Paris, like so many other North African boxers in the later 1920s and 1930s. Having rapidly established himself as national champion, he became world flyweight champion in 1931, retaining his title until the following year. However, Perez was destined to die in the concentration camp at Buchenwald, to which he was deported by the Nazis in 1942 (Rauch 1992, 367 n. 201). If Jewish sportsmen from North Africa were hailed as champions of France in the 1930s and again after the Second World War, the period of the Vichy administration was markedly different. As Jean-Louis Gay-Lescot (1991, 1992), among others (see Dine 1998), has demonstrated, the Vichy period was a crucial one in French sports history in that the regime was the first national administration, with the partial exception of the short-lived Popular Front government of 1936–38, to establish a leading role for the state in the management of sport in France. To this end, it established France's first ministry for sport, the Commissariat général à l'education générale et aux sports (CGEGS), headed by the former tennis champion Jean Borotra, very shortly after the catastrophic French military defeat in the summer of 1940. The sporting component of Vichy's reactionary project of "National Revolution" was characterized by the encouragement of mass participation, the suppression of professionalism, a preference for traditional and regional sports, and, above all, unprecedented public investment in sporting personnel and infrastructure. However, Vichy's approach to sport also reflected the racist orientation of both the collaborationist regime and its German masters. The banning from competition of the Algerian champion Alfred Nakache, France's leading swimmer, on the basis of his Jewish family origins, is the most obvious example of this policy's impact on targeted individuals and groups (Gay-Lescot 1991, 182, 208). Like Victor "Young" Perez, Nakache was also subsequently sent to Buchenwald, but miraculously survived.

Vichy's impact on Algerian sport went further than this, however, with Borotra's tour of North Africa between 18 April and 5 May 1941 in what was undoubtedly the high point of his period of office. As Daniel Hick explains, Borotra took 150 athletes across the Mediterranean, with major events in Algiers, Oran, and other major urban centers, attracting thousands of spectators.

The tour's function as a major propaganda initiative was reflected in the presence of the twenty-five journalists from metropolitan France who accompanied Borotra, not to mention their colleagues from the local press and a newsreel team from France actualités. A propaganda film entitled *Messager du sport,* with an Arabic soundtrack, was subsequently shown across North Africa by state-funded mobile cinemas (Hick 1992, 59). The impact of such propaganda on indigenous Algerian participation in sports, specifically in athletics, is inherently difficult to assess. However, it is perhaps no coincidence that the postwar years were marked by the rise of Algerian track stars, of whom Alain Mimoun is certainly now the most famous.

Both Bernadette Deville-Danthu (1992a, 1992b, 1992c, 1992d, 1992e) and Daniel Hick (1992, 39–41) have made the point that athletics was particularly favored by successive colonial administrations and throughout the French Empire as a suitably "uncomplicated" means of indoctrination and integration: a "sporting primary school" that in addition had the advantage of requiring little in the way of costly equipment and infrastructure. Hick notes that the number of athletic clubs, beginning with their introduction to North Africa in 1900, grew to forty-six in Algeria by 1908. Moreover, "athletics was a great spontaneous success, initially among the European population, but it soon found favor with the Muslim population as well, notably in cross-country, long-distance and middle-distance events" (1992, 39). Algerian athletes would achieve considerable success remarkably early on, with Djebalia, for instance, coming second in the Paris marathon in 1914. Hick goes on to explain that in preparation for the marathon at the Berlin Olympic Games planned for 1916, Pierre de Coubertin's Union des sociétes françaises de sport athlétique (USFSA) organized qualifying events in six French towns, including Algiers, before holding a final selection event in Paris. Eight of the thirty-five competitors came from Algeria, with Mouloud of the Racing club d'Alger winning the race and another three Algerians in the top five places. The subsequent victory of El Ouafi—originally from Biskra, but in the late 1920s an employee of the Renault car company in Paris—represented Africa's first gold medal in the same event at the 1928 Olympic Games in Amsterdam, although another Algerian runner, Khaled, was the highest-placed "French" runner in the marathon at the infamous 1936 Berlin Olympics (Hick 1992, 41). He thus, in his own way, contributed to the antiracist message most loudly and famously delivered by Jesse Owens and his black American teammates.

Algeria's (and Africa's) second gold medal for athletics was not to come for another two decades. Alain Mimoun was from El Telagh, a small village in the Oran region, and he joined the Gallia sports d'Alger before coming to prominence during his military service (Hick 1992, 43). He won the first of his thirty-two national championships in 1947, following service in the French army during the war years. Mimoun's Olympic career was a particularly remarkable one: he took the silver medal in the ten thousand meters at London in 1948 and then again at Helsinki in 1952, also coming second in the five thousand meters into the bargain. However, it was his stunning victory in his first ever marathon at the 1956 Melbourne Olympic Games—where he defeated his friend and rival, the great Czech runner Emil Zatopek—that transformed Mimoun into a French national hero. Having opted definitively for France as the land of his birth erupted into violence in the war for independence, he would actually go on to meet the man destined to grant Algeria its independence. Telling the story in a recent interview, Mimoun noted that de Gaulle told him: "Mimoun, you and I have at least two things in common: a love of France, and longevity!" (Mimoun 2000, 47). In 1999, Mimoun was made a Commandeur de la Légion d'honneur, the first ever Frenchman of North African origin to receive such an award. Later the same year, the readers of the specialist magazine *Athlétisme* voted him "French athlete of the century." However, Mimoun's status as an icon of successful colonial integration through sport is perhaps best captured by the statistic that no fewer than forty sports stadiums, fifteen streets, and a number of other buildings spread across his adopted homeland have been named in his honor.

In the same interview in 2000, Mimoun suggested that the FLN made no attempt to "pester" *(enquiquiner)* him during the 1954–62 conflict, so well known and, indeed, accepted was his pro-French stance. As he put it, employing the third-person to describe himself in a manner oddly suggestive of de Gaulle's own portentous style, "Mimoun was left untouched. How could they possibly have forgotten that I had fought for seven years for France, the country of my choice, a choice that the FLN respected? Besides, when I came back to Algeria for the first time, in 1988, to see my mother, I received a magnificent welcome" (2000, 48).

Mimoun's stance on the Algerian War was diametrically opposed to that of sportsmen such as Rachid Mekhloufi and his fellow Algerian footballers, who chose their homeland and the struggle for its independence over a seemingly assured future with the colonial power. However, there can be no doubt that this great runner belongs to an indigenous athletic tradition that started around the Great War and continues up to the present day. Indeed, such international track stars as Hassiba Boulemerka (Olympic gold medalist in 1992 and world champion in 1991 and 1995 in the fifteen-hundred-meter run) and Noureddine Morceli (Olympic gold medalist in 1996 and world champion in 1991, 1993, and 1995 in the fifteen hundred meters) may be regarded as the culmination of a century-long Algerian engagement with distance running. Thus regarded, the two runners' simultaneous domination of both the men's and women's fifteen hundred meters—the so-called metric mile and as such often regarded as the "Blue Riband" of modern athletics—in 1991 and 1995 represented an undoubted high spot for sport and society as a whole in an independent Algeria then traversing one of its darkest periods since the 1954–62 conflict.

Sport may not be the most immediately apparent route to an understanding of colonial Algeria or to an appreciation of the causes and circumstances of the rise and fall of *Algérie française*. However, as I have suggested, an examination of the deeds of the territory's gymnasts, swimmers, boxers, athletes, and *turfistes,* is significant. Although football and related activities may not, after all, teach us everything that we need to know about morality, this quintessentially modern cultural field certainly does have its own distinctive contribution to make to the colonial historian's "grammar of perception." In the final analysis, as Fred Inglis once explained in a pioneering study of modern games in general, "Sports tell us stories; they make sense of the world" (1977, 71). This is as true in the French colonial context as it is in any other.

4 "Unknown and Unloved"

The Politics of French Ignorance in Algeria, 1860–1930

SETH GRAEBNER

IN 1930, the European population of Algeria celebrated what no one could have suspected was the last centenary of *Algérie française.* Among the hundreds of articles and books published for the occasion, one in particular caused a small sensation among reviewers in the Algerian press: a book-length study by the French novelist Jean Leune, titled *Le miracle algérien.* The book itself was little short of miraculous, according to one Algiers reviewer, a windfall for the colony: "M. Jean Leune has managed to discover Algeria, and not the Algeria of feasts [*diffas*], fantasias, and other Orientalist trappings [*bamboulas*], but the real Algeria, the Algeria of workers that already looks—and in the future will look more and more—like old France; he deserves the gratitude of the Algériens" (["M. Jean Leune"] 1930, 4). Chapters from the book, already serialized in the Paris daily *Le Temps,* soon appeared in Algerian papers as well. Leune's book, it seems, was everything the European Algériens wanted and rarely got in French news coverage.[1] In the year devoted to celebrating their culture and solidifying their political position vis-à-vis France, they felt that Leune had managed to see through a screen of false images to the true Algeria, the one that colonialists of 1930 hoped would continue forever. He had succeeded in "knowing" their country, which the Algériens felt was perpetually unknown and unloved in France.

Leune set himself apart from his counterparts by explicit treatment of the colony's self-perceived public-relations problem. In a staged dialogue between the narrator and his Algérien interlocutors, he shows his firm grasp of the Algériens' feelings on the subject, a position that could only endear him to them. In

1. Throughout this article, I use the term *Algériens* to designate those to whom it referred from 1860 to 1930: people of European descent born or living permanently in Algeria. I am less comfortable with the parallel term *indigène* for Algeria's ethnic majority, though I do occasionally use it. Mostly, I have resorted to the descriptive "Arabs and Berbers" to mean those we would now simply call Algerians.

course of the staged conversation, the Algériens express their doubt about the narrator's commitment to obtaining solid information about the modern colony, despite his assurances. In a bitter outburst, one of them says that it is useless to give a French visitor real data or serious points of view:

> "You are boring the gentleman. No, no, I'm sure of it. Tell him instead about the marvels of El-Golea, the beauties of the deep south, the mysteries of the Hoggar. . . . Talk to him about art, literature, and antiquities: I bet he would like details on Elissa Rhais!"
>
> This time, I could not remain silent. I had to defend myself and refute these intentions or desires, which they ascribed to me.
>
> —"What," asked one of my interlocutors, stupefied, "so you really won't rush off to El-Golea as soon as you get off the boat? You say it's our work, our achievement, what we do, that interests you primarily? But, my dear sir, you are breaking all the rules of the game: camels first, Algériens second." (1930, 4)

The Algériens, it seems, had a publicity problem. No one knew the "real" Algeria, "our" Algeria as these colonists call it, the Algeria beyond deserts, camels, and palms. This country, they felt, lay outside the scope of exotic literature like that of the *juif indigène* writer Elissa Rhais or of the widely read French visitors to North Africa. Despite the huge proliferation of books on North Africa, the Algériens complained bitterly and constantly that "their" country was unknown in mainland France. They implied that out of either hostility or laziness, the French did not listen to their endlessly repeated declarations of Algeria's economic strength, cultural vitality, and strategic importance. Algeria, they felt, was thoroughly misrepresented, mostly unknown, and probably unloved. What exactly the problem was and what lay behind its constant reiteration changed over time and required some analysis. For now, it is enough to say that texts by Algériens that spoke of factories, vineyards, and farmers accused their French readers of ignoring them and wanting instead *diffas,* dunes, and dancing girls. These texts promoting the colony—whether histories, travelogues, pamphlets, literary prefaces, or editorials—argued that the problem was a gap between French perceptions and reality.

Analysis of a wide range of the self-justifying literature and journalism coming out of the colony suggests, however, that the problem was also a gap between self-perception and desire. A disjunction between the various kinds of procolonial discourse prevented the Algériens from producing a coherent message to the French about themselves. Although Algériens writing proud articles in the Algiers press about wine production or iron mining resolutely privileged only the most modern aspects of the land and its people, the colonial propaganda machine (there was one, as we shall see) was not nearly so single-minded. Publications by the promoters of *Algérie française* typically criticized the shallowness of French perceptions of the country, still mediated in the 1920s and 1930s by a flourishing production of exotic travel literature. The Algerian-born promoters of the colony preferred to call attention to their own cultural and economic creations rather than to the vestiges of Arab grandeur emphasized by French travel writers. Yet they themselves often referred to French travel writers as authorities and routinely fell back on the very descriptions they had denounced as clichés irrelevant to the grand future of French Algeria. The texts complaining of metropolitan ignorance of their country in fact allowed readers to glimpse a hidden uncertainty about the cultural identity the Algériens themselves wished to promote. What was the most worthy and representative image of modern Algeria, the minaret or the office block? To what extent were the Algériens, as they often argued, really Europeans building a Latin empire within the continuum of Mediterranean civilization?

The Algériens' expressions of malaise about the misperception of them in the metropole and their endlessly reiterated frustrations at not being able to control representations of themselves were symptoms of their own internal cultural debates. They also constituted part of the ongoing discussion between France and its colonies about the latter's place in the French world. Laments about being unknown and unloved were less an attempt to correct a problem with a descriptive discourse than a central component of the discourse itself. In the efforts to elaborate an independent cultural identity for themselves consistent with greater political respect and autonomy from the metropole, Algérien writers and polemicists found that their status as "unknown and unloved" offered much more than the solace of self-pity. Promotional literature proposed this status as a stimulus to cultural production in the colony and a central argument for the recognition of a distinctive identity within the French Empire.

"Tout a été dit sur Alger"

To account for the stakes of the discourse of an Algeria misrepresented, we must examine the nineteenth-century French writing about the colony to which this discourse reacted. Nineteenth-century guidebooks and travel narratives, with peculiar ways of commenting on their own place within the growing body of knowledge about Algeria, laid out the conditions for later contradictory messages. By the middle of the nineteenth century, books about Algeria had adopted one of the typical habits of French travel writing at the time: the conventional acknowledgment that previous accounts had left little undescribed in the areas the narrators visited. The first regularly updated guidebook for Algeria (which became Hachette's famous *Guide bleu* to the country) declared, "tout a été dit sur Alger" (everything has been said about Algiers) (Piesse 1862, 5). The author in fact gave almost no description of the city in his own voice; rather, he cited long passages from previous travelers, notably from the journalist Xavier Marmier's *Lettres sur l'Algérie* (1847). The guide then embarked on a kind of cataloging that supposed long familiarity both with the commonplaces of Algerian description and with the systems of urban description in France. The author accounted for all the monuments of the city by category: walls, squares, streets, mosques, palaces, each with a history already rehearsed in any number of previous descriptions. The sheer number of these previous descriptions, more than six hundred of which had been published as books between 1830 and 1860, may have suggested such a cursory and allusive procedure.[2] The colonial mechanisms for gathering and disseminating information on the conquered territories were, it seemed, working overtime.

The repeated descriptions nevertheless could not produce quite the coherence they seemed to promise. The legibility of the colony depended on accurate, comprehensive reception of previous descriptions by new authors and the reading public. Few texts suggest that this was happening, and many visitors to Algeria wrote as if it were not. Even where travel writers declared certain facts "well known" and therefore needless to repeat, their texts reproduced the information in sketchy form as if it were nonetheless unknown. To comment that "everything has been said about Algiers" in a guidebook to the city was in fact to engage in preterition on a very large scale, saying, "we need not tell you that . . ." before proceeding to tell. By the 1860s, preterition had become an essential device for writing about Algeria. The publicist Charles Desprez, whose *L'hiver à Alger* (1860) and *Alger l'été* (1863) set out expressly to destroy negative myths regarding the colony in order to promote tourism, declared that traditional Moorish houses had been "too often described already for me to wish to analyze here the ogival arches, twisted columns, and circular galleries" (1863, 63). On the contrary, however, almost no one in fact "analyzed" such architectural features. The most academic historian of Algeria at the time, Louis-Adrien Berbrugger, tended simply to list them, even in the monumental folios of *L'Algérie historique, pittoresque et monumentale* (1843). However, unlike classical preterition that presents what it purports not to mention, colonial preterition merely made brief allusion to preexisting descriptions that themselves consisted mostly of more

2. The Bibliothèque nationale de France catalogs under a single rubric the majority of nonfictional works published in France before 1860 concerning Algeria: 666 of them, almost all after 1830.

preterition. Descriptions of Algeria, detailed though they were, had a way of eliding details and analysis, and if readers had looked elsewhere for the more complete descriptions the texts alluded to, they would generally have found them similarly "not mentioned." Algiers had always already been described, but these descriptions had mostly already been elided.

This situation suggests some counterintuitive aspects of the process of distributing colonial knowledge, which many historians have suggested was a major part of creating what pro-colonial feeling there was in nineteenth-century France. Because descriptions of Algeria proceeded by "not mentioning" what everyone supposedly knew, it could be difficult to learn anything other than obliquely or telegraphically. Not everyone followed the same discursive pattern, of course, and new details did come up from description to description. Still, it is often easier to learn from the travel literature what sorts of things one was supposed to know already than to learn anything new or concrete one did not know yet. For instance, the guidebooks told readers that they already knew that one found ogival arches and twisted columns in Algerian design, but almost never told them what these things were or how they were used. Another contemporary traveler noted that "it is felt to be too easy to make a description of the metropolis [of Algiers] itself; and Algiers . . . is almost as unknown as the capital of Japan" (Dubois 1861, 7). Though the author seems unaware of his insight, these two observations were nearly cause and effect. Although we have little information on the readership or circulation of these volumes, a few authors directly address the distribution of information on the colony. The perceptive traveler Louise Vallory, prefacing her 1863 travelogue, acknowledged that "since 1830, so much has been said about Algeria that it seems as if everything has been told, and it takes true temerity to bring yet another book to this mountain of volumes titled *Souvenirs de l'Algérie*. . . . [But] even if people have spoken a great deal about this country, does that mean that we really know it?" (1863, 1). This would be precisely the problem of which Algériens would later complain. Already in the first thirty years of its existence, *Algérie française* had become "so close to us, and yet so little known" (Dubois 1861, 5).

Even with this new knowledge about how Algerian topographic texts presented (or did not present) information, it still seems odd to hear Algeria called "little known" in 1861. The production of Algerian descriptions in all genres was very substantial, and not all of these books resorted exclusively to quoting each other's ellipses. There was indeed significant information on Algeria within reach of the mid-nineteenth-century reader. However, good colonial publicists understood that they could not rest while the reading public "knew" only what it had already been told was important to know; they had in addition to make their audience understand the political and economic importance of colonization.[3] The sort of *connaissance* these texts tried to spread was often specifically oriented to the immediate goal of promoting the further colonization of Algeria. Talk about "knowing" the country already had political implications, and the patterns of reception, transmission, or ignorance of that knowledge would play a significant role in the later emergence of colonial Algeria's cultural identity.

"Déformations Littéraires"

All but the most sophisticated historians writing during the colonial period tended to assert that the *indigènes* lived outside the flow of historical development. They were what they had always been, stuck in millennial customs and modes of thought. Looking today at the discourses of colonial self-justification, we might be tempted to say something similar about Algerian colonialists. What they wrote in 1930 seems at first very much like what they wrote in 1860. Certainly, a *mission civilisatrice* had appeared in the meantime, but one could forget its existence when reading many of the celebrations of the achievements of European Algerians. The texts of the 1920s and early 1930s, the halcyon days of colonial certainty, inherited in some ways very directly from nineteenth-century texts that promoted "interested" colonial knowledge. That the twentieth-century writers frequently attempted to distinguish themselves sharply from their predecessors does not invalidate this characterization. Several things had nonetheless changed substantially, in ways that transformed the production and reception of texts about Algeria. French visitors were no longer the only ones producing novels, descriptions, or promotional literature about Algeria. The population of Algériens had grown sufficiently to constitute both a small, vocal pool of writers and a public for their work. In fiction, several new schools of colonial literature arose between about 1900 and 1930 to respond to this demographic development and its cultural consequences. Novelists such as Louis Bertrand and Robert Randau took the lead in developing new notions of cultural particularity for the colony, ideas rapidly taken up outside fiction.

The proponents of these new schools of thought diverged significantly in their chosen emphases in the new Algérien culture. The *académicien* Louis Bertrand started the new waves with his notion of *Afrique latine*, an ideological construction of North Africa that systematically devalued Arab or Berber contri-

3. The stated goals of the many ephemeral periodicals promoting Algeria in the nineteenth century demonstrated this felt need. See, for example, the prospectuses of the weekly *France algérienne* ("Prospectus" 1845), the organ of Governor-General Bugeaud, or the *Bulletin de l'Algérie* ("Prospectus" 1855).

butions to Maghrebi history in favor of the "Latins" Bertrand found more culturally compelling and politically promising: the colonists, who in his view inherited the mantle of imperial Rome. Others, such as Randau's Algérianiste school, took a view at least ostensibly wider and set to work glorifying all things properly Algerian in their view. Finally, by 1930, the young poet Gabriel Audisio, transplanted from Marseille, had begun to theorize a wider Mediterranean nature of Algerian culture. All these different literary currents set themselves up in opposition to earlier literature by passing visitors, led by the likes of Théophile Gautier, Eugène Fromentin, and Alexandre Dumas *père,* but ultimately including the whole crowd of nineteenth-century travelers exemplified by Marmier, Vallory, Dubois, and Desprez. The new theorists derided this material as "stopover literature"; this derision was their common point of origin, whatever their later divergences (Randau 1929, 419–20).[4] The Algériens explicitly blamed literary exoticism for metropolitan ignorance, and texts denouncing one very often complained of the other. To counter this literary travesty and its fixation on palm trees, camels, and "timeless" Arabs, the Algérianistes and their ilk focused instead on farms, cities, and "active" colons.

"So Close and Yet So Far"

The objection to books by literary travelers aimed at the shallowness of their authors' knowledge; the Algériens demanded a "deep knowledge" difficult if not impossible for visitors to obtain. Other texts, however, suggest that this knowledge, in the form of historical and statistical detail supported by inevitable citation of nineteenth-century observers, was not in fact what colonial promoters of 1930 hoped for as an antidote to the ignorance perpetuated by literary exoticism. Even a title such as *Le miracle des sables* (Juchereau de Saint-Denys 1934) was hardly going to make a bone-dry book of statistics and warmed-over history effective promotional material, so the Algériens turned to other forms of description, marked with a number of tropes to remind readers of the material's political and cultural significance. One such commonplace was the proximity-to-France argument. By the centenary, stressing Algeria's nearness to France had become virtually de rigueur in literature promoting French North Africa. From the largest, most academic tomes to the smallest works for hurried tourists, the phrase "24 hours from Marseille" echoed across first pages and introductions (Despiques and Garoby 1930, 3; A. Bernard 1931, 1). The proximity-to-France trope appeared in very diverse genres of writing, and the concerns of the tourism industry seem inadequate to explain its prevalence. Significantly, remarks on the

4. See also Louis Bertrand's fulminations on the subject (1930, 10; 1938, 21).

physical closeness of France and Algeria often occurred in the same text as complaints about the way the metropole ignored the colony. The phrase "so close yet so far" and its variations came to serve a political and cultural purpose in debates over the proper image and status of the colony.

According to the French novelist Antoine Chollier, the "terre latine" of North Africa was at once "so close, because it is linked to the whole history of our Greco-Roman civilization" and "so distant because its role as the lair of merciless pirates, which illuminated its image for centuries with a bloody mirage, is still reflected on its face" (1929, 10). Accepting Africa as in some way Latin espoused at least some element of regionalist identity for French Algeria, in forms that varied principally in the way they conceived of the *indigènes'* place in history. Fanatics of *Afrique latine* relegated the *indigènes* to a footnote, at best a destructive interregnum in the advance of Latin hegemony. The more numerous moderates on the *Afrique latine* question paid at least lip service to the idea of Arab and Berber contributions to North African culture and spoke of their assimilation as the ultimate cultural product of the Greco-Latin Mediterranean melting pot. Either view could serve to distinguish a particular regional identity for Algeria within the French Empire. The rest of Chollier's reasoning invoked the consensus regarding the historical origin of the colony. Even in 1930, discussions of the 1830 invasion still spoke of a necessary reparation for an affront to French dignity, which could not suffer the outrage of piracy in the Mediterranean. This explanation legitimated French actions as reprisal for outlawry, Chollier's "bloody mirage." It also suggested a continued need for vigilance: the reflection of this past was somehow still visible on the face of the country. The Algériens had to police the people still so illuminated by ideas of the pirate past; this perception justified a panoply of special judicial and administrative measures governing the *indigènes.* These measures routinely came under attack from the progressive opposition, and 1930 saw a concerted effort to end them. The rhetoric of Chollier and others allowed Algériens to suggest (however disingenuously) that such governing campaigns stemmed from metropolitan ignorance. Only those ignorant of the past and therefore of the historical distance between France and the colony, they asserted, could seriously suggest that Algiers be bound by rules set down in Paris. No single point of contention between colony and metropole was more acrimonious than this.

Stressing the paradox of physical proximity versus cultural distance was thus closely linked in these texts with accusing the French of ignorance about the colony. The two tropes together allowed proponents of greater autonomy for the colonial administration to suggest that the colony's special needs were unknown and unmet by its French guardians. They logically concluded that only "native"

Algériens or highly perceptive and like-minded visitors would be able to manage the country properly. This argument was of a piece with efforts to assert control over ever larger allocations from Paris. Substantial sums of money were flowing into the colony to fund activities connected with the centenary, the occasion that colonial promoters said would attract even larger sums in the future ("Dégageant la signification économique des fêtes" 1930).

"Une Belle Leçon des Choses"

The descriptive and polemical texts produced for the centenary of 1930 envisioned the occasion as an object lesson in all things Algerian, a show put on for France and the world to convince everyone that the Algériens had arrived as a thoroughly modern, technically capable, and culturally mature people. It was also supposed to prove once and for all that France possessed a *génie colonisateur* just as great as its rival colonizing powers and that *Algérie française* was worthy of French nationalist pride. Despite heated debates about the intent and impact of the commemoration, most Algérien promoters agreed that the greater good of the whole affair would be a remedial propaganda campaign. Even though hundreds of books and articles that had attempted to enlighten the French public over nearly a century, few in Algeria doubted the need for such lessons, even at the most basic level.[5] Everything about the centenary was calculated to provide such lessons, from exhibitions to concerts to parades, all designed to draw a crowd and to be extensively reported on both sides of the Mediterranean.

Many Algérien commentators wrote as if they hoped for an imminent change in French thinking, but they frequently emphasized that it still was not happening. Given the actual content of much of the propaganda, it is hard to see how it could have. Despite claims to the contrary, exoticist imagery continued to dominate even official propaganda exercises, notably in the "manifestations culturelles du Centenaire" sponsored in mainland France. The first official soiree in Paris devoted to the centenary, a dramatic reading and series of tableaux of the conquest, took place in April 1930. Three young French women in Arab costume (students at the École professionelle de jeunes filles in the rue Ganneron) represented the three *départements* of Algeria, while a blind actor by the name of Edouard d'Armancourt, "wearing the burnous of a caïd from a notable family,"

5. The *Dépêche algérienne,* the largest-circulating daily paper in the colony, ran a regular column titled "Alger-Paris-Alger" by a correspondent in Paris named Cluny, who used the occasion to reflect on Algerian affairs as seen from the capitol. He regularly claimed to be surprised by the "ignorance des choses algériennes" (ignorance of things Algerian) in France (Cluny 1930a, 1930b).

recited poems translated from Arabic (*La première fête du Centenaire de l'Algérie à Paris* 1930, 13). Nothing whatever evoked the contemporary Algériens' efforts or cultural influence; the program of this soiree seems calculated for an audience that would not appreciate a lecture on wine production or, for that matter, a dramatization from a Randau novel. The image of Algeria, for this audience, would remain exactly as the anti-exoticists complained it was: a set piece of Oriental figures. Without the slightest irony, however, the author of the article describing the event (in a periodical circulating in France) declared that the actor not only exhorted his audience to visit Algeria, but also succeeded in his efforts to "make [the colony] known and loved." Nor did planners restrict this kind of Oriental pastiche to presentations for French audiences. At home in the colony, the organizers of the centenary festivities served up equally exoticist extravaganzas in places where visitors from mainland France were surely few. In the distant desert town of Beni-Ounif, centenary celebrations included "graceful dancers [*almées*], covered with silk and jewelry, [who] presented scenes from the Thousand and One Nights" ("Grandes fêtes sahariennes" 1930). The government of a colony in which the intellectual elite repeatedly denounced such images as deleterious literary fantasies thus officially presented an Orient à la Pierre Loti as the celebration of French Algeria. The complacency of these descriptions may have stemmed from their appearance in a review circulating in France; other accounts of the same events condemned them (Mélia 1930c). These scenes expressed exactly the vision of Algeria that most Algérien promotional texts accused of obscuring reality and furthering metropolitan ignorance. From the Algériens' point of view, the more Algeria was promoted by the contradictory messages of official propaganda, the more it would remain unknown. To the more critical editorialists, those who most consistently made the familiar complaint of the misrepresented colony, even the centenary celebrations seemed a losing battle.

The Political Uses of Ignorance

If fighting metropolitan ignorance was such a hopeless proposition, the rhetoric devoted to it was hollow and useless. What good could it possibly do to publish denunciations of that ignorance in places where the putative ignorant (according to the accusers themselves) would never read them? Furthermore, the vehemence of the rhetoric often exceeded that which the situation apparently called for. These texts begin to make sense only when we realize that commenting on metropolitan ignorance in the colony was less an effort to end it than an attempt to use Algériens' ideas about it to further a surprising range of political and cultural goals. Almost the entire spectrum of political opinion attempted to use the idea of "Algeria unknown and unloved" to support their views on everything from ethnic assimilation to administrative autonomy. These positions demonstrate the looming discord both between colony and metropole, and between Algériens and *indigènes*. Even the extreme flexibility of tropes in colonial discourse ultimately failed to reconcile this discord because many writers in 1930 had more interest in recognizing difference than in resolving it.

In the Algerian right wing, editorials ran particularly hot early in 1930. One demanded nothing less of the centenary than "the definitive retort to the ignorant, as well as to the saboteurs of French Algeria" (Charles-Collomb 1930a, 1). Even if we allow for this columnist's usual hectoring tone, his vehemence in speaking of "the ignorant" and "the saboteurs" in the same breath seems to betray motivations far beyond the issue at hand. Were the uninformed really sabotaging colonial strength with their ignorance, or were the saboteurs a different group, lumped together with the ignorant for political purposes? Associating saboteurs with the ignorant in France certainly suggested how widespread and insidious they allegedly were. As for who the saboteurs actually might have been, Charles-Collomb linked metropolitan ignorance with "softness" on one very specific issue: the physical and political danger to the Algériens of being radically outnumbered by hostile Arabs and Berbers. To forget or "ignore" this would be to sabotage the future of *Algérie française* (Charles-Collomb 1930a). Because the French word *ignorer* means both "to ignore" and "to be ignorant," the ignorant here might be willfully so. In any case, assimilation and other political compromises with the colonized majority were the dangerous delusions of the ignorant. This ignorance called less for informational campaigns than for repressive measures because the Arabs and Berbers, Charles-Collomb (1930b) warned, would exploit it cynically. He seems nevertheless to have only limited interest in ending metropolitan ignorance because it was a useful argument for locally decreed repression.

Despite the fears of a virulent right-winger, the Arab and Berber press in fact bemoaned metropolitan ignorance of Algeria in ways very similar to the Algérien press. The editor of the weekly *Voix indigène* complained about an article in the *Dépêche de Toulouse* in much the same terms as a member of the "unknown and unloved" camp: "if France spent 400 million so that it could hear such rubbish, it was hardly worth it. . . . It is too bad that the author did not give us an exact description of the harems he must have visited in the countryside, between belly-dance sessions" (Zenati 1930). The waste of money was particularly galling to the *Voix indigène,* which had earlier called for spending centenary allocations on schools for Arabs and Berbers, more effective than parades for ending ignorance ("Le centenaire" 1929). The paper railed at this perpetuation of ignorance (here, both metropolitan and colonial) in the same pages in which it lobbied for the effective recognition of political rights for which the editors hoped in 1930. This campaign could only suffer from stereotypes about exotic Oriental *indigènes*. Whereas the colonial administration had no interest in presenting anything else, the Arab and Berber press lost no opportunity to point out how modern and assimilated their readers were and to publicize the abuses they suffered daily. Unlike many Algériens, they had a genuine interest not merely in denouncing metropolitan ignorance, but in actually remedying it. By doing so, they hoped to attract sympathy in France for their sufferings, which they felt were otherwise insufficiently well known.

Of any group in the colony, the Algerian Left had the most conflicted stance regarding the political use of metropolitan ignorance. The complex coexistence of the colonial Left's cultural projects and political goals led to a variety of positions regarding the discourse of Algeria misrepresented. Some of the editorialists most committed to the cultural promotion of *Algérie française* (theoretically the least likely to appreciate the mixed messages of official festivities) occasionally had tactical reasons of their own to pronounce themselves momentarily satisfied, despite their objections. The *Presse libre,* a left-wing Algiers daily, wrote that "already" Parisian news coverage of Algeria showed "a sympathy inspired . . . by a healthier appreciation of reality. They no longer dare serve up to their readers the trumpery of puerile exoticism, which used to pass for colonial documentation. This is already progress" (["Succès du Centenaire"] 1930). "Already," indeed, readers at the time may have felt a certain déjà vu. French journalists had already been traveling to Algeria for decades to inquire about "Algerian realities"; the point for the Algériens was that such inquiries had not helped. New information about Algeria had always had great difficulty getting into the established body of knowledge and imagery regarding the country, something the *Presse libre* columnist could not have missed. His choice of phrasing suggests that his position owes more to cultural politics shaped within the colony in advance of the centenary than to actual observation of the Parisian press in the spring of 1930. The real debate in which the *Presse libre* was engaged actually had little to do with its Parisian colleagues. The argument was more for internal use than for external recriminations or praise. These pronouncements carried much more weight in the colony, where they encouraged *Algérie française* to think of itself as a modern, hard-working, and culturally distinctive region, able to stand on its own within the French Empire. The dozens of variations on this message (i.e., "the French are finally beginning to understand us, but more efforts are still needed," or "the French still are only beginning to understand us, despite all our efforts"), adaptable to every nuance of pessimism or optimism, did not actually differ much in their basic thought. Most such expressions added up to the same thing: a perpetual exhortation regarding the colony's self-image.

Among the Algerian Left, the messages bound up with arguments about metropolitan ignorance addressed the colonial self-image in both political and cultural projects. Writers on the left and right used allegations of ignorance in France as thinly veiled arguments for greater financial and administrative autonomy for the colony. For many, French ignorance of the colony was at once the worst stumbling block and the best justification for increased autonomy. This was as true in Algérien cultural polemics as it was in politics; there could, for example, be no better reason to publicize books by Algerian-born writers, as the leftist *indigène*-sympathizer Jean Mélia (1930b) vigorously did in the *Presse libre*. For those on the left, it was not a question of breaking entirely away from the metropole, but rather of spreading an adapted version of French republican values that would guide the new cultural production. Metropolitan ignorance served as a trope to be invoked to justify or emphasize portions of this project. Mélia, a major exponent of Algérien intellectual pride, published an article protesting both continued ignorance and staged Orientalist fantasies (two sides of the same coin, for him); it carried the headline "New Fantasias and New Fireworks—Nothing in Honor of the Work of Frenchification of Algeria" (Mélia 1930b). This all-important "Frenchification" meant the elaboration of a French-language, republican culture by the Algériens. It was the major plank in the platform of the Algerian Left, and although its justification stemmed from a recognition that Algeria had a problem controlling its own representation in France, it could actually be pursued quite satisfactorily in an atmosphere of continued French ignorance or apathy.

In the end, some of the most perceptive promoters of a distinctly Algérien culture recognized that there would have to be several ways of dealing with metropolitan ignorance. They hinted, moreover, that the colony had just as much of an interest in continuing to proclaim that ignorance as it had in actually addressing it. Audisio, the poet who argued for a Mediterranean cultural identity for North Africa, warned of going too far in fighting exoticism. The old "Oriental" imagery, even faked, could be useful:

> We all agree that Algeria is not the Orient, and that the era and especially the illusions of the romantics are obsolete. But we must not hide from ourselves the fact that tourists come to Algiers looking not for port installations, but for the Kasbah . . . not the neo-Latin race so dear to Louis Bertrand (and to some others I know) but the Arabs.
>
> I believe the two ideas are not irreconcilable, and can work together to create this obsession with Algeria. In all commercial circles, we should praise the constructive power, labor, and modernism of the colony, masterpiece of France, but for the tourists, we should still reserve the Barbary spices for which they are eager. (1930, 12)

For those debating the appropriate cultural identity of the colony, Audisio's recommendation went far beyond a prescription for what sort of propaganda to use in varying commercial milieus. His text instead suggested that Algeria adopt a compromise in its self-portrait, one that in any case had already been adopted by the French press, which had been producing both "modernizing" and "exotic" views of Algeria concurrently for years. Audisio pointed out the distinction between the country's developing self-image, which it could control, and its long-standing external representation, which it could not. He as much as proposed that the colony perpetuate externally what others called French ignorance, even as its intellectuals continued to proclaim internally the colony's modernism. In other words, he suggested that the Algériens continue to produce the kind of narrative about their country that had been going strong since at least the 1860s, while at the same time inventing a very different one for themselves.

Saying "the French do not know us" was thus not meant to make them do so, but rather to convince people on both sides of the Mediterranean that this was so in order to further a wide variety of political and cultural designs, some of which we have just seen. The "obsession de l'Algérie" Audisio called for may have been what publicists wished to create in France, but it was even more necessary as a force for cultural creativity in Algeria. Faced with a metropolitan culture disinclined to recognize regionalist difference, the Algériens would have to pursue such distinctions single-mindedly themselves. Creating a cultural scene based partly on an idea of what the French did not know, however, created a political situation in the colony with which the metropole could not sympathize. Algeria unknown did in fact progressively become Algeria unloved, both by the Arabs and Berbers and by the metropolitan French. When the "obsession with Algeria" actually did strike France thirty years later, it was not a matter of celebrating another anniversary of *Algérie française,* but of ending it.

5 Assimilation, Cultural Identity, and Permissible Deviance in Francophone Algerian Writing of the Interwar Years

PETER DUNWOODIE

When I say that I am French, I give myself a label that all Frenchmen refuse to give me. I express myself in French, I was educated in French schools. I know as much as the average Frenchman. But who am I, for heaven's sake? Is it possible that, as long as labels exist, I don't have one? Which is mine? Tell me who I am!

—Mouloud Feraoun, *Journal*

I am a hyphen linking West and East, Christianity and Islam, Africa and Asia, and other things besides! Poor Arab, where were you, reduced to being a string of hyphens!

—Abdelkebir Khatibi, *La mémoire tatouée*

IDENTITY IS NOT A GIVEN, yet, as Feraoun protested, it can be withheld. The role of go-between is often valorized, yet, as Khatibi's sardonic humor highlights, it bears within it the mark of nonbelonging, hence the danger of marginalization when the voluntaristic dynamism of the go-between is nullified by a hegemonic discourse that repositions (hence disempowers) it as ineffectual in-between. The dual practice of Othering at work here, which produced these figures of the unacknowledged and the interstitial, was the single most obsessive issue of colonial Algerian writing—endlessly (re)negotiated under the label *la question indigènes*. In somewhat summary fashion, one can say that in the sixty years after the invasion of 1830, first under military then under civilian rule, this "question" was confronted as part of the European monologue about the (future of the) *indigène* in the colony; and the "solutions" envisaged ranged from physical extermination to assimilation (its cultural embodiment). With the appearance of Algerian francophone and arabophone newspapers from the late 1880s, launched by some of the first Algerian Arabs, Berbers, and Jews to have undergone acculturation, the subaltern voice of the colonial Other interrupted that monologue by interjecting a number of alternative responses to the "question."

In rigidly categorizing those inside and those outside colonial civil society (Européens/Indigènes), the process of artificial polarization and homogenization actually masked the global practices of deterritorialization at work in the Algerian colonial arena. These practices were modifying the makeup not only of the indigenous population, but also of the newcomers, in particular the immigrant non-French Europeans, who were forced to confront many of the influences that were undermining traditional Islamic society—despite the racially inspired socioeconomic advantages the newcomers enjoyed. Because Algeria was French by right of conquest, immigrants from Italy, Spain, Majorca, Malta, and elsewhere, "uprooted" and "transplanted," were, like the indigenous population, forced to undergo a process of acculturation and personal/collective identity (re)construction characterized more by slippage, hesitation, and permeability than by the illusory safety of ethnic boundaries protecting stable, clearly differentiated communities—a delocalizing process with far-reaching destabilizing effects.

La question indigènes, as posed by the French in colonial Algeria, thus actually begs the question because it was articulated within what was initially perceived as a monologue of domination, promoting only a self-valorizing French model. The consequence was an oversimplification of the process of construction of a collective identity in a tumultuous, unbalanced society-in-formation, which aggressively foregrounded differences between European and *indigène* collectivities as a polarizing device. This collective identity was exploited, in part, to elide differences, imbalances, and the multiple modes of accommodation within the rival immigrant groups (where change was most rapid) and, in part, to enclose the Muslim population within its difference (where change was commonly said to be painstakingly slow or impossible).

This chapter offers a brief investigation into the written record of the key problems confronting the Muslim majority within that rigidifying process, against the background of contemporary developments in metropolitan France and, in particular, a rapidly modernizing society's administrative processing of identities (both personal and collective).[1] The issue is one of de/construction of cultural identity via the modalities of identification, integration, and exclusion

1. On general issues of cultural identity, see, for instance, Abbou 1981. I take *cultural imperialism* to mean the policy of controlling and shaping the culture of a colonized group. Its objective was assimilation.

imposed in colonial Algeria, as articulated by a sample of texts by francophone Muslim journalists and novelists from the interwar years who projected alternative positionalities.

One of the earliest references to the emergence of a francophone group among the indigenous population of colonial Algeria, referred to as *évolués,* seems to have been that of E. Doutté and W. Marçais in an article published in 1901 in the *Revue des questions diplomatiques et coloniales.* Doutté argued that the group's objective was the "modernization" of Islam and feared their future involvement in the pan-Islamic movement; Marçais located their motivation in the drive to gain access to the advantages open to Europeans and argued that this drive should be encouraged because it would inevitably lead to the adoption of French attitudes (see Ageron 1968). Their identification as a group was facilitated by the clubs and associations that developed rapidly around the turn of the century, whether those of former pupils of French schools, such as la Rachidia (1902) or debating societies such as the Cercle salah bey (1907), a "société d'études littéraires, scientifiques, économiques et sociales." These associations constituted a forum in which a group identity could be forged, hence facilitating its emergence, and their positions entered the public arena via the numerous bilingual newspapers launched between 1893 and 1935. Despite limited resources and circulation, as well as the systematic opposition offered by both settlers and the colonial government, these papers constituted a declaration of both existence and intent, ensuring that the *question indigènes* became an issue that could not be resolved simply by colonial European diktat.

The first piece of extended prose on the subject was Ahmed Bouri's "Musulmans et Chrétiennes," serialized in the Oran newspaper *El Hack* in 1912; but the first novel to deal with it was *Ahmed ben Mostapha, goumier* (1920), the fictionalized account of First World War experiences, imprisonment in a German prisoner-of-war camp and internment in Switzerland, written by the Saint-Cyr-trained officer Si Ahmed ben Chérif (1879–1921). A dozen more novels were published in metropolitan France and Algeria by 1948, by Abdelkader Hadj Hamou (1925); Sliman ben Ibrahim and Etienne Dinet (1926); Chukri Khodja (1929, [1928] 1992); Saad ben Ali and René Pottier (1933); Saïd Guennoun (1934); Mohammed Ould Cheikh ([1936] 1985); Aïssa Zehar (1942); Rabah Zenati and his son Akli (1945); Djamila Debèche (1947); and Malek Bennabi (1948).[2] The output was thus not extensive and was dwarfed by that of the Euro-

2. On texts in which a (colonized) writer engages with representations made of him by others (the colonizer), see Pratt 1992.

peans of the "Algérianiste" movement of the 1920s and 1930s (of which Hadj Hamou was a vice president), but it is instructive when analyzing the channels of acculturation, not least because of its status as autoethnographic fiction.

The genre had no antecedents in preconquest Algeria and was therefore itself a sign of estrangement, especially because its adoption in the colony by francophone Muslims was governed by strict conformity to normative French models—within which, nevertheless, themes had to be reoriented to allow Muslim Algerian self-representation. As far as the French were concerned, these works deserved attention precisely as a sign of France's success in inculcating these models. Paratextual evidence—in introductions, for instance—reveals that the emerging indigenous novelist was sponsored by metropolitan professionals and marketed by French publishers on the basis of conformity to metropolitan moral and aesthetic norms—in short, as proof of successful assimilation. Readability was promoted, however, via their difference, as *témoins* or authentic insiders in an "Oriental" world. The respectability of ethnographic veracity, in which contemporary "Algérianiste" novelists grounded their superiority over earlier orientalizing fiction, was thus also attached to francophone colonial production and, indeed, used to justify publication of a novel such as *Bou-el-Nouar,* which, according to the foreword, "is not merely a novel that can provide enjoyment or a distraction. It is also a unique study of the family mores of Algerian Muslim Society. It is above all a sociological study of the Algerian problem, which hinges indubitably on the 'Native question' " (Zenati and Zenati 1945, iii).

The recognized function of such texts was thus to confirm established tropes/knowledge and to serve as a "supplement" to metropolitan and colonial writing in a process of reiteration of the constitutive (unequal) relationship between European viewer/reader and colonial spectacle/informant.

The *évolué* authors remained francophone, not French, however; hence, their production is also the site of an alternative self-representation that, necessarily, reworked the dominant, French-imposed themes and sociocultural issues of the day (freedom, identity, marriage, interpersonal relations, and so on). This subjective repositioning in the face of (largely derogatory) colonial representation was treated directly in novels about the problems confronting the *évolué,* so this chapter looks primarily at two of these novels: Rabah and Akli Zenatis' *Bou-el-Nouar, le jeune Algérien* (1945)[3] and Chukri Khodja's *Mamoun, l'ébauche d'un idéal* (1928). Both are bildungsromane: the first pitting the (modernizing) influence of the ideal Father (an *évolué qadi,* two French schoolteachers, and a re-

3. The *qadi* ("son confidant, son père spirituel" [Zenati and Zenati 1945, 158]) sees in turn the ideal Father in the "contrôle paternel d'une France débonnaire" (163).

formist Muslim scholar) against the weight of tradition concretized in the figure of the well-to-do peasant father of the eponymous young hero; the second charting the failure of assimilation in its hero, whose fruitless search for the kind of employment his French education should have made accessible is accompanied by a moral fall, through alcohol, adultery, and hashish.

The second half of the nineteenth century in France was a period of far-reaching and radical modernization and centralization, both in areas such as schooling and the army (where linguistic and cultural homogenization was a central factor in the construction of a republican and national identity) and throughout *l'administration* (which covers structures from local government to the police, civil service, and so on) (see Noiriel [1988] 1996). As compulsory military service from 1889 (1912 in Algeria) and the development of modern public-health and hygiene measures drew ever-increasing numbers into the state's bureaucratic network, rights—hence registration—became a major social and political issue, while identification, surveillance, and restraint of the outsider/foreigner became of paramount concern. This movement gave rise in the 1880s to a countrywide polemic about naturalization and the rights of the individual within French territory. It culminated in the first Nationality Code in 1889—the year in which, in Algeria, automatic naturalization was introduced for all persons of European origin born in the colony. Yet the issue, despite its impact on colonial society, is never engaged with directly in the francophone fiction, authors resorting instead to euphemisms such as *entente, understanding, cooperation, union, brotherhood* and to the vision of a future in which, after an interlude as "Frenchmen who temporarily do not dress in the same way" (Zenati and Zenati 1945, 71), "all the Arabs will become French at heart" (ben Ali and Pottier 1933, 248).

Demands for compulsory registration and more stringent controls were reinforced around 1912, when, probably as an offshoot of the longstanding middle-class obsession with *les classes dangereuses,* newspaper campaigns exploited widespread fears that France faced a major social crisis—concretized in the figure of the *nomades* who roamed the territory unchecked and unregistered (see Chevalier 1958). The impetus for such a campaign came in part, no doubt, from the massive influx of workers required in response to birth rate and labor crises after the Franco-Prussian War (and in conjunction with increasing Great Power rivalry), which helped to make freedom of movement synonymous with a disquieting lack of both ties and control, and vagrancy synonymous with immorality and criminality (see Foucault 1991). In Algeria, the already well-established dichotomy between the valorized figure of the sedentary, hardworking Kabyle *(assimilable)* and the devalorized figure of the nomadic, slothful Arab *(réfractaire)* was exacerbated by these metropolitan developments.

Where procedures of identification, hence categorization, enhanced central control and conformity in metropolitan France, and thus facilitated the republic's homogenizing nation-building efforts, they became not only key instruments of government in Algeria, but the tools with which a European minority—culturally and nationally mixed, hence highly unstable—sought to imagine and mold an exclusive, collective identity that would repress their differences and guarantee their superiority, while, of course, they jostled among themselves for the controlling positions that would allow different immigrant groups (Spanish and Italian in particular) to impose as exemplary their own cultural models.

Annexation in 1834 had dictated the legal position for Algeria's four million Muslim majority: no longer foreigners, they became French "subjects." In practice, as Jean-Robert Henry (1987) has shown, they were distanced by reference to both religious and ethnic categories and to the systematic use of the terms *indigène* and *musulman* to imply nonnationality. As "subjects," they fell under French sovereignty, but, primarily because of the role of Koranic law in all aspects of Muslim life, they were governed under a *régime d'exception.* Although this position recognized and protected their individual identity via a *statut personnel* as Muslims, it also excluded them from full French citizenship and political equality. Reforms in a decree of July 1865 gave them French nationality, but again not citizenship: "The Muslim native is French," it declared; however, only by renouncing Islam could he or she "benefit from the rights open to a French citizen." This abnormal category of "French national noncitizen" was made permanent in 1881, when Algeria was fully absorbed into the metropolitan administrative system. By the turn of the century, the colonial party—opposed to Paris's policy of assimilation—envisaged the National Code as a framework for a future of separate development through "association"—namely, permanent subordination and heteronomy within *l'indigénat.* As the reformist Muslim newspaper *La France islamique* protested in 1913, "The two ethnic groups remain politically distinct because the thinly disguised pedestrian ideal of the majority of the men who, over a third of a century, have been able to control the destiny of Algeria, often despite France itself, was to maintain a watertight barrier between the two societies there."

That position was grounded in the thesis that Arab "backwardness" was endogenous and Kabyle assimilability slow to materialize.[4] More pragmatically, it grew from the fact that the primary settler objective was guaranteed superiority and control via differentiation—by the army, then by the police and *l'administra-*

4. On French attitudes toward Arab and Berber, see Ferrié and Boetsch 1992 and Lorcin [1995] 1999a.

tion. The general classification of non-European *(indigène, musulman,* Arabe) was perceived as an adequate everyday marker of difference/subordination in the face of the destructive social, economic, and cultural impact of settler implantation itself (see Hamel 1890; Makaci 1936). Oppressive land laws, expropriation, and repeated famines drove millions off the land, and newspapers and political debates were dominated by issues of law and order, beggars, and the tens of thousands of day laborers wandering the colony in search of work. In the imaginary of Algeria's Europeans, the nomadism deplored in both metropole and colony was reinforced by fantasies of being submerged (indeed "eaten") by "outlaws" and "starving hordes." When opposing demands for the naturalization of soldiers returning from the battlefields of the First World War, for instance, a settler paper such as *L'echo d'Alger* warned in 1919 that French culture would be "engulfed, drowned in the mass" and that in a process of regression the French could be "submerged in a new race," which could then in turn be "absorbed by the primitive race" ("La question indigène: Electeurs" 1919; "La question indigène: Heur" 1919).

For the very small percentage of urban French-educated indigenous males concerned, the key issue therefore was how to negotiate a place in this civil society, how to effect the passage from the subordinate status of *indigène/colonisé* to the supposed equality of citizenship offered by the republic to the *évolué.* More specifically (and more problematically), the colonial subject had to confront the sociocultural issues raised by the acculturation *(assimilation)* demanded as proof that the *indigène* merited entry into French citizenship, considering that the debate involved a confused and constantly shifting interaction of the ethnic, the political, and the cultural (especially religion). The French of the colony dismissed the possibility of assimilation for the majority and demanded of the few the internalization of French models to the exclusion of Arab or Islamic alternatives: intellectual (through schooling in the values of the republic and Western rationalism); sociocultural (through Western practices such as monogamy); economic (new structures and professions); and political (parties, elected representatives, etc.).[5] The rigid Manicheanism that motivated settler cultural hegemony satisfied both the European population, firmly convinced that difference was the product of morphotypes, not mentalities, and the majority of the indigenous population, for whom Western mores were totally alien.

The dominant trope in Algeria's self-valorization was that of the "melting

5. Although official colonial policy at the Congrès colonial international of 1889, assimilation was already decidedly unpopular by the time of the Marseilles Congrès colonial of 1906. The policy lasted longer in colonial Algeria. See S. Roberts 1929.

pot"—but only for the colony's Mediterranean immigrants. Such a trope reflected essentialist colonist thinking in its status as aggressive antonym to cultural *métissage,* turning the cultural difference of the non-European Other into an ontological barrier to integration, while proclaiming that "Frenchness," grounded in conformity and homogenization, could be acquired only by abandoning other cultures and values. In short, where Muslim *évolués* (and some liberal Paris intellectuals) spoke of retarded evolution and the need for development (hence acknowledged that identity is a process of representation and construction), colonial opponents argued somatic difference, the fixity of racial superiority, and threats to (the myth of) ethnic and cultural homogeneity (see, e.g., Hutin 1933). Eliding the real history of French nation formation, this monolithic mindset defended its unicity (and, of course, its privileges) via the figure of the "Français de race," while actively opposing the elision of difference generated by assimilation and, in particular, by mixed marriage. By eliding the past of the Muslim, deriding his present condition, and dictating his future, the settler strategy of exclusion sought to reify him within a disabling, atavistic "fanaticism"—well exemplified fictionally in the figure of the biological father in *Bou-el-Nouar,* who "believed he was perpetuating the ancient traditions of his family by leaving nothing to chance and remaining wary of anything new, considering that what his ancestors had accomplished was highly respectable. . . . 'The ancestors have said, done, and foreseen everything. It would be unhealthily vain to upset the centuries-old order, to abandon the old customs in favor of habits from outside that have not yet been shown to be useful and that, above all, are not ours' " (Zenati and Zenati 1945, 47).[6]

In adhering to such rigid frames, which conveniently treated the *musulmans* as a homogeneous block, the settlers avoided the need to envisage a dialogic relationship with its most progressive fringe, a relationship that of necessity would have destabilized (defensive) categories and frontiers by revealing something of the discontinuities of the social formation. Instead, as European Algerian politicians and journalists reiterated daily from behind the ramparts of noncommunicability and reification, the relative positions of settler and *indigène* were fixed, nonnegotiable. The necessarily dialogic and processual nature of assimilation could thus be denied.

Such positions were designed to negate the more flexible psychosocial categories being constructed by the *évolués,* to block their progress, and to marginalize them in colonial debates, depriving them of any legitimacy by impugning their

6. *Fanaticism* rapidly became synonymous with adherence to Islamic beliefs; the refutation of the charge is a leitmotif of francophone Algerian newspapers.

good faith and projecting onto them a radical, hostile, and "foreign" political agenda, frequently attacked as pan-Islamism or religious/Arab nationalism.

Islam was, for the Europeans, not only the founding factor of Arab (and, to a lesser extent, Berber) identity, but the primary cause of Arab "backwardness" and the key obstacle to successful assimilation. This leitmotif of settler discourse is amply illustrated by the following assertions by one of the colony's most influential spokesmen, the *député* André Servier:

> The only thing the Arabs ever invented is their religion. And this religion is, precisely, the main obstacle between them and us. . . . Islam . . . is a homeland; and if the religious nationalism in which every Muslim brain is steeped has not yet been able to pose a threat to humanity . . . it's because the peoples linked by it have fallen, as a result of its rigid dogma . . . into such a state of decrepitude and misery that they are incapable of fighting against the material forces placed at the disposal of Western civilization by science and progress. (Servier 1923, 14–15)

In the face of the settler's autovalorization of a dynamic *peuple neuf,* constructing itself out of adversity and diversity, indigenous cultural memory/practice was stigmatized as fossilization and *dégénérescence.* Essentialized as static and resistant, not only backward but also doggedly backward looking, it was said to mark the refusal or the congenital inability to accept the benefits of France's (clearly superior) civilization.

Islam also became a subject of controversy between the pro-Western, promodernization *évolué* group known as the Young Algerians and the Islamic reformists or ulemas. Yet accusations of the "ignorance and prejudice" of a Muslim population "like ours, long decadent" are frequent not only in Young Algerian texts such as *L'Algérie française vue par un indigène* (1914) by Chérif Benhabilès, a *naturalisé* who was president of the Amicale des magistrats et officiers ministériels musulmans, but also in ulema publications that deplored the deleterious effect of Ottoman rule and the population's slide into the superstitions of maraboutism. Despite radical differences in the alternative models proposed, the calls for the "moral regeneration" of Algeria's Muslim population—a leitmotif of *naturalisé,* Young Algerian, and ulema positions until the mid-1930s—were thus in effect partly complicitous with the dominant divisive discourse of colonial hegemony. In Khodja's *Mamoun,* this complicitousness appears as the hero's distaste for the "barbarous visions of the countryside, the rudimentary morals of the Arab" ([1928] 1992, 88), and in *Bou-el-Nouar* as the rejection of "ancestral ignorance" and the "weight of illogical and crass customs" (Zenati and Zenati 1945, 100, 130). It is implicit even in articles of the pro-ulema *Voix du peuple* when arguing for instance that if the French had dealt equitably with Algeria since 1830, "Algerian Muslims would have been educated, civilized, and emancipated long ago" (*La voix du peuple* 1933–34).[7]

The distinction often foregrounded between Muslim traditionalists and reformists was declared irrelevant not only by their settler opponents, but by an *évolué* such as Rabah Zenati, a member of the Association des instituteurs indigènes, who argued in *Comment périra l'Algérie française* that the primary source of resistance to change in the colony was not the masses (said to be evolving through enforced contact), but both the conservative marabouts and the religious party of the ulemas. Dismissing the latter's reformist rhetoric, he condemned it as fundamentally anti-Western and antimodern, endeavoring to "rise against everything that develops through Reason and drag everything back to blind faith, to sectarian fanaticism and the living standards of the first centuries of Islam. Is it not attempting to hamper our evolution, to detach us from France and to deprive us of the benefits of modern Science?" (1938a, 13).[8] Such *assimilé* positions largely replicated those of the European majority and showed that their objective was primarily to find the means to open the Islamic world of the sacred (of tradition, submission, and community) to the European world of reason and modernity (the secular and individual).[9] In the process of acculturation, such *évolués* had learned, of necessity, to privilege the republican model of society and in particular its secular grounding. Yet, as Zenati's writings reveal, they continued nevertheless via two distinct approaches to opt for the systematic projection of Islam as a central and positive constituent in their characters' individual identity. The first is evident in Zenati's essay *Le problème algérien vu par un indigène:* "We recommend neither apostasy nor a brutal transformation, which is always harmful. . . . Those intellectuals capable of becoming French have neither to abandon their simple, beautiful religion nor to renounce their mores and traditions where these are fine and noble. They will evolve as Egypt and all the peoples of the Orient have evolved" (1938b, 46). For Zenati, the issue was neither to abandon nor to reform Islam, but to restrict its impact. Turkey was the most frequently quoted model for such evolution because "it has carried out something prodigious: it has separated the spiritual and the temporal" (1938b, 68).

7. The complicity between such discourses is well demonstrated in Chatterjee 1986.

8. Historians such as Julien, Nouschi, and Merad have concluded that the Young Algerian movement was fundamentally legalistic and assimilationist.

9. Many *évolués* became primary-school teachers, joining the ranks of France's militantly republican and secular *hussards noirs*. For the ulemas, assimilation meant conversion.

> Behind this example of the way forward for Islam stood France, obviously, in a relationship made explicit in Khodja's *Mamoun,* via an overt lesson by the narrator: Dogmatic Muslims have been seen to speak out forcefully against the path followed by regenerated young people, arguing that Islam was about to undergo a deformation, which would devastate its prestige and its grandeur. That is a meaningless alarm signal, the sole objective of lucid young people has been to adapt the Koran to the vital requirements of the era, and they draw from the Sacred Text the arguments needed to support their praiseworthy action. Ah! How right the Turks are to keep religion out of government, they are bravely following the example of France, that fine and tolerant nation. ([1928] 1992, 81–82)

Although no such "adaptability" was seen in the Koran, separation of religion and government was widely supported by those who deemed the obligation to renounce Islam as a delaying tactic on the part of the settlers, largely because it was expected that what Max Weber calls the "disenchantment" induced by secularization and rationalism would eventually lead to abandoning the irrational, the traditional, the religious.

The second approach is evoked in *Bou-el-Nouar* in a lengthy narratorial insert on the Salafi reformist movement and in particular on the impact of Djamal Edine El Afghani and Rachid Ridha, presented as "the loftiest expression of Islamic thought" (Zenati and Zenati 1945, 156). In discussions with a second ideal Father (reformist Muslim, rather than Western/ized), the movement is said to be "convinced that the Koran contains the seeds of all the accomplishments of which Europe is so proud" (160). The narrative context is a period of three years at the Tunis university of El Zitouna, "to return with new weapons that will allow an attack on the edifice . . . that keeps Islamic society within the rigid framework of an intolerance, which, sadly, is no more than the fruit of decadence" (169). The key argument is that Muslim intellectuals were now turning for inspiration to Cairo rather than to Paris and in particular to publications such as Rachid Ridha's *El mannâr,* which was "very open to modern ideas, but displayed fierce intransigence over anything that concerned the integrity of Mohammedan doctrine" (157). This position is close to that of the ulemas, who sought systematically in the late 1930s to limit recognition of positive French involvement, hence European epistemic dominance, to the realms of science and technology. In the novel, the position is concretized in the fictional figure of Bou-el-Nouar's ideal Muslim Father and can be summarized via Rachid Ridha's introduction to his history of relations between Europe and Turkey, *La faillite morale de la politique occidentale en Orient:* "I certainly do not underestimate the role of

European civilization and the magnificent results it has brought in the material field. . . . But material civilization becomes a destructive force if it forgets that it is merely a phase on the path to the heights of moral perfection" (1922, 11).

And for the old scholar of El Zitouna in *Bou-el-Nouar,* "This doctrine can be summarized as follows: evolve, but toward the purity of early Islam; produce, invent, rise to the level of civilized peoples, but by drawing on the roots of the Koran; learn, acquire Science in all its guises without turning away from authentic Islam" (Zenati and Zenati 1945, 160). In furthering this aim, the ulemas increasingly based sermons and articles on cultural memory and alternative, Islamic values. By referring consistently to pre-1830 Algeria and by glorifying the Muslim past, they tacitly excluded the French and their teleological, universalizing view of history in which the 1789 revolution was a key moment on the (historicist) path to progress, freedom, and civilization. Their slogan made the indigenous and founding values—national, religious, and cultural—of a non-westernized identity quite explicit: "Algeria is my homeland, Islam my religion, Arabic my language."[10]

Although rejecting the Europeans' claim to *moral* leadership and seeking to define an identity that fused modernity and Islam, the ulemas also demonized those aspiring to embrace that imported culture, especially the *naturalisé,* who was forced into denial in order to reemerge in strict conformity with a singular, secular, valorized model. It is this colonial creation, product of a *culture mixte,* which Bou-el-Nouar's Muslim ideal Father portrays while setting out the acceptable limits of their social and cultural endeavors:

> You are bad believers because you have an urgent need to submit to the light of reason things that precisely transcend reason. Descartes, Rousseau, Voltaire have sown in your minds seeds you no longer wish to banish. Is it your fault if you stand out in the midst of Muslim society? You are products of your mixed culture and cannot be otherwise. . . .
>
> You will never be a true believer. Don't forget that henceforth you are a slave to Western Reason and a fervent practitioner of scientific thinking. . . . All that can reasonably be demanded of you is that you love Islam, respect the faith of your fathers, and do nothing to help reduce it for the benefit of another religion. (Zenati and Zenati 1945, 185, 187)

By the 1940s, that median position or modus vivendi had been largely discredited, and the collective counteridentity grounded in Islam was proclaimed

10. The forced uniformization within Arabic and the insistence on Islam show the impact of colonialism on the debate on identity because they are imposed as key features of a single coherent national Subject, despite the country's actual diversity.

openly in *Lebbeik, pèlerinage de pauvres* (1948), a thinly fictionalized account of salvation through Islam, by Malek Bennabi, who belonged to the ulema movement and wrote in the early 1950s for *La république algérienne* and *Le jeune musulman.* His novel reveals the aggressive deadlock colonial relations had reached and pushes into the background everything European—at the time seen as a source of restrictions and corruption. The (Muslim) hero is a drunk whose behavior has already alienated his wife, family, and neighbors. Thus, like the hero of *Mamoun,* he is a totally negative image of the marginalization produced by colonial contact, but, unlike Khodja, Bennabi inserts no plea in favor of the benefits of assimilating French culture: "However degenerate, a Muslim soul when it has fallen retains . . . a certain dignity; thanks to this feeling of shame Brahim felt the shame which overcomes that illicit category of people who, raised in the days since life acquired a modern slant, wander without roof or family, on the margins of . . . Muslim society and European society" (1948, 22).

The novel is a declaration of the position of the reformist ulemas and in particular their call for recognition of " 'la nationalité MUSULMANE' in the face of a dirty and 'foul' civilization . . . of prostitution and alcohol," aided and abetted by a "sordid maraboutism" ("La colonialisme" 1933, emphasis in original). The hero's sudden reawakening to the call of the muezzin after yet another night's drunkenness (Bennabi 1948, 11–29), despite its blatant artificiality, opens a path to repentance, reintegration in the community, and salvation via the return to Islam and the pilgrimage to Mecca (29–99). In the narrator's words, the hero rediscovers "the fraternal ties of Islam, while reproaching himself mentally for having been so long a kind of renegade" (50). Subsequently, a discussion between one of the ship's crew and "one of those bilingual intellectuals one comes across in Algeria" (64) on the interdiction concerning wine and pork provides the context for clarifying the lasting opposition between religion and reason, the spiritual and the temporal: "It is civilized society that, out of self-interest, first transgressed the elementary rules of happiness. Today it is striving to replace them by artificial rules. But there is no ersatz for happiness. . . . Or for truth. . . . Science and politics will never rebuild what has been destroyed in the human soul" (65).

The religious component of *évolué* identity was thus an insurmountable problem for a colony such as Algeria precisely because the Enlightenment had made of secularization the touchstone of French republican progress, and French intellectual traditions demanded conformity to a rational, skeptical position and a historicist approach in which the sacred is gradually overcome by Reason. Under colonial law, the *évolués* had the right to seek full French citizenship, provided they renounced their *statut personnel* as Muslims. Hence, until an ordinance of 1947 envisaged naturalization "dans le statut," citizenship always disrupted the *uluma,* or Islamic religious community. Prevailing attitudes toward those who were perceived as having abandoned Islam in favor of French citizenship, pilloried as *christianisation,* were openly marked in the pejorative terms used to stigmatize them: *renégat, apostat, m'tourni.* In *Bou-el-Nouar,* for instance, rejection of them is clearly articulated in the real father/ideal Father debate when the young hero asks permission to join the *qadi's* sons at the local French school. For the biological father, education or progress is not the issue here, but rather "an opportunity to trample on the immutable rules of Muslim morality" because *évolués* belong to "a category of individuals set well apart, far from Islam and often in rebellion against God . . . [they] straddle two religions . . . destroying through their libertinage the bases of our beliefs" (Zenati and Zenati 1945, 48).

In the face of European rejection and Muslim distrust, progressive Arab/Berber intellectual circles were forced to reformulate the "question," seeking to define a permissible deviance via cultural convergence rather than acculturation, merger rather than loss, mutual enrichment rather than blanket homogenization—seeking the dosage of mimicry and resistance required for entry into a modernity dictated by Europeans. Marginalized by both communities, they defended an alternative self-image as modernizers who had absorbed both "Islamic sciences and the positive sciences of Western civilization," were educated into "a marked taste for everything French, [but] without nevertheless forgetting the respect [they] owed to Islam" (Zenati and Zenati 1945, 54, 100). The Young Algerian movement, for instance, which grouped a significant number of these intellectuals who were key interlocutors for (and threats to) the colonial authorities, argued that the process of modernization undertaken in Algeria was producing not only a *français musulman,* but an elite capable of acting as agents in France's "civilizing task." Such a claim was in itself disruptive because in demanding a role in civil society, they were declaring their allegiance to a culture in which the social agent was defined by roles and not by the positions allocated to them by divine right or religious tradition. The self-designated role was that of *trait d'union* or *intermédiaire* (Zenati and Zenati 1945, 54), selflessly linking the conflicting camps. The francophone *évolué* sought to anchor his self-representation in this (still unappreciated) figure of the intermediary working in favor of the idealized notion, as promoted, for instance, by the narrator in the novel *El euldj:* "rigorous mutual respect and convergence toward a happy medium made up of a synthesis of the qualities of both sides" (Khodja 1929, 130). This convergence remained, at best, an unequal synthesis, as revealed in the bias of the much-praised Burgundian teachers in *Bou-el-Nouar,* who denounce racism but construct a fantasized fusion in "a homogenous people with solidly French traits" (Zenati and Zenati 1945, 98).

Such change, clearly, could only hasten the disruption of traditional society and the development of a new elite. For groups such as the Young Algerians, for instance, progress could be achieved by greater equality via the abolition of the Code de l'indigénat and an increase in both French/Arabic education and Muslim political representation. This progress was to be entrusted to the enlightened minority, hence removed from the *notables* and other traditional Muslim "representatives" who were recognized by the colonial authorities, but derided by the emerging educated elite as "Vieux Turbans" and "Béni-oui-oui," self-serving and ignorant yes-men (municipal councillors, *qadis,* court interpreters, school principals, and the like).[11]

The long-term aim, as voiced in indigenous Muslim newspapers such as *El Hack* (1893), *El Misbah* (1904) *Ikdam* (1919), or *L'entente franco-musulmane* (1935), was agency for the elite through citizenship and equal participation in civil society. This position was widely supported before the First World War and strengthened in 1911, when a Paris committee of legal experts ruled that nothing in French law excluded the possibility of extending citizenship to Algeria's Muslims under the formula *naturalisation mixte.* This projected figure of a "Franco-Musulman" sat more easily with *évolué* valorization of the principle of *liberté* (rather than secularization) in France's self-congratulatory republican self-representation and, moreover, with the political conception of citizenship as collective contract or consent in which religious adherence is a purely private matter. In this notion, the *évolués,* like their liberal European interlocutors, challenged the convenient ethnic classification in which "community" or gemeinschaft (place/group belonging) was grounded (in the easily demonized structures of *tribu* and *çof* or *confrérie*). Instead, they insistently relocated the debate within a more modern, egalitarian concept of gesellschaft, of free/equal individuals within a society based not on tradition but on merit—a resistance maneuver of organic intellectuals that Gramsci ([1949] 1996) termed a "war of position."

Settler resistance thwarted metropolitan policies and exhausted the goodwill of most *évolués,* however, and assimilation remained grounded in the insistence on a singular, superior identity and conformity to a valorized French model. It was, therefore, an alienating univocal experience of ablation and loss of some of the key constituents of cultural identity: tradition, valorized history, and memory. In particular, history and the memory from which it is written were bowdlerized

11. Young Algerian demands that all candidates for elected posts should be holders of the Diplôme d'études françaises automatically excluded traditionalists and many ulemas.

as French education and intellectual domination led many to accept the annexation as a fait accompli and, in the process of identity building, to take as their starting point the French invasion of 1830 and its positive impact on North African, Ottoman-inspired "decadence" and the struggle for modernization. The historical past was thus commonly reduced in the novels to (unspecified) traditions and customs or, as in Mohammed Ould Cheikh's *Myriem dans les palmes,* to reminders of the "pays barbaresque de naguère," the "insécurité", and "régime discrétionnaire" finally overthrown by the French (1936, 242–46). Only the Zenatis and Ben Chérif, in *Bou-el-Nouar* and *Ahmed ben Mostapha,* respectively, actually attempted a fictional resurrection of the glorious Islamic past: *Bou* via labored conversations with the *qadi* at El Zitouna; *Ahmed* via equally artificial inserts in which a young French officer teaches the hero about the Arab heroism and nobility that he has, naturally, inherited.[12]

The most assimilated *évolué* of colonial Algeria was thus a double victim: of systematic "cultural co-optation" through the devalorization and loss of autochthonous culture when absorbed by the dominant French culture; and of (varying degrees of) what Edouard Glissant (1981) terms "néantisation mimétique," the identificatory void generated when the individual can only ever reproduce the dominant culture (see also Nandy 1983; Miller 1993). For most, the outcome was a fluctuating, double alienation, following a double rejection, articulated in a feuding, always incomplete, and hence unstable persona: *from/within* both an indigenous culture and the acquired European culture. Khodja's 1929 novel *El euldj,* a story of (unsuccessful) conversion set among the Christian captives of the sixteenth-century Barbary Coast, portrays the troubled existence (and, here, the final madness) that overwhelms the *m'tourni* (turncoat or renegade), although the most radical depiction of the pathological form of that alienation was to be found a year or two later in an attack on Europeanized intellectuals by one of the reformist ulema newspapers, *La voix du peuple* (1933–34): "They promote themselves as . . . representatives of Muslim Algeria. Yet, to various extents, they have all cut themselves off from it. Furthermore, it is in their midst that you will encounter the most poisonous secret hatred of Europe, of France, that they copy, they ape, in such servile manner."

The article condemns the objective of the "Franco-Christians" as the "de-Islamization of Algerian Muslims through Frenchification" and argues that when the acculturation is actually successful, the *européanisé* "repeats aggressively that he is French because he feels dimly that, at bottom, that cannot be true. He

12. A much more ambiguous (and orientalizing) past is evoked in both *Khadra* (Ouled Naïl dancing/prostitution) and *Aïchouch* (Berber legends).

throws himself on anything European because the voice of the blood, that he is unable to silence altogether, proposes another direction. Yet simultaneously he hates, he hates every day a little more that for which he is obliged to lie, that object for which he stifles his own nature and which turns him into a rootless being."

In the fiction, this view is clearly articulated in both the narratorial comment and the internal monologue of the hero of *Mamoun,* who, "at twenty, no longer had anything Muslim about him" (Khodja [1928] 1992, 32). The alienation is acknowledged vis-à-vis colonial society and the indigenous population, but cannot be openly recognized vis-à-vis the model he seeks to emulate, hence the slippage from individual "Français" (the Subject in the eyes of whom he nevertheless remains déclassé) to compensatory abstraction, "la France":

> He acknowledges, to his detriment, that the scattered elements of science acquired . . . had simply made of him a perfect déclassé. . . . I know perfectly well that I am an aborigine, held in disdain. I am fully aware of the deep divide between me and an Arab of the Sahara; between me and a native of Blida, there's an entire world. . . . The Frenchman, what is he in relation to me? A foreigner? No. France . . . is the mother protecting all the children that nature deigns to place under her tutelage. (Khodja [1928] 1992, 113, 167)

It is that alienation and the contemporary theory of the incommunicability of cultures underpinning it that the narrator twice describes in *Bou-el-Nouar* in generalizing terms such as the following:

> Each of us is the product not just of his epoch, but especially of the milieu in which he lives and the culture to which he is subjected. Like all young Algerians, Bou-el-Nouar was to be caught between the two civilizations confronting each other in North Africa. . . . It is in the hope of avoiding this inner drama that French-educated Muslim intellectuals engage in a prodigious balancing act in an attempt to *reconcile the irreconcilable.* (Zenati and Zenati 1945, 141, my emphasis)

Francophone texts of the interwar years thus show that assimilation was not merely a conflict *between* cultures, a question of negotiating a passage from one to the other or of serving as bridge or go-between. It constituted, instead, a site of contradiction *for* both: on the one hand, between the republic's "civilizing mission" (figured by the devoted French teachers in both *Bou* and *Mamoun*) and the pragmatics of rejection and discrimination (experienced by Mamoun and acknowledged by Bou's *évolué* ideal Father); and, on the other hand, between the *évolué's* anchorage in Islamic traditions (the continuity of the El Zitouna scholar) and the claims of European modernity (the *rupture* accepted by the *évolué qadi*).

The contradiction in both *Bou-el-Nouar* and *Mamoun* between idealizing, assimilationist discourse and closing narration confirms the irresolvable conflict. Although Bou's Burgundian wife proclaims that "for us there are no Natives and Frenchmen, we have a foot in both *çofs,* as you call them, we shall love them all, that will suffice" (Zenati and Zenati 1945, 226), they are obliged to retreat to metropolitan France, "far from racial and religious prejudices" (225). Although the hero of *Mamoun* can declare, "I owe a great deal to France, thanks to a feeling of gratitude in the innermost core of my personality" (Khodja [1928] 1992, 170), his failure is total, and the novel ends with his death, a "poor disoriented native" (167). A similar closure signals the failure of the converted captive Ledieux in *El euldj,* condemned by his *(métis)* son as "a man who failed either to retain his first religion, by standing by his nationality, or to be satisfied with his second creed, avoiding shame" (Khodja 1929, 163).

One other mode of "assimilation" was available, yet rarely discussed in francophone newspapers.

In France, until the early nineteenth century, debates on assimilation of the Other had focused on the notion of *métissage* or biological hybridity, and the majority equated *métissage* with degeneration on the grounds that it entailed a loss of purity. The penalty for "going native" was thus excommunication and ostracism for the product of such miscegenation, the *métis*—a figure of undecidability and indifferentiation, and a threat to the certainties grounded in both religion and science. The *métis* displayed the collapse of boundaries by dissolving the categories themselves. In a culture in which tracking degrees of nonwhiteness and deviance exploited a vertiginous vocabulary of difference, and in a century obsessed with categorization and registration (and with purity and lineage), the *métis* was the ultimate Trojan horse, infecting the colonial imaginary, which, in order to protect its own stability, privileged a radical Othering as guarantor of a phantasmatic purity/rationality. Insofar as the *métis* was the embodiment of both mixity and transgression, he or she exacerbated the nineteenth century's campaign against the irrational and the early-twentieth-century colony's obsession with corruption (concretized in venereal disease and prostitution, the marketable form of "Oriental lasciviousness").[13] The colonial trope of the fear of being "submerged" by the native masses was thus complemented by fear of the collapse of alterity if "infected" by them because purity and rationality—construed as ethnic qualities—came to be perceived as dangerously prone to penetration and dilution.

In colonial Algeria, assimilation via biological *métissage* was actually rare because sexual contact (in mixed marriage and concubinage) was itself extremely

13. See Berque 1970. On disease and colonialism, see Edmond 1997.

rare and surrounded by severe constraints and general disapproval. Its psychological significance for the *évolué* is suggested, however, by the fact that the majority of novels in this corpus portray such contacts between French and Arab/Berber characters, and nearly all also include *métis* or *m'tourni* characters or both. Outside prostitution, the barrier of Islam—and what Albert Memmi first called "heterophobia"—blocked the availability of non-European partners. As for those few Muslims who were swayed by Christian proselytizing, they were largely integrated into the European community—as was the case, for instance, with the children raised in the orphanages and "Christian villages" founded by Cardinal Lavigerie after the famines of 1866 and 1867 (fictionalized in the figure of Mamoun's mistress, Mme. Robempierre).

A Muslim Algerian male could marry a non-Muslim, as do the heroes of *Bou-el-Nouar* and *La tente noire* (ben Ali and Pottier 1934), but only if he renounced the practice of polygamy. A European male could marry a Muslim, but only if he converted to Islam, and such a marriage is a key plot element in two francophone novels: Khodja's *El euldj,* where the Christian captive converts and marries his master's daughter; and Ould Cheikh's *Myriem,* where the (unconverted) French officer's insistence that his children be raised as Christians contradicted in the text by the assertion that, as a free-thinker, he wanted "ni Coran ni catéchisme" for them (1936, 22, 21).

As traces of Ould Cheikh's attempt to "concilier les inconciliables," such disruptive narrative slippages inscribe in the novel the tension between the discourse of equality/fusion and the practice of segregation/differentiation.

In cases of mixed marriage, the administrative and legal systems actually endeavored to ensure that any offspring was raised as French (through French schooling, for instance), although in law they were deemed to belong to the father's religion. Consequently, the exceptional situation of the brother and sister *métis* protagonists of *Myriem* is no doubt motivated by Ould Cheikh's stated assimilationist objective: "Western education having borne fruit, the new French and Muslim generations, unlike the 'old' ones that remained for a long time mutually hostile, are beginning to understand and love each other" (1936, foreword, n.p.). The novel ends not on the dilation of psychologically coherent new beginnings, however, but on the sleight of hand in the marriage of both *métis* to traditional Muslims, despite both their introductory characterization as involved in " 'modernism,' which is the enemy of all religion because it corrupts those who overindulge in it" (23), and the text's condemnation of their parents' (mixed) marriage as a failure, an "impossible fusion because they had neither the same faith nor the same ideal" (22). Ideological position and fictional mise en scène thus remain mutually incompatible, and, at best, these novelists can only point to a future (idealized) resolution contradicted by past and current attitudes and practices—one in which the cultural conflict between religion and modernity would be either bypassed or suspended.

The figure of the *métis* in fiction of the interwar years can best be understood, therefore, not merely as transgressive, but as evidence that identity is the result of a process—of identification, of permanent (re)appraisal of fixed notions. Because the identity of the biological *métis* was not a given, it openly and disruptively displayed the mechanisms and resistances at work in the construction of the cultural *métis* and their always-incomplete absorption—when identification was thwarted. Settler insistence on the static, defunct nature of Islam (interjected as the essential constitutive factor of Arab identity) was thus a means of ensuring that the *process* of identification was practically unenvisageable. A conclusion by L. Gauthier in the *Bulletin de la société de géographie de l'Afrique du Nord* of 1906 put the position succinctly: "if the Arab, the Berber, are morally unassimilable, it is only insofar as they are Muslim." Equally peremptory was the conclusion to a 1919 text on the "conquête morale" of the indigenous population: "Muslim society, if it evolves within the Koran, will not evolve" (Delassus 1913, 19).

If education is domination by consent, as Gramsci argued, then the *évolué* Muslim Algerian was expected to demonstrate that internalized condition and to function as a pliable instrument of control of the masses. Unfortunately, by educating them into the republican principles of *liberté, égalité, fraternité*—however grossly distorted these principles became in Algeria—the colonial authorities were providing the concepts of a community of equals that settler society actually denied in both theory and practice, yet that, according to the narrator of *Bou-el-Nouar* in a subtle correction of European prejudice, the *Muslim* population was spiritually conditioned to implement (Zenati and Zenati 1945, 149). This modernizing system itself thus provided some of the tools of resistance and progress for these reformers, while locking the majority of them, less sanguine about Islam, into the colonial epistemology. The constructive dialogue they offered remained ineffectual, not least because, when calling for *coexistence, fusion,* or *rencontres,* these *évolué* intellectuals were putting an idealized France and the rights of the individual before colonial self-interest and the homogenizing impact of the republican model.

Such appeals to ideals and the creation of the phantasmatic figure of the *trait-d'union* are clearly instruments of resistance in a historical context in which, because identity was both a collective fiction and the arena of open conflict and unfinished negotiation, the colony was unable (unwilling) to rethink *la question indigène* in dialogic terms capable of integrating the differences of religion and culture required to absorb a permissible deviance. By imposing a nonnegotiable secular model and essentializing the subaltern status of those who did not conform (and, indeed, of many who did), this obstruction countered the French-educated elite's ambition to become agents in the colony's development. The problematic hero of many of the francophone novels of the interwar years embodies that quest, and the failure of their authors' "generous illusions" (Zenati and Zenati 1945, 226) is displayed in the stories, which undermine or contradict their narrators' pro-French positions.

It was in response to the metropole's fluctuating, ineffectual policies and to the colonists' systematic opposition thereto and in order to recover (construct) a collective identity that had been bypassed or denied in the process of identity building in the colony that in 1936 the Association des oulémas published a "Déclaration nette," which reclaimed for the Arab/Berber majority their past, present, and future. This declaration was to become a nationalist manifesto, foreclosing further debate. It condemned *naturalisé* positions as abandonment and betrayal, dismissed *métissage* as an aberration, and delivered a final, uncompromising Muslim Algerian response to the colony's unresolved "question." From its starting point in debates on absorption, then on cultural integration and political equality under the auspices of the French Republic, this response had finally evolved into an assertion of a countermodel by an urban elite skillful enough to turn the republican model against the republic and to appropriate for its own benefit the processes of differentiation exploited by European epistemology—and long disguised or displayed in the colonial rhetoric of *moral regeneration, rapprochement, assimilation,* and *association:*

> We have searched both the present and the pages of history. And we have realized that the Algerian nation was born and exists just as all the nations of the world were born and exist. This nation has its own history, marked by innumerable noble moments; it is united through religion and language; it has its own culture, traditions, and customs, with their strengths and weaknesses, just like all other nations.
>
> And so we declare that this Muslim Algerian nation is not France; it is impossible for it to be France. It does not wish to become France, and were there any such desire, it would be impossible. On the contrary, Algeria is a nation far removed from France through language, custom, ethnic origins, religion. Algeria does not want assimilation. (Association des oulémas 1936, 191)

6 The Politics of Solidarity

Radical French and Algerian Journalists and the 1954 Orléansville Earthquake

YAËL SIMPSON FLETCHER

ON THE NIGHT OF 8 SEPTEMBER 1954, the residents of the French colonial town of Orléansville, Algeria, suffered a devastating earthquake.[1] The colonial administration was completely unprepared for the estimated 1,400 dead, 5,000 injured, and 40,000–50,000 homeless. Hundreds of witnesses testified to the widespread destruction in Orléansville, but many of the villages in the Chelif region were hit by even more severe tremors. In Pontebo, Ténès, Oued-Fadda, Beni-Rached, and numerous *douars,* stone huts collapsed on the peasant inhabitants, livestock, and grain stores indiscriminately, leaving the survivors to face the coming rainy season without food, water, or shelter.[2] The first reporters in the area described scenes of desperation, with predatory birds circling overhead (*Alger républicain* [*AR*] 1954, 12–13 Sept., 1).

By 1954, all signs pointed to the end of the age of European empires. Britain had granted India independence, nine years of fierce fighting had defeated French forces in Indochina, and the French government had begun negotiations with nationalists in the protectorates of Morocco and Tunisia. In contrast, and despite decades of organization in France and Algeria, the Algerian anticolonial nationalist movement seemed weak and divided, effectively repressed by the settler state. Juridically part of France, the three departments of Algeria had two populations who identified as Algerians: (1) the descendants of European immigrants—some now big landowners, others workers, but all with full political,

1. Orléansville, now Ech-Chelif, is due south of the port of Ténès and equidistant between Oran to the west and Algiers to the east. It was the site of an even more severe earthquake in 1980. See further "Chelif, Ech-," *Encyclopedia Britannica,* available at http://search.eb.com/eb/article?eu=23126, accessed 7 May 2002.

2. A *douar* consisted of a cluster of huts housing some fraction of a tribe and was attached to a French settler administrative unit. See further Ageron 1991, 23, 54–55, 69–70.

social, and economic rights; and (2) the dispossessed and disenfranchised Arab and Berber population majority, for whom even drastic electoral reform would bring little in the way of improved living conditions and political representation. By September 1954, unbeknown to all but a few militants, the secret organization that was to become the Front de libération nationale (FLN, National Liberation Front) had already chosen the date for insurrection.[3]

Scholars have noted how earthquakes in major cities have sparked movements for social transformation and political reform.[4] With hindsight, it is possible to see how the Orléansville earthquake exposed the weakness of the colonial regime and revealed subterranean movements among the most dispossessed, the peasants of the *douars.*[5] At the time, the Communist, labor, and anticolonial leftist press publicized the plight of these earthquake victims, who suffered the sometimes fatal consequences of the government's harsh, corrupt, and inept food- and shelter-distribution policies. This publicity and the concurrent appeals for donations of financial and material assistance provide a valuable window onto the Left's views of Algerian identity(ies) in the final moments before the visible eruption of the armed struggle for independence.

This chapter focuses on accounts filed by reporters at the earthquake scene from two leftist/labor papers: the French weekly *La vie ouvrière* (given as *VO* in citations) and the French-language Algerian daily *Alger républicain. La vie ouvrière* was one of the official organs of the French Communist-led federation of trade unions, the Confédération générale du travail (CGT). The CGT included trade unions in Algeria, consistent with the colony's juridical status as part of France. Although a sector of the Algerian labor movement close to the CGT published a weekly page, "Le travailleur algérien," in the *Alger républicain,* and despite intermittent funding from the Parti communiste algérien (PCA, Algerian Communist Party), this daily maintained its political independence. The editorial staff included left-wing Algerian nationalists and European anticolonial journalists as well as members of the PCA. With a circulation of about twenty-five thousand, *Alger républicain* represented a left anticolonial coalition (Khalfa, Alleg, and Benzine 1987, 88–95, 153–64, 166). This chapter explores the modes of solidarity expressed in the reports of these two newspapers, paying particular atten-

3. For a full discussion of the nationalist politics leading up to the decision to begin the armed struggle, see Douzon 1986, 383–405, and Ruedy 1992, 153–61.

4. The 1972 Managua, Nicaragua, and 1986 San Salvador, El Salvador, earthquakes gave impetus to movements to overthrow authoritarian regimes in Latin America. The major tremor that hit the center of Mexico City in 1986 sparked self-help organizations that later formed part of the democratization movement. See Poniatowska 1995.

5. For example, see Khalfa, Alleg, and Benzine 1987, 181–82.

tion to the articulation of bonds of gender, class, and nation. The discursive strategies employed by the correspondents reveal the fault lines in Franco-Algerian identity, the limits of internationalism, and rifts within the Left on the question of the "oppressed Algerian nation."

The Family of Man

From the first days of coverage, *Alger républicain* editorials contrasted the immediate outpouring of funds, goods, and assistance from Algerians of "all origins," united by a profound "feeling of human solidarity," with officials' delays and seeming indifference (*AR* 1954, 12–13 Sept., 1). Clearly excluded from this humane Algeria was the colonial administration. Articles characterized the general public's aid as solidarity based on a relationship of equals rather than as charity based on the beneficence of a superior. An appeal to a common humanity, transcending race, class, and religious difference, suffused early reports of the disaster. Veteran *Alger républicain* staff Yvonne Lartigaud and Abdelkader Choukhal filed the first accounts of the impact of the earthquake on Orléansville and nearby villages.[6] In the hope of arousing "not only Algeria, but also all the countries of the world moved by the same feeling of fraternity that strikes all men before universal catastrophe," the reporters used tropes of universal loss to represent the human tragedy (*AR* 1954, 10 Sept., 1).

Lartigaud and Choukhal anthropomorphized the city as a way of communicating the distress of its residents: "twisted, mangled, destroyed, tortured as after the most intense bombardment, with disemboweled houses resembling an exposed still-beating heart" (*AR* 1954, 10 Sept., 8). This image no doubt resonated with memories of bombed cities, from Guernica to Coventry, in which the main tropes of representation were the totality of destruction and the innocence of the victims. In the "still-beating heart," it celebrated the survival of the city, but also suggested the tenuous nature of that survival and added urgency to the call for emergency assistance. Lartigaud drew on this image for a striking metaphor of personal loss: "And most tragic among the broken stones are the broken hearts, invisible to indifferent eyes" (*AR* 1954, 11 Sept., 8). As well as giving the banal phrase "broken-hearted" visible form and truly catastrophic content, Lartigaud placed herself in the scene as an empathetic and observant witness. *La vie ouvrière* reporter Madeleine Riffaud drew on nature itself to represent the tragedy:

6. Abdelkader Choukhal anchored the sports page and the human interest stories *(faits divers)*. Yvonne Lartigaud was one of the non-Communist staff, with responsibilities similar to Choukhal's. They both participated in fund-raising tours that accompanied sports events such as the Tour d'Algérie, a bicycling race (Khalfa, Alleg, and Benzine 1987, 104, 108–109, 156).

"An ocean of distress, unfathomable, unexplored, beyond imagination, difficult to conceive of, where those who have lost everything except their lives wander like the blind, eyes wide open, across the dead city in search of their loved ones" (*VO* 1954, 14–20 Sept., 3).[7] Riffaud's vivid image extends the destruction beyond rational comprehension, making it an event biblical in scope. This melodramatic rendering, however, emphasized the victims' helplessness and cast the reader as a spectator in a mythic drama.

In the following weeks, the coverage continued to evoke the human tragedy of the disaster—children orphaned or lost, homes destroyed, and families without shelter. Significantly, the focus of both papers was the suffering of the Arab population, ignored in the mainstream press. *Alger républicain,* in particular, tended not to identify individuals by ethnicity, religion, or race, but simply by name—on the one hand an indication of respect, but on the other a denial of significant differences. Any Algerian reader, however, would recognize that the only residents of *douars* were Muslim Algerians and that any reference to a peasant could only mean, again, an Arab or Berber agricultural worker.

On the fourth day after the earthquake, several reporters, including Choukhal and Riffaud, made it to the Arab village of Beni-Rached, twenty-five kilometers from Orléansville. The epicenter, it had suffered mass destruction and death, leaving survivors with no food or water, let alone shelter. After describing the sickening smell of corpses still trapped in the rubble, Choukhal and his colleague Mohammed Ferhat focused on helpless and injured children: "We have seen children wearing blood-stained clothes. . . . We have seen unconscious children." The emblematic nature of this terrible scene is highlighted by the cadence of the writing and the lack of specificity regarding any particular child. At the same time, the repetition foregrounds the *Alger républicain* reporters' role as witnesses to a terrible tragedy. The passage ends with a declaration of remembrance: "Not one of us could ever forget such visions!" (*AR* 1954, 12–13 Sept., 1). The accusations to follow gained in force from this exposure of official neglect.

The next day Yvonne Lartigaud filed a report from the children's ward of the Mustapha Hospital in Algiers, one of the places where children from Orléansville and the *douars* had been evacuated. She listed the Arabic names of a number of children and gave details of each child's injuries, experience, and situation in the hopes of recognition by some friend or family member, fitting in with *Alger républicain*'s policy of publishing messages about "missing persons." Although the information presented by Lartigaud had a practical purpose, the details also

7. Riffaud knew Algeria and had frequent contact with *Alger républicain* staff (Khalfa, Alleg, and Benzine 1987, 100).

made each child into an individual, easily pictured by the reader. Indeed, over the coming weeks, dozens of offers of adoption poured into the newspaper's office. She contrasted a heartwarming tale of how Zorah Choucha, a little girl orphaned by the earthquake, "adopted" as her mother a widowed nurse, Mme. Halima Attab, with a heartrending description of the injuries of an unclaimed infant from Beni-Rached. She called for those responsible for the abandonment of the villages to suffer "this nightmare image that pursues me, so that it will haunt their days and nights like an eternal accusation" (*AR* 1954, 14 Sept., 6). With this declaration, Lartigaud, like Choukhal, claimed her role as a moral witness.

Also focusing on homeless Arab women and children, Madeleine Riffaud highlighted her own interactions with the earthquake victims. Thus, addressing herself to French workers, she declaimed, "S.O.S. for these mutilated families, these children who are naked and who have been covered with clothes bloodied from those who have died! S.O.S. for these children without milk, whose eyes lit up with silent desire, unbearable, when we gave them bread brought from Algiers for our own snack!" (*VO* 1954, 14–20 Sept., 3). Riffaud's dramatization of the same scene described by Choukhal placed her as an intermediary, speaking for the silent *douar* children, rather than as a moral witness. Her act of giving up her own food emphasized the children's need and provided an example for her French readers.

Like Lartigaud, Riffaud filed a report from the Mustapha Hospital in Algiers. The *La vie ouvrière* reporter, however, focused on "X . . . native child," a severely injured toddler from Beni-Rached. Filed more than two weeks after the first shocks, the article was framed as a response to official denials of the extent of destruction and newspaper accounts belittling the Arab victims. It included a photograph of Riffaud holding the child. She reiterated commands to the reader to look at and even display this image representing "all the little victims of colonialism." With eyes swollen shut, "X" could not see Riffaud, but Riffaud imagined these other children returning the reader's gaze—and not just any reader, but a personal friend (*ami lecteur,* addressed in the familiar voice) (*VO* 1954, 28 Sept.–4 Oct., 5). Riffaud employed toddler "X" as a symbol of the deprivation of Algerian children before the earthquake and of the official "criminal abandon" of the *douar* victims after the earthquake. She used herself as an example of human solidarity. Her cradling of the dying Algerian child was for the explicit purpose of impressing the image on her readership. Indeed, she hailed these readers as trade-union activists, ready to take on the task of organizing aid. The contrasting use of vivid imagery of injured infants signified the national difference between the two reporters. Riffaud called on her French comrades to remember and act, whereas Lartigaud called for remembrance in a rhetorical move directed at the officials—she had no doubt that her Algerian (without distinction between European and Arab) comrades would not forget.

Articles in both newspapers drew out the emotional significance of the destruction of all homes, however humble (*AR* 1954, 16 Sept., 1; *VO* 1954, 21–27 Sept., 3). In addition, *La vie ouvrière* reporter Madeleine Riffaud brought out the particular issues that the loss of a residence raised for Muslims. For example, she included the words of a homeless peasant concerned about the physical distress of his family out in the open, with little food, but also about "his wife and mother mixing with *tout le monde.* Our customs, our religion, demand that women have a place to themselves" (*VO* 1954, 21–27 Sept., 3). This specificity contributed to the vividness of Riffaud's account, but also exoticized the earthquake victims for her French readers. This sense of otherness was heightened further by the reference to the Arab word for "nothing" in the title of the article, "The Word *Oualou,*" a word used repeatedly by officials in response to villagers' requests for food, medicine, and tents. Riffaud's appeal to a human universalism relied on a recognition of difference between French and Arab.

By the third week of September, when Riffaud filed this report, the rainy season was imminent. The inadequate distribution of tents and building supplies to the *douars* meant that the homeless villagers had to improvise shelter on their own. Both Riffaud and *Alger républicain*'s Abdelkader Choukhal considered the inequities in the distribution of food, medical aid, and shelter to exemplify French colonialism. By the end of September, while *douar* residents were still trying to get the materials to rebuild their homes, much ordinary business had resumed. One of the most striking images used by both Choukhal and Riffaud contrasted the households' "little donkeys, weighted down with branches . . . arduously climbing the tracks" to the "heavy tanker trucks that spread out in all directions to take the wine of the big growers to safety" (*AR* 1954, 26–27 Sept., 5; *VO* 1954, 5–11 Oct., 8).

Two weeks after Choukhal's story, five weeks after the earthquake, *Alger républicain* veteran journalist Paul Galéa reported on the frustration and anger of the residents of Orléansville and the nearby hamlets who were still awaiting tents, aware that their makeshift shelters could not withstand the rains for long.[8] Galéa's list of homeless included French, Spanish, Italian, and Arabic names. He aroused the reader's sympathy by linking the lack of tents to the question of life

8. Paul Galéa specialized in labor issues; for some years he edited the "Travailleur algérien" page. Like many of the other European Algerian long-term staff members, he was committed to a dream of a future independent, democratic, multiethnic Algeria (Khalfa, Alleg, and Benzine 1987, 93, 121).

and death for infants threatened by exposure, such as the cold "little babies of M. Mohammed Boughedad, of Rambia, and M. Djillali Madaouf, of La Bocca Chattia, who could be ripped away from the love of their parents" at any moment (*AR* 1954, 15 Oct., 6). The next day he named the *douars* where "young children have nothing to cover themselves, nothing to sleep on, and often nothing to eat" (*AR* 1954, 16 Oct., 1). Only the police, sent to keep order, had tents.

Over the month of postearthquake coverage, the articles showed a definitive shift in topic from all earthquake victims generally, urban and rural, European and Arab, to those in the *douars* specifically. All the correspondents foregrounded the material impact of colonialism on the villagers. Subtle variations in the rhetoric of the coverage, however, exemplified the two newspapers' different aims. *La vie ouvrière* was determined to bring the situation in Algeria to the attention of its French readers, whereas *Alger républicain* was committed to showing how the hardships in the *douars* were a direct consequence of colonialism.

Women Together

Popular literature and film have portrayed Algerian woman as either mysterious figures shrouded in white or nationalist militants unveiling for the sake of the revolution. In the aftermath of the earthquake, however, both *Alger républicain* and *La vie ouvrière* showed Muslim Algerian women speaking for themselves, not just as victims seeking assistance, but also as agents of their own destiny, taking action. Both newspapers called for solidarity on this basis, going beyond a passive sisterhood of wives and mothers. Nevertheless, there were significant differences between the newspapers in how this appeal was couched: the *Alger républicain* correspondents focused on collective action, whereas Madeleine Riffaud of *La vie ouvrière* concentrated on individual consciousness.

On 16 September, *Alger républicain* gave voice to several homeless Orléansville women, with names indicating varied backgrounds. Each rejoiced in the immediate survival of her children, but expressed fear of a future without food or shelter. Mme. Madani Chérifa made clear the expectation that women could identify with each other as mothers: "if all the mothers of Orléansville would unite their voices [to demand aid], we would give a day of joy to the children whom we have wrested from death" (*AR* 1954, 16 Sept., 6). Reverberating with the tropes of loss and motherhood in other articles, this statement introduced the idea of women organizing together on the basis of motherhood. Women of both the city and the *douars* did indeed unite in local committees that became increasingly vehement in the face of government inaction.

In early October, for example, *Alger républicain* published an account from "Myriam" that reported on "a delegation of women from the farthest reaches of the *douars*" who had come to Orléansville determined to put their demands directly to the administration. The correspondent described the four delegates as "peasant women from Ouled Larbi . . . who had had enough of putting their children to bed under threatening skies, of having nothing to eat but bread and salt, and of seeing their sisters give birth in the open air, living for days under nothing but fig trees with their newborns, with no type of care or medicine" (*AR* 1954, 9 Oct., 5). Their maternal role and identification with other mothers seemingly galvanized these women into action. This delegation was not a spontaneous creation, however. One of the four women was actually the "secretary of the local Committee of Victims," and the trip itself was undertaken with "the help of sisters from Algiers" (i.e., Communist and trade-union women activists). The column ended with a call to the women readership to join the effort (*AR* 1954, 9 Oct., 5). Assistance no longer consisted simply of food, clothes, and emergency aid, but also addressed the question of organization, strategy, and tactics.

By the third week of October, the rainy season had begun, and tornados and heavy downpours had washed away many of the makeshift shelters in the *douars*. Mixed-sex demonstrations in Orléansville swelled to more than one thousand, forcing the mayor to release some hundreds of tents. Choukhal described the mostly Arab Algerian women as "mothers of families, magnificently confronting the police [who were] attempting to arrest the young union leaders" (*AR* 1954, 24–25 Oct., 6). The next day one "mother of a family," waiting with her three young children to claim assistance, "was thrown to the ground and trampled by the police" guarding city hall. She then formed part of a protest delegation with representatives of the CGT, PCA, and the nationalist Mouvement pour la triomphe des libertés démocratiques (MTLD, Movement for the Triumph of Democratic Liberties) (*AR* 1954, 24–25 Oct., 7). The cooperation of these organizations represented an ongoing, informal anticolonial alliance.[9]

On 28 October, local and national women's groups joined together to send yet another delegation to the mayor's office demanding temporary housing, food, medicine, and financial assistance. The seven hundred women, "mostly mothers accompanied by their children," were greeted enthusiastically by the general population, according to *Alger républicain*. The march left from "the camp of the intersyndical committee of the CGT," and the women protested the arrest of a

9. The MTLD was openly for nationalism and democracy, and secretly for independence. Its membership included Muslim Algerian intellectuals, small property-holders, peasants, and workers. By 1954, the PCA had been "algerianized" to the extent that more than half its members were Muslim Algerians (Douzon 1986, 307–10, 319). For information on the MTLD, see also Ruedy 1992, 153–55.

"Travailleur algérien" correspondent covering the demonstration, thus showing the close connection between these women's groups and the organized workers' movement (*AR* 1954, 29 Oct., 1, 5). The newspaper offered a vision of reciprocal solidarity between mothers, organized around basic welfare rights, and male workers, represented by union leaders. The language of the articles rendered any fissures between European and Arab Algerian invisible.

Although Madeleine Riffaud of *La vie ouvrière* frequently praised French workers—or, more specifically, CGT members—for their generosity and solidarity, she also focused on the bonds between French and Muslim Algerian women. Emblematic of the link, Riffaud portrayed herself as the representative of French women to the earthquake victims, thus both calling for sisterhood and performing it. She dramatically embraced the dying child of an injured mother, writing that the hug was "for all of you moms [*mamans*] who read me, handkerchief to your eyes" (*VO* 1954, 14–20 Sept., 3). At the same time, Riffaud authenticated her role as spokeswoman for these women by emphasizing her participant observer status. She slept on the bare ground with those still homeless weeks after the earthquake and was woken up, like them, by the threat of a storm (*VO* 1954, 21–27 Sept., 3; 5–11 Oct., 8). In her prose, Riffaud brought the French woman worker to life in the imagination of both her reader and the Muslim Algerian women with whom she took shelter. Riffaud compared an orphaned young girl, Malika, resting her head on an orange tree, all she has left, to the working-class reader ("as you sometimes support yourself on your sewing-machine to dream, and, so, of what do you dream?" (*VO* 1954, 5–11 Oct., 8). Her parenthetical aside and her use of the familiar *tu* created the same intimacy between herself and the reader as between her and Malika. In the correspondent's narrative, Malika's flowered pink dress, donated by the CGT, inspired the girl to ask to be told about her French benefactors. Riffaud framed her response by, again, addressing herself to the reader: "So, I spoke of you, who live in the houses of our working-class neighborhoods, off stairways noisy with children, behind windows where oft-washed and mended laundry dries. I imagined for Malika the life of the unknown working girl who, in solidarity, had donated her dress." The vivid details of daily life not only painted a picture for Malika, but also constructed the readers as class-conscious female workers or wives of workers. This approach was emphasized when Malika responded with enthusiasm, saying that when she married, " 'I will never hold back my husband from striking' " (*VO* 1954, 5–11 Oct., 8). Riffaud marked the difference between herself—and by extension her French readers—and the Muslim Algerian women, however, when she noted Malika's illiteracy and, more significantly, the other women's incomprehension; Malika had to translate Riffaud's words into Arabic. Riffaud blamed this lack of education on French colonialism and suggested that she, in her role as CGT representative, both made up for this lack and sparked the awareness of the benefits of (class-conscious) knowledge for Malika and her neighbors.

Riffaud's highlighting of the differences between Arab and French women added to the significance of these particular bonds of "sisterhood." In contrast, *Alger républicain* correspondents noted the desire for organization among the women victims and in a classic coalition-forming maneuver focused on shared issues, which erased any hint of difference, even between rural and urban women. The articles in both newspapers, however, portrayed the leadership as coming from their own movements, the CGT in Riffaud's case, the anticolonial labor Left in the *Alger républicain*'s case.

Class and Nation

The political and scholarly debate over the question of the French Left's attitude toward Algerian nationalism is longstanding. In 1938, Maurice Thorez, the leader of the French Communist Party, clearly rejected Muslim Algerian claims of cultural autonomy and political independence in favor of a vision of a European Algerian worker-led state tied to a socialist France. This anachronistic vision continued to hobble the French and European Algerian Left in the aftermath of the Second World War. In contrast to the official leadership of the Communist and other left-wing parties, labor movements were directly challenged by North African workers in both France and the Maghreb, a difference reflected in the pages of the labor press.[10] The articles of both *La vie ouvrière* and *Alger républicain* displayed a complex and sometimes contradictory understanding of the relationship between class and nation in France and Algeria. Correspondents agreed that the Orléansville earthquake provided an opportunity for French workers to express their opposition to the colonial administration in Algeria and to educate the Algerian people about the existence of this oppositional France. This opportunity involved, however, the projection of a particular vision of Algerian identity. *Alger républicain* also noted how the devastation and lack of official response spurred the politicization and organization of the Muslim Algerian masses outside existing networks of labor and party politics, but it still characterized the fissures solely along class lines.

After the earthquake, the CGT was among the first organizations to respond. With a confederated structure that spanned the Mediterranean, it was able to

10. On the tensions between the French Communist Party, the PCA, and nationalist movements in Algeria, see Sivan 1976 and Joly 1991. On the question of the French and Algerian labor movements, see Ageron 1996, 326–31, and Khalfa, Alleg, and Benzine 1987, 120.

mobilize personnel and material assistance rapidly for the victims. In France, *La vie ouvrière* launched in Arabic and French the CGT's appeal "for solidarity with our Algerian comrades." It expressed sympathy and solidarity in the name of the "French working class . . . to the Algerian people." Funds collected from French unions and other organizations went directly to the CGT offices in Algiers (*VO* 1954, 14–20 Sept., 4). An *Alger républicain* editorial articulated the significance of this immediate "active solidarity" of the French workers: it represented "the effective, powerful friendship that unites the workers' democratic France with oppressed and indomitable Algeria" (*AR* 1954, 11 Sept., 1). Both newspapers marked the difference between France and Algeria by the shift in the terms on either side of "solidarity": workers or the working class on one side and a unified people on the other. How far "solidarity" should extend remained unclear. Even the opposition between democratic France and oppressed Algeria served only to exclude the European Algerian settlers from French identity.

Not surprisingly, considering its audience, *La vie ouvrière* emphasized the Algerians' appreciation for the CGT aid. Madeleine Riffaud quoted a homeless *douar* resident, "the husband of Aïcha" (one of women who shared their sleeping space on the ground with the reporter): "Over there, in France, the workers collect aid. The boats, loaded with crates of solidarity by the dockers of Marseilles are unloaded by the dockers of Algeria and our comrades distribute them. In this country where the earth itself does not cease trembling under our steps and where anger grows with each day's anguish, one thing is sure and positive: it is the active solidarity of the workers, it is this fraternal chain that has been thrown up from one shore to the other across the sea to relieve our distress" (*VO* 1954, 21–27 Sept., 3). Assuming the authenticity of this quote, it is hardly an artless response. The use of the terms *comrades, solidarity,* and *fraternal* demonstrates an exemplary class consciousness—making this Arab man the perfect recipient for French workers' aid. Although it is clear that the "comrades" were exempted from the peasants' anger, where, exactly, this anger was to be directed was left vague. "Distress" was under siege rather than colonialism. The words were also remarkably lacking in national consciousness for a man who had just explained to Riffaud the importance of the seclusion of women for Algerian cultural identity.

In an article the following week, Riffaud made explicit the value of the CGT aid for political education. She wrote that the children of the *douars* would remember the "union militants, those whose origins are French, like the Algerians of overseas ancestry, coming all the way to them with crates of solidarity: bread, milk collected across the seas, not like charity, but like the assistance of a brother to his brother" (*VO* 1954, 28 Sept.–4 Oct., 5). Here again Riffaud envisioned a fraternal chain from French worker to European Algerian worker to Muslim Algerian victim. The very acceptance of this aid created understanding. It was essential for her argument that recipients not only saw the spirit underlying the material donations, but also recognized their own struggle as fundamentally the same as the French workers. Riffaud imagined "village elders" telling the children: " 'Over there, in France, the workers are exploited by the same bosses as we are. Look, [the workers] help us, they love us. It is in misfortune that you know who is your brother' " (*VO* 1954, 28 Sept.–4 Oct., 5). Despite the explicit statement of common exploitation, the shift in this passage from workers' aid to assistance based on love and brotherhood implies a consciousness of difference not transcended by class solidarity. There is a certain ambiguity in Riffaud's construction of Algerian identity; it was relatively simple to claim that the workers, whatever their origins, were the same as those in France, proletarian brothers, but this equation was problematic for the peasants of the *douars*.

Alger républicain correspondent Paul Galéa also commented on the joy with which the *douar* residents greeted the CGT distribution of aid donated by "workers of the cities." He noted in addition, however, "in their gaze an indictment of the absence of all aid from the central government." He repeated the term *acte d'accusation* (indictment) for each count of the charge—delays in housing, food, medical assistance—thus escalating the severity of the crime. Galéa, however, presented a quite different view of the *douar* residents than Riffaud. He focused on their assertion of the right to assistance, reporting that "in firm and fearless voices, the peasants declare that 'we are ready to demonstrate. Our distress is too great. We must have aid!' " (*AR* 1954, 19–20 Sept., 5; see also 16 Oct., 6). Indeed, the peasants not only demonstrated, but organized themselves into earthquake victims' committees that directed attempts at self-help, the fair distribution of donated aid, and collective demands on the administration.

Alger républicain editorials reiterated the increasingly vehement demands by PCA deputies Pierre Fayet (Algiers) and Alice Sportisse (Oran) for immediate and adequate assistance to the *douars* and for aid distribution that gave responsibility to local committees of survivors (for example, see *AR* 1954, 21 Sept., 1). In October, André Ruiz, top official of the Union général des syndicat algériens (General Association of Algerian Unions), affiliated with the CGT, declared on the newspaper's "Le travailleur algérien" weekly page that "[i]t is only through organized action that the victims will grab their rights." [11] Ruiz saw this struggle for benefits as just the first step in the struggle against the "exploitative colonial

11. Ruiz was director of the Union général des syndicat algériens, founded in June 1954 on the basis of an autonomous committee of Algerian unions that included many nationalists. It affiliated with the CGT in July 1954 (Khalfa, Alleg, and Benzine 1987, 121).

regime." He promised, "Brothers and sisters, workers and peasants of the regions of Orléansville, Ténès, Duperré, you can count on the support of the working class of Algeria and that of France, on the support of the international working class" (*AR* 1954, 12 Oct., insert "Le travailleur algérien" no. 256). This clear statement of solidarity actually delineated the fault lines that would emerge over the next decade of Algerian history—along gender, class, and nation. Ruiz's main concern was to bring the urban and rural workers of Algeria together in the struggle against colonialism. His assumption of a continued close bond between the Algerian and French working classes was indicated by both group's rhetorical opposition to the "international working class"; Algeria might gain independence, but somehow it would not be a separate nation.

Riffaud, in the concluding article to her series on the victims of the earthquake, returned to the theme of the suffering of children, but this time she described the "babies with rickets, with swollen stomachs and matchstick arms" forced to work because of their families' routine poverty. She attacked the colonial regime for robbing the Algerian peasants of their land and livelihood in the past and for inhumanity in the face of tragedy in the present. By characterizing colonial officials as "monsters . . . not men," Riffaud detached colonialism from French identity. It became, rather, a universal evil that required a universal response. And, indeed, although Riffaud reiterated the CGT position in support of independence for colonial peoples in the context of a class-conscious joint struggle, she universalized the goal and redefined the movement: "After the catastrophe, Algerians and French of all opinions have gathered together, uniting hands, often for the first time, in order to combat death. We must also stay together for happiness. For lifting from our countries these heavy stones: oppression, misery, war. . . . Because NOTHING is as strong as the bare arms of men" (*VO* 1954, 12–18 Oct., 13). For Riffaud, this shift to a masculinized universalism was the only way of including Muslim Algerian peasants and incorporating the challenge they posed for a purely class-struggle view of the world.

In contrast, Paul Galéa, in his final article from Orléansville, ranted against the colonial administration for ignoring the recommendations of the Comité national algérien d'aide au sinistrés d'Orléansville (Algerian National Aid Committee). He characterized the government's actions as a refusal to "nationalize the problem of solidarity, of rescuing the victims." He called for "a total change of orientation, of practice, of methods" in aid distribution—ultimately a political transformation. Emphasizing the respect and justice owed to all the victims, with the only criterion being "urgency of need," he demanded that the government welcome the participation of "all the men, all the women, from all walks of life, from all professions, of all origins, through the agency of their representatives in union, social, cultural, or other organizations" (*AR* 1954, 20 Oct., 6; 21 Oct., 5, for program of Algerian National Aid Committee). The inclusion of women, professionals, and people of "all origins" in this statement suggests how this movement of solidarity transcended divisions based on gender, class, and national identity. At the same time, the separate recognition of social and cultural organizations outside the labor movement surely indicated Islamic fraternities and political parties more religiously oriented than the MTLD. Whereas Riffaud emphasized the unique aspects of Muslim Algerian identity in the interests of an abstract French-Arab class solidarity, Galéa and Ruiz downplayed European and Muslim cultural difference in order to build a viable anticolonial movement within Algeria.

This difference in each newspaper's sensitivity to the anticolonial forces at work in Algeria is exemplified in the contrast between an article in *Alger républicain* published on the eve of the insurrection and an article by Riffaud published several weeks later. On 30 October, *Alger républicain* reported "the vast deployment of repressive forces" south of Constantine following the sighting of " 'bandits' [*fellagas*]" (*AR* 1954, 30 Oct., 1). The quotation marks around the term *fellagas* indicated the newspaper's assumption that these men were actually armed nationalists—anything more explicit would have brought down the censors. The editors of *Alger républicain* understood almost immediately the meaning of the insurrection of 1 November and continued to provide sympathetic coverage of the armed struggle, albeit in coded terms (Khalfa, Alleg, and Benzine 1987, 184–86). At the end of November, Riffaud repeated the CGT resolution calling for an end to repression and the liberation of all prisoners "in unity and in solidarity between French and Algerian workers." What is interesting, however, is that she returned to a 1952 interview with Ali, an elderly peasant from the Aures, to quote his "wise and perceptive words" regarding the inequities wrought by colonialism and the need for unity in struggle (*VO* 1954, 23–29 Nov., 6). This nonthreatening figure out of Algeria's colonial past could not be more different from the armed young "patriots" glimpsed in the pages of *Alger républicain* (Khalfa, Alleg, and Benzine 1987, 184).

The September 1954 Orléansville earthquake revealed the hardships faced by peasants living in the region's *douars*. In the process of publicizing the plight of these "forgotten" victims, the correspondents of *La vie ouvrière* and *Alger républicain* also revealed the unequal and increasingly polarized relationships among Arab Algerians, European Algerians, and the French. The urgent task of fostering solidarity animated their reports. This meant that Madeleine Riffaud of *La vie ouvrière* focused her efforts on educating and mobilizing her French working-class readership. She created vivid vignettes of the suffering, resilience, and appreciation of individual Muslim Algerians—among others, the infant "X," Malika, and Aïcha and her husband. To encourage donations, even couched as "solidarity" rather than as charity, it was imperative for Riffaud to emphasize the Muslim Algerian recipients' gratitude rather than colonial subjects' demands on a supposedly democratic government answerable not to them, but only to France's "European" citizens. By contrast, the correspondents of *Alger républicain* sought to galvanize their readers against the repressive settler-controlled municipal administration of Orléansville in particular and the French colonial regime in general. This goal of collective action required, on the one hand, the recognition of *douar* residents, both men and women, as agents of their own destiny and, on the other hand, the construction of political alliances that could overcome differences between urban and rural, European and Muslim, mothers and (male) workers. But it must be said that the journalists of both newspapers, despite their differences, gave us a complex and compelling record of a society in a moment of uncertainty between two earthquakes: the first physical, the second political. Their own courageous efforts to make sense of human suffering and struggle remained exemplary, even as they foreshadowed wider divergences between the Algerian and French Lefts.

Part Two · Memory or Forgetting

7 "They Swore upon the Tombs Never to Make Peace with Us"

Algerian Jews and French Colonialism, 1845–1848

JOSHUA S. SCHREIER

THE FRENCH ARMY'S OCCUPATION of the cities of the Algerian littoral during the first years of the conquest brought approximately thirteen thousand Jews under colonial domination (Ministre de la guerre 1839). Though a fraction of the country's total population of between three and four million people, this community of skilled tradesmen, small merchants, and the occasional wealthy trader constituted a significant minority in the newly captured cities. Military observers estimated, for example, that between one-third and one-half of Oran's ten thousand inhabitants were Jewish, and more than six thousand Jews lived in Algiers. The significance of this population, however localized, was not lost on military officers or French Jewish reformers, who soon began emphasizing the group's potential utility to the French occupiers in official correspondence and published journals.

To take advantage of these "natural intermediaries," reformers lobbied for a separate policy for the Jews. While pushing for specific measures, they emphasized Jews' distinctiveness from their neighbors, explaining Algerian Jews' "faults" by equating them with the yet-to-be emancipated *French* Jews of the prerevolutionary period—whose abasement was eventually reversed through a process of "regeneration." The campaign to "elevate" the indigenous Jews of Algeria thus materialized in both official policies and in an (enduring) Enlightenment-rooted narrative of redemption. By the 1840s, Jews were submitted to a separate legislation from Muslims, and in October 1870 the government naturalized Algerian Jews en masse.

The received narrative of a fallen race revived by imperial generosity has not received much serious scholarly attention. Scholars interested in French colonial myths have understandably focused their attention on policies toward the far more numerous Kabyles (Ageron 1968, 1:267–70; Lazreg 1984, 384; Lorcin

[1995] 1999a), and the meager work on the Jews that exists questions reformers' patronizing attitudes, but leaves in place the seamless narrative of Jews' " progress" from oppression and ignorance on the colonial periphery to fusion with the metropolitan Jewish community through naturalization and acculturation (Schwarzfuchs 1980, 1981; Abitbol 1985). This lack of attention has left even our best histories deeply tinted by the colonial era that produced them (C. Martin 1936).

I argue that the traditional rendering is flawed and that the episode deserves more attention. Many Jews resisted initiatives undertaken in the name of "civilizing," and the modernization narrative summed up by one author as the Jews' "march toward the west" (Chouraqui 1952) elides a complex history of violence and resistance. Algerian Jews often rejected French officials, and rabbis intended to oversee their "regeneration" refused the French *statut personnel* and attempted to maintain outlawed schools and synagogues. Furthermore, despite official explanations that reductively attributed resistance to religious fanaticism and ignorance, indigenous Jews actually articulated their complaints in a nuanced language that combined piety, commitment to "progress," and even the emancipatory promise of republicanism. Furthermore, this episode usefully illuminates another side of colonial myth making and how resistance to "noble" objectives (such as civilization and emancipation) was formulated. It also suggests that "civilizing" was a multipolar process whose metropolitan and colonial manifestations were simultaneous and interconnected. Algerian Jews furnish a particularly interesting focus not only because they were "successfully" civilized (becoming French citizens in 1870), but also because the process took place largely before the Third Republic, the period on which most recent work on the civilizing mission has concentrated (Conklin 1997).

The Consistories

The most conspicuous expression of France's civilizing mission as directed toward the Jews in Algeria was the governing community organizations called Consistoires Israélites. Although it was by Louis-Phillipe's 1845 decree that these institutions came to Algeria, the model for them originated in 1808 with Napoleon I's Jewish policy. Worried that after more than a decade since emancipation the Jews of France were still superstitious, corrupt, and essentially a "Nation within a Nation," Napoleon created a series of Jewish-staffed bureaus to govern local communities. They were intended to monitor, police, and ultimately guide the masses of Jews toward morality, economic utility, and assimilation.

This project of elevating and assimilating the Jews of France was called "regeneration," and it involved new schools, expanded surveillance of the rabbinate, suppression of certain rituals, and the forced closure of synagogues—all in the interest of raising the Jews up to accepted standards of morality. If the phrase *mission civilisatrice* was not yet employed, the language of regeneration *did* refer to the requirements of "civilization." Perhaps more important, it evoked the same oppositions that later came to be associated with Third Republic colonialism, including rational/fanatic, active/stagnant, and productive/unproductive. One Alsatian consistorial officer, for example, spoke of "occidentalizing" fellow Jews by targeting their "absurd prejudices" and "superstitious practices" that kept them in an "Oriental envelope" (Weiland 1837). Similarly, in the face of resistance to this project, officials used modifiers such as *fanatic* or *superstitious* to describe the offenders. One reformer tellingly accused the local rabbinate of being so backward as to belong "in Syria or Palestine, not in France" (*Univers Israélite* [*UI*] 1843–44, 2).

With the conquest of Algeria in the 1830s, Metropolitan observers argued that if consistories were extended to Algeria, they could "attach to France" a significant portion of the native urban population, thus transforming them into a pillar of colonial domination (Schwarzfuchs 1980). Through letters to ministers, press reports, and scientific studies, reformers convinced a sometimes skeptical or even anti-Semitic French government that Algerian Jews would be useful if "civilized." The effort to expand Jewish regeneration to the colonies bore legislative fruit on 9 November 1845, when the king established an Algerian Consistoire central des Israélites in Algiers, along with two provincial Consistoires Israélites in Oran and Constantine. Each organization was to be staffed by a French grand rabbi and three (French and indigenous) lay members (four in the central bureau in Algiers). Despite French reformists' hopes to place these new consistories under the supervision of the central bureau in Paris (itself under the wing of the minister of justice and religions), their Algerian counterparts reflected the colonial context: the new governing structures were placed under authority of the minister of war.

The consistories' place in the colonial administrative apparatus, however, did not prevent their backers from seeing a direct equivalence between their mission and that of their metropolitan "sister" institutions. Reformers drew on the metropolitan discourse of Jewish regeneration, combined with notions about Muslims and Islamic society that had gained currency in Europe, to fashion a certain mythology about their new charges. Like the preemancipation Jews of France who had been corrupted by years of persecution and medieval fanaticism, the indigenous Jews bore the scars of Islamic despotism and their history of persecution. Only with proper guidance could they be saved (Abitbol 1985). These ideas remained part of the consistories' legitimating ideology throughout the nineteenth century.

Reformers' (republican-tinged) understanding of the indigenous echoed debates of 1789 by associating Jews' "fanatic" religiosity with oppression. One early report in the best-known French Jewish journal informed its readership that "under the Turks," Jews were "the targets of the most oppressive humiliations and [that they were] crushed under the yoke of the most violent despotism. Nothing for them was made to elevate or suggest any human dignity" (*Archives Israélites* [*AI*] 1840, 477). A later report argued that the indigenous were still somehow "medieval": "During the middle ages, it was the Catholic clergy that spread instruction. The Israelites of Algeria are still in the middle ages. It is thus necessary to give them good rabbis and good schools" (*AI* 1848, 434). Remedies would have to reflect their conditions: "Above all," argued one report, "the manner in which we intervene in religious education will make French Israelites out of Algerian Israelites, as it is such a powerful force over the ardent population of this country. [The choice is to bring] these men to the level of others regarding civilization and morality, or leave them stagnating for years to come in a demoralized, fanatic state" (*AI* 1844, 691). Similar sentiments reverberated through consistorial discussions as well.

Certain military officers adopted this parallelism quite early. Having been convinced of the necessity of installing some agency to govern "a large portion of the civil population," the war minister informed the justice minister that the Jews of Algeria had been "the object of the most profound contempt by the Muslims, [a sentiment] mandated by the law of the Prophet. They were the target of taxes and humiliations, which they avenged, according to their custom, by usury and ruse, and by acting almost exclusively as intermediaries in exchanges of money and goods" (Ministre de la guerre 1839). Clearly, the officers' anti-Semitism did not preclude agreement with the basic arguments of Jewish reformers. Algerian Jews not only shared a history of persecution with their metropolitan counterparts, but also their deceit and usurious tendencies.

The unquestioned acceptance of Jews' history of brutal oppression also permitted reformers another argument of revolution-era emancipationists: the Jews' assured future fidelity if France were to adopt them. When the Central Consistory in Paris appealed to the minister of war to bring consistories to Algeria in 1836, its logic was straightforward: "The conquest of Algeria, in adding a new trophy to the glory of our nation, has torn from slavery a population stooped for centuries under the yoke of barbary." In contrast to the hostile and recalcitrant Muslims, "The Israelites of this new colony, long subjugated to persecution, feel all the stronger the benefits of French domination, in that they were so miserable under the despotism of the defeated former government" (Consistoire central 1836). In another example, Joseph Cohen, an Aix-en-Provence lawyer who played a key role in establishing the Algerian consistories, published a series of articles in the most prominent French Jewish journal emphasizing Jewish suffering in precolonial North Africa.[1] This experience, he argued, both sharpened their intelligence and made them reliable allies of the French: "among all the populations, Arabs, Moors, Kabyles, [there is] a common sentiment of hatred and repulsion. . . . The Israelite population, in contrast, which has only found in France protection and liberty, has attached itself [to France] with the ardor of sincere gratitude. [The Jews recognize that] if we left Africa, [they] would perish by the vengeance of the Arabs" (*AI* 1843, 26).

Reformers insisted that Algerian Jews, beyond their loyalty, were cleverer than Muslims and thus amenable to French instruction, culture, and language. Many Algerian Jews, for example, "pronounce French with a purity of accent such that many *provençaux* could well be jealous" (*AI* 1846, 131), whereas few Muslims had bothered to learn the language of the colonizer. Meanwhile, reformers insisted (despite archival evidence to the contrary) that Jews took advantage of any opportunity to send their children to French schools. Jacques-Isaac Altaras, the wealthy president of the Marseilles consistory and author of an influential 1842 report commissioned by the Ministry of War about the moral and political state of Algerian Jews, noted that their intellectual state was "markedly superior" to that of the Arabs, who "fearfully distanced themselves from our educational institutions" (Altaras 1842, 170). In a series of articles begun in 1843, entitled "De l'instruction publique parmi les Israélites algériens," Joseph Cohen argued that although Jewish faults are curable, it would be "vain" to "hope to vanquish this antipathy against all of our institutions, which animates the Muslim population" (*AI* 1843, 343).

One of the most striking ways reformers reified differences between colonial populations was through stereotypes regarding women's status and morality. It has been persuasively demonstrated elsewhere that Muslim Algerian sexual and marital behaviors occupied a privileged place in French legal, popular, and "scientific" literature that purported to explain Muslim's intellectual, cultural, and moral degeneracy (Clancy-Smith 1998). Thus, the widespread existence of prostitution, polygamy, and repudiation, along with the image of the sequestered Muslim woman, not only distinguished natives from the French, but also served as an argument for their continued disenfranchised status. Jewish reformists de-

1. I speak here of the *Archives Israélites*, which began publication in France in 1840. It had a strongly reformist slant and tended to support the consistories. *Univers Israélite* appeared in 1844 as a more conservative alternative. It has been suggested that the founding of a number of European Jewish journals in the 1840s was in response to the 1840 Damascus affair, in which local Jews were accused of and imprisoned for ritual murder.

ployed these understandings as foils against which to measure the advancement of the Jewish woman.

Among other places, this formulation can be found in Jacques-Isaac Altaras's report, mentioned earlier. "Although the Mauresques [Muslim women] remained enclosed either within narrow walls of their dwellings, or under thick veils, avoiding our civilization," he argued, "the Jewish woman goes out with an exposed face, or happily entertains guests in her home for friendly evenings" (1842, 84–85). In another example, in 1850 the consistorial grand rabbi Weil celebrated the religious initiation of a group of French-educated girls by giving a speech on "the condition of the woman." A local newspaper reported that he "eloquently raised his voice against the Muslim doctrine that relegates the woman to the condition of a brute" *(Akhbar,* 22 Oct. 1850). The educated and accessible Jewish woman became a civilized counterexample to their Muslim neighbors.

1848

These prejudices were soon policy. In keeping with the royal decree issued two years earlier and with the backing of the provincial prefecture,[2] the three lay officers of the Oran consistory, along with the French grand rabbi Lazare Cahen, took the reigns of the community on 22 June 1847. According to the decree that *organized* the Jewish religion in Algeria, a term referring to the establishment of the consistories, the members were to be chosen among indigenous and French Jews, with the position of grand rabbi being reserved for a Frenchman.

The choice of consistorial members itself challenges the unipolar modernization narrative. The officially designated "French" officers were Emmanuel Menahim Nahon, an interpreter already working for the military, as well as the Strasbourg-educated grand rabbi Lazare Cahen. The "indigenous" members were two wealthy merchants, Amran Sénanès and Abraham El Kanoui. The choice of Sénanès as an "indigenous" member reflected differing understandings of the term. He was a member of the six- to eight-hundred-strong Moroccan immigrant community in Oran (as was Nahon—a "French" member) (Schwarzfuchs 1981, 220). Many in the Oranais community saw him, indigenous or not, as an outsider with different allegiances and practices. The same dynamic emerged in local towns such as Mostaganem, where the consistory chose Moroccan representatives. "Regeneration" was to be a colonial project whose most visible agents in Oran were "indigenous" North Africans—who remained foreigners nonetheless.

2. The prefectures were the highest local authority in Algeria. The three Algerian prefectures corresponded to the three provinces of Oran, Algiers, and Constantine. They were responsible for the population in the "civil territories," and the military ruled directly elsewhere.

One of the consistories' first actions was to secure control of community finances. This act meant naming (and securing the tax revenue from) a limited number of *Schohetim* (kosher slaughterers) and merchants of kosher alcohol. After taking their own salaries, consistorial officers directed revenues into the community charity fund and burial society. The community's new government also appointed (or reappointed) ministers for various synagogues in both Oran and smaller towns in the province, such as Mostaganem and Tlemcen. The officers required owners of all the independent synagogues of Oran to register with the consistory and to obtain its permission in order to remain in operation.

In addition to imposing changes through the consistory, the French occupation also brought Jews into contact with a new cultural milieu. Oran was becoming an important port city in colonial Algeria, and its population of European settlers was rapidly growing. It swelled from less than 10,000 souls in 1830 to almost 23,000 in 1847, the year of the consistory's establishment (Julien 1964, 225). In addition to an estimated 4,763 Jews and 2,504 Muslims, the city counted 15,591 European immigrants. Although Frenchmen were not in the majority (the European population figure includes 8,520 Spaniards, 4,954 Frenchmen, and 1,056 Italians), they were hardly impervious to political events of the metropole. Notably, the revolution of February 1848 in France had a strong impact on the largely working-class European colonists of Oran. The civic activism and widespread proletarian participation in political clubs that characterized the early Second Republic in France (Amman 1975a, 1975b) was echoed in urban colonial Algeria (Emerit 1949, 16–19; Agulhon 1983, 38–40).

Although Paris was the epicenter of the 1848 revolution, political mobilization among colonists in Algeria was nonetheless significant. Masonic lodges served as centers of political discussion—occasionally leading to public demonstrations—and larger cities hosted a number of republican clubs. On several occasions, demonstrations by European colonists led to violent confrontations with the police. In Bône, for example, the disorders eventually resulted in the dismissal of the director of civil affairs for the province, and disorders in Oran brought about the mayor's downfall (Emerit 1949, 16–19). In addition, activists produced republican brochures and petitions, planned club meetings, and attended public gatherings throughout the colony (Julien 1964, 346). The highly active press, though regularly harassed by the military authorities, benefited from a judiciary that often sympathized with the journalists.[3] This civic activism was not

3. One should note that the political effervescence in Algeria differed from that in the metropole, shaped as it was by particularities of the colonial situation. Notably, despite the stratification of white colonial society and their differences in political perspective, racism against indigenous

contained within the boundaries of the French settler population, but was soon to influence the way Oranais Jews responded to what they regarded as violations of their community's religious integrity.

Signs of resistance among the Jews emerged in January. Deputies from the Oran Consistory encountered serious problems in fulfilling their duties in provincial towns such as Mascara and Mostaganem, and Jews in this latter city went so far as to expel the appointed rabbi from the major communal synagogue. On 18 February 1848, forty-four Jewish household heads petitioned the Oran director of civil affairs with the intention of ridding themselves of their consistorial officers. They complained of abuse of authority, religious transgressions, Moroccan representatives' disrespect to revered local rabbis, and even physical mistreatment. The protests did not remain limited to writing, and soon the civil commissioners of Mostaganem reported a "complete insurrection" of local Jews against the authorities, and the eruption of "disorders" (Commissaire civil de Mostaganem 1848). By early February, the Oran Consistory solicited the power of the colonial government to put down the disturbance at Mostaganem. President Nahon urged the civil commissioner of Mostaganem to set a "severe example" so that other Jews would learn that "obedience is due to laws, and the administration has the firm intention to see that they are respected" (Nahon 1848a). The prefecture of the province was not long to respond with orders to "repress severely" the uprising (Commissaire civil de Mostaganem 1848). Joining other Oranais, Algerian Jews were in upheaval.

Notwithstanding the repression, the disturbances spread to other towns. By mid-February, the duc d'Aumale, the soon-to-be-replaced governor-general of the colony,[4] commanded the director of civil affairs of the prefecture of Oran to investigate the complaints and in so doing to determine their "morality" (Gouverneur général d'Algérie 1848a). With the fall of the July Monarchy, the republican Louis-Eugène Cavaignac was appointed governor-general of Algeria.[5] Meanwhile, the insurgency increased in intensity. In March, fully one hundred Jewish heads of households in Oran petitioned the new officer, asking for the

---

Muslims had a unifying effect on the various social classes of white Algeria. Few European colonists actually wanted to overthrow the French administration in Algeria, for obvious reasons (Emerit 1949).

4. Henri-Eugène-Phillipe-Louis d'Orléans duc d'Aumale was soon to be replaced by Cavaignac, whom the provisional government did not fear might aid a House of Orléans-inspired royalist coup. By 3 March 1848, the prince was on his way to a self-imposed exile in England.

5. Cavaignac was a republican, though quite conservative and, like his predecessor, related to the Orléans. He was to become well known for brutally suppressing the uprising of Paris workers in June 1848.

complete overhaul of their consistory, and civil unrest continued to worry the authorities. On 7 April, the director of civil affairs wrote a concerned letter to the consistory noting that he viewed with "extreme unhappiness the conduct of the Israelite population" (Directeur des affaires civiles 1848c). The officers agreed and noted that the "rebellion" had spread to other parts of Algeria. In April, an article in the Oran newspaper *L'echo d'Oran* reported that troops had intervened to suppress the disturbances, resulting in numerous arrests. Similar problems were reported at Mostaganem, where Jews had "manifested a systematic opposition to the measures required by the organization of the Israelite religion" *(AI* 1848, 338). In Medea, the army was called in to back the appointed heads of the Jewish community (C. Martin 1936, 85). On 13 May, rioters tore down governmental posters and stoned the police. Around the same time, many wealthy Jewish notables of Oran chose to withhold their taxes in protest against the consistory (C. Martin 1936, 86).

Already by 29 March, events had tired the consistorial president Nahon to the point where he sent a resignation letter to the director of civil affairs. "The execution of the law of 9 November 1845 appears to me excessively difficult under the current circumstances" (Nahon 1848b), he wrote. Sénanès, referring to "this ungrateful population" (Sénanès 1848), also chose 29 March to resign officially. The director, however, concerned about maintaining public order, insisted that they stay at their posts (Directeur des affaires civiles 1848a). In mid-May, local Jews wrote to *L'echo d'Oran* and accused Nahon of dishonesty and a host of other faults. The impact was such that he felt obliged to reaffirm his honesty and devotion to the cause of regeneration to his superiors at the Direction of the Interior (Nahon 1848c).

The colonial administration's resolve to retain Nahon and Sénanès despite their resounding unpopularity endured no more than several weeks. With the tax strike by wealthier community members, the poor Jews who depended on the effective operation of the charity committee had become, in the words of the director of civil affairs, "turbulent" (Directeur des affaires civiles 1848b). Doubts arose about maintaining both Nahon and Sénanès to serve on the consistory, and on 27 May the director of civil affairs said as much to the new governor-general. This recently appointed official (the antirepublican Nicholas Anne Théodule Changarnier) was thus informed that because tensions "have been recently translated into material disorders," a policy change was necessary. To this effect, the director would meet with Oranais Jews and with them produce a tentative list of new candidates. The new members whom the director chose were indeed members, he admitted, of the "turbulent opposition" to the current consistory (Gouverneur général 1848b). The two colonial officers agreed to appoint them conditionally and to wait to confirm them in their posts until they had proven their fidelity to the administration. By August, the new members of the consistory had been brought in, namely local notables Mordekai Darmon and Abraham ben Aïm. Abraham El Kanoui and the French rabbi Lazare Cahen would also remain.

The changes at Oran lead to the appointment of new deputies in Mostaganem as well. On 26 May, (the Moroccan) consistorial appointees Salomon Sarfati and Isaac Ben Oliel resigned, and their opponents were installed in their place (Ben Oliel and Sarfati 1848). It appears that a similar trial period was accorded in Mostaganem, for there was no official act of instatement until 10 November. Nevertheless, the administration created a list of new deputies that included those previously active in the opposition: Jouda Smadja, Maklouf Troudjman, and Moïse ben Jacob Abou (Consistoire Israélite de la Province d'Oran 1848). Significantly, in both cities, the local notables already serving on the consistory were maintained, but those who had clearly entered into the administration as a consequence of military service were expelled. The Jews of Oran had, to a limited extent, made the French consistory Algerian.

The uprising itself complicates the received narrative wherein France "saved" the Jews, initiating a process leading inevitably to total assimilation. At the same time, examining the "transcripts" of the rebellion gives us even more insight into how both colonized and colonizer understood these events. As we shall see through "reading between the lines" of official correspondence and through petitions by the Jews themselves, the events resist the classification schemes applied by both the colonizers and subsequent historians.

"They Swore upon the Tombs Never to Make Peace with Us": Rebellion and Religion

The revolt was, first and foremost, articulated in religious terms. Rabbinical authority and the right to lead prayers emerged quickly as a point of conflict. In February 1848, Jews of Mostaganem asked that Salomon Sarfati, a "Moroccan" consistorial appointee, be replaced by someone of their choosing (Jews of Mostaganem 1848). Not only was he corrupt and ignorant, but also during the high holidays the previous year he had forced the venerated Rabbi Mordekai Abédia out of his functions and replaced him with a rabbi of his own choosing. In another instance, Sarfati had interrupted the prayers when he noticed they were following local customs and not the Moroccan rite to which he insisted they conform. Later, it was reported that the same community had forced his appointee out of the main synagogue and into a smaller local meeting place. The reason given was that they wished to choose their own religious leader (Commissaire civil de Mostaganem 1848). Sarfati himself confirmed some of these accusations. The opposition, he wrote, "act in solidarity with the previous chiefs, who support them energetically" (Ben Oliel and Sarfati 1848). He also complained that the locals constantly changed the times of prayer in order to avoid him and the other consistorial representatives.

Opponents of Sarfati sought the support not only of the local rabbinate, but of the dead. They convened in the Jewish cemetery of Mostaganem, where, according to the embattled representative, "they swore upon the tombs never to make peace with us" (Ben Oliel and Sarfati 1848). Although it is impossible to know the exact nature of the oath, one may imagine that it was on the graves of a departed rabbi (or rabbis), whose spiritual strength the opposition hoped to garner for their struggle.[6] In another colorful episode, it was the spiritual strength contained in holy books that entered into the dispute with the consistorial deputy. In the petition to the director of civil affairs at the prefecture, Mostaganem's Jews noted that Salomon Sarfati had invited catastrophe upon Mostaganem by mishandling old holy books that, according to many in the community, protected the city (Jews of Mostaganem 1848).

Religious competence was of great importance for Oranais Jews as well. Grand Rabbi Cahen was accused of being ignorant of local custom and for not speaking the language, rendering him "completely incapable" of fulfilling his community responsibilities (Jews of Oran 1848). They also interpreted as corruption his charging for rabbinical services, such as marriages, in addition to his salary (it should be pointed out that consistorial president Emmanuel Nahon was also seen as corrupt for using community funds, destined for charity, for his salary). They were particularly unnerved that Cahen's previous official appointment was at a prison in Nîmes. They insisted that although he may have been well suited for the prison, he was "totally out of place" in Oran (Jews of Oran 1848). The religious revolt against the consistory was also one against a series of practices understood to be corrupt.

But the centrality of piety in the revolt should not obscure the fact that indigenous Jews drew on a "French" political lexicon. Just as European colonists organized in support of the new republican government in 1848, hoping to replace the military "Regime of the Sword" with local, civilian rule in the colony (Emerit 1949, 16–19), the indigenous Jews of Oran also saw in republicanism the potential to reacquire local control. In their letter to the republican General Cavaignac, they wrote, "[We] saluted with joy the appearance of the Republic," and "we [now] take advantage of the freedom of thought acquired with this Re-

6. Praying by the graves of departed holy men to strengthen one's prayers is not an uncommon practice in many Jewish communities.

public, and dare to hope that you will receive [our] complaints and remedy them" (Jews of Oran 1848). As in France and among the Europeans in Algeria, expanded suffrage was a prominent demand among Jewish petitioners. For instance, they wished for a new grand rabbi who "will have obtained the most votes in elections" and alternative consistorial officers who would also be selected "by way of election." Furthermore, the petitioners demanded the elimination of the paid position of the office of the consistory president (Jews of Oran 1848). The Oranais' answer to the religious abuses of its officers was a "republican" consistory.

The Jewish opposition also seems to have shared techniques, if not technologies, with the republican movement among colonists. According to President Nahon's report to the director of civil affairs, the Jews of Oran were coordinating their actions with other communities, using print media, and organizing into groups. Whether or not the Jews of Oran organized political "clubs," as did so many Parisians (and urban colons), consistorial officials remarked that they did achieve a degree of coordination. One note read that "tumultuous meetings have taken place, and flyers have been sent to Israelites in all the localities of Algeria in order that the rebellion be the same all over. [They do this so that] its uniform and generalized character gives it more power" (Consistoire Israélite de la Province d'Oran 1848). They also produced posters that appeared in synagogues throughout the province and published defamatory articles about the consistorial president in a local paper (Nahon 1848c). The movement of indigenous Jews was no more isolated from the political agitation that surged among the wider civil population than it was unreceptive to the potentially liberating aspects of the ideologies of this unrest.

Indigenous complaints often rang with liberalism in addition to explicitly republican sentiments. The letter from the Jews of Oran concluded with the words, "these events infringe on our beliefs, our habits, or customs, and the free exercise of our religion" (Jews of Oran 1848). Similarly, Mostaganem's Jews warned of the potential failure of civilizing because Sarfati's chosen rabbi "could exercise no influence on our coreligionists"; considering that he "personally merits neither respect nor consideration . . . the Consistoire reaps none of the benefits that it could expect from enlightened administrators" (Jews of Mostaganem 1848). Accepting that the Algerian Jews were to be "influenced" and "attached to France," the petitioners urged the government to find better representatives.

Indigenous demands that called upon principles of progress or republicanism unsettled French officers whose power was justified by their mission to civilize. The consistory—on letterhead newly embossed with the words *liberté, égalité, fraternité,* and with standard salutations replaced, at least temporarily, by

"Citoyen!"—argued that its monopoly on power should not be compromised by indigenous people who demanded "liberty." The message to the (republican) minister of war was clear: indigenous Jews did not understand the real meaning of *republic:*

> These words "Liberty," "Republic" which have come to resonate so powerfully in all French hearts, have also been heard by the Israelite population of Oran. Unfortunately, they do not wish to understand the true meaning of the words. They have misinterpreted them.
>
> For [this population], [these words] signify the abolition of all existing laws, the ability of everyone to do as he pleases, or to not do what does not please him. [They mean] the absence of any brake and of all authority, that is to say anarchy and license (Consistoire Israélite de la Province d'Oran 1848).

At the much-celebrated height of expressive liberty in the first half of 1848, newly appointed "republican" officials were charged with containing "liberty" within the borders of the nation. The question naturally arises regarding how such officers charged with "civilizing" and "enlightening" harmonized their mission with orders to repress a movement calling for religious freedom, local democracy, and "enlightened" officials. President Nahon's explanation of the revolt sheds some light on the issue: "Among some of the agitators it is jealousy, [but] among almost all of them it is [also] ignorance" (Nahon 1848a). Despite indigenous Jews' claims to uphold common values, Nahon assured the prefecture that the consistory needed to continue the difficult task of "enlightening." In response to the incidents in Mostaganem, the prefecture of the province told the local authorities to use "moderate firmness" to "assure the deputies [of the consistory] the respect and obedience that is owed to them and repress severely the spirit of insubordination that has animated several agitators." Interesting to us here is how the same letter asked the local authorities to "please continue, by the combined effort of persuasion and force, to enlighten [*éclairer*] the Israelites" (Directeur des affaires civiles 1848a). In this conflict, "enlightenment" demanded greater freedom for the insurgents, but among officials it had taken on a meaning approximating obedience.

"Enlightenment" as a policy response to objectionable behavior among marginal groups recalls revolution-era emancipators who rooted French Jewish "degeneracy" in centuries of oppression and ignorance. French officials made basically the same argument regarding the Jews of Algeria, who were similarly emerging from what was seen as the oppressive yoke of immutable Islam. This view both explained resistance and neutralized calls for self-government. Nahon, in one of his reports, for example, argued that because of their long years of "abuse" and "oppression" under "Turkish" despotism, "the Israelite population of Mostaganem is still, we must say, incapable of appreciating the advantages it may reap as a result of the royal ordinance of 9 November 1845" (Nahon 1848a). Elsewhere, he lamented: "this population that I wanted to raise to the level of our French co-religionists request now to remain crouched in the morass of ignorance and superstition" (Nahon 1848b). Rejecting any alternative routes in the march of progress, consistorial officials demanded a monopoly on the mantle (and meaning) of "enlightenment." "Fortunately for [the Jewish population of Algeria]," consoled Nahon, "it is being forced to accept and submit to the work of regeneration" (Nahon 1848a).

Parisian Parallels

As mentioned earlier, the ideology and campaign of "regeneration" targeted French Jews before extension overseas as a "colonial" ideology and campaign in Algeria. It is perhaps not surprising that metropolitan communities, faced with similar forms of control, also resisted the consistorial structure in ways that exposed cracks in the vision of enlightenment embedded in that structure. Interestingly, Parisian activists, like their coreligionists across the Mediterranean, also found in republicanism a useful vocabulary with which to mobilize to protect the religious integrity of their communities during the 1848 revolution.

Immigration to Paris had both augmented and diversified its Jewish population in the years leading up to 1848. From a small, unregistered community of several hundred at the time of the revolution, the Jewish community of Paris at midcentury had grown to be the country's most significant minority at around twenty thousand. Recent consistorial efforts to impose a tax on kosher meat, to repress unauthorized prayer meetings, and to institute controls on the practice of circumcision had angered local Jews (Consistoire Israélite de la circonscription de Paris 1843; *UI* 1844–45, 245, 275; Cohen Albert 1977). Several years earlier, in May 1844, the government had enacted a new centralizing decree that established a strict rabbinical hierarchy and gave lay officers the power to change rituals if they were deemed incompatible with civilization. This was just a year and a half before the November 1845 decree "organizing" the Jewish population of Algeria.

Many French Jews and even the more conservative reformers who otherwise supported aspects of "regeneration" responded critically to the new ordinance. In 1848, a group of self-identified working-class, religious Jews organized along the same model as many of their non-Jewish neighbors and formed a republican political club. The Club démocratique des fidèles was led by a merchant named

Abraham ben Baruch Créhange, who had vocally opposed various consistorial abuses for years. Much like the Jews of Oran, the Club démocratique laced its vigorous defense of traditional Judaism with republican themes of democracy and free expression.[7] Créhange insisted, for example, that Moses and the prophet Samuel were both republicans and that such a form of government was the only one truly blessed by God (Créhange 1848). Like their Oranais counterparts, the Parisians acted in the name of piety and complained about how consistorial officers were chosen—Créhange noted their elitism and that voting "notables" were chosen exclusively by wealth. By the beginning of April, the club had decided to address their complaints about the consistory to the provisional government *(La Vérité* 1848).

On 9 April 1848, the same month as the Oranais Jews sent their petition, the Club démocratique sent a petition addressed to the "Citizen Members of the Provisional Government of the French Republic" (Club démocratique des fidèles 1848). The letter noted that the May 1844 reform decree effectively limited suffrage in elections for consistorial officers to a list of "notables" so exclusive that in the elections of December 1847 only 111 people were allowed to vote. "A consistory named in such a manner," declared the petition, "is not the expression of the mass of Israelites of the jurisdiction because it is precisely this mass that is not permitted to vote" (Club démocratique des fidèles 1848). The Parisian petition, much like the Oranais one, called for the dissolution of the local consistory and its reconstitution by universal (male, Jewish) suffrage.

Like in Oran, the movement to which these complaints were attached did win some ground. The consistories in France were briefly and partially democratized, but in the wake of the "June days" of 1848 restrictions on suffrage were renewed. Ultimately, the Paris and the Oran consistories never truly became representative organizations, but were altered by political mobilization on the part of those they were attempting to "regenerate." These similarities were not lost on reformers. Reporting on the uprising in Oran, one reporter joked that as of yet there was no Club des fidèles in Algeria *(AI* 1848, 338). His joke underscores the limits of the traditional unipolar narrative positing assimilated French Jews as the unified source and model for "civilizing" Algerians. "Modernization" was not a process completed in the center before being exported to the periphery.

7. The club also blended religious themes with discussions of class politics. For example, in one of Créhange's publications, he argued about God's concern for labor relations: "The fourth commandment of God [observe the Sabbath and keep it holy] is a proof of the benevolent concern of the Supreme Being for the workers" (Créhange 1848).

Conclusion

The events of 1848 in Oran suggest that the received history of the Algerian Jewish encounter with French colonialism glosses over intense ambivalence regarding French colonial institutions. Many Jews regarded the consistory not as emancipatory, but rather as an intrusive and impious force usurping power from their communities. Furthermore, in addressing what they saw as religious infractions as well as the marginalization of venerated rabbis and their replacement by "foreign" representatives regarded as incompetent if not venal, Jews of Oran used liberal or even republican terms. Their demands to be rid of consistorial control appealed to the defeat of monarchy, the right to vote, the right to progress, and guarantees of religious freedom. This blending of a French political language with graveside oaths and rabbinical support represents a fascinating counterexample to treatments that trace the steady path of a submissive and fanatic group toward assimilation with metropolitan Jews. The rebellion's parallels to simultaneous events in Paris; officers in Oran who were frequently Moroccan immigrants with different customs and practices; and the fact that nonlocal but nonetheless indigenous North African Jews represented the civilizing ideology to local Oranais Jews suggest that the "civilizing" project, although conceived in France, was conducted and resisted by Jews on both sides of the Mediterranean.

Moreover, the events suggest that an important chapter in the history of colonial myth making has been left out of discussions of French Algeria. Notably, the short-lived "Kabyle myth" of the late Second Empire and Third Republic was preceded by a successful "Jewish mythology" that initiated policies based on the "fact" that Jews were less "barbaric" than Muslims and that their history would follow the same theme as the history of the Jews of France. Of course, this chapter's look at the events of 1848 also adds some nuance to our understanding of this early civilizing ideology. Even as Algerian Jews adopted French themes and discourse, their protests were interpreted as the anarchic passions of uncivilized and fanatic men. The truly *éclairé,* wrote the consistorial officers, would welcome the institutions of colonialism. For colonial officers, the term *enlightenment* was often understood as obedience.

8 Entering History

The Memory of Police Violence in Paris, October 1961

JOSHUA COLE

17 October 1961

ON THE EVENING OF 17 OCTOBER 1961, six months before the end of the war for Algerian independence, perhaps thirty thousand people—most of them Algerian laborers and their families—gathered in Paris for a demonstration.[1] The immediate target of their protest was a police curfew that prohibited Algerian Muslims from circulating freely between 8:30 P.M. and 5:30 A.M. For many of the demonstrators, however, the planned march was also a rare occasion to demonstrate solidarity with nationalists fighting the French army in Algeria.[2] The police responded with extraordinary brutality. Nobody will ever know the exact number of people killed by the police on 17 October and in the days that followed, but recently published estimates range from thirty-one to two hundred (Brunet 1999, 329; Einaudi 2001, 11).

1. I thank David Bell, Patricia Lorcin, Neil MacMaster, Mary Louise Roberts, Todd Shepard, and Daniel Sherman for their helpful comments in preparing this essay for publication. Jean-Luc Einaudi and Jean-Paul Brunet agreed to meet with me in Paris, and I thank them both for their frankness and generosity. Parts of this chapter come from a related article published in *French Politics, Culture, and Society* (fall 2003), and I thank the editor of this journal, Herrick Chapman, for his help in clarifying the argument in key places.

2. Literally hundreds of articles about 17 October 1961 have appeared regularly in French and Algerian newspapers since the early 1980s (see, e.g., "17 octobre 1961" 2001). Books, in chronological order, include: Levine 1985, Amicale des Algériens 1987; Einaudi 1991, 2001; Tristan 1991; Brunet 1999; Le Cour Grandmaison 2001; and Einaudi and Kagan 2001. Papon (1988) addressed the events of October 1961 in his memoirs. Other books that contain important discussions of 17 October 1961 are Haroun 1986, 359–77; MacMaster 1997, 199–201; and Gastaut 2000, 17–35. In addition, the events of October 1961 have played a part in several novels written in the past two decades, including Daeninckx 1983; Kettane 1985; Lallaoui [1981] 1986; Benaïcha 1992; and Sebbar 1999.

Prefect of Police Maurice Papon had called the curfew as a response to the Front de libération national's (FLN) attacks on police officers in previous months, but it was also an attempt to break the nationalist organization's hold on the Algerian immigrant population in the city—some 150,000 people.[3] The Fédération de France du FLN collected a small weekly contribution from every Algerian laborer in France, and this cash was an important source of revenue for the struggle against the French. Because the curfew interfered with the collection of these contributions, the federation had to challenge it, and their only weapon was to publicize its discriminatory nature with a large demonstration.[4]

The federation also had a political incentive. In the last year of the war, a split between the military leadership of the FLN and the politicians of the Gouvernement provisoire de la République Algérien (GPRA) threatened to destabilize plans for building an independent state.[5] The Fédération de France hoped to play a mediating role in this conflict, but to do so it would have to increase its own stature within the movement. Such stature came only with direct participation in the struggle against the French, and the demonstration of 17 October would give proof of the organization's willingness to confront the enemy at home, in the French capital.[6] Such thinking certainly lay behind the occasional threats and coercion employed by the federation to ensure a high turnout for the demonstration (Brunet 1999, 175–78).[7]

Maurice Papon's official report after the demonstration listed three deaths: two killed by the police acting in self-defense and a third attributed to cardiac arrest. The Archives of the Prefecture of Police show that 11,538 people were arrested on that evening alone, and by the end of the week the number was more

3. Brunet gives the following figures for assassinations of police officers in France by the FLN: 1958, 12 killed and 22 wounded; 1959, 4 killed and 10 wounded; 1960, 9 killed and 29 wounded; 1961 (January-October only), 22 killed, 76 wounded. Total figures: 47 killed and 140 wounded. Brunet 1999, 82.

4. For the planning of the demonstration see Levine 1985, 82–83; Haroun 1986, 361–65; Einaudi 1991, 92–96.

5. On the formation of the GPRA, see Ruedy 1992, 170–74; Harbi [1980] 1993, 218–23; Nouschi 1995, 226–31.

6. On the politics of the federation's decision to call the demonstration, see Tristan 1991, 41, and P. Bernard 1999.

7. The FLN leadership must have expected casualties on 17 October. The last time Algerian nationalists had demonstrated in the capital was 14 July 1953, when Messali Hadj's Mouvement pour le triomphe des libertés démocratiques (MTLD) chose Bastille Day to demonstrate for Algerian independence. Seven people were killed, and forty-eight were injured (Einaudi 1991, 46). Benjamin Stora gives as six the number killed on 14 July 1953 (1991, 134).

than 14,000.[8] Many witnesses on 17 October told of seeing the police hoisting demonstrators up over the parapets of the city's bridges and dropping them into the Seine.[9] In the days that followed, dozens of unidentified bodies were pulled from the Seine and deposited at the morgue.[10] Although many family members filed missing-person reports in the coming weeks, judicial authorities classified these unidentified bodies as *sans suite*—no follow-up.[11]

The government's effort to hide the extent of the repression culminated in Charles de Gaulle's 1968 amnesty of all military and police personnel for war crimes and acts of treason committed during the French-Algerian War.[12] No police officer was ever charged with murder in connection with the demonstration of 17 October, and the Prefecture of Police did not permit historians to view the police archives relating to the demonstration until 1999. As a result, there is still a persistent uncertainty about the most basic facts, including the most fundamental question: How many people died? Uncertainty about this question has been deftly translated by irresponsible commentators, beginning with Papon himself, into an uncertainty about the event as a whole.

From 1961 to the early 1980s, few people in France ever spoke about the event, but when they did, they usually mentioned something close to the original

8. Archives de la Préfecture de police, Ha 110, Manifestation du 17 octobre 1961, Subfolder: Manifestation du 17 octobre 1961, Comptes-rendus. Official figures for arrests are contained in a document entitled "BILAN DES OPERATIONS EFFECTUEES A LA SUITE DES MANIFESTATIONS DES 17, 18, 19 OCTOBRE 1961."

9. See, for example, the testimony of Édouard Durand, Daniel Mermet, Yvette Teurlai-Quéval, Guy Gauthier, Krib Abderrahmane, Robert Chamayou, Pierre Gervaux, and Roger Blanc as reported to Einaudi (2001, 172–74, 192–94).

10. Gérard Monate, a police officer who in 1961 was secretary general of the Syndicat general de la police, told Einaudi that more than one hundred bodies were brought to the Institut medico-légal in the immediate aftermath of the demonstration, but that many of them were simply thrown back into the river, which ran alongside the morgue (Einaudi 2001, 205).

11. In the lawsuit that Maurice Papon filed against Jean-Luc Einaudi, archivist Brigitte Lainé testified that although one-third of the relevant judicial records are missing, she was able to find records of 103 cases opened at the Tribunal de grand instance in Paris, concerning 130 individuals. From these records, 32 of the cases, concerning 40 individuals, were classified as *sans suite*. She also cited a brief dated 30 October 1961 that concerned the deaths of 63 North Africans, of which 26 could not be identified. All of these bodies had been found in the Seine or in canals near Paris since September 1961, and in the majority of cases their hands had been bound, and they had been strangled or shot (Pereira 1999).

12. Among the works about October 1961 subjected to censorship were two books by Paulette Péju (1961a, 1961b). A censored film by Jacques Panijel, *Octobre à Paris* (1961–62), has still never been distributed in France.

estimate of two hundred deaths given by the FLN at the time.[13] Constantin Melnik, a somewhat shadowy government fixer who worked closely with Michel Debré (prime minister in 1961), shocked many of his former colleagues in 1988 when he suggested in his memoirs that the number of deaths on 17 October was at least one hundred, and this figure was often cited in the years that followed (Melnik 1988, 220–21). A new consensus emerged in 1991, especially in the media, following the publication of a book by Jean-Luc Einaudi, *La bataille de Paris, 17 octobre 1961.*[14] Einaudi relied on the testimony of witnesses, information from the FLN on the number of people who disappeared, and corroborating evidence from the archives of the Paris morgue to come up with an estimate that largely confirmed the FLN's original estimate of two hundred deaths. Journalists often cited this figure until the mid-1990s, and Einaudi's version of the event seemed poised to become the standard reference among historians.[15]

In 1997, however, the controversy over 17 October converged with a growing media storm over another scandalous aspect of Maurice Papon's extraordinary career: his participation as a young provincial official in the deportation of nearly fifteen hundred Jews from Bordeaux to Auschwitz during the Second World War. Einaudi's 1991 book on the events of 17 October received renewed public attention in October 1997, when prosecutors called him to testify at Papon's trial for crimes against humanity.[16] Einaudi's detailed testimony was widely quoted in the press, and commentators began to speak of a trial within the trial, a second tribunal that brought the history of the French-Algerian War together with the history of France's Vichy regime under the occupation (Conan 1998, 28–30; Dumay 1998, 49–53; Golsan 2000, 224–42). The court eventually convicted Papon and sentenced him to ten years in prison in April 1998. While his case was in appeal, Papon sued Einaudi for libel, but lost. In February 1999, the court recognized Einaudi's right to use the word *massacre* in writing about police violence on 17 October 1961.[17]

13. In 1961, the Fédération de France du FLN estimated 200 deaths, 400 disappeared, and 2,300 injured ("Entre 30 et 200 morts" 2001).

14. Einaudi's was not the first full-length book to be published about 17 October 1961 (see, for example, Levine 1985), but it was the first to be widely reviewed and discussed, and it was the first to have made much impression on the community of professional historians in France.

15. For example, the entry "Manifestation du 17 octobre 1961" in the most widely used historical dictionary of twentieth-century French political life largely follows Einaudi's version of events, with only a few caveats (Pervillé 1995).

16. Einaudi's testimony can be found in *Le procès de Maurice Papon* 1998, 1:225–44.

17. Lainé's and Grand's participation in the trial got them in trouble with their superiors at the Archives de Paris, who believed that they had violated their professional obligations to remain silent

Faced with these sensational trials, Prime Minister Lionel Jospin and his cabinet were forced to break the government's longstanding silence on the "official" version of the events of 17 October. The Ministry of the Interior released a report after the verdict in the first Papon trial of 1998, suggesting that no more than thirty-two people were killed by the police on 17 October.[18] The Ministry of Justice, however, suggested in May 1999 that there were at least forty-eight deaths on 17–18 October and probably more.[19] The Justice Ministry report also noted that the week of 17 October was only a peak in a year that saw 246 bodies of North Africans pulled from the river and registered at the morgue, including 37 in September and 105 in October, though the average had never been more than "a dozen" in previous months (Herzberg 1999).

In the meantime, the Prefecture of Police gave permission in the spring of 1999 to Jean-Paul Brunet, a historian who holds positions at both the École normale supérieure and the University of Paris. Brunet's book *Police contre FLN: Le drame d'octobre 1961*, published at the end of 1999, reinforced the lower figure given by the Ministry of Interior's report and criticized Einaudi's reliance on unverifiable testimony by eyewitnesses. Ever mindful of France's libel laws, journalists have now resorted to the unwieldy formulation of "between thirty-two and two hundred" or simply "dozens" to speak of the number of dead. It is not difficult to see how painful such approximations are to the families of victims, nor how much comfort they give to those whose political interests still require a degree of damage control.[20]

A Long Silence

In France, 17 October is now officially a day of remembrance, but a large part of what is now remembered is the forgetting of 17 October 1961, a public event that

---

about the contents of archives that are not open to the public. They were subsequently reassigned and removed from many of their former activities that brought them into contact with researchers at the archives (Thibaudat 2001).

18. The Interior Ministry report, authored by Dieudonné Mandelkern, was commissioned in October 1997 immediately after Einaudi's testimony in the Papon trial, but Jospin's government withheld publication until after Papon was convicted in April 1998 (P. Bernard 1998).

19. Jean Geronimi, reporting for the Ministry of Justice, quoted in Herzberg 1999. Geronimi's report was not made public until August 1999.

20. In October 2001, after gaining access to the police archives, Jean-Luc Einaudi reaffirmed his commitment to a higher figure of deaths and documented a pattern of murder perpetrated by the police throughout the months of September and October 1961: "393 dead and disappeared in September and October 1961, of which 159 after 17 October" (cited in Garcia 2001). Garcia's article cites Guy Pervillé and Jean-Paul Brunet as historians who continue to disagree with Einaudi's figures.

literally happened in plain sight. Algerians commemorate this date as well, but their memory of it is beset with difficulty for the opposite reason. Those Algerian Muslims who marched in Paris in 1961 were separated from their nationalist compatriots in Algeria because they were emigrants, so their relation to the story of national renewal was already once removed. From both perspectives, then, what makes 17 October 1961 exceptional is the fact that it occurred in Paris. This fact made the subsequent effacement of the demonstration all the more necessary and makes it all the more paradoxical for those who want to explain the event's curious afterlife in history and memory.

Commemorations of 17 October 1961 also disturb the narratives of national renewal that both France and Algeria settled upon after the war ended in 1962. Charles de Gaulle obviously had no wish to dwell on the excesses committed by Parisian police in the summer and fall of 1961.[21] In signing the Evian Accords, he sought to recast decolonization as a transformation of France's relationship to Algeria rather than its the termination of that relationship. Meanwhile, the dynamics of the civil war that accompanied Algerian independence brought Ahmed Ben Bella, the new nation's first president, into conflict with the GPRA leaders who had signed the accords in the spring of 1962. The Fédération de France du FLN took the side of the GPRA in the immediate postindependence struggles, and Ben Bella's regime later punished the federation's leadership for their association with those who had opposed his accession to power.[22] Militants whose power emanated from the emigration in France found themselves excluded from Ben Bella's inner circle, even as the new president moved to establish a more cooperative relationship with a French administration that was anxious to retain some influence over France's former colony.[23]

The split within the FLN at the moment of independence deprived Algeria of many of the most prominent leaders of the revolutionary movement—Mohamed Boudiaf went into exile in Morocco, and Hocine Aït Ahmed retreated to his home base in Kabylia to create a new opposition front, the Front des forces socialistes (FFS) (Ruedy 1992, 201–2; Nouschi 1995, 243–47). Aït Ahmed's departure underscored the extent to which the conflict between Ben Bella, on the one hand, and the GPRA and the Fédération de France, on the other, overlapped a

21. Kristin Ross offers an important discussion of these narratives of national renewal (1995, 1–13).

22. On the divergences of the GPRA, the FLN, and the Fédération de France in 1962, see the comments of Omar Boudaoud, former head of the five-member committee that directed the activities of the Fédération de France ("Entretien" 1992).

23. On the relationship of France and Algeria under Ben Bella and more generally since independence, see Naylor 2000, 47–73.

persistent ethnic split between Arabs and Berbers, especially Kabyles, within the nationalist movement.[24] The leader of the GPRA, Benyoucef Ben Khedda, was a Kabyle, and for historical reasons Kabyles were generally overrepresented among those who emigrated to France from Algeria. Berber concentrations in France included the Paris suburbs of Nanterre, Puteaux, Courbevoie, Saint-Ouen, Saint-Denis, and the eighteenth *arrondissement* of Paris, precisely those neighborhoods that provided many of the protesters on 17 October. These neighborhoods were also key to the organization of the Fédération de France, which recruited many of its militants among immigrants in these areas. The effects of these splits were to have long-term consequences for the memory of 17 October because Ben Bella's victory over the GPRA and the Fédération de France in 1962 set the stage for his ambitious program of *arabisation* and *islamisation* after independence, a movement for cultural renewal that sought to build a common sense of Algerian national identity around religion and the Arabic language. Ben Bella's overtures to Islamic leaders and to those who favored Arabic over French made sense as a way to deflect the criticism that his endorsement of cooperation with de Gaulle's government constituted a capitulation to neocolonial interference. For many Berbers who continued to speak their own dialects of Tamazight, however, Ben Bella's cultural policy relegated them to second-class status within their new country. Because Algeria lacked the kinds of political institutions that could resolve these persistent splits within the national community, Ben Bella and his successor Houari Boumedienne turned to a mythologized history of the revolution as a way to create at least the illusion of a unified national identity. In this mythology, they presented the nationalist revolution as a spontaneous uprising of rural Algerians against the French military throughout the countryside of Algeria (Stora 1991, 121–84). Conspicuously absent, however, was the story of urban workers in the emigration and the role of the Fédération de France in supporting the struggle for independence.

A break in this relative silence came in 1968, when Boumedienne's government celebrated for the first time a new holiday on 17 October, the Journée nationale de l'émigration.[25] Even here, however, the Algerian government did little to give voice to the victims of the French police or to the veterans of the Fédéra-

24. On the distinction between Kabyles and Arabs and its importance for colonial policy in Algeria, see Lorcin [1995] 1999a. Estimates of the number of Kabyles among the total Algerian emigration in France ranged from 84 percent in 1923 to 75 percent in 1938 and then to 66 percent in the 1950s (MacMaster 1993, 22). On Berbers in the Paris region, see Harbi [1980] 1993, 64.

25. The original idea for the holiday came out of the November 1967 meetings of the FLN-sponsored Amicale des Algériens en France ("Journée nationale" 1990, 21).

tion de France. Instead, the holiday was largely designed to serve the ideological needs of Boumedienne's authoritarian government in the aftermath of several years of crisis following his military coup in 1965 (Nouschi 1995, 268–78). In this political context, the very public celebration of the Journée nationale de l'émigration served primarily to bolster the government's position as the only legitimate representative of Algerians, both at home and abroad. In fact, however, Algerians in the emigration remained problematic for Boumedienne. He continued to require exit visas of all Algerians who sought to move to France, and although he remained publicly committed to the policy of "reinsertion," he was forced to recognize the Algerian economy's growing dependency on the remittances sent home by emigrant laborers abroad (Naylor 2000, 64–65). The FLN's official newspaper, *El Moudjahid,* continued to use 17 October as the moment to celebrate the nationalist commitments of the emigration, but this did not mean that the regime had rehabilitated the leaders of the Fédération de France.[26]

The first substantial work on the role of the Fédération de France in the revolution was Ali Haroun's *La 7e wilaya: La guerre du FLN en France, 1954–62,* published in France in 1986. Haroun's book, occasionally dismissed by French commentators as an apology for the FLN, is in fact an attempt to rehabilitate only one particular part of it—the Fédération de France. Haroun claimed that the Conseil national de la révolution algérienne (CNRA) consecrated the federation as the seventh *wilaya* or military district in the summer of 1959—the six *wilayas* being the primary units of the struggle against the French in Algeria. Haroun asserted that this status—which elevated his own position within the movement as one of the five directors of the federation—was "hidden, and then unrecognized, as soon as independence was acquired and the faith of militants was so often replaced by political opportunism [*arrivisme politicien*]" (1986, 8). Haroun's implicit criticism of the FLN establishment as it had developed since 1962 was part of a series of works that appeared in the 1980s—all published in France—that sought to reclaim the legitimacy of a revolution that had been diverted from its course by Ahmed Ben Bella and his successors, Houari Boumedienne and Chadli Bendjedid.[27] This need to stimulate discussion of the Fédération de France's role in the revolution also explains why Haroun gave Jean-Luc Einaudi the archive of

26. Jean-Luc Einaudi noted that when he first traveled to Algeria in the 1980s to research the 1961 demonstration, nobody, including the official veteran's group, the Organisation nationale des moujahidine, had ever bothered to undertake a systematic collection of firsthand accounts by witnesses or victims of police violence ("La mémoire" 1991; Marion 1991).

27. See Aït Ahmed 1983, 2000; Abbas 1984; and Harbi [1980] 1993. For a list of other texts by Algerian nationalists, see Stora 1989.

federation documents that the French author used to write his 1991 book on the events of 17 October.

The publication of Ali Haroun's *La 7e wilaya* in 1986 coincided with the onset of a serious political crisis for the FLN regime in Algeria. Economic stagnation and widespread dissatisfaction with the government in the early 1980s forced the government of Chadli Bendjedid (1979–92) to undertake economic reforms that had been postponed under his predecessors. The result was a period of increasing instability and unrest in Algeria that culminated in civil war in the 1990s. Bendjedid sought to shore up support for his policy of economic liberalization by wooing conservatives and leaders of the *arabisant* movement, even as he alienated the FLN cadres who were reluctant to give up the socialist vision upon which the revolution had been founded. The difficulty of this balancing act was illustrated by outbreaks of unrest in Kabylia in 1980 and strikes throughout the country after 1985, when falling oil prices forced Bendjedid's government into an austerity program that it could ill afford. These disturbances, serious though they were, turned out to be only a prologue to the dramatic conflicts that broke out in October 1988, when thousands of rioters clashed with security forces in Bab-el-Oued, a poor and densely populated suburb of Algiers. After several days in which the chaos spread to other Algerian cities, the government declared a state of siege and gave troops the order to shoot on sight. By the time it was over, the government forces—especially the greatly feared Sécurité militaire (SM)—had killed between two hundred and five hundred protesters. In addition, thirty-five hundred young people were arrested, many of them literally children. Most disturbing to those old enough to remember the war years was the fact that many of the young people arrested in Algiers in October 1988 were tortured by the FLN security forces (Stone 1997, 64–67; Naylor 2000, 165–67).

October 1988 revealed the gulf that now separated the FLN regime and the Algerian population—the FLN regime now stood accused of crimes that were comparable to those perpetrated by the French. Ten days after the declaration of martial law in Algiers, the country observed the twenty-seventh anniversary of 17 October 1961, and in official publications such as *Actualité de l'émigration,* published by the Amicale des Algériens en Europe, the FLN regime tried to deflect international protests over its treatment of protesters by invoking the 1961 massacre and the larger history of colonial violence.[28] One need not interpret

28. A typical example is the following statement: "So many voices cry out now in October 1988 to denounce and condemn Algeria after the recent riots in Algiers; but no voice is raised to remember 17 October 1961, and still fewer show the images of the ferocious repression between 1954 to 1962" ("Octobre à Paris" 1988, 40–41).

such efforts as cynical attempts to co-opt the memory of 17 October to meet other needs—one hears rather the accumulated bitterness at decades of international silence over the French government's wartime policies, broken only when the Algerian government revealed itself to be capable of a similar brutality. Still, the fact that the repression in 1988 occurred so close to the anniversary of October 1961 forced many to ponder the connections.[29]

This uncomfortable juxtaposition was soon followed, however, by a change in the Algerian coverage of 17 October. The 1988 demonstrations also created pressures for reform, pressures that forced Bendjedid's government to allow for the development of legal opposition parties. The result was a brief experiment in a more pluralistic society, culminating in the formation of Sid Ahmed Ghozali's government in June 1991. Ghozali's administration had at least the appearance of an independent secular administration with a social democratic complexion. In this atmosphere, former members of the Fédération de France were able to create their own veteran's group, the Association des moujahidine de la Fédération de France du FLN in 1990. On the thirtieth anniversary of 17 October, members of this group appeared alongside members of the Organisation nationale des moujahidine at a colloquium in Algiers, and the history of the *septième wilaya* was given wide attention.[30] This opening up of the commemoration to members of the Fédération de France continued in 1992, when for the first time 17 October was celebrated as a national holiday with the same status as other key dates in the official calendar.[31]

By this time, however, it was too late for those who hoped that a more complete rendering of the history of the war years would foster a renewed sense of civil society in Algeria. For the younger generation that had grown up since independence, neither the traditional myth of the FLN nor the rehabilitation of the Fédération de France had any effect on their dissatisfaction with a regime that had grown increasingly opaque. Lacking viable political alternatives for an Al-

29. During the mid-1980s, the *Actualité de l'émigration* had become accustomed to running a special issue devoted to 17 October every year on the anniversary, at times running to more than forty pages of interviews, historical summaries, and photographs, including the front cover. In 1988, in contrast, there was only a brief note of several paragraphs, accompanied by several photographs in the interior of the magazine.

30. In 1991, seeking to compensate for the years of neglect, the Conseil national of the Organisation nationale des moujahidine passed a resolution recognizing the important role played by the Fédération de France du FLN and highlighting the importance of 17 October 1961 in the struggle against the French ("Le 17 Octobre" 1991; "Résolution" 1991).

31. See, for example, the long article published on the 1993 anniversary of 17 October in *El Moudjahid* ("La Lutte" 1993).

gerian future they could believe in, many people turned to Islam, and it was the Islamic party, the Front islamique du salut (FIS), that profited the most from increasing democratization in the early 1990s. In January 1992, Bendjedid's government collapsed on the eve of elections that the FIS seemed poised to win. Following the suspension of elections, military leaders imprisoned thousands of Islamic militants and brought back Mohamed Boudiaf, the long-exiled former leader of the FLN, to serve as president. In June 1992, Boudiaf himself was assassinated, perhaps by factions within the military who resented his attempts to root out corruption. The resulting civil war claimed tens of thousands of lives, and among the many groups targeted by Islamic militants for assassination—secular intellectuals, women, journalists—were the once-venerated *moujahidine,* veterans of the war with France. The FLN's long attempt to create a unified national identity around the myth of the first nationalist revolution had failed completely.

Entering History

Beginning in the late 1980s and continuing in the 1990s, then, 17 October entered history: in France by way of the glare cast by Maurice Papon's trial for crimes against humanity, and in Algeria in the aftermath of a political crisis that challenged the FLN's monopoly on the history of the nationalist revolution. The demonstration has now been the subject of several films, both documentary and fictional, that appeared on television or in movie theaters in France, and these films continue to be shown in both France and Algeria on the anniversary of the event.[32] In May 1999, Lionel Jospin's government publicly called for archivists to relax the restrictions that had kept the archives of October 1961 sealed, and in large part this wish has been fulfilled in the ensuing years.[33] Meanwhile, associations such as Au nom de la mémoire, 17 octobre 1961 contre l'oubli, and Mou-

32. Films on 17 October 1961 include: *Le silence du fleuve* (Agnes Denis, 1991), *Secret History: Drowning by Bullets* (a British Channel 4 production, shown on 13 July 1992), *17 octobre 1961: Une journée portée disparue* (Philip Brooks and Alan Hayling, 1992), and *Vivre au paradis* (Bourlem Guerdjou, 1999). See note 12 on the status of Jacques Panijel's 1961–62 film *Octobre à Paris.*

33. By law, the Ministry of Culture has authority over archives of government documents in France, but each individual ministry and government office still retains the right to determine which documents are consigned to the archives and for how long they are to remain closed to the public. It is possible for historians to consult documents that are closed to the wider public, but only with special permission. The process of demanding this permission—called a *dérogation*—can be long and at times confusing for researchers. In practice, certain archives, among them the Archives de la Préfecture de police in Paris, have operated with a great deal of autonomy and without much supervision from the Ministry of Culture. Jospin's call for greater accessibility was an attempt to establish some standardization and transparency in this process. I should add, however, that when I requested per-

vement contre le racisme et pour l'acmitié entre les peuples (MRAP) all maintain web sites with information on 17 October, including testimony by witnesses and statements of support from prominent personalities. There is evidence, too, that the message of these *militants de mémoire* has penetrated mainstream political parties. One of the founding members of Au nom de la mémoire, historian David Assouline, is now an aide to the socialist mayor of Paris, Bertrand Delanoë.

It is not clear, however, that the event is understood by the general public in France. In 1992, a poll undertaken by the Ligue de l'enseignement and the Institut du monde Arabe gave some grounds for hope: the poll revealed that although only 22 percent of young people in France age seventeen to thirty could name a leader of the Algerian revolution (usually Ben Bella or Boumedienne), fully 55 percent of the respondents knew that on 17 October 1961 "about a hundred Algerians who were demonstrating peaceably were killed by the police" and that "numerous corpses were thrown into the Seine" (P. Bernard 1992). But at the end of the decade, a CSA agency poll revealed that less than half of all French people had heard of 17 October, and only one out of five "knew what the demonstration was about" (Bernard and Garin 2001).

Meanwhile, the controversy over the opening of the police archives and the publication of the first works of history by those who have had access to these archives has not settled debates about the extent of the repression or about the responsibility of the prefect of police, Maurice Papon. On the side of those who claim that Papon must bear full responsibility for the massacre that occurred in Paris, the works of reference remain Jean-Luc Einaudi's 1991 book *La bataille de Paris* and a second book that he published in 2001 after he was finally given permission to examine the archives, *Octobre 1961: Un massacre à Paris.* On the other side, Jean-Paul Brunet's *Police contre FLN: Le drame d'octobre 1961* remains the work of choice for those whose political loyalties lead them to avoid any suggestion that they might agree with the FLN about anything.[34] Einaudi stands by his initial estimate of two hundred people killed, whereas Brunet wrote that he could be reasonably certain only about thirty-one deaths attributable to police action. Too much attention to the disagreement about numbers, however, has distracted commentators from the fundamental differences of approach that each of these works takes, differences making it inevitable that the confrontation between their respective accounts will merely serve to prolong debate, rather than settle it.

---

mission to see the documents in the police archives regarding the 17 October in the spring of 2002, I found the staff to be very cooperative, and the permission was granted in a matter of weeks.

34. See, for example, the review of Brunet's book in *Figaro* (Roussel 1999).

The Prefecture of Police refused to give Jean-Luc Einaudi access to the police archives because he was not an academically trained historian. He was (and is), however, a prolific author who had already published several books. He wrote *La bataille de Paris* based primarily on the testimony of eyewitnesses. He treats these sources largely as individuals, without seeking to place their various political engagements in context. His technique is to convince by the accumulated weight of testimony, and it is as important for him to give voice to those whose stories have long been ignored as it is to attribute responsibility for the deaths to French officials. Einaudi's desire to let these voices be heard without being challenged was no doubt responsible for his willingness to report allegations that have little or no corroborating evidence, such as the reports of poison gas being used in the Palais des Sports and the Stade de Coubertin (Einaudi 1991, 190–93). It is safe to assume that Einaudi's relatively uncritical attitude toward the testimony of witnesses guaranteed a higher estimate of the number of dead.

In Einaudi's work, one can detect the echoes of an opinion that has become widespread among those who organized themselves to commemorate the anniversaries of October 1961 in recent years—that the distinction between memory and history is neither fixed nor absolute, and that attempts to define such clear delineations are always context specific and political. In other words, people make distinctions between history and memory because they want to accomplish something, as the Prefecture of Police did when it concluded that what Einaudi published was not "history" and therefore that he was not entitled to see the police archives related to the demonstration. From this perspective, any attempt to preserve a pure and idealized realm of historical practice, free from the interference of ideology and politics, will ultimately fail because historical pronouncements about complex societies are inevitably bound up in the labeling of collectivities and in the examination of individuals' places within them, acts of definition that themselves have political consequences. The various organizations involved in commemorating 17 October accept these political consequences and indeed seek them out—their goal is to foster a broader sense of citizenship and belonging in France by commemorating the sacrifices and sufferings of groups that were targeted for persecution in the past. Accepting such a position does not mean, however, that one should give "memory" free rein—Einaudi has disassociated himself from commemorative organizations that label the demonstration of 17 October an example of "genocide" because he does not believe that police actions that day merit that label (Einaudi 2001, 66–67).

Jean-Paul Brunet, in his 1999 book *Police contre FLN,* explicitly opposed this view in the name of a historical practice that actively seeks to protect itself from the intrusion of politics. Brunet is a professional historian who has written many books on twentieth-century French history, including books on the police, on the working-class suburb of Saint-Denis, and on the socialist and communist movements in France. In the introductory chapter to *Police contre FLN,* he claims that he took it upon himself to write a book about 17 October because of a personal conviction that the story had been distorted by a Manichean opposition between those who sympathized too much with the FLN and the self-exculpating testimony given by Papon himself in his memoirs. Brunet also feared that a consensus had been established around Einaudi's 1991 book that was not firmly based on reliable evidence. He set about to rectify this situation with a book that is both a model of verifiable empirical procedures and at the same time a profoundly and unself-consciously political book that refuses to acknowledge either the extraordinary privilege he enjoyed as one of the first three historians to be granted access to the archives or the position that his book occupies in a larger debate about the relationship between history, memory, and citizenship in contemporary France.[35]

Brunet's work examines in minute detail the available evidence on the number of protesters who were killed on 17 October, and in many ways his caution is commendable. He details with care the reasons for including each case in his final tally, and he concludes the book with a summary: thirteen cases where he is certain the police were responsible, eight likely, four probable, six possible, making for a total of thirty-one. Admitting that his sources may have been incomplete, he hazards a range of between thirty and fifty, with the probability of accuracy decreasing as one moves up the scale. The difference between this estimate and Einaudi's count of two hundred can be accounted for by their different attitudes toward witnesses' testimony. For example, Einaudi reports without question the testimony of Gérard Grange, a seminary student who was doing his military service at the Fort de Vincennes in October 1961 and who was called along with his unit to the detention center at the Palais des Sports to help with the distribution of food to the prisoners. During the day, he witnessed the beatings the police gave to prisoners on their arrival, and in the evening a captain, whom he did not know, took him to a room where he saw the bodies of nine prisoners (Einaudi 2001, 221–24). Brunet mentions Grange's testimony but concludes that because these bodies were never registered at the morgue, Grange must have seen nine inanimate but still living prisoners (1999, 228, 268). Likewise, Brunet several times cites the testimony of police officer Raoul Letard to illustrate the mood and attitudes of the police on the evening of the demonstration. He does not cite, how-

35. See Brunet's explicit refusal to justify or explain the fact that he had been chosen among the original three historians who were allowed in the archives (1999, 17–18).

ever, Letard's assertion that after the "manhunt" in the Colombes housing complex near the Neuilly Bridge, a police van had collected the bodies and returned to the police station with "more than a few corpses [pas mal des morts]."[36] Nowhere does Brunet question what became of these bodies, and in his final tally he dismisses such accounts as unfounded rumors (1999, 329).

With witness testimony that tends to support his larger argument about the FLN's responsibility, however, Brunet is more indulgent. For example, in his account of the crucial confrontation on the bridge at Neuilly, in which shots were fired and several demonstrators hit, he cites first the testimony of Pierre Mézière, the police commissioner from Puteaux, who directed the operations on the bridge, and two civilian witnesses, both non-Algerian French citizens. Mézière reported seeing the flashes from the muzzles of guns among the protesters before his forces opened fire in return, and Brunet corroborates this account with the testimony of "witness C.," a businessman from Colombes who happened to be passing by and joined the police on the bridge after perceiving them to be outnumbered by protesters, and of "Mme A.," a resident on the third floor of a nearby apartment building. Without dismissing the possibility that provocateurs among the ranks of the protesters sought to incite a violent response from the police, one should simply note that Brunet's account is the result of inevitable decisions made about who to listen to and who not to hear. The accumulated weight of these decisions results in his overall conclusion that many fewer people died than is commonly supposed and that the responsibility for these deaths is shared by the FLN. In fact, Brunet's criteria for including deaths in his account guaranteed that his result would be substantially lower than Einaudi's.

The political nature of Brunet's narrative is accentuated by his decision to use the term *Algerian* to refer to the protesters without ever mentioning the fact that they were still "French" in 1961 and without examining the political context that framed their presence in metropolitan France at the time—that is, the facts that many of them had been actively recruited for their labor and that they were the focus of a concerted effort of social assistance that both contributed to their segregation and facilitated the work of the police in keeping them under surveillance. Brunet might argue that such details were irrelevant to the task he set for himself—of examining empirically Einaudi's charges that two hundred people had been killed by the police on 17 October—but by carrying this work further and attributing responsibility for the deaths, he unavoidably entered into the difficult and intractable debates about the French state's relationship to this population and the degree to which protesters on the street in 1961 could be held

36. For Brunet's discussion of Raoul Letard, see Brunet 1999, 87–88, 90, 180–81, 184, 260.

accountable for the actions of FLN militants. Brunet concludes that the FLN leadership bears a large part of the responsibility for the tragedy because they ordered the demonstration at a moment when "France was in a state of war. . . , a war that the FLN had imported to France" (1999, 338). But the logic of this argument only works to attenuate the police hierarchy's responsibility if one assumes that France and Algeria were two qualitatively different places and that what happened on one side of the Mediterranean had no relationship at all to what happened on the other. Brunet's argument assumes that the war somehow belonged only in Algeria, and the fact that French troops were there had no relation to the situation in the metropole. One does not need to take the FLN's side to point out that the cycle of violence that bound the French and Algerians together during this period was a great deal more complicated than Brunet characterizes it here, and to make this assertion is to slip into precisely the Manichean opposition that he so earnestly sought to reject at the outset of his book.[37]

17 October 2001

In October 2001, the socialist mayor of Paris, Bertrand Delanoë commemorated the victims of police violence on 17 October 1961 by placing a plaque on the St.-Michel Bridge, where the fourth and fifth *arrondissements* come together. The plaque reads: "To the memory of Algerians who were victims of a bloody repression during a peaceful demonstration." The location of the memorial is symbolically central to the city: the bridge is only two blocks from Notre Dame Cathedral, and the street that crosses the bridge runs in between the Palace of Justice and the Prefecture of Police. On the left-bank side of the bridge is the Place Saint-Michel, where hundreds of protesters were beaten and arrested on 17 October 1961. In spite of all this, the choice of a spot was inevitably dictated by municipal politics: the plaque was placed on the side of the bridge that fell in the jurisdiction of the fourth *arrondissement,* whose mayor, Dominique Bertinotti, was a socialist. The other side of the bridge falls in the fifth *arrondissement,* ruled by the former Gaullist mayor of Paris, Jean Tiberi (Bernard and Garin 2001).

This commemoration fulfilled a promise that Delanoë made while campaigning for the mayor's post earlier in the year. Much to the disappointment of human rights activists, Delanoë elected not to speak at the dedication of the plaque, though he was accompanied by other members of the Paris Municipal Council. Official invitations to the ceremony included all 163 municipal council members, the fourth *arrondissement's* legislative delegation to the National Assembly, and

37. Two recent works sensitive to the need to go beyond the tendency to treat this history in terms of fixed oppositions between "French" and "Algerian" are Le Sueur 2001 and Shepard 2002.

a range of human rights organizations, including MRAP, and the Ligue des droits de l'homme. The municipal council's right-wing members boycotted the ceremony, and Prime Minister Lionel Jospin, a socialist like Delanoë, sent no representatives from his government. Delanoë's staff insisted that only the minister of the interior, Daniel Vaillant, had been invited in his role as a member of the Paris delegation to the National Assembly. But Vaillant did not come; the minister of the interior still has authority over the police in France, and the major police trade unions had strongly opposed the placement of the memorial, including those who had protested against the violence in 1961.[38]

Meanwhile, in addition to the official ceremony organized by the mayor's office, a separate demonstration organized by a coalition of human rights groups and political activists gathered at 6:00 P.M. at the Rex Cinema and marched to the Pont Saint-Michel in memory of the victims and against what they called "a crime against humanity." More than sixty organizations were represented in the coalition, including the Ligue des droits de l'homme, MRAP, and Act Up, as well as trade unions and various parties from the left, including Lutte ouvrière, Ligue communiste révolutionaire, the Greens, the Communists, and the Paris federation of the Socialist Party ("40e anniversaire" 2001). The League of the Rights of Man noted its satisfaction "that the Mayor of Paris recognizes forty years after the fact the reality of a massacre that had the approval of the political authorities of the time" (*La Polémique* 2001).

The Parisian Right protested bitterly. Claude Goasguen, of the center-right Démocratie libérale stated: "I expect the mayor of Algiers to dedicate at the same time a plaque commemorating the assassination of dozens of thousands of *harkis* whose throats were cut" ("La polémique" 2001). When a Green Party municipal councilor, Sylvain Garrel, spoke of "a large-scale crime ordered and covered-up by the highest state authorities," citing Charles de Gaulle, Maurice Papon, Roger Frey, and Michel Debré, members of the right-wing parties briefly walked out of the National Assembly chamber (Bernard and Garin 2001).

If this debate is evidence of anything, it is that the Manichean opposition Jean-Paul Brunet sought to avoid still structures all attempts to talk about what happened between the French and Algerians between 1954 and 1962. No matter

38. Just as significant as Daniel Vaillant's absence, perhaps, was the fact that the current prefect of police, Jean-Paul Proust, commented publicly on the affair, making him the first person in this office since Maurice Papon to mention 17 October 1961 at all. Proust stated, "One can only deplore certain offenses committed in October 1961." Aware of the anger of the police unions, Proust sought to strike a balance, insisting that "memory should recognize all the victims of the French-Algerian War. . . . I also have a duty to remember those police officers who died in the line of duty during the Algerian War." See "40e anniversaire" 2001.

how one decides to tell this story, it seems impossible to render it on its own terms. What would these terms be? When one relates the events of 17 October 1961, can one really discern if the protesters were Algerians demanding independence or French people demanding the rights to public space in the city or simply frightened laborers and their families with few options, caught between the fear of punishment by the FLN for not participating and the fear of certain violence from a police force that had been unhinged by attacks on its members? All of these options are both more or less possible and more or less inadequate to address the complexities of a situation that cannot be entirely mastered by any particular historical account—or by any particular act of commemoration. It is clear, however, that the opposition we are now faced with, between the "militant journalism" of Jean-Luc Einaudi and the cautious but unself-consciously political empiricism of Jean-Paul Brunet, will not be resolved until both sides recognize the extent to which their claims for historical veracity are inseparable from the political controversy that engulfs any discussion of the memory of 17 October. The work of history, like the work of citizenship, requires an ability to hear the multiplicity of voices that constitute the social realm and to be self-conscious about the ways in which the necessary institutions of public life—governments, universities, archives—determine which voices are more easily discerned and which are forgotten.

9 Memory in History, Nation Building, and Identity

Teaching about the Algerian War in France

JO McCORMACK

REMEMBERING THE ALGERIAN WAR (1954–62) in contemporary France continues to prove highly problematic forty years after the end of the conflict. The events surrounding the publication in May 2001 of General Paul Aussaresses's *Services spéciaux: Algérie 1955–1957* (2001b) highlight this fact. In France, there has been "a very polemical and media-orientated reactivation of the memory"[1] of this period, which confronts commentators with a number of paradoxes. On the one hand, the war in Algeria was a hugely significant event in recent French history. Yet, on the other, it is a conflict that unlike the two world wars was rarely referred to in the public or private spheres in France until very recently. It is a memory that for a long time was characterized by "absence of the 'Algerian war' " and "apparent forgetting" (Stora 1994, 131), yet that has recently been extremely present in the media (at least for a period). Much of what Aussaresses "revealed" had already been discovered and published by activists at the time of the war and by some historians since, yet the book appears to have shocked many. This chapter attempts to explain these paradoxes by pointing to the lack of transmission of memories of the Algerian War through a case study of one vector of memory: public-school history classes. It also suggests that continued concern (especially by the state) of the high stakes of the Algerian War has hindered greater discussion of the period, leading to the violent "return of repressed memories" currently being witnessed. Further difficulties occur concerning finding an appropriate public-sphere arena in which to remember together where "the traditional model [of commemoration] has shattered" to be replaced by "a broken-up system, made of disparate commemorative languages, which assumes a

1. See Jack Lang's 29 August 2001 speech at http://www.education.gouv.fr/discours/2001/algeriejl.htm.

different relationship with the past, with more room for choice and less obligation, which is open, plastic, alive and constantly changing" (Nora 1992, 985, 983–84).

This chapter focuses on history classes not only because they are an important form of transmission of memory in their own right, but also because they lie at the intersection of memory, history, nation building, and identity. By looking at the way the war is taught, we can comment on these relationships. Alfred Grosser has made the point that collective memory is effectively "transmission via the family, school and the media" (quoted in Durmelat 2000, 175) rather than an actual memory. The historian Henry Rousso in his book *Le syndrome de Vichy* describes textbooks and school history programs as "the mode of social transmission par excellence" of memory (1990, 253). This comment immediately foregrounds the link between memory and history because it is history that is taught. Rousso also refers to historiography as "scholarly memory" (1990, 253). Furthermore, it is historians who have been called upon by France's political leaders Lionel Jospin and Jacques Chirac to investigate recent revelations about torture.

Education has long been established in France as a central pillar of the republic. The role of subjects such as philosophy and history has been primordial since the Third Republic and the reforms of Jules Ferry that made primary education secular, free, and compulsory. This role has certainly changed and evolved, but it remains extremely important. In particular, history classes are still viewed as playing a role in creating or maintaining present national unity and cohesion (nation building or nation maintaining) and in forging identity. As the authors of the latest history program in France state: "the role of a history program is vital for insertion in the city, through the discovery of what constitutes the basis of a human community" (Berstein and Borne 1996, 136). They also say the history program should "provide young people with those elements of a national memory which forge their identity" (Berstein and Borne 1996, 142). In *Vingtième siècle,* Dominique Borne, who designed the 1989 program and cochaired the group that designed the 1998 program, likened school history programs to "[the national photo album] that binds together a community like the family album gives depth to families" (1989, 104). The historian Philippe Joutard, commenting on a huge media debate at the end of the 1970s around the teaching of history, stated: "This crisis and its favorable outcome for the place of history teaching in schools proves, if this were necessary, *the strength of the historical component in French culture and identity*" (1995, 51, my italics). So the history program is clearly important in transmitting memories and thus influencing national cohesion and identity, but what is included in this history?

By examining what is taught, we are able to "read" the program and see to what extent the common history between France and Algeria is included in the view of France's past proposed to pupils. What information on the Algerian War is deemed inherent to pupils' identity? How are the various conflicting memory groups brought together, given that "[t]he teaching of history aims to transform individual and group memories into a common memory" (Peyrot 1990, 10)?[2] To what extent does the Algerian War have a place in the official narrative of France's past? Overall, what do we deduce from the treatment of the Algerian War about Algeria's role in the construction of a French sense of cultural identity? Indeed, in the only previous collection that focuses on the question of identity in Franco-Algerian relations, Jean-Robert Henry does discuss history and school textbooks when addressing French-Algerian identity exchanges (1993, 7).

To answer these questions, my corpus includes interviews with two French historians (Jean-Pierre Rioux and Serge Berstein), eighteen teachers who work in Lyons (some of *pied-noir* origin), and twelve pupils (two-thirds of whom are of Algerian descent). This sample is obviously small. The disadvantage of this approach is that the sample can never be representative. Conversely, it allows more detailed questioning in a qualitative analysis and represents the first time that teachers and historians have been interviewed in this way on this subject. In addition to cochairing the group that designed the 1998 history program, Berstein was for many years the editor of the school textbook published by Hatier. Jean-Pierre Rioux edited *La guerre d'Algérie et les Français* and is currently *inspecteur général de l'éducation nationale* (civil servant involved in educational inspections). The interviews were conducted between 1998 and 2000 and constituted much of the interest and originality of the project. The chapter also draws on written sources such as textbooks and examination questions. The study is limited to the *terminale,* the final year of high school, in order to focus on the year that crowns French secondary education and at the end of which pupils sit the ever-important *baccalauréat.*

To begin with, one can argue that too little use has been made in the history program of the knowledge amassed on the Algerian War by historians in the 1980s and 1990s. This fact leads me to believe that the writing of history is not the main problem in evoking the Algerian War; rather, it is the diffusion of these findings and their discussion. Such diffusion involves both effective transmission and reception. Although I believe reception (e.g., reading the books written or watching the films made about the subject) to be a major obstacle in wider French society, transmission is particularly problematic in the educative sphere. Indeed,

2. Jean Peyrot was president of the Association des professeurs d'histoire et de géographie for many years.

in 1983, when post-Second World War history began to be taught in *terminale,* historical knowledge on the Algerian War was very limited. Speaking in 1983 at the Agoras méditerranéennes in Marseilles, the historian Guy Pervillé (1986) pointed to the absence of scientific debate on the war. In the early 1990s, an article in *Le Monde* characterized progress in historiography in the early 1980s as barely begun—"recherche à peine entamée"—and in the early 1990s as having begun—"recherche entamée" (Kajman 1992, 15). In the early 1980s, the only properly scholarly work in French on the Algerian War as a whole was Bernard Droz and Evelyne Lever's *Histoire de la guerre d'Algérie 1954–1962* (1982). Historiography then was characterized by "témoignages pour la politique" (testimony written with a political motive), "témoignages pour l'histoire" (testimony for posterity), and a few books written by journalists, rather than by much scholarly work.[3]

The writing of the Algerian War has been a slow and long process. Charles-Robert Ageron wrote in the early 1990s that it was not then possible to write a scientifically acceptable history of the Algerian War (1993a, 155). The principle obstacle was lack of access to written archives. Restricting access to archives is one way the French state has been able to occlude the war. The political situation in Algeria was also a hindrance, putting more archives out of reach and making collaboration between French and Algerian scholars extremely difficult. Memory too was an obstacle: "Thirty years after this tragedy, wounds remain unhealed and passions blaze each time memories are called upon" (Ageron 1993a, 155). Hence, we can begin to understand the difficulties in researching (or teaching) such a subject. But scholars have published some excellent work on the war, particularly with the gradual opening of archives. For example, the late 1980s saw *La guerre d'Algérie et les Français,* edited by Jean-Pierre Rioux (1990), and the mid-1990s witnessed *La guerre d'Algérie et les Algériens* edited by Charles-Robert Ageron (1997). The 1990s saw increasing access to archives. In this way, since 1992 it has been quite common to read in the *Annuaire de l'Afrique du Nord* (which annually includes a very useful bibliography of work published on the Algerian War) comments such as, "The author retraces the history of the Algerian War thanks to recent access to French military archives," or "The documentary work, which draws on varied sources, was facilitated by the progressive opening to the public of archives" (*Annuaire de l'Afrique du Nord* 1993, 865, and 1995, 1096). Yet even by the early 1990s nearly seventy Ph.D.s had been

3. See the *Annuaire de l'Afrique du Nord* annually for an appreciation of historiographical developments concerning the Algerian War.

written on the Algerian War in France (see *Mémoire et enseignement* 1993, 159–64). Since then, many others have appeared. Work by new scholars such as Claire Mausse-Copeaux, Sylvie Thénault, and Raphaëlle Branche has been published. Nonetheless, during this time Ageron stated that it was "still not possible to write a history that would be accepted by all Algerians and all French people" (1997, 4).

Yet as historiography has developed, the amount taught on the Algerian War in the *terminale* history class has dramatically decreased, as indicated in various school textbooks. Studying textbook content reveals a significant difference between pre- and post-1998 editions' presentations of information on the war in Algeria. In 1998, the program was changed. For the 1998 editions of different textbooks, the average number of words on the Algerian war was 950—that is, about 1.5 pages of text—to which can be added on average eleven documents (roughly 2 pages of documents). Such textbooks typically run to between 350 and 400 pages. In 1995, in contrast, the average coverage of the Algerian War was 1,500 words, about 2.5 pages of text, to which were added on average sixteen documents. There was therefore significantly less coverage in 1998, all the more so if we also take into consideration the findings of Guy Pervillé and Paul Fournier, who in 1983 talked of an average of about 9 or 10 pages on the Algerian War, ranging from 2 to 20 pages (see Pervillé and Fournier 1986, 893–98). The Hatier textbook, edited by Serge Berstein and Pierre Milza (1983–98) (which is highly instructive given the place of Berstein in the group that designed the 1998 program), experienced perhaps the most pronounced changes between 1983 and 1998: in 1983, it had 3,500 words on the Algerian War, but in 1998 only 600 words.

Teacher comments during interviews confirm these findings. The change in program in 1998 reduced the coverage of the Algerian War. One teacher said: "I know that this year I'm dwelling less on, let's say on details, or rather on particular points. And the Algerian War, if we study it, involves going into detail" (Teacher 12). On the change in program, another teacher stated: "we are asked to insist on long time periods in a much more general fashion. Therefore, in fact, we are asked to go into less detail." She also said: "We should spend less time on decolonization. We should cite the Algerian War only as an example of a colonial war, but without going into much detail" (Teacher 11). Events were dropped owing to the change in program, and those events still studied were dealt with more quickly and superficially. Whereas in my pre-1998 sample, teachers on average spent 2.5 hours studying the Algerian War, after 1998 this figure fell to 1.5 hours.

Furthermore, because the Algerian War ended only forty years ago, many of the participants are alive, so there is a tremendous potential for testimony to be given in class on the war. Millions of people living in France were in Algeria during the war. However, this resource is not used. Only two of the teachers in my corpus had invited veterans of the Algerian War into class. One of the two teachers had done so more than ten years ago. The meeting involved a veteran and an Algerian to get two viewpoints on the war and lasted two hours. Above all, the discussion created much interest and many questions—notably on the everyday life in Algeria as well as feelings and opinions at the time of the war. That meeting took place twice in the early 1980s, and according to the teacher has not been done recently since: "It has not been repeated because in the old programs we had more time, and so since we had less time in these programs, it hasn't been done again" (Teacher 4).

Another teacher said that he had not been able to invite a veteran of the Algerian War to give a testimony in class owing to time and practical considerations, but would have liked to. He said in the interview that he would have liked to invite a man called Bernard Gerland, who has written a monologue on his experience as a soldier that he has been presenting since 1995 (Gerland 2001). Gerland gives a fascinating and very memorable narrative that I was lucky enough to see in a theater in Lyons in 1997. It is, however, a hard-hitting account as, after a somewhat positive introduction to his time in Algeria, he suddenly begins to describe how he executed a prisoner in a *corvée de bois* (illicit summary execution after interrogation). Clearly, he has never recovered from this act.

An overall picture of the way the Algerian War is taught thus emerges here in even this small study. Textbooks contain little on the Algerian War; most include a preponderant number of documents but relatively little text. The war has an ambiguous position in the program. It can be dealt with in the section on *decolonisation* or in the section on *histoire intérieure* on the Fourth and Fifth Republics. The war certainly figures in the program and has done since 1983. It is studied in different subjects, yet it is not really studied in its own right and actually ends up being marginal.

When asked about the lessons, pupils said: "it wasn't particularly on Algeria, it was global"; "we didn't do a special lesson on the Algerian War"; "we didn't study it as such" (Pupil 8); and "it isn't the Algerian War itself" (Pupil 12). Teachers concurred: "The Algerian War isn't really studied in its own right" (Teacher 1). When the Algerian War is evoked in the chapter of the program on decolonization, the aim "is to show the overall problems of decolonization and how that translated for France" (Teacher 2). Alternatively, in the chapter on the Fifth

Republic, "we see the main stages, but in the middle of an analysis of Gaullist achievements at that moment" (Teacher 1). Another teacher said:

> The objective is the examination—the *baccalauréat*—so the content of class has to help them to answer questions; they don't simply get questions on the Algerian War, so what we do in class helps them to answer questions on decolonization—France and decolonization or decolonizations in general—or on the French Fifth Republic. The Algerian war is always studied in the context of other subjects. (Teacher 7)

Hence, although it is true to say that the Algerian War is studied in *terminale,* closer inspection reveals that the study of the war is very partial. The program deals with certain aspects of the war, and in general the conflict is used to explain wider phenomena such as decolonization and French political evolution. As a teacher who talked me through a chronology taken from *Le Monde* said, "There are a lot of things that are dropped, that are often not done" (Teacher 10). As he indicated, elements of the war given in the chronology but not studied in class include the creation of the Mouvement national algérien (MNA); the decision to call up again soldiers who had already done their military service *(les rappelés);* "la journée des tomates" (when Guy Mollet was angrily received during his visit to Algeria); the massacre of French conscripts in Palestro; terrorist attacks in Algiers; the hijacking of Ben Bella and others; the massacre of MNA supporters by the Front de libération nationale (FLN) at Melouza; the bombing of Sakhiet-Sidi Youssef; the Jeanson trial; the "Manifeste des 121"; Charonne; and the massacre of European settlers by the French army in rue d'Isly in Algiers. Many of the most painful and divisive events in the Algerian War are thus not studied.

Examination questions reflect this emphasis. Questions set at the *baccalauréat* are generally on decolonization or on the French Fourth and Fifth Republics in mainland France: "the emancipation of colonies since 1945," "France and decolonization," "assessment of the Fourth Republic," and "De Gaulle's presidency." Between 1983 and 1999, in mainland France in the June sessions of different *académies,* the Algerian War was central to only 3 out of 450 questions. Outside metropolitan France, however (i.e., in the Départements d'outre-mer-Territoires d'outre-mer [DOM-TOM] and *lycées français à l'étranger*), more questions are given that concern the Algerian War: "France and the Algerian problem"; "De Gaulle and the generals' putsch"; "France, the French, and the Algerian War"; "the Algerian problem and its impact on the political life of the Fourth and Fifth Republics"; "De Gaulle and the Algerian question"; or "the Algerian national movement."

In France, a general overview of the war is performed, which excludes detail. Torture is one aspect of the Algerian War that is not studied in detail in class. One teacher said: "We can't go into the details of either military operations or in fact this or that significant detail, like for example the role of torture. We speak of the problem of torture, but we cite it quickly; we don't need to go further" (Teacher 5).

In the interviews, teachers often highlighted the lack of time to study this war. Phrases such as "we have to go very quickly," "in *terminale* I can't find the time," or "it's extremely quick" punctuated all interviews. The *terminale* history program is huge.

Lack of time also severely limits the use of audiovisual sources in class. Numerous excellent documentaries have been produced on the Algerian War, including Yves Courrière's *La guerre d'Algérie* (1972), Peter Batty's *La guerre d'Algérie* (1984), Benjamin Stora's *Les années algériennes* (1991), and Bernard Tavernier and Patrick Rotman's *La guerre sans nom* (1992a).[4] The *harkis* (Algerians who fought on the French side during the war) and the pro-colonial Organisation armée sécrète (OAS) have also been the subject of recent documentaries and many films dealing with the Algerian War. Some teachers used documentaries or films in the past, but can no longer. While teaching about torture, one teacher used a section of a documentary on the subject in which there were interviews with soldiers and Algerians. She stopped doing this four or five years before 1998 owing to time constraints, and more recently in class had instead "tackled torture rather randomly, in a haphazard fashion" (Teacher 15). Another teacher used films more in *première* (the year before *terminale,* in which teachers have more time for some subjects) and in *terminale* used *bande d'actualité*—for example, film footage of 13 May 1958 or bits of de Gaulle speeches. Teacher 9 would like to show Tavernier and Rotman's *La guerre sans nom* but cannot find the time. Teacher 4 had shown the film *Avoir 20 ans dans l'Aurès* four times in class before 1983, but in a citizenship class *(instruction civique)* rather than in history class. He said there was no time to do so in current history classes. In short, films exist, but are not watched (in full) owing to time constraints resulting from the nature of the *terminale* program. Hence, education mirrors society insofar as the tremendous amount of information available on the Algerian War is largely ignored.

Perhaps most important, this overall treatment of the Algerian War reflects the fact that there is or was no *volontarisme de mémoire* (will to remember) concerning the Algerian War. To invite veterans or to show films requires more time. Given the spate of developments recently in remembering the war, this situation

4. For a full appreciation of the wealth of film on the Algerian War, see Dine 1994.

may be changing, as the holding of a *université d'été* in August 2001 on the subject suggests (organized by Jack Lang, France's minister of education). Other developments such as naming the war and an *hommage aux harkis* also point to greater recognition of the importance of the war and the need for a greater *travail de mémoire* (work of remembering), to use Paul Ricoeur's (2000) expression. For Rioux, there is neither a *volontarisme de mémoire* nor a *volonté d'occultation* (will to forget) in the history program on this subject. In my opinion, the Algerian War is not deemed sufficiently important in itself for a more detailed study in the current history program in France. Hence, it has become only a small part in "global history" and has been lost. According to Berstein, who cochaired the group that designed the 1998 program, "the Algerian War as such almost never appears in the program. The program is France from 1945 to the present day. So the Algerian War is bound to be in there, of course. But the war doesn't appear as such in the program" (Berstein 2000).

Yet we know the historical importance of the Algerian War, the aims of the program, and how important the conflict is to understanding contemporary France. So is not the time given to it in the program therefore rather inadequate? The different aims of the program seem to be incoherent: giving students a memory and helping them to understand the present necessitates a more detailed study of the Algerian War, but this cannot be done if "global history" is to be studied, with shorter events avoided.

What is more, the divisive nature of the subject may be one reason why so little is taught about it. For Rioux,

> The republican school in France does not think we should favor the Algerian War to the detriment of other events also so as not to take the risk, because the school authorities do not want this, of inflaming the memory conflicts that exist and that one can detect in class, evidently, so as always to bring them back to elements of knowledge and knowledge acquisition for all pupils on a phenomenon like the Algerian War. (2000)

In 1995, Rioux gave an interview on French collective memory of the Algerian War in France in which he stated: "There is too much tension at present to feed a memory of the past" (1995, 90). He also said: "The work of grieving will be finished when the dispersion of memories is less pronounced. And that will occur over time, as the generations that lived through the Algerian War disappear. Today it is too early" (1995, 91). Hence, (divisive) memory can inhibit the teaching of history. The place of the Algerian War in the program contrasts strongly with the amount of teaching currently devoted to the Vichy period.

The study of Vichy and the Second World War occupies a huge place in the program, about one-quarter of the year. Textbooks typically have four chapters on this subject, totaling about eighty pages in textbooks that have four hundred pages. These chapters address crucial subjects such as collaboration and extermination. Film and testimony can be used in class to illustrate the history of Vichy. Pupils interviewed in my sample had visited the Centre d'histoire de la résistance et de la déportation in Lyons. Examination questions on the subject are given very regularly. This subject was reintroduced in *terminale* in 1998 largely because of the actions of Resistance veterans who were very unhappy that this period of history would not be sufficiently studied at the end of the year in *première*. The Algerian War does not benefit from such a *volontarisme de mémoire*. Nor do supporters of a greater study of the Algerian War, including veterans, have such influence. A tremendous amount of effort has been put into remembering Vichy, and the program has reflected wider French society in integrating this essential study.

Hence, one can conclude that the Algerian War as a subject is still too divisive to discuss in greater depth, in a way that the Vichy period no longer is. Such a point was mentioned in an article in *Libération* in June 2000. The historian Pascal Blanchard was defending the Musée des Arts Africains et Océaniens (MAAO) as a possible *lieu de mémoire* (site of memory) to "refresh the memory of a France that has forgotten its past as a colonial power." He said:

> unlike the somber pages of collaboration and the French Vichy state, the republic still does not assume its colonial history. . . . Today it is the state (and the Republic) which is/are the obstruction. . . . The time has come to propose in the only republican symbolic site soon to be available, the MAAO, a veritable area of knowledge of this past, which is the first indispensable step toward breaking the infernal machine of the de facto "nonexistence" of these "populations" within the republic. . . . [I]t is through a move toward global awareness (not only media-oriented), which draws on memory and knowledge of our common past that mentalities will change. (2000)

Education is clearly still important in nation building or nation maintaining, as comments by the program designers themselves bear out. In the *terminale* history program, the divisive memories born of the Algerian War are to be brought together, but only through a cursory study of the war. Furthermore, the educative vector of memory is influenced by other vectors (such as family transmission of memory), and we can speculate that only when greater discussion of the period occurs in France can more be taught in class. In my 2000 interview with Berstein, he said that what was taught changed over time and depended on "the information that society has had about the phenomenon in the meantime," influencing "what is acceptable to include [in the program or in a textbook]"; he also argued that a textbook's "purpose is not to shock a part of society" and is linked to a "phenomenon of respecting society" (Berstein 2000). I believe this means that if trials took place examining crimes committed during the Algerian War or the conflict was commemorated more, to take only two examples, it would become easier to teach certain aspects of it. Forgetting is still necessary for cohesion in society, as Renan argued over a century ago (as given in Bhabha 1990). In a somewhat Halbwachsian perspective, memory (selective memory) and history seem to be the necessary glue for society.

What does the case study tell us about exclusion and inclusion, French identity and Franco-Algerian culture exchanges? To my mind, it shows that this aspect of French identity—a colonial identity, clearly influenced by a seven-year war of decolonization in Algeria and modified still further by emigration from this area in the whole post-1945 period—is not sufficiently included in official French history. Yet the subject is present in the classroom. For example, one teacher stated: "In the school on the outskirts of town where I teach, nearly 20 percent of the pupils are of Maghrebian descent. I think it's interesting to teach them this part of their history, which is also our history. Similarly, we attempt to spend more time on Islam and on Maghrebian societies, or rather on Islamic societies in general, in the context of the program—which deals with these issues fairly well—but as much as possible . . . we try to talk about these things in more depth" (Teacher 1).

Initiatives have been taken to teach more on immigration and Islam. The Haut conseil à l'intégration (HCI, High Council on Integration), in its December 2000 report *Islam in the Republic,* recommends "a new approach to cultures of origin," a knowledge of which must be "transmitted openly and to the whole of the school community in order to facilitate a 'living-together' spirit [*le 'vivre-ensemble'*]" (Ternisien 2000, 10). Ségolène Royale in particular engaged with the idea of changing the program to include more on the history of immigration (Guibert 2000). There has also been increased questioning of the teaching of the Algerian War. As noted earlier, one *université d'été* entitled "Apprendre et enseigner l'Algérie et le Maghreb contemporain" (Learning and Teaching about Algeria and the Contemporary Maghreb) was organized by Jack Lang and held in August 2001. Its aim was to examine the teaching of the Algerian War and to identify its strengths and weaknesses.

In the teacher sample (eighteen teachers) for this study, nearly all the interviewees knew someone in their family or workplace who had been involved in the Algerian War. Three teachers were of *pied-noir* origin, either French settlers in Algeria themselves or descended from settlers. One of these teachers had lived in

Mostaganem until 1962. Another had lived in Bab-el-Oued. A third was not born in Algeria, but his mother was a *pied-noir.* Before 1998, these teachers spent five or six hours on the Algerian War, which is significantly more than their colleagues. In the pupil sample, two-thirds of the pupils were of Algerian origin. The fact that they volunteered for the interview suggests that they are more interested in the subject, something the teachers also noted. Opinion polls have also shown the importance of family history in dictating interest in subjects (see Cornette and Luc 1985). Fascinating differences emerged in interviews between information obtained from the family and that learned in class. However, in some cases little information had been obtained from the family. One pupil's father had fought on the French side in the Algerian War, and it is known that such veterans are generally critical of the place of the Algerian War in textbooks. Their associations have examined textbooks, and they have written to textbook editors—such as Serge Berstein and Minister of Education Jack Lang. In a survey published in 1992, 80 percent of the young people interviewed said they felt that the Algerian War had not been discussed enough at school (see P. Bernard 1992). What would this figure be now given that significantly less is taught on the war?

A rare exception to the standard teaching model described earlier—indeed, an alternative model—can be found in an article in *Le Monde* describing a teacher who works in a French secondary school who, with her pupils, published a book entitled *Mémoires des migrations* in 1996 on the family histories of her pupils (Guibert 2000). She worked in a *lycée professionnel* with Brevet d'études professionelles (BEP) and *bac pro* pupils, whose history program is much easier than the ordinary *baccalauréat,* where time limitations prevent such an initiative. The teacher talks of the "extraordinary wealth" of her pupils in terms of their family histories. Their parents come from many countries, including Algeria. Such histories are not well represented in the traditional history program, but they should be, given that the program is supposed to "[g]ive pupils a memory, . . .[and] help to constitute the patrimony that allows each pupil to find his or her identity."[5] Immigration to France and decolonization have profoundly changed France and French identity. The teacher herself was born in Algeria. In the article, she said that she had "felt like Robinson on his island" after her family left Algeria in 1954 and moved into a small flat in Paris, but that "this experience [in class] allowed me to go forward." So the project helped her to have her history acknowledged, too.

Some identities are therefore unrepresented or underrepresented, particularly in the *voie générale* of the *terminale* history program. In an interview published in

5. Wording taken from comments by the program designers and quoted in Rioux 1996, 50.

the French review *Hommes et migrations,* the eighteen-year-old son of a man who was thrown into the Seine in Paris on 17 October 1961 (see chapter 8) and who was a witness at the recent trial in which Maurice Papon brought proceedings against the journalist Jean-Luc Einaudi for slander, spoke of how he had learned of these events: not at school, but more through his father. Throughout the interview, he shifted between various pronouns when talking of the French and the Algerian War, despite the fact that he himself was born in France: *on* (we), *ils* (they), and *eux* (them). The person who conducted the interview identified what she called his "difficile identification" with France. She said: "This difficult identification can be seen in the vocabulary used by Slim. When he says '*We* had the Jews in 1945,' he associates himself with France. 'But in 1961 however *they* were capable of starting again': 'they' represents France, when he distances himself and sees himself as Algerian. This double identity shows itself at another point in the interview: 'In France, *we* denounced the Germans, but *they* don't denounce what *they* did with the Algerians" (Marchaut 1999, 62, emphasis in the original).

Here memory is clearly linked to concerns in the present and to identity. Repression and denial in wider society have led to what the interviewer called the interviewee's "difficile identification" with France and the French. Interestingly, such considerations can be the subject of *beur* novels. Tassadit Imache's *Une fille sans histoire* (1989) examines representation, identity, and the construction of "history." In school, the protagonist "had heard nothing there about almost a century and a half of colonialism" (124). We follow her attempts to construct her own story in order to fill in the silences in dominant representations of Franco-Algerian history, to combat her erasure from history, and to reclaim her history. Leïla Houari's *Zeida de nulle part* (1985) concerns the search for collective memory. Zeida undertakes a similar effort to discover her past and her origins. Regarding such an effort, Claude Liauzu has argued that "[c]oncerning Algeria, a third of a century later, the official amnesia remains full of consequences. It leaves the way clear for opposing memories; it covered serious violations of republican values in a French society, which dumped the Algerian burden. It leaves young people of foreign descent in an identity crisis, bars them from history, and prevents them from inclusion in national history. This can only increase ethnic tensions" (1999, 24).

Some historical events are not sufficiently assumed, such as the use of torture, summary executions, or *regroupment* (large-scale, forced movement of people). In 1998 textbooks, torture is mentioned in one or two phrases, and a document might be included. In one 1998 textbook, for example, we read, "Progressively, the violence became widespread, the countryside was controlled and covered [by the army], suspects tortured, even executed, despite protests by intellectuals," and "Even though successive French governments began conscription, covering the increasingly systematic use of the torture . . . they could not halt progression of the nationalist cause" (Marseille 1998, 260, 216). The document provided in this textbook is an article from *Le Monde* that examines "[t]he dilemma of journalists" (224). The same textbook makes no mention of the *harkis,* the bombing of Sakhiet-Sidi Youssef, or the massacre at the rue d'Isly. The events of 17 October 1961 are simply mentioned: "on 17 October 1961, the police [*les forces de l'ordre*] in Paris killed about one hundred Algerians" (272). This reflects official political discourse on the Algerian War—for example, Jacques Chirac's comments at the first Journée d'hommage national aux harkis (National Day of Homage to the Harkis) on September 25, 2001—which, although recently addressing the Algerian War (after many years of occlusion), has often fallen short of the acknowledgment of wrongdoing some wish to see. Alain Madelin, president of the political party Démocratie libérale, said he was disappointed not to hear an admission of fault (Zappi 2001, 17). Also after the publication of General Aussarresses's *Services spéciaux,* both Chirac's and Jospin's comments on torture used by the French in the war were ambiguous. For Raphaëlle Branche, the latter "refused to recognize the responsibility of the authorities of the time, by arguing that the state was not called into question in this affair and that acts of torture had been 'a minority' [of the total war action]" (2001, 433).

To some extent, memory encourages the writing (and teaching) of history. As Pierre Nora has put it, "History writes while memory dictates" (1989, 21)—that is, history is written because it is deemed important in society. Researchers are given funding, and their work is accepted by directors of research or publishers. Politicians call for more history to be written and for greater access to archives. In contrast, actors literally write it themselves. In an article in *Libération,* Stora writes of "l'homme du Sud" (the man from the South), who, he argues, allowed an opening (i.e., a greater discussion of a previously taboo subject) in the early 1990s to take place in two ways: first, in his country of origin by letting filmmakers actually work in Algeria and, second, in France by the research, filmmaking, or book writing of people whose parents came from Algeria and who have provided much of the impetus for studying this period of French history by doing it themselves (1992, 5). In terms of teaching, such an opening can be created through increased interest in the subject, which will lead to more time given to it. However, memory can also inhibit history: when it creates *polémiques* (controversy) and division, writing it is highly problematic (Ageron) as is teaching it (Rioux). Here we enter the realm of nation building and nation maintaining.

There is a tremendous amount of interest in writing and teaching the history of the Algerian War. As Pierre Nora points out,

> What today we commonly call memory, in the sense that we talk of working class, Occitan, or feminine memory, is on the contrary a defunct tradition achieving a historical consciousness, the reconstruction and recuperation of a phenomenon that we left behind and that interests principally those who feel themselves its descendants or its heirs; a tradition that the official history had never felt the need to take into account because the national group had more often than not been constructed on its hushing-up, on its silence; or because that history simply hadn't come to the fore in History. But a tradition that these groups now in the process of being integrated into national history feel the urgent need to reconstitute with whatever means are available, from the most basic to the most scientific, because it constitutes their identity. This memory is in fact their history. (1992, 997)

In her book *Fast Cars, Clean Bodies: Decolonization and the Reordering of French Culture,* Kristen Ross argues that there is a tendency in France to keep the two stories of modernization and decolonization separate, as if "France's colonial history was nothing more than an 'exterior' experience that somehow came to an abrupt end, cleanly, in 1962. . . . [C]olonialism itself was made to seem like a dusty archaism, as though it had not transpired in the twentieth century and in the personal histories of many people living today, as though it played only a tiny role in France's national history, and no role at all in its modern identity" (1995, 9). The way the Algerian War is taught reflects such a narrative. The war is "ancient history." It occupies a small place in the history program. It does not play a big role in the national narrative. Surely the time is now ripe for this to change. Many developments point to a changing position of the Maghreb, Islam, and the Arab world in French identity, including an integration of France's common history with Algeria. Until such changes take place further, I support Jean-Robert Henry's argument that "Algeria generally plays a less prominent role in the construction of a French sense of cultural identity" than France plays in Algeria's identity (1993, 7).

10 *Pieds-Noirs, Bêtes Noires*

Anti–"European of Algeria" Racism and the Close of the French Empire

TODD SHEPARD

THERE ARE HISTORICAL REASONS why "memory work" has proven so central to the many discussions in the past decade about the Algerian Revolution in French history, some of which have become topics of historical and political debate in France and elsewhere. Among the multiple starting points for this recent spate of studies, those focused on the *pieds-noirs*—the people who in French Algeria were known as colons, "Europeans," settlers, and so on—have embraced invocations of memory almost without exception. This work includes films such as Brigitte Roüan's *Outre-mer* (1990) and Alexandre Arcady's *Là-bas mon pays* (2000); literary echoes of the period in novels such as Claire Messud's *The Last Life: A Novel* (1999) and Jean-Noël Pancrazi's *Madame Arnoul* (1995), as well as the posthumous publication of Albert Camus's *Le premier homme* (1994b); studies of *pied-noir* writing; and studies based primarily on oral sources, such as Jeannine Verdès-Leroux's *Les Français d'Algérie: De 1830 à nos jours* (2001).

Historians of the *pieds-noirs* during the last years of French Algeria have been particularly attentive to the usefulness of memory. Joëlle Hureau's *Mémoires des pieds-noirs de 1830 à nos jours* (1987) is the most recent book-length study, and Jean-Jacques Jordi's work remains the most in-depth combination of archival sources and memory, in particular his book *De l'exode à l'exil: Rapatriés et pieds-noirs en France* (1993) and subsequent article "Les pieds-noirs: Constructions identitaires et reinvention des origines" (2002). The term *exile* plays a key role in his analysis. If Benjamin Stora (1991, 1999) seeks constantly to challenge, even undercut, the political valence of "*pied-noir* memories," Jordi's exegeses foreground memories that are more usable in French public discussions. His histories seem destined to allow *pied-noir* understandings of their victimization to be considered outside of the far-right political language that has so tarnished their reputation.

This chapter maps out some of the certainties that continue to haunt the Algerian War as a "realm of memory." It looks back at the last months when Algeria was French and focuses on public debates in metropolitan France about, first, why the *pieds-noirs* were not French and then on why they were. This history emphasizes how the troubling assertion that "Algerians cannot be French" emerged in a particular and particularly intense and brief moment, when who was Algerian and who was French remained very uncertain. It is quite fitting, in the context of this collection, that a book by Pierre Nora is one of the chapter's key sources—not in terms of methodology, but as primary document.

Throughout the late 1950s, the hegemony of republican political idiom impeded most French politicians and intellectuals from accepting Algerian nationalists' demands for liberation. Indeed, the fact that all of Algeria was part of France and that all people from Algeria—Muslims, Europeans, "natives," or "settlers"—were French nationals became more rather than less a "fact" during the course of the war. The Constitution of 1958 recognized that all people born in Algeria were French citizens (Article 75) and announced the end of all territorial distinctions—either in laws or in regulations—between the now fifteen departments of Algeria and the Sahara and the ninety metropolitan departments.

A few short years later, at the end of 1961 and in early 1962, what allowed people in metropolitan ("mainland") France finally to articulate why Algerian departments (legally part of the French Republic) and Algerians (since 1958, all full citizens of the French Republic) should become independent was a growing hatred of some of those people in Algeria, the so-called "Europeans of Algeria," the "settlers" or *pieds-noirs*. Rather than engaging with arguments from the Front de libération nationale (FLN, National Liberation Front) or other Algerian nationalists that the so-called Algerian Muslims were not French, metropolitans focused on a different problem: the threat posed by terrorist Organisation armée sécrète (OAS, Secret Army Organization) activists. For metropolitans at the end of the Algerian War, the OAS came into focus as violent *pieds-noirs*. Metropolitan media and politicians presented the activists as the emanation of a subtropical subculture that racist and colonial structures of domination had perverted. Public recognition of *pied-noir* decadence made clear how different those people and that land were from France (Agulhon 1991; Heurgon 1994).[1]

1. On European understandings of how the tropics produced decadence in settlers, most famously evoked in Joseph Conrad's work ([1902] 1991), see Kennedy 1990 and Bleys 1996.

The "New Left" and the Eruption of Anti–"European of Algeria" Racism

It was the New Left that most aggressively demonized the *pieds-noirs* as "not French" in the months before the Evian Accords. This presentation was key to the New Left's emphatic recasting of the conflict as a Franco-French civil war. In late 1961 and early 1962, they shared an analysis of surging popular mobilization against defenders of French Algeria as revelatory of a nascent revolutionary solidarity inspired by the Algerian struggle. The February 1962 Métro Charonne protest and the mass demonstration that followed the martyrdom of eight Parti communiste français (PCF) militants convinced them that history was on the move. In acts and writings, militants and in particular New Left journalists thus chose to privilege attacks on the OAS and "European" Algerians over their long-held critique of the French state and society.[2]

Writers of the New Left recentered their struggle against "fascism"—which previously had focused on de Gaulle, French society itself, or Western imperialism—on the OAS and, in an easy elision, on the "Europeans of Algeria." Accusations that the *pieds-noirs* were under the sway of neofascistic impulses buttressed a growing assumption that the *pieds-noirs*—like all people from Algeria—were not French. *Pied-noir* fascism also suggested that it was their irrationality and violence that had produced "French" wartime abuses, such as torture. France needed to stop the *pieds-noirs* by getting out of Algeria, for neither was French.

In a deforming but reassuring recasting of Frantz Fanon's identification of the colonized as the equivalent of Marx's proletariat and the colonizers as the bourgeoisie, New Left writers in these months decided that it was only the "colonists," the *pieds-noirs,* who dominated and exploited. Although often invoking Fanonian wording, their styling broke with the revolutionary's careful knitting together of colonist and colonial excess with the metropole and, indeed, Western culture. Sartre, in his preface to *The Wretched of the Earth,* had warned against this move, however ([1963] 1991, 43–44). In *France-observateur* and in other New Left journals *(Esprit, Témoignages chrétiennes),* writers enthusiastically joined in fighting the newly identified enemy of the people.

The template for New Left representations of the *pieds-noirs* at the war's end

2. The Reseignements généraux suggested this distinction in an analysis of the explosion of books published during the war, noting a shift from books that addressed "the Algerian War" as a phenomenon to, later in the war, those that responded to "the existing political context" and focused on different elements that could be addressed distinctly, such as "partisans of French Algeria, the OAS, the situation of repatriates, etc." (RG 1963, 2).

was the 1961 book *Les Français d'Algérie* (The French of Algeria) by historian Pierre Nora (1961). Usually cited as a scholarly study, prefaced by the prominent historian of Algeria Charles-André Julien (one of the first in France to break with the "colonialist school" of imperial history), the book synthesized a racist and self-righteous anti-*pied-noir* discourse among French intellectuals. Nora foregrounded a defense of the rights of those referred to as colonized "Arabs." Yet, like those who would take up his anti–"French of Algeria" jeremiads, the radical possibilities of such a project in fact served to assert a definition of France from which two groups of "Algerians" should be excluded: "Arabs," as different from the French and equally deserving of a state, and the "French of Algeria," as, despite their name, different from the French and dangerous to the republic.

Nora had come to public attention as a journalist for *France-observateur,* but he presented *The French of Algeria* as the work of a university-trained historian. The book, however, as American historian of French Algeria David Prochaska notes, "is not so much a work of history (it is not based on original research and is devoid of the usual scholarly apparatus) as a personal account written in a passionate, powerful style" ([1990] 2004, 6).

Nora's study explained that the "French of Algeria" were wholly different from the French. That is, rather than the 1950s pro-independence dialectics of French colonizer/Algerian colonized à la Fanon and Sartre, or Raymond Aron's assertion of obvious noncongruence between French people and "Algerian Muslims," the Algerian difference Nora sought to explain was between metropolitan French and the "French of Algeria." He presented this difference in starkly hierarchical terms. Metropolitans embraced this definition of what separated France and Algeria.[3]

Nora explained that the most fervent *pied-noir* partisans of French Algeria inhabited *le bled,* the Algerian countryside, where "they have suffered the influence of their Arab milieu." Sharing the "same climate and the same lives, they have finished by adopting the same habits." This is what allowed them, he ar-

3. This new vision of a society uniquely racist has contoured some of the most compelling Anglo-American analyses of French Algeria. The influence of Nora can be seen, for example, when Prochaska argues that "[i]n making Bône a European city in the nineteenth and early twentieth centuries, moreover, the settlers blocked social evolution, attempted to contain history" ([1990] 2004, 26). A second important example of the influence of *The French of Algeria* mars Neil MacMaster's excellent *Colonial Migrants and Racism: Algerians in France, 1900–1962,* which assiduously presents a Marxist and convincing argument that anti-Algerian racism in France was always and everywhere a result of the actions of capitalist elites. The only exception is the *pieds-noirs,* who when they arrived in the metropole during the exodus, MacMaster argues, "injected a particularly virulent strain of racism into French society" (1997, 1).

gued, to embrace the French government's post-1956 policy of "integration," which "permits them to imagine that they will resuscitate their link with Europe and to recover that precious Western essence that they largely have lost" (1961, 51).

At the heart of the "French of Algeria" sickness was their relationship with Algeria itself, a relationship based on the exploitation of the land and of its people, the "Arabs." For the historian, this second connection also condemned the "French of Algeria" to a nonindustrial future; like Marx's peasants, their rejection of industry here referred above all to human relations, to the gathering together of workers: "men scare them" (Marx 1926; Nora 1961, 252). Their double exploitation of Algerians and Algeria paradoxically produced a sick society and allowed it to soldier on: it was only their certainty that they "all were better than the Arabs that allows them to survive," for all "would be little or nothing in the metropole" (Nora 1961, 175).

Nora posited that all "French of Algeria" should be considered as a powerful elite, but an elite the French should disdain not simply or even primarily because they exploit, but because they are without culture or education. Only the urgent need to prove that the "French of Algeria" were not French can explain the publication of his work. Such visions of the irrationality and foreign-ness of the "French of Algeria" would shape not just New Left analyses, but also official media and propaganda.

On 19 March 1962, the day following the announcement that representatives of the FLN and the French government had signed the Evian Accords, the noon report of metropolitan radio station Europe 1 detailed the stark difference between the calm that reigned in the "Muslim neighborhoods" and the scene in "European" Bab-el-Oued: "one thousand men, but only men, in the streets, who look at everything, inspect everything," streets littered with "light barricades made of broken bottles and crates" (Commandement supérieur des forces en Algérie [CSFA] 1962b). A government minister spoke of "the atmosphere of insecurity, the attacks, the street-fighting, the closing of schools—often by bombing—that brings mothers of families to send their children to the metropole, the economic difficulties, without mentioning the fear many of [these women] experience." The government continued to insist that most French citizens of Algeria would choose to stay in the soon-to-be-independent Algeria. France's secretary of state Louis Joxe noted that those who were arriving in the metropole were "almost all women and children, coming to France, mostly still for summer vacations" (*Journal official de la République Française* 1962, 1398).

French horror at the actions of the OAS accompanied a growing sympathy for the Algerian people, the oppressed Arabs and Berbers. It seemed clear that the same *pieds-noirs* who were now killing French young men, soldiers seeking merely to oversee the peace accords, were responsible for the brutalization of the Algerian people. They were to blame for the ongoing involvement and the activities that had sullied France's reputation.

In the face of OAS terror, the French saw an army protecting "women and children" from other violent and questionably French men. The armed forces' new vulnerability tempered images of brutal irrationality with which previous charges of torture had tainted them. OAS brutalities allowed the French army to appear as defenders of the weak and of French values. Depictions of the OAS offered an explanation that could elucidate earlier French use of torture. It was not, as discussions of military torture had suggested, a crisis of French values or the republic that provoked abhorrent behavior: it was Algeria.

This was the ultimate certainty conveyed by the outpouring of New Left anti-*pied-noir* sentiment. Again, Nora's book was exemplary. The preface by Charles-André Julien presented France's history in Algeria as marked by the metropole's making good-hearted and civilized efforts, a mission the "French of Algeria" had always deformed. (Nora went so far as to claim that torture and "excesses" on the part of French army soldiers during the early 1830s resulted from "French of Algeria" refusal to condemn such acts. Yet no "French" or "European" settlers had yet arrived in Algeria [Nora 1961, 88 and 252].) Julien portrayed civil servants in Algeria as "traitors" to the metropole. They had been "mostly recruited there or quickly converted by the milieu." What "gave the French of Algeria strength," he explained, was "their refusal of the liberal tendencies of the metropole" (1961, 26–27).

The only way to save France and Algeria was to end their unnatural bond. Referring only to the "French of Algeria" and not to Algeria's "non-European" majority, French New Left intellectuals articulated a sensible definition of how "Algerians" were different from the French, an explanation that reaffirmed French superiority. Although it was New Left writers who largely vehicled the presentation of *pied-noir* difference, their efforts buttressed government activity that worked to separate legally the Europeans of Algeria from France. What such understandings could not explain was the exodus—that is, "Algerians" coming to France after the war.

The belief that the *pieds-noirs* necessarily would end up in Algeria was tenacious. As late as May 1962, government experts in the Hexagon continued to plan on no more than three hundred thousand repatriates from Algeria staying for good in Europe. Official reports from Algeria maintained that, as the head of the Gendarmerie in Oran wrote in early June, "Although many Europeans try to convince themselves that staying in an independent Algeria is impossible, it is certain that in their heart of hearts they hope to stay." Noting the "massive exodus of Europeans toward the metropole," he highlighted the "small number of them who declare that they are giving up and leaving definitively." The rest, he presumed, would return to Algeria (Koch 1962b, 7).

The arrest of former general Raoul Salan dates, empirically and symbolically, the beginning of what would be recognized as more than a variety of discrete phenomena, distinct departures, and conjunctural developments, but rather as an event: the exodus. From 20 April on, what would prove to be definitive departures to the metropole went up markedly and did not drop until the exodus ended. As a year-end chronicle asked, "Coincidence or consequence? For the first time, the 21 April, the constabulary had to refuse entrance to the airport of Maison-Blanche, where numerous Algérois [inhabitants of Algiers] wanted to board. Two thousand people were able to leave. The rest, pushed back, camped in their cars" (*L'année politique, economique et sociale* [*APES*] 1962, 282). Salan's arrest not only removed the individual who had embodied popular hopes for a victory for the forces supporting French Algeria, it also marked the collapse of any semblance of OAS unity and of the organization's across-the-board support of a republican project for France (Shepard 2002, 44–77). After Salan's capture, the exodus began, it did not stop, and it was definitive.

The exodus began in the *bled.* If military and government observers first remarked the segregation of urban neighborhoods, they soon took note that Algeria's interior was emptying quickly of its European population. This process had begun even before the cease-fire, but the accords accelerated a "regrouping in villages or large cities" of "the near totality" of European *bled* dwellers; then came the "abandonment of towns where the ALN [Armée de libération nationale] will station, in order to take refuge in large cities," which later led to "another movement involving Europeans leaving by air or sea." Officials first remarked on and explained such departures in "the countryside and small towns, where insecurity is greater." In cities like Oran, however, as gendarmerie commander Captain Koch reported, departures to the metropole were said to concern "certainly a rather small percentage" (Koch 1962a, 2). One officer in Algiers relied on material proof to ground his assertion that "certain symptomatic indicators allow us to think that the exodus is going to become general in the weeks ahead." He remarked that "wrapping paper of all kinds, cardboard, and twine have become unavailable necessities" (Cavard 1962, 4). Koch related that whereas movement within Algeria concerned "entire families," that toward the metropole, although affecting "all social classes," was "primarily women and children. The head of the family generally stays behind" (Koch 1962a, 2).

In the Constantine, where concerns about "Jewish" departures had introduced the term *exodus* in 1961 (Shepard 2002, 255–92), it was in late April that military intelligence first announced that "definitive exodus to the metropole" was what "many" Europeans now planned. The reasons suggested were, first, a growing realization of "the uselessness of all the [pro-French Algeria] demonstrations"; second, the "persistent fear of future exactions by the Muslim masses or administration"; and finally, the pressure of " 'taxes' that are imposed on them by the FLN since the cease-fire" (Genestout 1962, 2). The previous weekly summary, like those before it, had made no mention of such reasons, analyzing instead the "stupor" of the "European" population confronted with "the referendum in France, and the installation of the Provisional Executive," which "will determine their future but in which they play no role" (Serafino 1962).

Explaining the Exodus

Speaking before the National Assembly on 30 May 1962, government representative Gérard Wolff explained to the deputies that the "rhythm of retreat to the metropole at present is around five thousand people a day." Whatever the deputies might think, he cautioned, "what I would like to inform the Assembly is that this rate is exactly the same—for various reasons, of course—as [it was] at this time last year: 99,522 in May 1961, around 100,000 now." The government was not quite suggesting, as Ile de France deputy André Laffin interjected, that "no one is leaving!" It asserted, simply, that nothing irreversible was happening. More important, nothing was occurring that needed explanation. After their vacations, *(pied-noir)* "Algerians" would go back to their now independent homeland (*Journal official* 1962, 1408).

Even internal government documents referred straightforwardly to vacations, perhaps envisioning the summer as a cooling-down period. In late May, the prefecture for Oran, calling attention to the masses of people "descending on the port of Oran and waiting day and night on the docks," urged the minister of the interior "to organize the transportation to France of thousands of women and children for summer vacation" (Parat 1962, 1–2). Others, although asserting that Europeans were "pretending to go on summer vacation" in order "to save face," still drew attention to "their hope that they will be able to return [to Algeria]." The proof Captain Koch pointed to was that "the heads of family remain in Algeria" (1962b, 7).

Like the government, claims made in the name of the OAS would dispute the reality of the "exodus" long after the movement had become a veritable groundswell. The OAS Zone III (Oran) refused to accept the early June Susini-Mostefai Agreements and sought to establish a "territorial platform" governed by the OAS and independent from the French Republic as well as Algeria. In mid-

June, a communiqué explained: "we have asked that certain zones be evacuated, and the slightly more numerous departures of the last few days are the result of the evacuation of some families from the interior." By "families," they meant women and children: "The Men Are Staying Put. They Are Ready To Fight," a claim that reinforced an image that the government, reversing itself, had begun to combat (OAS Zone III 1962).

By the end of June, official observers joined the French press (e.g., De la Gorce 1962, 7) in accepting the existence of "the exodus," and some recognized that the cause, rather than being conjunctural, was structural: "The collapse of hope among the European community in an OAS victory, which would keep Algeria French, plunged them [in May] into deep despair and provoked an exodus verging on panic." Despite earlier estimations that this movement was "seasonal" or simply irrational, in June one officer detailed that "departures to the metropole, in any case, have not ceased and their numbers are far beyond previous records for vacation-related voyages: 225,000 passengers recorded, versus 88,000 for June 1961" (CSFA 1962a, 11).

Previously certain that Europeans would not leave and faced with the total failure to convince them that they could remain French in Algeria, French officials confronted enormous difficulties in mobilizing to counter what one officer identified as the "psychosis of the exodus" with transportation and accommodations (Cousin 1962, 26). By June, top government officials in Algeria were ready to predict, as the prefect of police in Oran explained to Minister of the Interior Frey, that "we are going, if the general tendency does not reverse itself between now and July 1, to have a fairly important exodus of Europeans." It was time to face "the problem of organizing their departure, by sea and air, of transportation, of arrival in Marseilles and Port-Vendres" (Biget 1962, 2).[4]

The exodus had begun. The Pompidou government would have to manage a situation that resulted from the failure of French policies—ranging from the creation of repatriate status in 1961 to the guarantees of the 1962 Evian Accords, meant to keep almost all Algerians, "French" as well as "Muslims," in Algeria (Shepard 2002, 214–54). After enumerating for the interministerial Committee for Algerian Affairs the diverse measures that needed to be taken (and paid for), Robert Boulin emphasized that "for psychological and political reasons" it now was "essential to go before the Parliament to detail the massive effort asked of the Nation." The secretary of state's words signaled the beginning of what would become a significant public mobilization to welcome the repatriates. It should be noted that he presented the calling on "the Nation" in wholly cynical terms, ex-

4. For an overview of June, see CSFA 1962a, 11.

plaining to his colleagues that "any other policy might lead the Assembly to reject a budget judged derisory" (1962, 2).[5]

Metropolitans and the French press were fixated on the exodus. The reactions varied enormously, although the press was much more welcoming than the people. *Paris-Match* consistently urged its readers to welcome "the repatriates of Algeria," and its editorials, photos, captions, and articles struggled to fabricate what, before the cease-fire, an early editorial had assured was "the only guarantee" French Algerians needed: "the friendship of French people for French people" ("La seule garantié" 1962, 27). Every element of the photo-weekly's 2 June cover worked to produce compassion: blond baby holding a stuffed animal; a young, tall, dark (but not too dark) and handsome man; a young, petite, Jean Seberg-coiffed woman in a suede vest; the couple in profile, leaning on a ship railing, eyes fixed on land (Jarnoux 1962, 1). The headline read, "France, Does She Still Love Us?"—with the promise of a "Major Report" not on, but "with the repatriates from Algeria." The front-page caption explained, "They met and were married in Algeria, he, a military man, she, *pied-noir.* They were teachers, today they return to the coasts of the *mère-patrie.*" Who could think they were in any way connected with France's enemies? A white band at the top of the page, the bold-faced caption "The Judges of Salan," reminded all that the enemies were being dealt with, and the first sentence of the first article explained that the judges had "looked to the future" ("Il n'y a pas assez" 1962, 6). For others, particularly on the left, the problem posed was less social and economic than political. If socialist (Section française de l'internationale ouvrière [SFIO]) leaders were, according to the Reseignements généraux (RG), "preoccupied" by "the problems posed by the repatriation of refugees from North Africa" (RG 1962b), the left-Christian union Confédération des Travailleurs Chrétiens (CFTC) warned its locals to be on guard against the threat of "infiltration by repatriates" (RG 1962a, 2). In *France-observateur,* the letters-to-the-editor page was filled each week of early 1962 with criticisms of the *pieds-noirs,* the repatriates, and what many readers felt was the weekly's too sympathetic coverage of their situation. Mr. H. C. from Paris, "one of your earliest subscribers," questioned whether the "exodus" was well founded, given that "the French government has done everything to guarantee their safety and their property." Opposed to offering any assistance to the repatriates, he worried that they would "reinforce metropolitan activism that, according to the press, is getting stronger and more violent" (H. C. de Paris 1962).

5. On the various agencies put in place, see Jordi 1993, 1995; Viet 1998, 163–302; Jordi and Temime 1996.

"Does France Still Love Us?" Reaffirming the Frenchness of (European) Repatriates

As the overwhelming number of repatriates became clearer, so did moves to prepare the French nation for their arrival. The emerging official line, cobbled together once the collapse of all previous previsions became undeniable, urged metropolitans to welcome the *pieds-noirs*. The mythic heterosexual family was the principal register of such appeals. Days after the "exodus" exploded, *Paris-Match* responded to "the announcement that some families from North Africa have begun to settle in the metropole." The editors dragged old-time pronatalism out of its post-1945 *bébé boum*-provoked retirement with an editorial titled "There Are Not Enough French People." The editors wrote that "today, economic progress depends on abundant manpower and the number of solvent consumers." In these months, "[h]ave confidence in the future," the editorial's final line, was the mantra of *Paris-Match* ("Il n'y a pas assez" 1962). Although not historically unprecedented, the use of familial descriptions to explain official responses to the exodus was particularly intense, working to extricate the OAS from *pieds-noirs* and acting to reinsert the latter in classic, comforting, and hierarchized gender relations. Men joined their women and children in metropolitan France, thus countering evocations of the separation between men, fighting for the OAS in Algeria, and women and children in France, waiting to return to Algeria, that were so apparent in anti-OAS arguments after the announcement of the Evian Accords. These arguments had contributed too successfully to producing people who were foreign to French understandings of the French.

Images of "whole" families, men with women and children, were repeatedly produced to describe the people coming to France. Both pro-government and pro-*Algérie française* deputies worked to distinguish the innocent French refugees flooding into the metropole from vividly described violent anti-French fanatics, who like the refugees were "Europeans" and from Algeria. Deputies from all sides of the hemicycle, except the far Left, called for French fraternity and solidarity. One Gaullist deputy urged, "it is necessary for those who returned with pain in their souls, with bitterness on their lips, who are somewhat maladroit because they suffer—they must be welcomed like distressed members of the same family." More than mere words, there was an institutional vector to this discursive deployment, as the state sought to cement depictions of the refugees as French families (*Journal official* 1962, 1440).

The government announced that its repatriation program had opened "15,000 dossiers for heads of families"; "we have had 19,000 families, about 50,000 people . . . each head of family receives 50,000 old francs, each person in their charge 20,000." One Algerian deputy called into question the functionality of such a system: "I would like to say to M. the Secretary of State for Repatriation, that in order to receive these allocations, it is necessary that the head of the family has come to the metropole. It would be just, it would be reasonable, that these benefits be equally available to repatriated families where the head of the family has not come" (*Journal official* 1962, 1404, 1488).

The particular genealogy of this dispute is compelling. As we know from the work of Susan Pedersen (1993) and others, directing payments to the male head of the family was not the norm for French social spending. It was only in the 1930s, after the collapse of the Popular Front governments that the Daladier government under great pressure from the traditionalist Catholic and royalist right began to utilize familial allocation of welfare benefits. Earlier in the twentieth century, the French government repeatedly had opted to give money to needy mothers directly, whether married or not. Thus, although the deputy's complaints made sense within the recent history of France, their political origins were novel. The pro-French Algeria Right, not the secular Left, was calling for a policy that ignored family status. The government's "pro-family" choice suggested that although French Algerian men on their own were undeniably citizens, legally entitled to enter the metropole, it was only as "heads of family" that they could be welcomed.

Rather than a reflection of ahistorical privileging of the natural familial order, this criterion was forged in discursive necessity. Indeed, within weeks, certain payments to repatriates began to be distributed whether or not the male "head of the family" had arrived. Yet the government's initial policy—which broke with standard political and bureaucratic practice—suggests how critical it was, in responding to the unexpected "exodus" of "Europeans," to present them as grouped in heterosexual families. Representations of the *pieds-noirs* as irrational, deviant men had been widely convincing understandings that offered vivid proof that they were not French and were a threat to France. To be male and *pied-noir* in these months was enough to be associated with fascist terror. If in late 1961 and January 1962, government reports on departures from Algeria had specified how many of those concerned were "Israelites," in June and July 1962 RG reports on "repatriates from Algeria arriving in France" distinguished the number of "men older than seventeen" (RG 1962c, 1).

Counterrepresentations that normalized these men as heterosexual were at the heart of efforts to provoke metropolitan solidarity with people who, although from Algeria, were in fact French. This familial language worked to assert that the *pieds-noirs* were directly linked to other French people, that they were "members of the same family." Familial images were readily articulated to disentangle the mass of *pieds-noirs* from the actions of the OAS. As one Algerian deputy noted, evoking the Holy Family itself, "Already, in spite of official declarations and proclaimed optimism from the higher ups, stories abound of facts that shame us. . . . In Marseilles, the [repatriates] have to sleep on the roadside before packed hotels or ones that refuse to accept refugees" (*Journal official* 1962, 1427). Through the multiple resonances of familial imagery, the refugees were positioned not as violent, but as weak, as themselves children, and as profoundly French—all exemplified in the words of one deputy on 11 July 1962, urging his audience to look at the exodus and understand:

> Today, you can see the French who arrive on the docks of Marseilles, or the grounds of our major airports. [They are] poor and often miserable, with for their only baggage several sacks in which they were able to save their modest belongings; over there that was all they owned. One needs only to look at them to know that these are Frenchmen of the lower middle class, little people for whom life consists of work, of effort, and suffering. . . . [D]o not forget that these French, our compatriots, our brothers, are the children of those who went before, pushed more by the need to give [to France] than greed. (*Journal official* 1962, 2353)

The family—above all the necessary place of males within it as fathers, brothers, and even children—was a privileged trope, mobilized to cleanse the *pieds-noirs* of the OAS stain and to guarantee their Frenchness.

In the midst of the exodus, as French Algeria not only ended, but also seemed abruptly to disappear, new definitions and understandings of who was French became important. Shifts in terminology were concomitant with changing legal, institutional, and bureaucratic assessments of the relationship between Algerian and French identities. Familial discourse offered tentative resolution to one of the key questions the Algerian revolution forced France to address: Who could be French and why? It emerged as obvious, seeming common sense, that some people from Algeria—the "Europeans"—were a priori French, whereas others—Arab and Berber "Muslims"—were Algerians. The war's close allowed the Gaullist government to reaffirm national boundaries as not only hexagonal, but distinctly "European." For *pieds-noirs,* this meant they were included within the family of France, at least officially. The place where they were born, however, was not simply no longer part of France, but a place that had never been France. Produced under enormous duress, these clear definitions of what territory and which people were French were wrought with tensions. Debates in late 1961 and 1962 about the *pieds-noirs* (among others) make this clear. The centrality of "memory work" in recent studies of the *pieds-noirs'* Algerian War experiences suggests that historical explorations of this past have much to offer to understanding post-Algeria France. As French philosopher Etienne Balibar recently reaffirmed, to insist that France and Algeria were one nation—as many in France did for more than a century—was an imperialist manipulation. Yet, pretending today that France and Algeria are and were simply "two wholly distinct nations" impedes analysis of how formative colonialism was for both France and Algeria: "the impact on the so-called West as well as on colonized peoples" (1997, 12).

11 The *Harkis*

History and Memory

WILLIAM B. COHEN

THE ALGERIAN WAR, one of the most brutal conflicts France has been involved in, left behind deep scars. The memory of the war was experienced in different ways by different participants; each group harboring its own understanding of what occurred while often contesting the memory of others. One of these vectors of memory has been the *harkis,* a much-neglected group, which both the French state and public, ill at ease with the record of their treatment, have tried to disregard.

Shortly after the Algerian War broke out in November 1954, the French started to recruit local auxiliary forces. Several units were established, the largest being the *harkis.* Their name stems from *harka,* meaning "movement" in Arabic, suggesting the roving bands they formed. *Harki* became the generic term for all auxiliary forces; 120,000 auxiliaries (and an additional 60,000 Muslims in the regular army) served the French at the end of 1960.[1]

The use of *harkis* reduced the number of French draftees, already very large, that would have had to be called up. It brought into the field young men who knew the region they were fighting in and were familiar with the local topography and the habits of the inhabitants. Furthermore, the existence of these forces was useful in the propaganda war. It could be argued—as it was—that more Algerians supported the continuation of French rule than who wanted independence, for the number of Algerians enrolled in the auxiliary forces was nearly four times the number fighting for the nationalists, the Front de libération nationale (FLN), within Algerian territory.

1. There are conflicting figures owing to the lack of clarity on the status of these troops and the dates at which they were measured. Méliani claims that on the eve of the cease-fire in March 1962, 160,000 auxiliaries and 65,000 Muslims were serving in the regular army (1993, 26). Ageron, however, finds a total of 120,000 Muslims (including 40,0000 *harkis*) serving in the French forces at the time of the cease-fire (1993b, 11, 1995, 3–20).

The reasons why young men joined auxiliary forces were varied. Some joined to seek vengeance for an act of terror that might have been committed by the FLN against their village.[2] Others joined as a result of traditional enmities between villages and clans: if one joined the FLN, the other by reflex signed up with the French. Many joined because of French military pressure. French officers bullied and threatened young men to become *harkis;* they also deliberately compromised villagers, making them appear to be collaborators, so that, in defense, young men had to sign up with a *harka* if they did not want to suffer the fate of those suspected by the FLN of treason (Ferdi 1981). Yet others found in the pay they received from the French, modest though it was, a regular form of income that could keep hunger and want at bay from their families.

The French military viewed the recruitment of *harkis* and other auxiliaries as a useful tactic in revolutionary warfare, a method of depriving the FLN of potential supporters and helping tip the population toward the French. According to Charles-Robert Ageron (1994, 1995), there was little belief in their intrinsic military usefulness. There were doubts about *harki* loyalty; they were therefore poorly armed and commanded by a large number of French officers. Paid a daily wage, 750 (old) francs, they were viewed as day contractors. Although the desertion rate was low, many did not sign up for renewed contracts. *Harkis* were suspected of contributing part of their wages to the FLN, of avoiding battle with FLN troops, and of showing insufficient zeal in rounding up FLN suspects. Documents from the war suggest that the *harkis* did not see themselves as soldiers. In explaining why they were not denouncing the presence of FLN soldiers, one group of *harkis* declared in October 1960, "We are laborers and nothing more." Yet even if the *harkis,* as much of the Algerian population, held an attentiste attitude, unsure for which side they should opt, Algerians viewed them as traitors (Ageron 1994, 1995).

Charles de Gaulle took power in June 1958 on the premise that he would preserve Algeria as French; by late 1959 or early 1960, he concluded that Algeria had to be granted independence. Reflecting the winding down of the war and a desire not to compromise more Algerians, the *harki* forces were reduced in size; the total number of Algerians serving as *harkis* and in other military branches of the French army by 1 March 1962 was 120,000 (80,000 of whom were auxiliaries) (Ageron 1993b; Faivre 2000, 131).

Various planning organs considered the implications for the *harkis* of France leaving Algeria. One military position paper in 1961 decided that the *harkis*

2. The FLN itself recognized that some of its actions led villagers to volunteer for *harki* service (FLN directive, November 1961, quoted in Harbi [1980] 1993, 259).

should be disarmed for fear that if they were left with their weapons, there would be something like a "revolt of the Sepoys." It was feared that the *harkis* would turn their weapons on the French to win last-minute recognition as patriots and to gain favor with the newly independent government ("Problèmes posés par les harkis" 1961).

Officials had contradictory information on the risk to the *harkis* of reprisals once Algeria became independent. A preliminary study, conducted in 1961, assumed there would be few reprisals. A position paper considered the extent to which pro-French Moroccans had suffered after their country's independence and found that few were victimized. Other information, however, was more alarming. When the prefects in Algeria were asked in October-November 1961 about the best way of assuring the safety of French loyalists, they reported that they should be transferred to France (Faivre 2000, 113, 133).

The planners determined that to protect the French loyalists, the government of an independent Algeria would be required to issue an amnesty to them, and France would have to issue a unilateral guarantee that anyone who wished to leave Algeria would be helped to settle in the metropole, although it added that "settling in France is neither to be anticipated nor encouraged." The number of loyalists coming to France was assumed to be very low, numbering a few thousand at the most. Even the alarming December 1961 report by the prefects that suggested that virtually all loyalists were in danger stated that few felt themselves threatened (Faivre 1995, 83–84, 2000, 133).

When the French government and the FLN finally negotiated an end to the war on 18 March 1962 at Evian, a cease-fire was announced for the next day, and mechanisms were put in place to transfer authority to the Algerians, leading to independence in July. At Evian, the issue of the *harkis* was not dealt with specifically, however. Both the FLN and the French government declared that no one would be persecuted for his position during the war.

At the end of the war, the French disbanded the auxiliary troops. French officers were supposed to offer the auxiliaries three choices: (1) sign up with French army, (2) be part of the local forces that were about to be formed, or (3) go home with a bonus. The first option was available only for those without dependents, and most were married. As one historian of the *harkis* claims, it is likely that few were told of these options; instead, they were simply disarmed, given their bonus, and sent home (Faivre 1995, 184).

In the spring of 1962, the French had intercepted FLN correspondence indicating that the *harkis* were at risk. The party directed its members to "show themselves conciliatory toward the *harkis* in order not to provoke their departure for the metropole, which would allow them to escape the justice of independent

Algeria." By April, harassment and killing of *harkis* had begun, although not to the extent that was to occur in July and August. In April, the secretariat of the Ministry of Algerian Affairs noted that "Muslims [are being] tortured" (Faivre 2000, 137, 198, 222, 317; Pervillé 1999, 65). It was clear all was not well. *Harkis* were fleeing to French military barracks asking for protection. Individual French officers, who had led *harki* units, offered *harkis* protection on their own initiative and transported a number of them to France.

Higher-up officials were opposed to the possible inflow of potentially a million French loyalists (*harkis* and other auxiliary troops, elected Algerian officials and civil servants, and others who had shown support for the French cause) and their families. Although some were highly "Frenchified," the *harkis* were least so, coming from rural areas and being often illiterate. In various letters in April, the minister of Algerian affairs, Pierre Joxe, confirmed that *harkis* could enjoy the protection of the French army, but he appeared to put a limit on their right to come to France by saying they could qualify only if their lives were in danger. On 12 May, he issued a decree, backed up by a circular from Colonel Buis, head of his military cabinet, and leaked to the press, which forbad the repatriation of *harkis* outside any official plan (Faivre 2000, 135–136, 225; *Combat* 1962, 23 May; *Nation* 1962, 23 May; *Le Monde* 1962, 24 May; Hamoumou 1993, 273). This decree effectively excluded most from coming because the officially organized plan admitted only a small number.

Until independence, all the populations of Algeria were French citizens and should have had the same rights to move between Algeria and France. However, whereas Algerians of European origin, the *pieds-noirs,* could arrive freely in metropolitan France, that was not the case for the *harkis*. In May 1962, when some *harkis* arrived in Marseille through nonofficial channels, they were sent back to Algeria (*Figaro* 1962, 23 May). As far as French officials were concerned, there were two categories of citizens.

The only public explanation for the reluctance to accept the *harkis* was Minister Joxe's claim that they might be employed by the French terrorist organization, the Organisation de l'armée secrète (OAS), committed to keeping Algeria French. Many army officers had been involved in challenging the government's policies in Algeria and, given the personal loyalties that many *harkis* felt toward their officers, such a scenario was within the realm of the possible, and it therefore found some echoes in the press (Pervillé 1999, 67). But, then again, toward the end of the war, although the *pieds-noirs* nearly unanimously supported the OAS, they were not hindered from reaching French shores (Duranton-Crabol 1995, 113). The most likely explanation was provided by Joxe in a letter to the prime minister warning of the danger that *harkis* might be used by the OAS and stressing "the particular habits of these elements." In a cabinet meeting, he described them as "undesirable," alluding most probably to their purportedly unassimilationist nature (Peyrefitte 1994, 136; Faivre 2000, 199).

There was little sympathy for the *harkis* in the government. Once de Gaulle had convinced himself that the FLN incarnated Algerian nationalism, its opponents, such as the *harkis,* became unworthy. In a cabinet meeting, he described the *harkis* as "flotsam and jetsam" and as "soldiers of fortune" who served no purpose and should be got rid of as soon as possible. De Gaulle was indifferent to any danger the *harkis* might be facing: "if the people kill each other, it will be a matter for the new authorities," he told the cabinet (Pervillé 1999, 66; Peyrefitte 1994, 166).

With independence on 3 July, any constraints that Algerians might have felt were gone, and a full-scale assault was unleashed on the *harkis* and their families. There were reports of *harkis* and their dependents being hacked to death, set on fire, and even boiled to death. Some were taken prisoner and forced to carry out life-threatening tasks such as removing the mines the French had laid on Algeria's borders with Tunisia. There is no consensus as to the number killed, but it was in the tens of thousands. One of the first estimates in November 1962 came from the journalist Jean Lacouture, who evaluated the number of *harkis* killed by then to have been ten thousand, reflecting French official sources at the time (*Le Monde* 1962, 13 Nov.; "Atteintes aux accords d'Evian" 1962). *Harkis* and their sympathizers often mention 150,000 victims, a figure based on the extrapolation of a report by the subprefect of Akbou, who thought that maybe 750 *harkis* or even 1,000 had been killed in his *arrondissment* and surmised that the number was double in other *arrondissements.* Because Algeria had seventy-two *arrondissements,* the 150,000 figure was arrived at. After a careful demographic study, however, the historian Xavier Yacono (1982) categorically rejected the 150,000 figure as far too high, although he did not suggest an alternative number (see also Hamoumou 1993, 246–48; Méliani 1993, 34–35). Thirty years after his initial estimate, Lacouture (2001) revised the figure to 100,000. In 2001, the official historical Algerian agency devoted to the history of the war, which was probably liable to downplay the number of casualties, came up with a surprisingly high figure, suggesting between 75,000 and 100,000 victims (*Quotidien d'Oran* 2001, 4 Oct.).

After 3 July, all Algerian Muslims became Algerian citizens; until 1 January 1963 they could ask a French court to recognize them as French citizens, but they had to be on French soil to do so. With regard to *harkis,* who were now obviously in danger, the government adopted a legalistic position: they were not of interest to the French government because they were not French. When Minister of Defense Pierre Messmer reported on 25 July that *harkis* and other French loyalists were claiming that they were in danger, de Gaulle remained indifferent, telling the cabinet, "We cannot accept all Muslims who claim they are not getting along with their government" (quoted in Peyrefitte 1994, 196).

In Algeria, the French army was aware that the *harkis* were being persecuted. The superior commander noted to his subordinates on 24 August that the "crimes and brutality" suffered by the *harkis* justified the reception of the four thousand who had fled to French military camps. But no more could be accepted, and officers were forbidden from looking for former *harkis* or their families (this part of the copy of the order in the archives was underlined in red). The camps in France were full, and the experience with the *harkis* was "disappointing"—they were "inadaptable;" it was unclear how the camps in France would manage with winter approaching (Commandement supérieur 1962c).

Ageron has documented repeated expressions of concern by French authorities for the fate of the *harkis*. Prime Minister George Pompidou told the minister of the army that the auxiliaries who had sought asylum in French garrisons be transferred to France, and later he and his subordinates filed protests with the Algerian government for its maltreatment of the *harkis* (Ageron 1994, 5, 2000, 13).[3] But Pompidou, in line with other members of the cabinet, wanted to limit the number arriving in France. At a cabinet meeting in January 1963, Pompidou said, "We must not let ourselves be invaded by the Algerian labor force, even if it pretends to be *harkis*. If we are not careful, all the Algerians will settle in France" (Peyrefitte 1994, 396).

Government-organized repatriation programs, lasting from 1962 to 1967, brought twenty-five thousand *harkis* and other loyalists and their dependents to France; sixty-three thousand came by nonofficial means. Although these figures are in dispute, the one firm figure is that of the census of 1968, which shows that eighty-eight thousand "French Muslims" were born in Algeria (Jordi and Hamoumou 1999, 48–49; Faivre 2000, 142). Some of them were from privileged backgrounds, high civil servants, members of the liberal professions, and other important notables, but most were modest auxiliaries and their families. It is estimated that the French loyalists and their descendants, with a high birth rate, might today number around four hundred thousand, but there is no consensus on this figure.[4]

3. The Pompidou order, Ageron seems to believe, provides documentary evidence that the French were not reluctant to repatriate *harkis*. But Pompidou knew that this order would not mean that all *harkis* would be brought to France; the garrisons in Algeria were no longer accepting any more *harkis*. So the order applied only to the four thousand in the garrisons.

4. An official estimate of their number in the 1980s was already 400,000 (Report by secrétariat d'état 1984), but most estimates are lower and widely fluctuating; *Le Monde* in 2000 approximated

Although the *pieds-noirs* were allowed to live among other Frenchmen in France, most of the *harkis* were segregated. Government policy toward the *harkis* was a mixture of paternalism and racist indifference. Some *harkis* were brought to what previously had been internment camps, such as Rivesaltes, Larzac (Aveyron), and Saint-Maurice-l'Ardoise (Gard). Surrounded by barbed wire and run like military camps, these camps had held Spanish refugees in the 1930s, then Jews in the 1940s, and during the Algerian War the FLN and still later OAS prisoners. There were few facilities; most internees lived in tents even though winter conditions prevailed. Larzac was closed in 1964, but Saint-Maurice l'Ardoise and Biais continued as camps to house those considered to be unassimilable: the chronically ill, the traumatized, the aged, and families with no male heads of household. The former camp functioned until 1975, the latter even longer. Some *harkis* were employed to do forestry work in remote areas, with their families housed in abandoned villages. Still others were housed in public housing near industrial towns, where they had little contact with metropolitan Frenchmen (Gaspard 1995, 37–39).

At the beginning of this period, many *harkis* appeared to be hopeful that they would be recognized as French. Interviewing *harkis* in a camp in 1963, *Le Monde* met a girl who proudly announced that her name was Yvonne, and families had to be dissuaded from changing their names to Pompidou (*Le Monde* 1963, 20 June). The television news program *Cinq colonnes* had a program on *harkis* and shared the news of the birth of a new Frenchman, the son of an *harki*; his parents had named him Jacques (*C'était les harkis* 1963). Such naming practices were quite common during the first decade after the *harkis'* arrival, but by the 1970s disillusionment with the possibility of assimilation had set in, and *harkis* reverted to giving their children Muslim names (*Le Monde* 1973, 4 July; Roux 1990, 22)—a natural response to the poor reception they received. When in the 1990s children of *harkis* evoked the practice of giving European names, they claimed the names had been imposed upon them by social workers; they could not imagine that their parents had freely and rather enthusiastically administered these names (Delarue 1992, 34).

The metropolitan population revealed the same prejudices and fears toward the *harkis* as it had toward Arabs and Algerians in particular. An *harki* daughter remarked that in the hiring process, employers, in deciding "between us and the French with the same qualifications, will take a French person; they don't like us. They fear us, maybe it's our looks" [*peut-être c'est la tête*] (radio program 1981).

---

their numbers at 250,000 (17 June 2000). A few months later it reduced the number to 150,000 (*Le Monde* 2001, 8 Feb.).

The son of an *harki,* who had taken on the very French-sounding name Jean-Pierre Guérin, reported that he would call a potential employer on the phone about a job saying his name was Guérin and would be encouraged to come for an interview, but when he arrived, the employer would tell him there was no job. Then there was the gaze of the Frenchman categorizing him; when he crossed the border, police would scrutinize him because he did not "look like a Guérin." He applied to the Conseil d'état to change his name, but was repeatedly refused. He was now stuck with a name that he did not feel suited the reception French society was giving him (Muller 1998, 1:70–71, 1999, 35–36).

The daughter of an *harki* bitterly remarked that she was not French; there was no point in insisting on that: "We were never liked, I am always an Arab." In a radio program in 1981, a second proclaimed, "From all points of view I am French, but we are kept out of the system." Yet a third complained, "We desire total integration; we should not be thought of as immigrants. We have no rights, we are called Algerians." One *harki* reflected some of the same despair, "I would prefer Algerian nationality, but it is too late. Here, one is always an Algerian," or, as another put it, "He who says I am French is a liar." Asked when he came to that realization, he said it was the moment a fence was erected around the camp in which he was housed (radio program 1981; see also R. Courrière 1985).

Anger at their parents for bringing them to or giving birth to them in a society that did not accept them as full equals and embarrassment at having parents who were often illiterate and incapable of assimilating to French society created generational conflict. Critical of her *harki* parents, one girl remarked, "They came to France, but they did nothing. They did not really learn the language. They did nothing to succeed." Another girl remarked, "Parents don't transmit anything to us. We have no past, no future, no present." Reflecting these disappointments and an inability to put their parents' choice in historical perspectives, many of the *harki* children confidently declared, "We would have made a different choice from our parents," and "They let themselves be duped." A son of an *harki* angrily told his interlocutor:

> My father is an idiot. A poor creature. He chose the camp of the defeated and he brought us here to live the life of a dog; I am ashamed of him. Look at what being French has brought us! We are held in greater contempt and treated worse than the authentic Algerians. . . . If I had been adult before 1962, I would have fought for my country, Algeria, not for the colonialists. I would have been a member of the FLN and everyone would have respected me.[5]

5. See Anglade 1976, 114; radio program 1981; and Muller 1998, 1:133, 1999, 69, for the quoted material in this paragraph.

Their parents' choices were to blame for the no-man's-land in which the *harki* children found themselves: "In Algeria we are traitors, in France we are Arabs" (Diop 1990, 35).

In the early years, *harki* children came home from school reporting that their classmates called them children of traitors, creating in them a malaise, a sense of guilt. And as for parents, "hardly ever do they speak in front of the [children] of events in Algeria, neither telling about their lives, nor exalting their battles. It is a terrible silence, born of the impossibility to communicate and from an acquired sense of guilt" (Muller 1999, 199; Méliani 1993, 42).

Fathers felt disgraced by often being unable to provide a living for their families and for having brought them to live in a country that treated them as outcastes. A pregnant silence enveloped *harki* families with no mention of the war or the circumstances that had brought them to France. When Mohand Hamoumou conducted his research on the *harkis* in the 1980s, much of it based on interviews with former auxiliaries, the children of the *harkis* would listen in and afterward tell Hamoumou that this was the first time they had heard their fathers talk about the war (Hamoumou 1993, 39). The son of one *harki* interviewed by Jordi and Hamoumou noted that "[m]y father was an *harki*. For a long time I did not know what that meant. My family did not speak of the Algerian War" (1999, 17; see also Muller 1998, 1:91, 186, 1999, 108).

Many *harkis* were burdened by the position they had taken in the war. Were they patriots or traitors? Hamoumou, in his three hundred or so interviews, discovered a fairly large number of former *harkis* who claimed to have been FLN sympathizers, favoring independence for Algeria. But, they said, they found themselves repelled by FLN atrocities or by some other form of misplaced zeal, or they had tried to join the FLN but were fended off by militants who did not want to share in the glory of being fighters (Hamamou 1993, passim). Although Hamoumou believes his interlocutors, it seems more likely that these explanations were memories created later, protecting the interlocutors from the charge of sedition that had been leveled against them. Also, the rural environment from which the *harkis* were recruited was not one in which a strong sense of nationalism flourished, especially in the early years of the war (see Stora 1986).

Another response to the charge of treason was loudly to proclaim one's Frenchness. Bachaga Boualem, the son and grandson of notables who had served France, had been vice president of the French National Assembly and recruited *harki* groups. He proclaimed his choice in the title of his book *Mon pays la France* (1962). Colonel Abd-el-Aziz Méliani, a graduate of Saint Cyr and an officer in the regular French army, wanted it to be understood that the *harkis,* born in Algeria, a territory that was French in 1830, were "French before our compatriots in Nice and Savoy and on the morrow after independence of Algeria chose to remain French" (1993, 11). In a television program, one *harki* proclaimed, "I am French; my grandfather fought for France, and in the Algerian War my brothers did. I have always thought I am French" (*Vaincre l'oubli* 1985). Many *harkis* and their supporters insisted that they could not have been traitors to the Algerian nation, for it did not exist until 1962. As an *harki* publication put it, how could *harkis* be considered traitors? "Our country is France and we have not betrayed it" (Méliani 1993, 42; *Le clin d'oeil* 1997; Muller 1998, 2:7, 33, 1999, 188).

Certainly a number of Algerians had felt strongly French and been well assimilated to French culture. Sometimes their expressions of loyalty to France were seen as representing *harki* sentiment, but on the whole *harkis* had had limited contact with the French and did not speak or read their language. Just as few of them had been Algerian nationalists, so they equally had not had a strong sense of attachment to the colonial power. The strong French patriotism, mostly absent during the Algerian War, was a product of the postwar era, an answer to the charges of treason and a means of assuring themselves of all the rights they were entitled to as French citizens.

Some *harki* children were pleased their parents had chosen France. The horrors in independent Algeria after the civil war that broke out in 1992 seemed to validate the French cause: "our parents did not make a bad choice. . . . We now know why our parents were *harkis*. We know why we are here. We can be proud of our fathers. They refused the terror that we now discover in Algeria." A number of *harki* women expressed gratitude for their fathers' choice of sides, for otherwise they would be growing up in a country where women were denied their rights (Anglade 1976, 121; Diop 1990, 35; Jordi and Hamoumou 1999, 123). Although such opinions were expressed, the overwhelming attitude was one of disappointment, of a sense of betrayal and a memory of betrayal. If some regretted they had chosen the wrong camp, others remembered how France had betrayed them. When in 1982 *L'honneur d'un capitaine* was filmed, the sons of *harkis* played their fathers. There was a scene in which a French officer addresses them and tells them, "We shall not betray you." One of the actors requested that the scene be changed with the French officer just saying, "We need you," explaining "especially not that word. For too long they swore not to betray us, and we have been widely betrayed" (Droit 1982).

The *harkis* had legitimate grievances; they had been told they could trust France's word: France would stay in Algeria, but instead it decided to leave, disarmed the auxiliaries, and abandoned them to be murdered by the FLN. The French had only reluctantly accepted the settlement of a few *harkis* and had been indifferent and even callous toward their plight after their arrival on metropoli-

tan soil. Yet it could also be argued that the emphasis on how France had betrayed them was a way of displacing the charges of betrayal the *harkis* had had to endure for so many years.

The *harkis* were generally ignored; their presence was an embarrassing reminder of the costs of decolonization. As Secretary for Repatriation Raymond Courrière put it in 1985, "The intent of the politicians was not to speak of this community and that it not be spoken of" (Courrière 1985). To the Gaullists, the *harkis* were an uncomfortable reminder of the failure to protect French loyalists and the reluctance to accept them into French society. To the Left, which had supported de Gaulle's policies in Algeria, they were also a poignant reminder of the costs of decolonization. Once the war was over, the *harkis* were a reminder of a conflict the French preferred to forget. Years later, the caricaturist Pancho amusingly summarized the case of the political Left and of many Frenchmen against the *harkis:* in the cartoon Marianne tells an *harki,* "You were wrong to help us when we were in error" (*Le Monde* 2001, 31 Aug.).

Frustrated by years of neglect, the *harkis* started to protest in 1974. They held hunger strikes, took officials hostage, issued manifestos, and gave interviews to the press. There were high-profile *harki* hunger strikes at the Madeleine in Paris in 1974 and again in 1983. In Narbonne, children of *harkis* rioted in June 1991, setting off a series of similar protests throughout the country. On the day before Bastille Day, five thousand *harkis* marched through Paris, carrying flags and wearing large badges inscribed with: "My country, France. Where is France?" (Muller 1999, 140). In the years that followed, they held publicized hunger strikes, and on 11 November 1999 a scuffle took place between *harki* organizations and police at the Arc de Triomphe. The media provided a voice to the children of *harkis,* who made clear the neglect and mistreatment of a population whose only transgression had been loyalty to the French nation (Muller 1998, 1:240; Jordi and Hamoumou 1999, 111).

With the passage of time, it was easier to confront the issues of the *harkis.* The Gaullist leaders who had directed affairs during the painful years of decolonization were replaced by a new generation that had had no role in the decision making of that period and hence could more easily confront the *harki* cause. During the war, the *harkis,* seen as tools of repressive policies, had been the subject of opprobrium from the left. Indicative of this view was the journalist Paulette Péju, who described the *harkis* as "mercenaries serving the occupier, they round up people, they rape, they pillage, they torture and they kill" (1961a, 7). But after the war, the Left saw the *harkis* as victims of exploitation and neglect and hence worthy of empathy. Socialist prime minister Michel Rocard in 1990 assured the *harkis* of his concern for them and "more generally [for] those who feel they have been the victims of history." Later, even the Communists empathized with the *harkis,* describing them as "victims of colonialism" (Méliani 1993, 190; *Humanité,* 29 Aug., 26 and 29 Sept. 2001).

In the 1980s, xenophobia, exploited by the extreme rightist National Front Party, made clear that there was a need to combat racism, in particular that aimed at Algerians and other North African migrants. Responsible political leaders from both the left and the right stigmatized racism and its discourses of exclusion. If immigrant workers and even their offspring born in France were viewed as foreign, that certainly could not be the case for the *harkis,* who not only had been French citizens (also applicable, of course, to Algerian immigrant workers), but also had shed their blood for France. As Prime Minister Jacques Chirac declared in 1987, "We must honor the debt we have for the blood that was shed" (quoted in Roux 1991, 334).

Political leaders, arguing for the inclusion of all people living in France regardless of background, made a special case for the *harkis,* for if they could not be included in the body politic, which Muslims would qualify? Even the National Front was sympathetic to *harki* inclusion, albeit not as a first step toward inclusion of those considered of non-French origin, but to claim that the party was not racist and to show its continuing support for French Algeria. Opinion polls revealed a consensus on the *harkis.* A 1992 poll showed that although 32 percent of Frenchmen thought the *pieds-noirs* had been unfairly treated upon their arrival in metropolitan France, 62 percent thought the same for the *harkis* ("1962–1992" 1992).

Official attempts were made to repair the prejudice that the *harkis* had experienced. By 1974, before the protests broke out, the French parliament recognized that the *harkis* had the same veteran rights as the French soldiers who had fought in Algeria. (Until then they had not because the French Parliament did not officially recognize the conflict as a war. Indeed, it did not do so until October 1999.) By giving *harkis* the same rights as regular soldiers of the French army, Parliament appeared to recognize the auxiliaries as having been comparable fighters, a change from the actual status they had enjoyed throughout the war.

Parliament also provided financial help; in 1984, it gave a lump sum of 110,000 francs to each of fifteen thousand *harki* families. In 1987, in 1994, and again in 1995, further indemnities, special loans, and training programs were established for *harkis* and their families. In 1994, *harkis* who were imprisoned or tortured by the FLN after 2 July 1962 because of their loyalty to France were provided with a pension and provision for medical services. In 1999, *harkis* older than sixty years of age and of low income were given a yearly pension of 9,000 francs. By 1999, 6.8 billion francs in aid had been disbursed on various government programs to *harkis* (Assemblée nationale 1999).

A number of symbolic attempts were made to register regret for the treatment of the *harkis* and to show gratitude toward them. In 1989, a stamp was issued in their honor, with the inscription, "Homage to the *harkis,* soldiers of France;" it sold 11.5 million copies. The need to include *harkis* in the national community led to a rewriting of the past; although during the war they had not been recognized as soldiers, now they were. Public regret was expressed for the policies of the past. At the ceremonial issuing of the stamp, a Defense Ministry representative declared: "Those who wished to reach France, unfortunately, were unable to do so. Those who were repatriated did so under difficult circumstances of which we cannot be proud. By this ceremony the Government of the Republic wishes to thank the veterans, tell their children and grandchildren they should be proud of their parents" (*Journal de l'union nationale des anciens combattants* 1990).

By a law of June 1994, Parliament unanimously declared, "The French Republic acknowledges its gratitude toward the repatriated former members of auxiliary or similar forces, or victims of captivity in Algeria for the sacrifices they made." In 1996, inaugurating a monument to "civilian and military victims who fell in North Africa, 1952–1962," President Chirac spoke of the auxiliary forces and the regular military as "fraternally united in the same fold of the flag" ("Inauguration à Paris" 1996).

Broad developments in general regarding memory and justice affected both the *harkis* and the attitudes toward them. In the 1970s, there was, as Henry Rousso puts it, "a reawakening of Jewish memory"; Jews and non-Jews to a greater degree focused on the Holocaust (1991, 132). The language of persecution and genocide commonly employed to talk about Jews was also appropriated by *harkis* and their supporters. Jean Bastien-Thiry, the would-be assassin of de Gaulle, at his trial in 1963 represented the killing of the *harkis* as a "genocide," before it had become common to do so (see Bastien-Thiry 1994, 127). Dominique Schnapper, a sociologist and the thesis director of Mohand Hamoumou's *Et ils sont devenus harkis,* herself Jewish, saw parallels between the treatment of *harkis* and Jews in the Second World War: "The treatment of the *harkis* constitutes a shameful page in the history of France, as was the establishment of the Jewish statutes on October 3, 1940 or the rounding up of Jews at the Vel d'hiv on July 16, 1942" (Hamamou 1993, 10). Colonel Méliani spoke of the *harkis'* "massacres, as having the dimension of a genocide" (Méliani 1993, 27; see also Méliani 1995). Ahmed Kaberseli, also an *harki* spokesperson, described the killing of the *harkis* as similar to that of the Jews, Armenians, and Roma peoples. If 120,000 *harkis* had been killed, why did French people care less about them than France's 76,000 Jews killed in the Second World War? If Philippe Pétain was held in opprobrium for killing the Jews, why was de Gaulle, responsible for a greater number of *harki* deaths, not cursed also (Kaberseli 1996, 5)? For a French military historian who as an officer had directed *harkis,* "There is no example of such atrocities carried out by a fanaticized population in the whole twentieth century" (Faivre 1994, 184).

Although nearly all *harkis* went through camps as part of the official processing, most stayed only a limited time before joining the labor force. But the camps became a focus of *harki* memories. They were seen as analogous to the Nazi death camps. One *harki* reminisced, "When one sees a film on the concentration camps, it reminds me of Saint-Maurice-l'Ardoise. . . . It is a different planet" (Méliani 1993, 128, 140). Another remembered the Biais camp "as resembling very much a concentration camp." The child of an *harki* noted, "I personally am traumatized. To spend one's youth in a concentration camp is not a piece of cake" (Delarue 1992, 33). Certainly some *harkis* did spend many years in such camps, but such an experience became emblematic of the whole *harki* experience. A spokesperson for the *harki* cause declared, "After letting us be massacred, we were put in camps to remain subcitizens, victims of crimes against humanity" (Chabrun, Lenoir, and Varela 2001, 14).

The heightened memory of the Holocaust, triggered by Jewish memory, led to an increasing role for the state in recognizing the horrors of Vichy's policies toward France's Jews. The courts were seen as a venue for meting out justice, but also for establishing the historic record. Beginning in the 1980s, the courts brought to trial for crimes against humanity Klaus Barbie, Paul Touvier, and

René Bousquet on charges of "crimes against humanity" for their role in the killing of Jews. The most important trial, however, was that of Maurice Papon in 1997–98, who as secretary general of the prefecture of Bordeaux in 1942 had helped deport fifteen hundred Jews. He was found guilty and sentenced to ten years' imprisonment (Golsan 1996, 2000; *Le procès de Maurice Papon* 1998). In between these trials, in July 1995, President Chirac made a significant gesture in a solemn ceremony by issuing an official apology for the role of the Vichy state in the Holocaust (*Le Monde* 1995, 18 July).

Harkis and their supporters, having equated *harki* fate with that of the Jews, came to expect a parallel remedy for their ills: a state apologia and the sanction of courts to bring to justice the authors of their misfortunes and to redress the historic record. If Papon could be tried for killing fifteen hundred Jews, what about the officials who had served de Gaulle and were responsible for the deaths of 150,000 *harkis,* asked one *harki* publication (*Le clin d'oeil* 1998).

The attraction of judicial action was heightened in 2000–2001 by a passionate debate that broke out on the possibility of bringing to trial, on charges of crimes against humanity, French police and army officials guilty of torture and other acts of brutality during the Algerian War (W. Cohen 2001). In the fall of 2001, an *harki* organization filed suit against the French government for committing crimes against humanity by having abandoned the *harkis* to their fate (*Le Monde* 2001, 29 Aug.) Most commentators quite rightly pointed to the Algerian state as responsible for the death of the *harkis* and to the unlikelihood that any court would accept the case because all acts connected with the Algerian War had been amnestied by a series of laws after the end of the war. Nonetheless, the case caught the attention of the press (Gacon 1995, 2000).

The need for a symbolic recognition of France's responsibility for what happened to the *harkis* was seen as crucial after an episode that took place in the summer of 2000. In June, Algerian president Abdelaziz Bouteflika came to France on a state visit. French journalists queried him as to whether *harkis* would be allowed to return to Algeria on a visit (most had been barred by Algerian authorities from doing so since independence). The president answered that the moment was not yet come: "it is exactly as if one asked a French member of the Resistance to shake hands with a collaborator" (*Le Monde* 2000, 18–19 June). The *harki* community was stung at being compared to Nazi collaborators and by the failure of French authorities to speak out for the equality of all French citizens. After all, Bouteflika had issued an invitation to *pieds-noirs* to visit their former birthplace, but was barring other French citizens from the same rights. A few weeks later, however, on the occasion of the yearly interview with the president of the republic on 14 July, President Chirac expressed shock when asked about Bouteflika's comments and affirmed the *harkis'* full equality with all other French citizens (*Le Monde* 2000, 16–17 July). But the pain inflicted on the *harkis* seemed to need a more forceful intervention—some national ceremony to recognize their contributions to the nation and to affirm their full membership in the body politic.

The *harkis,* believed to be four hundred thousand strong in France, represented a significant electorate that needed wooing, so their cause was also being exploited by political rivals. Alain Madelin, the leader of the centrist party Democratie libérale, called on the Fifth Republic to carry out "its duty of repentance" (the mention of the Fifth Republic was a covert reminder to voters that it was the founders of the Fifth Republic, the Gaullists, who bore the responsibility for the fate of the *harkis*) (Agence France presse 2000). In February 2001, President Chirac decided to hold a national ceremony in September to honor the *harkis*—a reparation for the slight they had suffered during Bouteflika's visit. It was also intended to neutralize the political exploitation of the *harkis.*

On 25 September in the presence of sixty *harki* organizations and the highest civilian and military officials, President Chirac gave a speech at the Invalides in which he spoke of the "debt of honor" France owed "these proud and courageous fighters" and of the need to recognize "the position that is their due . . . [and that] justice be rendered to their honor as soldiers, their loyalty and patriotism": "our brothers in arms expect of France, the fatherland they chose, that it defend their honor and express the gratitude to which they have a right."

Once again the obligations of memory took precedence over the historic record considering that the *harkis* had not been fully viewed as soldiers during the war. But history and memory coincided when Chirac mentioned the massacres of *harkis* and their families and noted that when leaving Algeria, the French had "not known how to prevent [these deaths]." He also spoke of the poor reception of the *harkis* in France, their segregation, and the poor schooling provided them, all of "which are still at the origins of important handicaps." And he promised that "the *harkis* and their children will have their place in the national community" (quoted in *Figaro* 2001, 26 Sept.; *Le Monde* 2001, 26 Sept.). Ceremonies were held in twenty-seven locations in France connected to an *harki* past, such as the camp at Saint-Maurice, or where there were large concentrations of *harkis,* as in Lille. A plaque was installed at the Invalides and in the provincial sites with the words of the 1994 parliamentary resolution, "The French Republic acknowledges its gratitude toward the repatriated former members of auxiliary or similar forces or victims of captivity in Algeria for the sacrifices they made."

This was an important symbolic act, but an editorial in *Libération* was correct in suggesting that success in resolving the problem of the *harkis* would occur when there no longer would be an "*harki* community, because they finally would be fully French. What are we waiting for?"

12 Language and Politics

A New Revisionism

HABIBA DEMING

ALGERIA'S POSTCOLONIAL HISTORY can be seen as a series of attempts to deal with consequences of the colonial past. Nowhere is this truer than in the cultural realm. Because of the brutality of the wars of conquest and liberation and the extent of the destructuration of society that occurred between these two events, colonization in Algeria resulted in greater social upheavals than in the rest of the Maghreb. The economic and social tectonic shifts that took place under French domination and the devastation they caused often obscure other forms of destructuring that are not easily measured, but may have longer-lasting sequelae. Aspects of the French colonial project that deserve closer attention are the colonial linguistic and cultural policies and how they continue to impact the country today. This chapter examines how the present linguistic debate in Algeria both stems from and reflects a revisionism of colonial cultural ideology.[1]

At the time of conquest, Algeria had an extensive infrastructure of Koranic schools (primary education) and *medersas* (secondary education) (Lacheraf 1963). These schools were funded by revenue from *habous* lands.[2] Education was

1. This chapter focuses on certain aspects of colonial linguistic policies aimed at disjoining vernacular Arabic from classical Arabic, the written language. For this reason, it does not deal with Berber vernacular languages such as Chaouia or Kabyle, for even in Berber-speaking areas the written language was classical Arabic (Berber vernaculars do not fully function yet as written languages, and there are ongoing efforts to codify them and debates over the use of Latin, Arabic, or Tifinagh characters to give them a written form). In Berber-speaking areas, both in Algeria and Morocco, the French colonial administration pursued another brand of cultural destructuring of traditional society, often referred to as *la politique berbère*. Its strategy was somewhat different in that it relied primarily on religious and ethnic mythologizing rather than on linguistic mythologizing. Berber speakers were constructed as quasi-pagan populations, superficially Islamized and descendants of Romans or Aryans and thus easily Christianized.

2. Also called *wakf*. These charitable foundations, constituted from lands willed by individuals, served to finance schools (Stora 1991).

conducted in classical Arabic and was traditional in the sense that it was grounded in religious, legal, and philological studies. Though the curriculum was old-fashioned and in need of modernization, it achieved a literacy rate in Algeria's population as high as in France and other agrarian societies of the time and produced cultured and effective leaders, such as Emir 'Abd el-Kadir (Lacheraf 1963).

The military conquest had devastating effects on Algeria's cultural resources, causing the deaths or permanent exile of a large number of Algeria's educated elite (Lacheraf 1963, 723). The anarchic and competing colonial practices that followed caused further disintegration of social and cultural networks in the country. According to Lacheraf, between 1850 and 1870 thousands of traditional schools were closed, leading to a precipitous and catastrophic fall in literacy rates. Massive land expropriations undermined not only the economic and social bases of society, but its cultural and linguistic foundations as well: the expropriation decree for *habous* lands acted, in effect, as a decree for shutting down schools.

Aggressive land-confiscation policies were not the only cause of the collapse of the education system; they were followed by a systematic policy of restricting and controlling access to schooling for the conquered population. Thus, the literacy rate never reached its precolonization level during the entire 132 years of colonization. In 1962, at the time of independence, there were still remarkably high rates of illiteracy: 85 percent of the population was illiterate (could not read Arabic or French), and 94 percent of men and 98 percent of women were illiterate in French (Lacheraf 1964, 1630; Stora 1991, 105, citing Germaine Tillion). A full assessment of the long-term impact of education policies during the colonial period has not yet been made, but such an assessment is critical for understanding the present linguistic debate.

In addition to negatively affecting the literacy of the population, the dismantling of the traditional Arabic educational system caused deep cultural and psychological damage by distancing written Arabic from spoken Arabic (Lacheraf 1964). Arabic shares with other languages a feature linguists call diglossia: it has classical (written) and vernacular (spoken) forms (Fergusson 1959, 1991).[3] Al-

3. The spoken Arabic dialects represent regional variations and deviations of the written language. Linguists have usually divided spoken Arabic into five dialects: the Arab peninsular dialect, the Syro-Palestinian dialect, the Iraqi dialect, the Egyptian dialect, and the Maghribi dialect. Although there are variants within these main dialects, they represent the main regional types. For a basic introduction to the structure of Arabic, see Yushmanov 1961. For a survey of Arabic dialects and their evolution and relation to classical Arabic, refer to Versteegh 1997. For a historical overview of the language, consult Chejne 1969.

though written Arabic is the same language across space and time (from medieval Arabic), spoken Arabic has several regional variants.[4] Throughout the Arabic-speaking world, classical and vernacular forms of the language represent the two poles of a linguistic continuum. The more educated a person is, the closer his speech is to the classical (written) end of the continuum, whereas a totally illiterate person's speech would be at the most distant point from the classical form. For an educated person, there is constant interplay between the classical and the vernacular forms.

In Algeria, as literacy rates fell, the interplay between classical and vernacular Arabic decreased, resulting in an impoverishment of spoken Arabic and an alienation from written Arabic. Although the situation thus created did not progress to a permanent alteration of the linguistic rapport between vernacular and classical Arabic, it did alter significantly Algerians' perception of these two forms. More important, the loss of literacy in Arabic displaced the authoritative discourse of high Arab culture, which served what Djait calls the "tenuous artery of classical culture" (1985, 12). This cultural foreclosure left Algerians with limited access to the historical context from which to articulate a resistance discourse.

In his article "L'interruption généalogique," Meddeb uses the term *interruption* to describe the end of the transmission of cultural values between the generations that immediately preceded colonization and the one that followed. He contrasts the poetry of Emir 'Abd el-Kadir—"la figure qui illustre la prégnance et la transmission continuée d'une éducation traditionnelle" (the figure that exemplifies pregnance and continuity of the traditional education) (1995, 75)—to that of the poet Si Mohand, whose work, less than a generation later, does not show the symbolic continuity present in the poetic language of Emir Abd el-Kadir. Si Mohand's poems already express, beyond the physical destruction of the war, the loss of a referential system, which made him a cultural "orphan." One might say that the interruption of the flow of symbols Meddeb detects in poems is a textual example of a phenomenon that became generalized in the culture at large and was mirrored in the disjoining of the linguistic structure itself.

4. Several terms are used to describe the written and spoken forms of Arabic. In French, the terms *arabe littéral* and *arabe classique* are often used interchangeably for the written form, and *arabe dialectal* and *arabe vulgaire* for the spoken form. In English, *classical* and *standard Arabic* are used for the written form and *colloquial Arabic* for the spoken form. There is also the expression *standard modern Arabic,* which also refers to written Arabic but distinguishes it from the more formal and complex *medieval Arabic.* In this chapter, I use the terms *classical* and *vernacular* when stressing the cultural context and the terms *written* and *spoken* when emphasizing the linguistic function.

As education in classical Arabic in Algeria disappeared, a limited number of schools were allowed to teach Arabic. Colonial authorities controlled the curriculum, limiting it to what was needed to produce colonial subalterns. By sentencing it to irrelevance and stripping it of its value to the society, these policies aimed at a slow atrophy of Arabic as a living language, treating it de facto as an archaic, almost dead language. As Boudjedra expresses with poetic bitterness, these policies worked to "la cloue au pilori de l'archaisme démodé, hors jeu," (nail it to the pillory of old-fashioned archaism, no longer in use) (1992, 32). As Arabic lost ground educationally and culturally, it began to be constructed as a marginal premodern language of limited value, one that with its bizarre script and archaic synthetic morphology had not evolved. The colonial discourse systematically debased Arabic. It was variously described as illogical, unlike French (because it is written from right to left), and at once too difficult yet not complex enough to signify modernity. The occulted remnants of this discourse are now like deeply embedded shards in the collective psyche, manifest in any debate about language in Algeria.

Although effectively banned or tightly controlled, Arabic was not replaced by French. The use of French is often mistakenly thought to have been widespread in colonial Algeria. On the contrary, despite the elimination and consequent atrophy of Arabic as the traditional language of education, French did not become entrenched in the population. The explanation lies in a contradiction inherent to the colonial project. Although officially a French department, Algeria in reality was what Stora calls a "faux modèle de la République" (a false model of the republic) (1991, 7). In a sense, it was a false France, with false French institutions and a false French educational system. It was neither a protectorate, able, like other regions of the Maghreb, to keep its language and a semblance of cultural continuity, nor a region to be transformed progressively through education in French into a French province (like Brittany or Alsace), with its people partaking of the rights of full citizenship.

The land expropriations that led to socioeconomic disintegration, the breakup of communities, and the atomization of individuals resulted in French domination over the public sphere.[5] However, to ensure permanency to the colo-

5. See the analysis on the impact of the breakup of arch properties in Laraoui 1995. The term *arch* refers to a type of property ownership. Islamic property law recognizes both individual ownership *(melk* property) and collective ownership, lands owned by a community as a whole (arch property). The colonial administration dismantled the arch property in order to bring the bulk of the land under French control. In Algeria, this was done by the passing of a series of laws (April 22, 1863, July 26, 1873, and February 16, 1897).

nial enterprise, domination over the private sphere was also essential, and with the obliteration of the country as a social, political, and economic entity, the only remaining evidence of the existence of an Algerian nation was cultural (Lacheraf 1963). If, as Laraoui asserts, French colonial designs were for Maghrebian society to survive essentially as a "réserve anthropologique" (anthropological reservation), the severing of the flow of Arab high culture became central to the colonial project. To accomplish this goal, as Laraoui very pointedly remarks, "L'idéal aurait été d'avoir devant soi 'un peuple sans écriture' et l'on prit des dispositions pour y arriver" (The ideal would have been to be faced with a "preliterate population," and measures were taken to reach this ideal) (1995, 318). Colonial cultural policy in general and the education policies aimed at Arabic in particular need to be considered in the light of this programmatic.

Laraoui's thesis about the manufacturing of a preliterate society can be deduced from the two-pronged policy pursued by the colonial administration. The first goal of this policy was to suppress written Arabic as a living language, confining it for most Algerians to liturgical use and restricting and closely controlling any other use. Efforts to achieve this goal resulted in what Ageron delicately calls a "small war": "la petite guerre faite aux écoles coraniques, tolérées mais tracassées n'est pas une page honorable de l'histoire française" (the small war waged against Koranic schools, tolerated but harassed, does not do honor to French history) (1968, 2:947). The second policy goal was to restrict the introduction of low-level French education to selected areas.

Most selected areas were in predominantly rural and Berber-speaking regions such as Kabylia and, to a lesser extent, in the Aurès region. To colonial administrators, the cultures of these areas seem to have approximated more closely their conception of the anthropological ideal of "a preliterate" stage where they thought a proto-French specimen could be developed to help permanently entrench colonization in the country. This policy was summarized in one education bureaucrat's declaration:

> Ce n'est pas par générosité que l'Université veut répandre l'enseignement en Kabylie, mais, disons-le bien haut, dans l'intérêt de la France. . . . Nous donnerons donc à nos élèves, par des leçons appropriées, des notions sur la grandeur de la France, sur sa force militaire, sur sa richesse. Notre situation serait bien plus solide si les Indigènes en arrivaient à penser: "Les français sont forts et généreux; ce sont les meilleurs maîtres [*sic*] que nous puissions avoir." [It is not out of generosity that the University wants to spread education in Kabylia, but, let us say it out loud, in the interest of France. . . . Thus we shall give our students, through an appropriate curriculum, an idea of the greatness of France, its military power, its wealth. We would be more solidly entrenched if the indigenous population

> comes to think, "The French are strong and generous, they are the best masters we could have."] (quoted in Lacheraf 1963, 729)

Focusing on antagonisms surrounding education policies in Algeria (the local colonial administration's opposition versus the Algerian population's reluctance), Ageron does not link specific policies to specific objectives. One may accept his seemingly genuine consternation at what he terms the "incomprehensible" pattern of school openings, but it is surprising that he would attribute this pattern to chance and to isolated, individual decisions by colonial administrators: "Que des villes françaises comme Philippeville par exemple aient refuser d'ouvrir la moindre école indigène jusqu'en 1914 alors qu'on avait créé huit dans l'Aurès, refuge de tous les archaismes, paraît aujourd'hui incompréhensible" (That French cities such as Philippeville, for example, have refused to allow a single school for the indigenous population until 1914, whereas eight were created in the Aurès, refuge of backwardness, seems incomprehensible today) (1968, 2:951). His attempts to explain this pattern are hampered by a failure to see how ideological and political goals affected education policy. Although he recognizes the prevalence of "une certaine conception militante de l'enseignement" (a certain partisan conception of education) (1968, 2:956) in the French educational enterprise in Algeria, he does not go on to relate its different constituent components to a broader ideological project.

Ageron focuses a great deal on the struggle between assimilationist educators and the local colonial administration. This traditional but superficial dichotomy, which pits a corps of liberal and dedicated cadres from France against a reactionary colonial administration vehemently opposed to educating Algerians, fails to account for the impact of the colonial educational undertaking irrespective of which approach prevailed. Although there were some differences to be considered, the approaches were not fundamentally in opposition in the sense that both were predicated on the cultural and historical erasure of Algerian society through the obliteration of its linguistic and cultural identity. One approach sought to achieve this result simply by destroying Arabic and Arab-Islamic culture, the other through the progressive replacement of them with French and French cultural ideals. In the end, both approaches were tried at various times with disastrous results for the population.

It is not in dispute that education in colonial Algeria was directed primarily by political rather than pedagogical considerations or that whatever policies were pursued were part of a process that can be described as ideological consolidation of the colonial project: "l'enseignement des Indigènes était une oeuvre politique plutôt qu'une oeuvre scolaire" (the education of the indigenous population was a political task rather than an educational one) (Ageron 1968, 2:932, citing a colonial administrator). The actual elimination of written Arabic was necessary but not sufficient for the manufacturing of a preliterate people, precisely because of the organic relationship between the classical and the vernacular forms of the language. Because the use of written Arabic had effectively ended, it could have been considered eliminated *in fact;* however, its virtual presence in the vernacular required a strategy to eliminate it in *thought* as well. As a presence in the vernacular ready to be actualized, classical Arabic could only be destroyed discursively. This discursive destruction required the elaboration of a colonial discourse that made written Arabic a "foreign" language. It was officially classified as such, and spoken Arabic was offered, optionally, under a variety of names, such as *arabe vulgaire* (common Arabic) or *arabe usuel* (vernacular Arabic) with some attempts to give it a written form using the Latin alphabet. This linguistic fiction was clearly recognized by educators and population alike: "Ce qu'on appelait donc arabe usuel écrit n'était que de l'arabe littéraire plus ou moins fautif" (Thus, what was called vernacular written Arabic was nothing but classical Arabic, more or less defective) (Ageron 1968, 2:924). Although the colonial scheme of classifying classical Arabic as a "foreign" language did not affect sociolinguistic reality and thus failed to detach vernacular Arabic concretely from classical Arabic to make it a "language" of its own, the mythology of this scheme has not been directly confronted or systematically dispelled since independence.

Thus, the lasting effect of the colonial discourse is not so much in the linguistic realm as in the "imaginary" realm, the internalized myths about what Arabic is and about how its vernacular and classical forms relate to each other. The reconfiguring of written Arabic as a foreign language in the colonial discourse failed as a linguistic myth. However, it succeeded in effectively disrupting the relationship between spoken and written Arabic and in devaluing Algerians, in their own eyes, as a people who did not have a "real" language, but only a dialect. By detaching Algerian culture from its Arab-Islamic moorings, the myth stripped the people of their ownership of written Arabic as a language of knowledge, abstraction, and universality and left them with an impoverished dialect, which could only serve as a vehicle for practical concerns and provincial values. Orphaned by the colonial discourse from the millenarian civilization they had participated in building, many Algerians internalized this linguistic and civilizational inferiority.

It would be difficult to overstate the far-reaching consequences of this state of mind, which in many ways continues to manifest itself. The cultural questions that Algeria faced at independence were similar, in some ways, to those experienced in other parts of the Maghreb. However, although the use of classical Arabic was marginalized in other countries of the Maghreb, alienation from the classical language in Algeria was almost total. Venerable institutions of learning in classical Arabic remained in existence elsewhere in the Maghreb, such as Zitouna and Qarawine (institutions of higher learning in Tunisia and Morocco, respectively), ensuring a continuity of traditional philological, religious, and philosophical teaching. Although diminished by colonization, these institutions still represented cultural and linguistic *lieux de transmission* (sites of transmission) to use Meddeb's term (1995).

After colonial encroachments, most Arab countries, even those in the Arab heartland, had to rebuild linguistically and culturally, but for historical reasons the work of cultural reconstruction in the Maghreb lagged behind the efforts undertaken in the Middle East. The impetus to Arabize and modernize in Algeria dates back to the 1930s and to the work of Ben Badis (1889–1940) in the context of the Nahda (Renaissance). It paralleled the efforts undertaken in the Middle East. As Djait explains, "[t]he immediate consequence of this movement, whose vital center lay in Egypt and Syria, was the emergence of a modern Arabic language and literature, hence an Arabization by the core of the Middle East" (1985, 138). The perception that only the Maghreb had to rebuild its culture and language is a mistaken one. This is not to say that the Algerian nationalists at independence did not face a more daunting task than most. The double task of building a country in the face of an extremely high illiteracy rate and after the mass departure of skilled workers and professionals, and then of rebuilding or reconstituting a national identity and culture was and remains to a large extent the burden of generations.

Algeria's postindependence education policy was marked by pragmatism. It was decided to alphabetize primarily in French, obtaining the necessary cadres through technical cooperation with France, while pursuing Arabization on the side. The expectation was that the country would inexorably progress toward replacement of French by classical Arabic (the written language) as the language of work. The difficulties were thought to be of a practical nature, related only to implementation modalities, not ideology. It was accepted that national independence required cultural independence and that cultural independence required a reconnection with the written language that would provide access to the Arab/Islamic cultural legacy and national patrimony. Arabization was not just about making classical Arabic the language of work; it was part of a conscious effort to reconstruct a cultural identity.

As mentioned earlier, at the time of independence, in 1962, Algeria was more than 90 percent illiterate in French, so it was independent Algeria that promoted French by making primary education in French widespread, thus allowing the emergence for the first time of a French-speaking generation. To appreciate the magnitude of this phenomenon, one has to remember that even on the eve of independence, after last-minute French reforms to increase schooling rates, only one-third of Algerian school-age children were in school, whereas twenty years later the majority of children in this age group were in school (Bennoune 2000, 223–34). Thus, efforts to Arabize occurred in a context of high literacy in French among children and young adults, which adversely affected the process of Arabization (Moatassime 1996).[6] Although problems with the implementation of Arabization programs have often been considered an exclusive and a particularly intractable Algerian problem, in-depth study of Arabization programs elsewhere shows similar difficulties in the rest of the Maghreb (Moatassime 1992).

Many people in charge of the Arabization programs were products of a French educational system and influenced by French models of education. The assimilation and internalization of linguistic norms specific to French had a bearing on the methodologies and approaches they used. Malika Greffou (1989) shows how a model for teaching Arabic was constructed from the model used to teach French as a foreign language. The mostly French-trained educators who designed this approach for Arabic in fact translated wholesale techniques developed for French-language instruction. Teaching Arabic was thus viewed through the linguistic prism of the French language and with the assumption that it was a foreign language for those learning it. Hence, Arabization resulted in a process of teaching classical Arabic in a vacuum, as if the dialect did not exist. Almost as if in reaction to the colonial approach, which tried to appropriate the vernacular in order to eliminate the classical, the Arabization programs ended up glorifying the classical and ignoring the vernacular. In a sense, the Algerian school system unwittingly pursued the colonial approach of severing the classical from the vernacular forms of the language, merely reversing the terms of the process.[7]

6. Moatassime demonstrates that despite the complexity of factors surrounding Arabization in Algeria, there is not an Algerian "exception": the linguistic problem throughout the Maghreb exhibits similar essential features.

7. Classical and vernacular forms have been a constant feature of Arabic since the language was codified, with the classical form commanding the most prestige. Colonization and Western cultural encroachment have disrupted the nature of the classical/vernacular rapport. Although Arabic speakers have always valued the classical over the vernacular, there is a distinction between precolonial natural valorization, a form of cultural elitism, and the colonial and postcolonial reactive valorization that must be considered in light of colonial cultural context. Arabic vernaculars (as well as Berber vernaculars), paradoxically, have been negatively impacted by colonial efforts to promote them at the expense of the classical language. Examples such as the reaction to the Dahir Berber in Morocco (1930) represent a deeply rooted suspicion of colonial cultural intervention aimed at the evisceration of the Arab-Islamic cultural and linguistic legacy of the Maghreb. See Delanoue's (1998)

Instead of logically bringing vernacular and classical Arabic together through a focus on the patterns of variations, classical Arabic was taught as a foreign language, and the vernacular form was ignored as "defective." The right methodology would have incorporated into the teaching of the classical form the phonological, syntactical, and lexical skills the child had already mastered when he came to school by virtue of knowing vernacular Arabic. The dialect was the natural springboard to understanding the classical form, and teaching the written form in isolation discouraged the development of skills that bridged the written and spoken forms naturally. In addition, because of the strong socioaffective content of the dialect for the child, any devaluing of it ended up devaluing the child himself. The desire to give classical Arabic its rightful place, although a valid national education policy, should have included a valorization of the dialect by stressing its kinship to the classical form.

For two decades, the challenges and debate concerning Arabization were primarily technical, focusing on the modalities and timetables of implementation. There was a consensus that Arabization was the cultural equivalent of political independence for the country.[8] Since the early 1990s, however, a new attempt has been made to recast the issue of Arabization from an essentially technical linguistic debate into a political debate about the policy of Arabization itself. Paradoxically, this revisionism starts by positing that education policies were politicized after independence and that the policy of Arabization, or more accurately re-Arabization, is really an instrument of political manipulation to legitimize power. Bennoune summarizes it in this manner: "Ainsi, dès 1962, l'éducation de nos enfants est devenue l'enjeu de luttes politiques et idéologiques acharnées pour le pouvoir" (Thus, since 1962, our children's education has been at stake in bitter political and ideological fights for power) (2000, 13). This point of view, of course, suggests that until independence, education existed in a space free from political and ideological concerns and that the instrumentalization of education was not a feature of the colonial system, but rather introduced later in independent Algeria. As we have seen, there was really no time in colonial Algeria when education policy was not used as a political tool.

This topos of a neutral educational space uncontaminated by ideological and

---

excellent analysis of the evolution of the rapport between the classical and the vernacular in Egypt before and after British and Western cultural intervention.

8. Dissensions from the broad Arabization consensus were generally muted or carefully disguised during the height of nationalist fervor following independence. Even the Kabyle Berbers' linguistic and cultural claims did not really become overt until the 1980s, as the country entered a major economic and political crisis.

political designs fits into the larger topos of an "open" and "secular" and "French-speaking" society that existed before Arabic was substituted for French. According to Grandguillaume, however, "[d]u point de vue culturel, le remplacement intégral du français par l'arabe pouvait suggérer la substitution d'une société ouverte, sinon laïque, par une société de type théocratique islamique" (from the cultural point of view, the complete replacement of French with Arabic could suggest the substitution of an open, if not secular society, by an Islamic, theocratic society) (1991, 399). If we scrutinize this statement carefully, we see that the key word is *substitution,* which seems to posit the existence of a society for which another one was put in its place. This statement occults two essential facts about Algerian society: the majority of its people were Arabic speakers and illiterate at the close of French rule, and it was never a secular society (its population having refused to renounce Islamic legal status). In fact, during the entire colonial period, Islam was the only identity (one might say the only nationality) Algerians were able to claim and have recognized as *Français-musulmans.*[9] This statement amalgamates the linguistic (Arabization) and the political and ideological (resurgent Islam) to contaminate the linguistic debate with the anxieties of the political debate, leaving out the fact that the only successful Islamic revolution and subsequent establishment of an Islamic theocracy took place in Farsi-speaking Iran and not in an Arabic-speaking country.

On the French side, the proponents of this revisionism, such as Grandguillaume, are not steeped in a self-congratulatory nostalgia about a mythical secular and French-speaking Algeria that never existed; rather, they are attempting to project a vision of the Algeria that never was into the one that might be. The rewriting of history, in this case, is not used for exculpatory purposes, but as a process of wish fulfillment. It functions as an incantatory formula that would will a French-speaking future for Algeria even from its dark colonial past. In this mythical future, French will be "again" the language of Algeria as it would have been were it not for the colonial system that never taught French to more than 90 percent of Algerians.

In France, the salient characteristic of this revisionism is that it started to coalesce in the late 1980s, when perceptions of cultural and linguistic encroachments by English were heightened. The place and future of French has since become a central subject of concern to a global francophone movement that often conceals neocolonial impulses under a multiculturalist discourse. It is at this conjuncture that a debate about national education policy became tributary of geopolitical calculations and of a former colonial nation's anxieties about global-

9. Stora (1991) calls Islam the only "homeland" that Algerian masses had under colonization.

ization and its perception of the imperiled status of its own language and culture. In Algeria, part of the revisionists' strategy has been to translate political interests into linguistic concerns. First, as we have seen, the revisionist discourse attempts to malign Arabization by linking it with political Islam, obscuring the fact that it was earlier put forward by the first Algerian government, constituted on the basis of a nationalist and secular (socialist) ideology. In the economy of the discourse, Arabization is made to stand metonymically for Islamic resurgence. This discursive configuration allows the fixation of political anxieties onto the cultural sphere, where they have become diffuse.

Although the revisionist discourse successfully articulates various political and economic interests into linguistic terms, it lacks originality when it comes to the linguistic challenge itself. It is just a variation on the colonial discourse, taking the colonial position that classical Arabic is a foreign language and that the "real" language of Algerians is vernacular Arabic. However, this time the vernacular is no longer called a "dialect," but instead is promoted to the rank of a full-fledged language. To posit that Algerian vernacular Arabic is a different language from classical Arabic rather than one of its spoken variants is a colonial myth, which like all myths is unaffected by such objective matters as morphological, syntactical, and lexical reality. As we have seen, this myth was promoted during the colonial period for the purpose of manufacturing a preliterate society by the elimination of the written language. This new revisionist avatar of colonial ideology aims at eliminating classical Arabic by the promotion of vernacular Arabic to the exclusive position of mother tongue.

An expansion and variation on the theme of the foreignness of classical Arabic is the view that Arabization is a disguised easternization. In this perspective, classical Arabic becomes the language of the Levant, whereas vernacular Arabic is the national language. Thus, for Benrabah (1995, 1999), behind the Arabization educational programs there was a government design not just to teach Arabic, but to alter Algerian children's identity in the sense of making it more Middle Eastern. He sees, for example, the replacement in textbooks of the word *hout* by the word *samak* (fish) as evidence of this attempt at the depersonalization of the Algerian child. Again, in this case, the ideological assumptions are contradicted by the linguistic reality. The word *hout,* commonly used in the vernacular, is not an "Algerian" word, nor is *samak* a "Middle Eastern" one; both words belong to the classical Arabic lexicon, but whereas *hout* refers to big fish, *samak* refers to any fish.[10] Rather than revealing ideological bias or political manipulation, the

10. The French transliteration of the quoted Arabic words has been retained here because the article discussed is in French.

introduction of the lesser-known term is based on sound pedagogy—namely, precise use of language, a standard objective for basic education in any language.

In an important way, Benrabah's approach mimics the old colonial mythologizing process. By dispensing with much of the complexities of linguistic reality, he attempts to elaborate a simplistic narrative of a conspiracy to disenfranchise and manipulate the population through Arabization. Such theories stand in sharp contrast to linguistic facts and practice. Tapiéro wonders: "Précisement, que faut-il entendre par 'arabisation' d'une langue déjà arabe, comme c'est le cas de l'arabe algérien? C'est d'abord l'introduction, pour remplacer les mots d'origine étrangère et les mots arabes impropres, de tout un vocabulaire nouveau provenant de l'arabe littéral moderne, c'est-à-dire l'arabe savant et commun à tous les Pays arabes" (Precisely how is one to understand "Arabization" of a language that is already Arabic, as is the case of Algerian Arabic? It is first the introduction of a new vocabulary from modern standard Arabic, in other words from learned Arabic common to all Arab countries, to replace foreign words and improper Arabic terms) (1978, iii). This is precisely what Arabization aimed to achieve, albeit in a difficult sociolinguistic context that juxtaposed a prestige language with a language going through the arduous travails of rebuilding itself. Not surprisingly, the results have been mixed, as many studies have shown.[11]

The revisionist discourse unravels from its inability to surmount a fundamental contradiction. Stating that classical Arabic is not the mother tongue of Algerians is stating an obvious fact while occulting the more important fact that it is the mother tongue of *no* Arabic speaker. Every native Arabic speaker's mother tongue is his regional vernacular Arabic, and he or she learns classical Arabic at school. The reality is that classical Arabic is not spoken naturally or used for normal everyday interaction by any person or group. It is reserved for writing (literature, poetry, newspaper articles) and for "high-culture" activities such as political speeches, university lectures, religious sermons, television and radio news. For this reason, mastery of classical Arabic for all Arabic speakers results

11. Elsewhere, Grandguillaume (1983, 1990) attempts to introduce another cleavage: written Arabic in the Maghreb is classical Arabic in its form, but its "reference" is now French (the Koranic linguistic reference having been displaced). This thesis is in part a look at the linguistic landscape of the Maghreb from the narrow linguistic prism of the French model and in part a kind of wishful thinking. Sociolinguistic studies show that the existence of diglossic tendencies, different linguistic registers, and the influence of dominant or prestige languages are common occurrences particularly but not exclusively in countries that have experienced some form of foreign linguistic oppression. The colonial scheme to disjoin the structure of Arabic was not successful in large part because of the Koranic reference of the language, which remains central; without it, an evolution scenario similar to that of Maltese would have been conceivable, even plausible.

from formal schooling and is not a function of the particular Arabic vernacular they speak at home.

The other significant contradiction in the revisionist discourse is the recasting of Arabization as an exclusivist policy of promoting monolingualism similar to or even inherited from traditional French "Jacobine" attitudes toward dialects. The obvious problem with such a comparison is that there are major differences in the linguistic realities of the two countries. The relationship between vernacular and classical Arabic is different from the relationship of Breton or Alsatian to French. Breton and Alsatian are markedly different from French, representing different branches of the Indo-European family. The Algerian vernacular (or more accurately the Maghrebian dialect of Arabic), in contrast, is one spoken form of Arabic and linguistically is in the same relationship to classical Arabic as the other Arabic vernaculars.

In Algeria, the revisionist discourse has progressively fetishized French as the language of an ubiquitous modernity from which emanates desirable values such as democracy, whereas Arabization is a transparently ideological operation used for legitimizing authoritarian states, and the Arabic language, with its sacral character and its pan-Arabist and pan-Islamic tendencies, is axiomatically other things than simply a language. French, in contrast, is just a language—neutral, universal, and unencumbered by ideological issues. There is total disavowal of the epistemic fracture and historical violence inscribed in the French language as a colonial language. So thoroughly has French been dehistoricized and sanitized from issues of power and control that Bennoune can affirm with simplicity: "Contrairement à certaines thèses énoncées dans le domaine politique, philosophique . . . l'apprentissage et la maîtrise de la langue et de la culture francaise n'ont aliéné qu'une infime minorité d'individus" (Contrary to some theories advanced in politics and philosophy . . . education in and mastery of the French language and culture have caused the alienation of only a small minority of people) (2000, 720).

It is difficult to assess to what extent the linguistic debate is culturally overdetermined, with factors of self-interest and cultural alienation reinforcing each other. Some Algerians have clear economic self-interest in the perpetuation of a French-language presence in some sectors of the economy, in particularly "intellectual workers" such as journalists, writers, and teachers able to perform their marketable skill only in French. Others, anxious about time lost to colonization, favor the use of French as a shortcut to modernization. Their utilitarian vision stems from an ethos of *usine clés en main* (turnkey factory construction), which in the 1970s fueled the euphoric desire for rapid industrialization. This notion, which has proved illusory in industry, is now being applied to the cultural arena.

To "borrow" a language that is already operating as a modern medium of communication is meant to avoid delays in economic modernizing and development. Implicitly, however, the shortcut to a ready-made language defers the real work of rebuilding linguistically and culturally. This utilitarian view is similar to the *usine clés en main* approach that in the seventies fueled the euphoric effort for rapid industrialization and may prove in the end just as illusory.

Part Three • Nostalgia

13 Tattoos or Earrings

Two Models of Historical Writing in Mehdi Lallaoui's La colline aux oliviers

MIREILLE ROSELLO

BY THE END of Assia Djebar's *L'amour, la fantasia* ([1985] 1995a), the female narrator has successfully woven a lyrical and multilayered historical narrative in which colonial wars in Algeria are intricately entwined with personal and collective stories of the War of Independence. Through a careful interlacing of fiction and history, individual memories and archival documents, old women's stories and autobiographical vignettes, Djebar proposes a poignantly transnational vision of what it means to write the history of violent conflicts when one is an artist. Telling stories of painful remembrances unavoidably leads to the invention of a model of what it is to tell such stories and of what it means to choose to witness. In the last few pages of the novel, the writer imagines herself as the fictional daughter of Eugène Fromentin, the painter who followed the French military expeditions and saw much more than a few "women of Algiers in their apartment":[1]

> Eugène Fromentin offers me an unexpected hand—the hand of an unknown woman he was never able to draw. In June 1853, when he leaves the Sahel to travel down to the edge of the desert, he visits Laghouat, which has been occupied after a terrible siege. He describes one sinister detail: as he is leaving the oasis which six months after the massacre is still filled with its stench, Fromentin picks up out of the dust the severed hand of an anonymous Algerian woman. He

1. The dialogue between Assia Djebar and French Orientalist painters had already started in 1979, when the title of a collection of short stories reclaimed and displaced Delacroix's "stolen gaze" on *Femmes d'Alger dans leur appartement* (see Djebar 1980, 172). Djebar's postface to the 1980 edition tells the story of how Delacroix obtained permission to spend a few hours in the company of women inside an Algerian house. The painting was completed later, after his return to France. The (sometimes antagonistic) conversation with Orientalism continues in Leïla Sebbar's *Shérazade, brune frisée, les yeux verts* (1982), where a character falls in love with the Algerian protagonist on account of her resemblance to the women portrayed in the Delacroix's painting.

> throws it down again in his path. Later, I seize on this living hand, hand of mutilation and of memory and I attempt to bring it the qalam. ([1985] 1995a, 226)[2]

In the very first sentence of the paragraph lies the painful paradox of all attempts to write an Algerian-French history that would not be separated into two camps by official national discourses. The passage begins with what could be a peaceful and welcoming gesture: "Eugène Fromentin offers me *a* hand [me tend *une* main]" ([1985] 1995a, 259, my emphasis). At first, it looks as if the painter himself is holding out his hand, and in French the only "unexpected" element in the sentence is the indefinite article. The long dead French painter seems to reach out to the twentieth-century female author in a gesture that usually connotes affection, or perhaps an invitation to join him, and most certainly connotes the willingness to greet an equal. The text never abolishes the possibility of such an interpretation even if the adjective *unexpected,* which at first might be taken to refer adverbially to the surprising nature of Fromentin's gesture, soon proves to be much more sinister: it signifies another (severed) hand. The presence of the dead woman's hand introduces a third space between the painter and the writer, so that unspeakable violence contaminates the apparently benevolent signal. Djebar's syntax turns the scene into a horrific mixture of imaginary historical dialogue and graphic details. The hands of two artists, who might be connected by a transnational and transhistorical fascination for what is around them, are suddenly separated by another protagonist, an excluded third whose tragic presence-absence is the symbol of violence and cruelty.[3] The severed hand, a hand that will no longer write, a hand that will no longer paint, comes between the hand of Fromentin the painter and that of Djebar the novelist as if to remind us that the writing of any story will now always be complicated by this unbearable Derridean supplement. The third hand is an excess. It is no longer alive, yet it cannot be buried or put to rest until its owner's story has been told. Djebar imagines that, across the centuries, Fromentin's gift becomes a responsibility, the duty to teach the ghost of the woman how to write her own untold story.

Djebar's powerful image is one possible model of history that *L'amour la fantasia* proposes as its own founding gesture, but the severed hand is not imposed as the only metaphor for history or even as the necessary image others should adopt. Here is a literary vision that allows literature to distinguish itself from official history while reflecting on the writing of history. The amputated hand held by a contemporary writer tells us what it means to write the literary history of colonial

2. All translations from French text are by the author.

3. In "Disorienting the Subject in Djebar's *L'amour la fantasia,*" Zimra calls the exchange between Djebar and Fromentin a moment of "textual and intertextual intercession" (1995, 156).

and postcolonial conflicts. And such powerful icons, which combine fictional imagination with an implied theoretical model of history, are the almost unavoidable by-products of the type of writing that I analyze in this chapter. Novels written by contemporary authors of Algerian origin often seek to remember the lives of individuals either swallowed by the ideological presuppositions of the colonial archive or later dismissed by the logic of official postindependence national histories. And they tend to arrive at a sometimes tragic, sometimes sarcastic, and always self-reflexive definition of what it means to remember a transnational, traumatic, ghostly past.

Novelists are obviously not the only writers whose interest in the French-Algerian conflict has led them to explore both the past and its difficult transmission—or, perhaps more accurately, the traumatic construction of a contested past. Benjamin Stora's 1991 analyses of silence and censorship in *La gangrène et l'oubli* makes suggestions similar to Djebar's recent *Le blanc de l'Algérie* (1995b): neither text allows official discourses to dictate the only legitimate list of heroes, or antiheroes as the case might be. Stora alternates chapters on France and on Algeria and suggests that both countries, in different ways, imposed a national version that systematically negated whole portions of the narrative.[4] France carefully guarded what Stora calls "the dark violence of family secrets," including the use of torture by the French military ([1991] 1998, 13–117). Meanwhile, the newly formed Algerian government refused to acknowledge that the myth of a "unanimous people" ([1991] 1998, 161) rested on the erasure of secret internecine rivalries that sometimes led to massacres within Algerian revolutionary movements.

More generally, francophone historical novels written about the relationships between Algeria and France during the colonial and postcolonial periods are part and parcel of a cultural turn or historical moment that may be said to culminate with the publication of Pierre Nora's *Realms of Memory* (1996c). The monumental construction of historical monuments is one of the textual symp-

4. Narratives change gradually, probably under the pressure of voices who insist that the past should be differently told rather than because of the passage of a supposedly neutral "time." Writing about Abane Ramdane, one of the leaders of the Algerian Revolution killed by fellow Algerians, Stora notes that in 1999 the new president, Abdelaziz Bouteflika, rehabilitated several historic names, announcing that "the airport of Béjaïa (previously Bougie) would be named after Abane Ramdane" (1999, 127). In *Le blanc de l'Algérie,* Djebar writes about Ramdane's last moments, about his thoughts, his murderers' reactions, and blames herself and her generation for allowing silence to prevail for so long: "Who among us, for thirty years, thought of writing Abane Ramdane's *tombeau* in Berber, Arabic, or French? We barely had a few interventions by political scientists, historians, polemicists" (1995b, 151).

toms of a collective attention to history as a discipline and to the multidisciplinarity of historical texts. Nora posits that at the end of the twentieth century, "Totemic history has become critical history. . . . The old symbols no longer arouse militant conviction or passionate participation" (1996a, 7). Instead, a self-reflexive relationship to one's own history, to one's own identity, becomes a mandatory practice. We have, he suggests, entered an age of "historicized memory" (1996a, 10), where each individual feels obliged to become his or her own historian. The atomization of memory (as collective memory is transformed into private memory) imposes on each individual a duty to remember. This "law of remembrance" has great coercive force: for the individual, the discovery of roots, of "belonging" to some group, becomes the source of identity and its true and hidden meaning (1996a, 11).

It may seem paradoxical to invoke Nora's work in an essay on Algerian memory considering that the historian deliberately excludes Algeria from his very corpus. As many critics have noted, Nora's monumental reflection on historical monuments shies away from nonhexagonal sites.[5] Emily Apter regrets that "even the most recent volumes. . . , with their New Historical attention to the mystificatory components of national identity, clumsily justify their choice not to include Algiers or Montreal as *hauts lieux,* or psychotopographies worthy of revisionist nostalgia" (1999, 2). And yet Nora's historical gaze and type of historical research is remarkably similar to the approach chosen by Franco-Maghrebi novelists who seek to redefine the narrative tools used by different generations in order to rewrite and manage their history. The process entails more than the freedom from censorship, the struggle against forgetfulness, or the absence of archival material because what must be "recovered" (i.e., written, narrativized) is not analogous to some raw material that one can hope to retrieve, unchanged, and to give (or sell) to an uncritical reader.

The novel I analyze in this chapter suggests that looking for the past means having a theory about the past and negotiating that theory not only for yourself, but also with your grandfather, with your community, with your neighbors, with the people you fall in love with, and with the strangers who become your allies. It also means (re)inventing a changing past, a new past, or, consequently, a new present, which, in turn, changes the individual who has embarked on the quest. No element of the equation is safe from metamorphosis; the present, the past, and the self are put into question. The imperative is not to fill a void, but to rethink the relationship between different types of narratives, including those that we have

5. In "The Arts and Sciences of Colonialism" (2000), Sherman notes that Charles-Robert Ageron's article on the 1931 Colonial Exposition is the exception to that rule.

traditionally called autobiographies, history, and fiction. Listening to those voices silenced by history is an admirable goal as long as "speaking for" does not ultimately replace "listening to."[6] And literature may become a form of "speaking for" if the reader starts imagining that a colonized character is a necessarily more reliable narrator than a fictional colonizer.[7] In Mehdi Lallaoui's *La colline aux oliviers* (The Olive Grove) ([1995] 1998), history itself is the hero, and different characters struggle between various models they think of as incompatible.

Novelist, filmmaker, historiographer, Mehdi Lallaoui—who describes himself as a child born in France to a family of Algerian immigrants—works on contemporary memory, continually straddling the Mediterranean. His first novel, *Les beurs de la Seine,* came out in 1986 halfway through the so-called *beur* decade and was followed by an album of antiracist posters published under the auspices of the Association black, blanc, beur (see Lionnet 1998). Not innocently, publication of the album coincided with the celebration of the bicentennial of the French Revolution in 1989. A few years later Lallaoui coauthored *Un siècle d'immigration en France* (with David Assouline, 1996a) before publishing two other novels: *La colline aux oliviers* and *Une nuit d'octobre* (2001b), a fictional account of the tragic events of 17 October 1961 in Paris.[8]

Lallaoui's *La colline aux oliviers* is as much about the "truth" discovered by the narrator as about the ways in which this truth is reached. The end of the book does allow the reader a satisfactory sense of closure, but to the literary critic the careful delaying of the ending is just as remarkable as the glimpse into a relatively unknown portion of colonial history. Consequently, writing about *La colline aux oliviers* is almost like explaining a magic trick, a sleight of hand: something gets lost in the process—the fascination of the performance, the pleasure of being deceived and enchanted at the same time. Yet, because the novel also talks about the necessity of coming to terms with loss and of renouncing the hope that history will magically restore the past, it may be less sacrilegious than it seems to start

6. Just as Abdelkebir Khatibi suggests that his "bi*langue*" is a "third ear" (rather than a third tongue) (1983, 11), historians who listen to voices that official history has excluded might be looking for a "bihistory" that only a third type of narrative, a third type of attention to testimonies, will be capable of hearing.

7. On what Guadeloupean author Maryse Condé does with or to Tituba, a "real historic" character whom the novelist transforms into an African witch involved in the Salem trials, see Moss 1999.

8. The night of 17 October 1961 has recently inspired quite a number of French novelists, including Leïla Sebbar (*La Seine était rouge,* 1999), Didier Daeninckx *(Meurtres pour mémoire,* 1983), and Nacer Kettane (*Le sourire de Brahim,* 1985). For a study of texts directly related to the events and their lasting effects, see Donadey 2001.

with the end and concentrate on how the novel arrives at certain revelations. At the end of *La colline aux oliviers,* the search for one of the ancestors who had disappeared from his village in Kabylia is finally over, and by the time the story reaches its satisfying narrative closure, it has also provided us with a fictional overview of events that span more than a century: it opens around 1871, the time of the Paris Commune as well as of the great Kabyle Insurrection, and closes in the 1990s, long after the end of Algerian War, at a time when France and Algeria are gradually coming to terms with the legacy of the conflict and preparing the fortieth anniversary of the Evian Accords.

In *La colline aux oliviers,* Si Larbi is the alpha and the omega of the plot not because he is the narrator or the main character, but paradoxically because his absence structures the novel: Si Larbi has been missing from the *colline aux oliviers* for more than a century. And at the very end of the book, it is finally revealed that the missing hero, who disappeared during the 1871 insurrection, was arrested by the French and deported to New Caledonia, another French colony. He stayed there until his death. As his story gradually unfolds, we learn that he did try to alert the members of the community that he was still alive and exiled, but the kind of message that he sent out to his brothers demanded a specific type of deciphering that the first generation of readers failed to realize. This lost or rather misinterpreted message is a historical text that the novel as a whole reconstructs, rewrites, and makes us understand through its own apprehension of history.

At the beginning of the novel, we thus listen to Baba Mous, the first I-person narrator, who spent all his life searching for his uncle Si Larbi, but failed to find him. Baba Mous is now an old man. He had not participated in the 1871 insurrection, but he lived through the First World War: he was drafted and fought in the French army. The old man's I-person narration is tightly interwoven with a second narrative voice that intervenes as early as the second chapter and transforms the novel into a duet. The second narrator, who also says "I," is Baba Mous's grandson, Kamel, a painter who has emigrated to Paris, a transnational *beur* who is not as physically rooted in the *colline aux oliviers* as his ancestors. For Kamel, the 1871 insurrection, the First World War, the Second World War, and even the Algerian War belong to history, a multifaceted history that he does not really know how to discover when pieces turn out to be missing from his grandfather's stories. Olive trees have become symbols of his native land and of his culture rather than a means of subsistence: Kamel is a painter. Both Kamel and his grandfather are the guardians of history, although they will construct very different types of stories. Kamel's different approach to history will finally enable him to let a new image emerge out of the mosaic of more or less reliable pieces of information stored in the villagers' memories.

Two significant narrative choices thus distinguish Lallaoui's text from other fictional historiographies that seek to displace official discourse. First of all, the events that the novel allows us to discover (the 1871 uprising in Kabylia)[9] are even less well known by the general public than the War of Independence. Then the novel tells us that it takes two generations to finally arrive at a complete narrative about the lost member of the community. In other words, this text also tells the story of a failure, of bad historiography. The second narrator himself, whom the novel places in the interesting position of the reader's docent, learns about the 1871 uprising and is therefore able to share his knowledge. We are reminded (or we discover)[10] that the famous 1871 Paris Commune has often eclipsed in the French history books the memory of a large-scale insurrection in colonial Algeria. Led by El Mokrani and Cheikh El Haddad, the insurrection was crushed by the French military. Rebels were executed or deported to New Caledonia, and countless Berber farmers lost their land. The 1871 uprising is often referred to as the so-called Kabyle insurrection, but, according to historian Marc Ferro, this description minimizes its significance:

> In fact, 250 tribes were involved in the uprising, almost a third of the Algerian population. Most of the leaders had been restless since the administration had deprived them of their power. . . . The multifaceted rebellion was greeted with harsh repression according to the "Algerian rule" and followed by massive expropriation: Kabyle songs started repeating: 1871 was our ruin, the year we became beggars. (1994, 291–92)

In the novel, Baba Mous is one of the villagers who had always lived by the olive grove and whose land was taken away after the insurrection. In the story, the loss of the land is compounded (but also symbolized) by the disappearance of one of the male members of the community, who joined the rebels, never to be seen again.

9. For historical accounts of Kabylia and more specifically of the 1871 uprising, see Dessaigne 1988; Mailhé 1995; Sicard 1998; and Lorcin 1999a, 173–83.

10. Jacques Thobie, author of *La France coloniale de 1870 à 1914,* notes the surprising indifference of the metropole: "On aurait pu penser que les événement d'Algérie relatifs à la liquidation par les colons du régime miliatire, puis à la révolte de Kabylie et à sa répression, eussent entraîné d'importantes répercussions dans l'opinion éclairée et la classe politique métropolitaine: ces affaires ne sont pas minces et de nature à engager résolument l'avenir. Les résonnances en sont plutôt modestes" (We would have thought that the incidents involving the elimination of the military regime by the settlers and then the Kabyle insurrection and its repression would have had important repercussions within the enlightened circles of public opinion and among metropolitan politicians. Those issues are not trivial, and they definitely have consequences for the future. And yet reactions were rather muted) (1991, 11).

This structuring absence of the missing anticolonial hero becomes the pivot on which the novel builds its own definition of history and, more important, of the evolving role of history and memory in the life of very different characters. At the beginning of the novel, the great energy deployed to bring back Si Larbi or at least to find out what happened to him is presented as an absolutely mandatory mission. According to the elders, telling the history of the village becomes impossible if the story of one individual is missing. Si Larbi's disappearance created "an unexplained void. . . . The continuity of a common history, founded on each individual's existence, was broken. To reconnect with our past, we needed to understand what had happened to Si Larbi" (Lallaoui [1995] 1998, 13).

The first striking proposal made by the novel is that the definition of history presented is based on a narrow or at least a specific definition of a "story." After all, we might agree that the account of Si Larbi's disappearance is already a story and that his absence can be the subject of numerous tales; the statement "and then, Si Larbi disappeared" functions grammatically as a perfectly acceptable part of a narrative. Instead, however, Si Larbi's absence, which all the characters constantly talk about, paradoxically becomes the ultimate metaphor for the absence of a tale, for the end of history.

The second idiosyncratic feature of the novel's definition of history is that the search for Si Larbi and for his story is presented as an enterprise of reappropriation of the land. Bringing Si Larbi back is supposed to be the equivalent of recovering the land stolen by the colonizer. If the villagers are so keen to find out what happened to him, it is not only because he is a missing link in a chain of individual stories, but also because his absence is imagined as the symbol of an original spoliation that will end with his return. This type of seemingly magic thinking is owing to the fact that the villagers rationalize Si Larbi's disappearance as the fulfilling of an old prophesy made by an astrologer years and years earlier. The astrologer did not belong to the village, but he had been rescued by the villagers after being left for dead by his previous employer. To thank his hosts, the guest had looked into the stars and made a prediction. As Baba Mous explains, "The scholar told Si Brahim that the fifth male of the fifth son of one his descendants would disappear. But he also predicted that later on, one of them would find the man and, from then on, the land would be ours forever" (71).

The imperative to discover the fate of one of the members of the community—that is, metaphorically speaking, the need for history—thus becomes linked to the hope to recover the land. The legend seems to promise that the possibility of telling the tale will somehow correspond to the reappropriation of the land itself. No war of decolonization is announced, and no promise is made about the birth of a new nation. The writing of history becomes the promise of a better history for the *colline aux oliviers,* a microcosm that seems completely divorced from larger national and international logic. As readers, we are left to wonder whether the prophecy can be read figuratively or literally. The search for Si Larbi ultimately does lead to the telling of stories that history books and national memories have regularly relegated to obscurity (stories about the 1871 insurrection, about the rebels' deportation to other far-off colonized islands, about their friendships with Parisian Communards such as Louise Colet). Filling the "void" left by Si Larbi's departure means the recapturing of cultural dignity, in itself a political gesture. But readers of the novel are never told, in the end, whether or not the land is indeed reappropriated by its inhabitants other than symbolically.

The issue of whether or not owning one's history is the exact equivalent of owning the land (a perspective that may seem hopelessly optimistic) is never clarified; the novel draws no clear conclusion about the power of history, and the ambivalence of that position spills over to two other issues. First, the text seems to hesitate as to which is the best method of reaching historical truth, and, second, the choice between methods raises difficult questions about whose history is being told. If there is a connection between telling one's history and getting one's land back, it is obviously crucial to determine which community can make a claim to which land, and it is also imperative to agree on ways to identify the rightful owners of the land in question. It is especially important when the group is small, self-contained, and not bound by a unique language or religion or nationality or citizenship. The inhabitants of the *colline aux oliviers* are not identified by a passport or an identity card: they recognize each other. In other words, the establishing of one individual's identity is just as important as the telling of his or her story.

How is identity defined in Lallaoui's novel? At first, legitimacy is defined as belonging to the land or to the hill, having been born there, and being attached to a metonymic olive tree as if by some sort of imaginary umbilical cord. Identity is not encoded as race, ethnicity, political belief, or even nationality. A simple and apparently straightforward construction of belonging unites all the villagers: each man is represented by one tree, and the olive grove functions as a physical equivalent of administrative records. "For each birth, a tree, and for each planted tree, a year, and a name" (10). An apparently simplistic definition of who belongs is thus created whereby the history of the village is the history of whoever has had a tree planted in the olive grove to symbolize him. Instead of "one man, one vote," the slogan might be "one man, one tree."

And I deliberately say "man" because one of the difficulties at the beginning of the novel is to know whether the bodies in question are really all male (the gendered specificity of the French language authorizes some possible negligence or unverifiable doubt). At first, we may not notice that history and memory are made up only of the story of male individuals. Si Larbi is a man; the prophecy mentions only males; and it seems as if the tradition of tattooing individuals who are about to leave the land for a long journey is also reserved to men. At the beginning of the novel, whenever a physical relationship between a tree and a human body is mentioned, the pronouns are ambiguous, and the reader must draw provisional conclusions about whether or not these legitimate bodies *must* be male.

What is not ambiguous, however, is the reciprocal bond between olive trees and human bodies. For each man, a tree is planted, and if a man travels, a tattoo recalls the exact location of the original tree whenever distance threatens to loosen the tie between the tree and the man. The tattoo can put the man back in his place physically and symbolically and attach him to his roots: the unerasable and unquestionable mark guarantees his identity. Si Larbi had such a tattoo. Baba Mous remembers:

> As the villagers did when any man left for a long and uncertain journey, they tattooed three olive leaves, a sun, and our birth date on our left shoulders with a thorn from a carob tree. Under each of the three leaves, a series of numbers: seven, nine and two for my father, seven, nineteen and five for me. The figures corresponded to the group of trees, the row and the place of the olive tree that represented us on the hill. This is how we had proceeded for as long as we could remember to permanently mark, in our flesh, our belonging to this land, to these stones, to the sky that brightened each of our homes. (49)

Yet this model of apparently impeccable simplicity is only one possible paradigm of identification, and the novel no sooner presents this narrative identity as a possibility than it immediately questions its straightforwardness. This clear relationship between men and memory, between land and men, is a dream that does not resist the reality of historical changes. Something always intervenes that compromises the integrity of a narrative whose truth is the equation between a man and a tree. And the blurring of the connection goes both ways: neither the tattoo nor the tree is a perfect guarantee. From the very first pages of the novel, memory entertains problematic relationships with the principle of substitution, with telling stories, with history; any claim to the land is therefore much more uncertain than it seems at first.

Baba Mous thus reveals that the original olive grove, the original record, no longer exists, and the history of the village is a palimpsestic forest: "Our hill, the olive grove had partly burned down. A portion of our memory escaped together with the six hundred trees that disappeared. It took ten years for Baba Ali, my father, to replace them all. . . . Century-old trees that had been destroyed by the devastating fire were thus replaced. And ancestors, who we thought had vanished with the trees, sprang up again in our memory" (12).

Strangely enough, the villagers do not seem to perceive the planting of new trees, the replacement of one symbol by another, as a problematic substitute. If the tree disappears, memory dissolves (the ancestors were "forgotten"), but planting other trees is apparently enough to restore memory, to recapture lost narratives. The tree that represented a man can be replaced by another tree that serves exactly the same commemorative function in spite of its different age. The loss of burned trees is not irreparable: unlike archival documents, this type of oral-vegetal history can be reconstructed from scratch. The image of *rejaillir* (springing up again) suggests that memory is interruptible and that neither forgetfulness nor memory are stable. Remembrance is willed; it is a product of the determination of a villager who plants new trees to commemorate old men. It is possible for memory to disappear and then reappear. But then it takes ten years to reconstitute the "realm of memory" that is neither a narrative nor a monument, but a practice (planting) and a desire to tell, a determination to respect and transmit what must be known.[11] One may of course want to ask if anything is lost, gained, or at least modified when the equation between the original tree and the original man is thus replaced by a copy, a simulacrum, a fiction. The novel does suggest that nothing is as simple as Baba Ali makes it sound and that even if trees are replanted, some slippage occurs owing not only to time but to errors, blurring, miscalculations. Baba Ali may be in denial because perhaps he does not pay enough attention to the function of the substitution, and the story of how the missing ancestor's story is eventually recaptured suggests that the replacing of one sign with another creates enough noise in the system to endanger the system itself.

For example, Baba Mous, the first narrator who will not succeed in spite of having sacrificed his life to find his ancestor, may have made the mistake of relying too much on the historical model based on trees or on tattoos. In France, he met a wounded Senegalese rifleman, a First World War soldier like him. And he noticed that the man had exactly the same tattoo as Si Larbi. When pressed about where he had met Si Larbi and why he had this tattoo, the dying man was only

11. In the introduction to the English edition of *Lieux de mémoire,* titled *Realms of Memory,* Pierre Nora gives us the origin of his own coinage: "I took it from ancient and medieval rhetoric as described by Frances Yates in her admirable book *The Art of Memory* (1966), which recounts an important tradition of mnemonic techniques. The classical art of memory was based on a systematic inventory of *loci memoriae* or 'memory places' " (1996b, xv).

able to mutter something that was interpreted as "Paris." We find out, at the end of the novel, that he really meant Bouloupari, the name of the town in New Caledonia from which the would-be "Senegalese" soldier had come.

Unaware that the puzzle was incomplete, Baba Mous spent years in the French capital, looking for his uncle, wasting his time on a wrong conclusion. I would argue that by playing on the resemblance and partial homonymy between "Paris" and "Bouloupari," the novel reminds us of the constant possibility of substitution and shows that slippage does occur between repetitions. Baba Mous, however, does not have the imagination of a possible substitution. The difference between Paris and Bouloupari is like the difference between the original olive tree planted when an ancestor was born and the second one that replaced the burned symbol. A mental leap is necessary to move from one tree to the other, and, in that distance, change as well as ideology and values are inserted, of which Baba Mous is not aware. For example, the fact that the sound *-pari* should immediately be heard as "Paris" rather than as "Bouloupari" is a very plausible case of Eurocentrism that prevents him from thinking of other colonized far-off islands.

Later, when Kamel will be asked to interpret the same story, his own historical perspective will have changed: although Baba Mous is drawn to the colonial metropole as though Paris can be the only center, the only pole of attraction, the second narrator is less eager to interpret *-pari* as Paris—to impose a Parisian subtext and logic. The novel never explicitly suggests that Kamel's ability to better decipher truncated words is a sign of his postcolonial condition, but the reader is obviously encouraged to compare the two hermeneutic activities. In this novel, the origin of the truncation is owing either to the exhausted soldier's inability to articulate or to the narrator's inability to hear properly. The text does not decide, but it hints at the far-reaching consequences of such literal misunderstandings between two different colonized subjects. Both possibilities (that the subaltern did not articulate or that his words were misheard) resemble but also differ from the phenomenon described by Jean-Paul Sartre in his preface to Frantz Fanon's *The Wretched of the Earth.* Sartre writes that intellectuals who went to school in the metropole go back home altered and alienated, producing "echoes" of Western culture repeated by colonized intellectuals: he imagines a situation where the colonized subject hears *Parthénon* and *fraternité* and repeats the words *thenon* and *nité* ([1963] 1991, 7).

In *La colline aux oliviers,* a long word is mispronounced and shortened, but the context and the effect of the misunderstanding are considerably different. Although *thenon* and *nité* mean nothing, "Paris" means too much and generates rich and complicated narratives and travels. "Paris" is not a defective and inferior rendering of "Bouloupari"; it is a creative and productive mistake that ironically makes us think about the possibility that Paris is a copy, a pale and incomplete version of Bouloupari. Errors, here, are more important than the illusion of correct repetitions: writing on the body is no more reliable that the repetition of words, and different generations react differently when confronted with the fuzzy sign.

And like the truncated word, the tattoo found on the black man's body is not a straightforward sign. In order to understand the message correctly, it is necessary to guess that the straightforward link between the body and the land no longer exists. The "devastating fire" that destroyed the trees has a historical equivalent: Berber rebels were exiled and deported to New Caledonia. Yet, just as Baba Ali replanted trees, the tattoo that originally appeared on the missing ancestor's shoulder could be replaced, or rather copied, inscribed, on someone else's body. The tattoo is a reproduction, and as long as the connection between the skin and the tattoo is not correctly reinterpreted and reassigned, Si Larbi's disappearance remains a mystery. Kamel, Baba Mous's grandson, will have to give up on the original meaning of the tattoo in order to understand its presence on the dying soldier's body. He will much later discover (but only after finding out that Si Larbi had been deported to New Caledonia) that his great uncle had tattooed his own signature on the shoulders of young men recruited by the metropolitan army to fight against the Germans. For Si Larbi, tattooing the young men who were about to be drafted was the equivalent of planting a new tree: it was his way of sending a message, of circulating his signature. And in order to be allowed to tattoo the young soldiers, he lied to their families and pretended that he could protect their children from death thanks to a magic tattoo.

Normally, his mark should have been unique, like a passport or modern official piece of identification. For a reader who knows the code (what the figures represent), the deciphering of the tattoo should require no interpretation. A simple act of recognition is needed. Whoever bears the mark belongs; his place is forever set. But in the novel, the sign, which seems so easy to read, reveals its polysemy and the possibility of distortion. When the disappeared Si Larbi marks other bodies with the mark he has on his shoulder, he modifies the purpose of the tattoo, turning it into a text, a message. Its meaning is unclear (Did he want to be rescued? Did he simply want to let people know that he was still alive?). The messenger does not know that he is carrying a message, and the message is not easily deciphered by its intended recipient.

Like archives, like testimonies, like remains found by people who search for historical truth, the tattoo is undeniable (it exists), and the sheer force of its existence makes it impossible to ignore that something must be discovered. At the same time, many errors are possible, and being satisfied with the presence of the archive is foolish. Baba Mous learns that the relationship between an event and a historical text is never direct. Eyewitnesses are storytellers, and we know that even photographic evidence can hide fabrication (not to mention that the camera's point of view is itself enough to change radically the meaning of a scene). The link between "what happened" and "what a text says happened" is always on the verge of infinite slippage, troubled as it is by the possibility of interpretation and false decoding.

When Baba Mous first talks to his grandson Kamel and tries to convince him that he must continue to search for Si Larbi, he himself has clearly failed in the task. Not only has he not found his uncle, but also his loyalty to the mission has forced him to betray the only woman he ever cared for. When in France, he fell in love with Marinette, a French woman, but was forced to go back to the village in Kabylia and married there, continuing his fruitless pursuit of Si Larbi in Algeria. The apparently secondary female character and the fact that she is left behind in the name of supposedly nobler causes are pivotal factors because at that juncture Baba Mous fails to perceive that he is making a choice between two different historical models. Unable to see that there are several definitions of history, he fetishizes the model that valorizes one paradigm at the expense of another. For him, history is about remembering the (male) ancestors who were born on the hill, about tattoos, and about reclaiming the land. This character's faith in that historical model is so deep that he is not even aware that an alternative narrative is available to him. And yet at least one voice is warning him that there may be no connection between finding Si Larbi and getting the land back: the voice of cheikh Iskandar, his beloved teacher and surrogate father.

In the text, Iskandar is the embodiment of another historical model. Paradoxically, he had been entrusted with the task to turn the child into a "learned man" to better prepare him for a mission that, as a teacher, he did not really believe in. Iskandar is not the guardian of collective myths. He does not seem to have faith in the stories that the villagers repeat. When Baba Mous is about to be recruited into the metropolitan army, he notices that Iskandar's position is different from his: "With the exception of cheikh Iskandar, we all thought that we could find Si Larbi's trail and perhaps, eventually, recover the olive grove" (48). Iskandar has a different definition of history, identity, and memory. But who is this skeptical educated man, and why does he not agree with the dominant creed? Why does he symbolize the possibility of another type of historiography?

Iskandar's presence in the village testifies to the existence of other possible models of "belonging," models not based on roots or on the relationship to the land. The learned man does not come from the village. A nomad whose origin is never explained, he appeared in the village "out of the blue and completely destitute" (33). But once he was granted hospitality, his role as Baba Mous's infinitely wise and knowledgeable teacher earned him a perfectly legitimate place among the villagers. The relationship that the child established with him was obviously much more meaningful than the superficial bonds he formed with other people from the village. Yet the master continues to represent a different form of identification. The absence of a tattoo on his shoulder symbolizes the possibility of different forms of identity that can be read as either a minus (he was not born there, he cannot claim the land) or as a plus (he is free from that bond, and he chose the hill). After all, the idea of writing on the body may connote something slightly cruel, as if the "belonging" is both privilege and curse because there is no escaping.[12]

I would argue that Iskandar stands for and advocates a different type of identity and a different type of history as well: he proposes another form of transmission of knowledge and of the past that will in the end turn out to be not incompatible with and may even be preferable to and complementary to the traditionally (male) conception of collective memory. Iskandar does not wish to mark his pupil, but he still gives him a chance to preserve what will become history. His way of dealing with memory is to make a gift that both will symbolize the past and his affection and will announce future gifts and future attachments. He does not write on the body, but rather gives a precious object that is another substitute for identity and a metonymic token of his presence: a pair of gazelle-shaped earrings. "This is my most cherished possession. They are for me what the olive grove means to you, the proof of our existence. . . . Guard them as you would guard your own life and give them to the woman who will bequeath them to your children" (51).

Whereas olive trees keep the memory of a dynasty of men whose contingent birth attached them to a land, Iskandar's earrings preserve memory while authorizing exile and exogamous relationships. He gives Baba Mous the right to choose who will be the recipient of the story, just as the novelist gives us the right to hear the story rather than forcing us to act like the soldier who thinks that his tattoo is protecting him when his body is really being used to carry someone else's message. The gift of the earrings does not claim to protect; it is not a talisman. In fact,

12. Writing on the body is a highly charged symbolic gesture whose valence may change depending on the context. Sartre, in the passage on colonial education cited earlier, also imagines that Western education is a form of "branding" ([1963] 1991, 7), a text cruelly and definitely inscribed on the body that will always bear the trace of the violence undergone by the colonized subject, a mark of uprooting rather than the symbol of belonging. Lallaoui seems keen on presenting us with a more nuanced perspective. In *La colline aux oliviers,* the writing on the body is not the exclusive province of the colonizer, nor is the sign thus produced reliable or dictatorial in its meaning.

when Baba Mous first gives the earrings to a woman, it is during a sad and tragic moment. Although neither Baba Mous nor Marinette know this, he is about to disappear from her life, just as Si Larbi vanished from the village.

However, it is to be noted that Baba Mous does not exactly follow his teacher's recommendation: he is supposed to give the two earrings to the woman who would be the guardian of his memory. Instead, he gives only one earring to Marinette. Disregarding his master's instruction, he splits the pair and modifies the double object's original purpose. Instead of representing the transmission of an intellectual and affective legacy, the half-gift is transformed into a promise that will not be kept: like the ancient symbol, the two parts of a loving couple are pulled apart by stories that they do not fully understand, by their different origin. At first, it seems as if the hill has won, as if history as gift has proven less powerful than memory as belonging. The two pieces of the original master's gift cannot be reunited until another generation comes along, ready to accept Iskandar's healthy skepticism.

Kamel, Baba Mous's grandson, will not happily step into his ancestors' shoes. For him, the search for the elusive Si Larbi is "utopian" (102). He is not sure that he believes all the legends that his grandfather has told him. "All this sounds like a fairy tale, I said, ironically" (72), and even when Baba Mous insists, Kamel feels very reluctant to accept a mission that he considers doomed and fruitless ("I was not going to spend my life like Baba Mous, towed by a ghost" [102]). Yet, in spite of his decidedly critical interpretation of the sacred legend, he will succeed where his grandfather failed. The novel manages to unite the two historical models proposed to the reader by suggesting that the ultimate discovery is owing to the felicitous encounter between two paradigms, Baba Mous's faith in the original script and Iskandar's generous ideal. If Kamel, who is on the verge of telling his grandfather that he will not look for Si Larbi, suddenly changes his mind, it is because Baba Mous has sent him the remaining earring. Touched by the gift, Kamel explains: "With this present, my grandfather was confirming his faith in me. How else was I to interpret the gift of a jewel that had never left him? Understanding his gesture, I was filled with shame. I hung the earring in full view, on the red kilim on the wall, and I tore up the letter" (104).

From then on, like his grandfather, Kamel becomes a devoted archivist, traveler, anthropologist, and interviewer—an interdisciplinary historian. But he discovers the truth only because this second model of historiography, symbolized by the dangling earring, manages to prevail. In a surprising denouement, we find that Anne, a woman with whom Kamel is slowly falling in love, is in fact Marinette's granddaughter. And it is upon finding the earring in Kamel's room and remembering that her grandmother owned a similar one that she is able to reunite the two portions of Iskandar's gift and to act as the conduit of the complete story. The earrings have finally served their purpose, across time and distance.

This second model of history thus contains an element that we might read as serendipity (or implausibility) if the deliberate rejection of gender out of the realm of history had not problematized the notion of "chance" here. On the one hand, it is an incredible stroke of luck that Kamel's girlfriend should be the granddaughter of the woman whom Baba Mous abandoned. That Anne should find the second earring at Kamel's and should suddenly recognize her grandmother's earring at the very moment when the two lovers can fit this last piece into the almost completely assembled puzzle is a fictional deus ex machina. At the same time, this narrative decision makes a point about the presence of women in this picture. Both Baba Mous and his grandson make the same mistake in eliminating gender from history.[13] Baba Mous leaves the only woman he ever loved because he thinks that his quest is more important. Kamel, like him, is convinced that Anne has nothing to do with his search, with his work as a historian. At worst, she is a distraction, at best a pleasant distraction. And yet Anne's discovery makes the point that her model of history, inherited from Iskandar, works perfectly. History as gift, history as transmitted by women and by people who do not necessarily belong to the *colline aux oliviers,* is just as successful as Baba Mous's stubborn determination. By turning his back on Marinette to devote himself to what he thought was history, he paradoxically was perhaps delaying a discovery that he would have made earlier had he been able to open his eyes to other texts and stories.

This does not mean that Kamel has given up on memory. Like an explorer looking for the one original spring of a large river, he admits that at a certain point his quest for a unique truth will have to take on an arbitrary quality. Perhaps, to refer to Gilles Deleuze and Felix Guattari's (1980) famous vegetal metaphor, he may find that the root he was looking for is closer to a rhizome that implicitly and ironically displaces the image of the olive tree. And yet it is the distance introduced between the two earrings and their subsequent reunion that constitute the solving of the riddle, as if, to paraphrase Edouard Glissant, it was not a question of "reversion" (to the roots, to the native land), but of "diversion" (1989, 14).

Memory as gift reconciled with a memory that tolerates substitutions proves more reliable than a tattooed memory.[14] At the end of the novel, the second nar-

13. For an analysis of the interconnection between gender and historiography in the Maghreb, see "Wild Femininity and Historical Countermemory" in Woodhull 1993.

14. As if Lallaoui's reference to tattooing is an implicit homage to and rewriting of Khatibi's autobiography (Khatibi 1971).

rator has demonstrated that a "trace" is not enough until it has been woven into a story and that "being given the *colline* back" will not magically happen as the result of the discovery of the archive. Through the searching, however, something was transmitted, not only to the grandson but to the reader, who, like the pupil receiving a pair of earrings from his master, has now been entrusted with the story of the *colline aux oliviers* and of its inhabitants. If the *colline aux oliviers* can be said to belong to Baba Mous's grandson, it is because he has critically accepted the responsibility for the search, because he has sat up all night listening to his grandfather's tales while others were asleep, and because he has spent hours in the library trying to connect memory and history, the local and the global, the colonial wars and contemporary situations that include his relationship to Anne, the granddaughter of a woman whose happiness was sacrificed to another idea of history. In the end, the book presents us with two models of memories, two versions of historical research, and suggests that it would be a mistake to eliminate one of them, especially if tradition leads to the rejection of history as gift or history as transmitted by individuals, including women, who choose to belong.[15]

15. Earlier versions of this essay were presented at the University of Cincinnati and at Duke University. I thank Michèle Vialet and Michele Longino for their hospitality. Thanks to Amy Settergren for her help with the final version of the chapter.

14 Generating Migrant Memories

ALEC G. HARGREAVES

THERE IS A LONGER HISTORY of mass migration from Algeria to France than from any other part of the Third World to Europe. Yet the historiography of this phenomenon has until recently been fragmentary at best.[1] The forces that have combined to submerge, repress, and more recently revive the memories of Algerian migrants are emblematic of the tensions and contradictions at work in the colonial project and in its contemporary legacy in both France and Algeria. The recent upsurge of interest in migrant memories is intimately connected with the generational structure of the family, which makes it a key site for the transmission of memory. If the past is to live on and be commemorated, its traces must be carried by generations who did not directly experience it, but who feel motivated to preserve it. The deep affective charges between parents, children, and grandchildren provide a major motivation of that kind. It is on this generational transition, especially among Algerian migrants and their descendants, that the present chapter focuses.

Until recently, the memories of Algerian migrants were almost wholly absent from the public sphere. They have entered that sphere mainly through a growing body of literary, cinematic, and historical work by second-generation members of the Algerian minority in France. The most frequently evoked episode in the history of colonial migration is the savage police repression of the demonstration of 17 October 1961, when tens of thousands of Algerian migrants took to the streets of Paris in support of the Front de libération nationale (FLN). It is now well known that information about the events of 17 October, in which an unknown number of unarmed Algerian demonstrators were killed by the police, was suppressed for a long period by the public authorities and a large part of the mainstream media in France. Subterranean memories of 17 October continued to

1. The overwhelming majority of scholarly research on Algerian migration and settlement deals with the period since the Second World War and more especially since the 1970s. For an excellent study of the earlier part of the century, see MacMaster 1997.

circulate among the Algerian minority as well as among majority ethnic political radicals and human rights activists. These memories have fed into the accounts of October 1961 constructed in recent years by second-generation Algerian writers and filmmakers. But it is far from clear that these accounts are direct representations of their parents' experiences.

Many second-generation Algerians have reported that their parents were reluctant to talk of their experiences during the colonial period and of October 1961 in particular (Gastau 2000, 33–34). Whereas Mohammed Rouabhi, who wrote one of several recent plays depicting the events of 17 October, says his parents often spoke of them, Mustapha Aouar, author of another theatrical representation of these events, reports that his parents were silent about them (Bédarida 2001). Aouar's experience seems to have been the more common of the two. Actress Fadila Belkebla, who plays an Algerian migrant caught up in the events surrounding the demonstration of 17 October, had never heard of them until she was cast in that role in Boualem Guerdjou's film *Vivre au paradis* (1998). It was only after making the film that she learned her parents had in fact participated in the demonstration ("17 octobre 1961" 2001). Similarly, the novelist Farida Belghoul learned of October 1961 not from her father, but from majority ethnic political radicals writing in left-wing magazines (see Belghoul 1988). And although Nacer Kettane's novel *Le sourire de Brahim* (1985) is almost entirely autobiographical, the opening chapter—in which the young protagonist sees his brother die in the arms of his mother during the 17 October demonstration—is in large measure fictional, for Kettane's family was not directly involved in those events. The generational nature of the migrant memories constructed by second-generation Algerians is thus twofold: they are at one and the same time grounded in a sense of fidelity to the older generation and yet newly generated by young men and women whose feet are fixed firmly in the present and whose eyes seldom stray far from future horizons.

Although the family nexus within which these memories are generated may appear at first sight to offer fertile ground for psychoanalytic interpretations, they are in my view structured more fundamentally by the social, political, and ethnic determinants of (post)colonial immigrant settlement. In the face of the stigmatizing gaze of the majority ethnic Other, inherited to a large extent from the colonial period, many second-generation Algerians have acknowledged that in seeking to find a place for themselves in contemporary French society, they have at times been tempted to bury or efface references to their Algerian ancestry. The writer-musician Mounsi is typical of many second-generation Algerians who as children or youths vowed never to resemble their parents (interview with Mounsi in Benguigui 1997b, 159). Like many other colonial migrants, Mounsi's father accepted the socially humiliating status that accompanied poverty and illiteracy with a docility that his children were determined not to replicate. But as the children of Algerian migrants have advanced in years, they have become more mindful—perhaps in part because of their own experience as parents—of the sacrifices made by their parents and of the sociopolitical context that conditioned them. Mounsi eloquently describes the importance of that context and the newfound commitment of second-generation Algerians to the restoration of migrant memories:

> As children of the Maghrebi periphery, we really need a thoroughgoing revision of the basic principles of psychoanalysis and Freudian thinking. The Oedipal complex is all about killing the father, whereas the need for us is to unearth him and bring him back to life. He was killed by the social forces of colonialism, war, and emigration. Instead of killing him, it's up to us, his children, to enable him to live again, to hold his head up high, proud and straight, just as he did when he went to have his photograph taken in his best suit so he could send it to his family back in the home country to reassure them all was well. (in Benguigui 1997b, 163)

The filmmaker Yamina Benguigui, who recorded these remarks by Mounsi while making her first full-length film, *Mémoires d'immigrés* (1997b), experienced a similar transition. Recalling the childhood memories of her immigrant mother on which she based her second feature-length movie, *Inch'Allah dimanche* (2001a), Benguigui told a journalist: "We felt ashamed of our mothers and didn't want to talk of them. This film arose from my realization of this" (Bouzet 2001b; see also Bouzet 2001a).

My analysis of this transition falls into two main parts. The first explores the reasons for the marginal status accorded to Algerian migration in public constructions of the past and suggests that three main sets of factors have been involved. Within France, the myth of a republican concept of nationhood inimical to the recognition of ethnic differences combined with the painful trauma of decolonization to render Algerian migration especially sensitive. In Algeria, the nationalists who fought for independence and who have since exercised power insisted until very recently that migration to France was a temporary phenomenon arising from colonization, the importance of which was destined to diminish with the consolidation of Algerian nationhood. Squeezed between these two blocks, Algerian migrants themselves generally lacked the will and in many cases the means to communicate their experiences publicly. Among the descendants of Algerian migrants, however, a new commitment to exploring the past has recently emerged in the work of writers, filmmakers, musicians, and historians such as Benguigui, Mounsi, and Mehdi Lallaoui. They are discussed in the second part of this chapter, which considers the complex interplay between the construction of family memories, on the one hand, and national memories, on the other.

Muffled Memories

Although the population of modern France owes more to inward migratory flows than that of any other west European state, there is virtually no acknowledgment of this fact in public monuments, the national educational system, or other public spaces. As Gérard Noiriel has observed, the myth of a republican concept of nationhood inimical to the recognition of ethnic differences has in effect made immigration a "non-lieu de mémoire" ([1988] 1996, 13–67). Moreover, as most economic migrants have lived and worked in places of relatively low social standing, unofficial sites of memory associated with immigrant settlement have often been bulldozed into oblivion. The now demolished *bidonvilles* that sprang up around many French cities during the 1950s and 1960s are obvious examples. The efficacy of France's republican model of integration is often said to be demonstrated by the thoroughness with which immigrants and their descendants have been incorporated into the nation, at the cost of obliterating any references to their foreign origins. If this environment is inhospitable to migrant memories in general, it is doubly hostile to minority ethnic groups—foremost among whom have been Algerians—who are perceived as unassimilable or threatening, or both, to the French nation. Practically the only publicly sanctioned markers of an Algerian presence in France lie in memorials scattered around the hexagon commemorating the role of colonial troops in support of French forces during the First and Second World Wars.[2] Until 2001, when the socialist mayor of Paris, Bertrand Delanoë, inaugurated a plaque to the victims of 17 October 1961, there were no public markers of the important role played by the Algerian migrant population in France in support of the struggle for Algerian independence (Stora 1992b). Economic migrants from Algeria have been present in France for more than a century, and their numbers grew rapidly after independence in 1962, but the trauma of the Algerian War and a widespread desire to leave behind the painful memories associated with it (Stora 1991) were powerful factors that led

2. On the role of colonial troops, see the special issue of *Hommes et migrations* titled *Aux soldats méconnus* (1991). During an official visit to France in 2000, Algerian president Abdelaziz Bouteflika went to some of the graves of Algerian troops who fell at Verdun (Tuquoi 2000). The grandest architectural expression of a North African presence in France, the Grande Mosquée de Paris, was constructed after the First World War at the initiative of the French government in close collaboration with an association of Algerian Muslims in recognition of the contribution of Muslim troops to the French war effort (Kepel 1987, 64–94).

many among the majority ethnic population in France to blot out any recognition of an Algerian dimension within French society.

Algerian nationalism has been a second major force curbing the recognition of the migrant experience during and after the colonial period. In the eyes of the nationalists who fought for independence and who ruled Algeria afterward, the expatriation of migrant workers was a temporary phenomenon caused by the inequities of colonization. It followed from this that the repatriation of migrants was to be expected as Algerian nationhood became consolidated. The promotion of national unity precluded virtually any recognition of the specificity of the migrant experience. For similar reasons, the bloody struggles that had divided supporters of the FLN and the Mouvement national algérien (MNA) in France were airbrushed out of official Algerian accounts of the war for independence (Stora 2002). Practically the only events involving Algerian migrants regularly commemorated in Algeria have been those related to 17 October 1961, which minister to a sense of Algerian national unity for precisely the same reasons that they embarrass and divide the French (Amicale des Algériens en Europe 1987).

A third set of factors inhibiting the expression of migrant memories lay in the experiences and aspirations of Algerian migrants themselves. Brought up in colonial Algeria, where educational provision was reserved mainly for Europeans, the overwhelming majority of migrants were illiterate when they left Algeria. Their low skills base and commensurately low incomes greatly limited the resources at their disposal for any form of public activity. They were consequently ill equipped to construct any public monuments to the migrant experience in France. In many cases, the motivation may also have been lacking. To a very large extent, Algerian migrants supported the struggle for national independence and expected to return to their country of origin eventually. Why should they commemorate their passage in France by building enduring monuments in a country that they regarded as a place of exile?

The Algerian sociologist Abdelmalek Sayad (1975) was one of the first researchers to begin recording oral testimonies among Algerian migrants in the early years after independence. His initial finding was that their preoccupations revolved around the idea of *el ghorba*—that is, exile from a homeland to which they expected to return. By the late 1970s, however, Sayad (1977) detected a shift in perceptions among the migrant population, with permanent family settlement beginning to replace the almost century-old rotation system of temporary labor migration. Central to this process of family settlement was the rise of a second generation of ethnic Algerians raised and in many cases born in France. These sons and daughters of Algerian migrants confounded the expectations of those on both sides of the old colonial divide who for diverse reasons had hoped that the end of empire would mark a clean break with the legacy of the past. Because these new Franco-Algerians were not only bicultural but also binational, juridically or affectively or both, they became a kind of battleground over which the old antagonisms of the colonial period were played out anew. In the eyes of the Algerian authorities, their birth and socialization on French soil represented a threat to the independence and national cohesion of postcolonial Algeria. To the extent that this new generation saw their futures in France, there was a risk not only that they would escape the orbit of the Algerian nation, but also that this view would weaken their parents' resolve to return to their country of origin. Unwilling to countenance the permanent integration of Algerians into French society, with all the historically charged symbolism that this implied, the Algerian government insisted that second-generation Algerians in France were part of the Algerian nation, with all the rights and obligations—including military service—that went with Algerian citizenship.[3]

In France, the colonial legacy weighed in the opposite direction. In a society where most of the majority ethnic population wanted to forget the trauma of decolonization, the highly visible rise of a growing minority of North African origin was an unwelcome reminder of the past, reopening old wounds and reenergizing long-held grudges. It is clearly no accident that the prime targets of racial discrimination and racist violence in contemporary France are Maghrebis and to a lesser extent other postcolonial minorities. They are the victims both of popular attitudes that owe much to racist stereotyping inherited from the colonial period and of factions of French society—most obviously those associated with the extreme Right—who see in the exclusion of France's Algerian minority a form of revenge for the loss of empire and the exodus of the *pieds-noirs* from Algeria (Stora 1999). Attitudes of this kind were key factors motivating those who supported the Balladur government's exclusionary reform of French nationality laws in 1993.

Caught in the cross-fire between these rival camps, second-generation Algerians have had to negotiate their way through a minefield of memories that are not directly theirs, but that permeate the spaces in which they live. Echoes of those memories resonate through many of the literary and cinematic works they have produced. Initially, those echoes were relatively muffled, but in the course of the past decade they have become much more pronounced. At the risk of overgeneralizing, I suggest that in the early wave of novels and films produced during the 1980s, second-generation Algerians tended to assume that staking out a future

3. For a typical expression of the FLN's position, see the article "Journée de l'émigration" (1989).

for themselves in France meant divesting themselves of the baggage of colonial history. By the same token, they relegated their parents to marginal roles. If in more recent years the emphasis has shifted, this shift would appear to be owing in part to a growing conviction that the younger generation of French Algerians cannot become fully part of French society until the majority ethnic population recognizes the historical role of their parents and its continuing significance today.

A Generational Transition

At the heart of this transition is a complex interaction, often contradictory in nature, between family histories on the one hand and national histories on the other. These contradictions are perhaps revealed most starkly in Tassadit Imache's novel *Une fille sans histoire* (1989), where the young protagonist's relationship with her Algerian immigrant father is destroyed by the ethnic animosities aroused in France during the War of Independence, which led her French mother systematically to conceal the paternity of her daughter. It appears that the only way in which the protagonist can become "une fille sans histoire," a girl with an uncomplicated life, is by insulating herself from those other *histoires* that are the collective national fates of France and Algeria. The replication of those national divisions within the family unit is particularly evident in this text because the protagonist's parents are of mixed ethnic origins. But even within monoethnic Algerian families, the act of migration destabilizes the conjunction of national and family histories. Born and brought up during and immediately after the War of Independence, second-generation Algerians in France were in the paradoxical situation of being natives of a country from which many of their parents had struggled to be independent. The schoolboy Azouz in Azouz Begag's *Le gone du Chaâba,* with his eyes fixed on his future in France, can see the benefits of a change of ancestry: "The teacher is always right. If he says we are all descendants of the Gauls, he must be right, and it doesn't matter if we don't have the same moustaches at home" (1986, 62). For similar reasons, in *Béni ou le paradis privé,* the sequel to *Le gone du Chaâba,* the eponymous Béni does everything possible to conceal his Arab origins as he seeks to win the heart of the blonde girl who has stolen his heart, symbolically named France. In the eyes of Béni's father, who tries unsuccessfully to marry his sons to brides from Algeria, exogamy is nothing short of treachery to both family and nation: "What? What? So you dogs want French women, do you! You want to dirty your name, dirty our race! You want to have children and call them Jacques. . . . Well, you go ahead and marry French women: when you're reduced to tears after they've called you a 'wog,' then you'll come back to your father who you think doesn't know anything" (1989, 109).

With little if anything to gain and much to lose from the inherited forms of racial stereotyping feared and at the same time perpetuated here by Béni's father, it was tempting for second-generation Algerians to gloss over the historical experiences in which they were rooted. The 1983 Marche pour l'égalité et contre le racisme typified in many ways the desire of second-generation Maghrebis to secure a legitimate place for themselves in French society. One of the participants, Bouzid Kara (1984b), in finalizing the account he wrote of the march, decided to omit a passage in which he had compared the racist killings of young Maghrebis during the summer of 1983 with the fate of Algerian migrants killed by Paris police on 17 October 1961. Explaining his decision to delete this passage, Kara stated: "That sort of rapprochement with the Algerian War might simply have added grist to the mill of people nostalgic for the old days of colonialism" (1984a, 9).

Gradually, however, writers and filmmakers of Algerian immigrant origin have turned more openly to their historical roots, and memories of October 1961 have been pivotal in this process. Brief and sometimes more extended references to the events on this date are made in many of the narratives they published during the 1980s (Hargreaves 1989). Those events are given pride of place in the opening chapter of Kettane's *Le sourire de Brahim* (1985) and feature prominently in Imache's *Une fille sans histoire,* which is driven by the narrator-protagonist's desire to recover the memory of her lost father and his Algerian origins. By the early 1990s, several organizations—foremost among which were Génériques and Au nom de la mémoire—dedicated to the memory of France's immigrant minorities had been established by young members of minority ethnic groups. Spurred by the bicentenary of the French Revolution in 1989, Génériques produced a richly documented exhibition and associated book tracing the history of immigrant-produced newspapers in France, many of which were intimately associated with the struggle for decolonization (*Presse et mémoire* 1990). The association went on to produce a meticulously researched multivolume guide to archival sources on immigrant populations in France (Génériques 1999) and has more recently been at the forefront of a campaign for the creation of a national museum of immigrant histories and cultures ("Rapport pour la création" 2001).

In 1991, Au nom de la mémoire played a key role in helping to focus public attention on the thirtieth anniversary of the events of 17 October, placing an unofficial marker in memory of those killed on the Pont de Bezons (Bernard 1991), a full decade before the ceremony in which the mayor of Paris unveiled an official plaque in the same place. Second-generation Algerian Mehdi Lallaoui, the moving force behind Au nom de la mémoire, has been a prolific author, producer, and publisher of novels, historical studies, and documentary films on colonial Algeria and on the contribution of immigrants to modern French society (see Lallaoui [1981] 1986, 1989, 1993, 1994, 1995, [1995] 1998, 2001b; Lallaoui and Denis 1991; Lallaoui and Langlois 1995; Lallaoui and Assouline 1996a, 1996b, 1997, 2001). Other high-impact films focusing on the memories of Algerian migrants include those of Yamina Benguigui (1997b, 2001a) and Boualem Guerdjou (1999).

The changes that distinguish Guerdjou's film *Vivre au paradis* from the 1992 narrative by Brahim Benaïcha on which it is based bear eloquent testimony to the heightened interest of second-generation Algerians in their parents' experiences. Benaïcha's autobiographical text was narrated from the viewpoint of its second-generation protagonist, and the events of October 1961 were just one episode in a much longer and more diffuse narrative. The screen adaptation shifts the center of consciousness to that of the boy's immigrant father, Lakhdar, and is constructed climactically around October 1961.

Like the father in Imache's *Une fille sans histoire,* Lakhdar is caught between the dictates of family on the one hand and those of nation on the other. In Imache's novel, the father loses his daughter because it proves impossible to reconcile his commitment to Algerian independence with the aspirations of his family within metropolitan France. Lakhdar's failure is the obverse: in his determination to provide for his family, he refuses to commit his scarce resources to the nationalist cause and as a consequence finds himself deeply isolated when Algerian independence is eventually celebrated in the *bidonville* where he and other migrants have settled in Nanterre.

Whether fighting for family or nation, Algerian migrants made many sacrifices to which there are few public memorials, and one important motivation behind the recent upsurge of work by second-generation Algerians documenting those sacrifices is a sense of debt toward their parents that sometimes shades over into guilt. Guilt is a key element driving the protagonist in Mehdi Lallaoui's *La colline aux oliviers* ([1995] 1998) to research into the ancestry of his immigrant family. His grandfather, Baba Mous, entrusts him with the task of finding out the fate of the old man's uncle, who disappeared without trace in colonial Algeria many years before Baba Mous was born. The young protagonist would much prefer to get on with building his own life in France instead of running after some lead-dead ancestor, but he feels he cannot refuse the old man's request, for the burden of guilt would be too heavy to bear. As he works his way back through successive generations, the grandson uncovers the history of Algerian migrants in France and the colonial territory in which they had their origins, finally learning that Baba Mous's uncle was among a group of Algerians deported to New Caledonia following the insurrection of 1871 against French rule in Kabylia. These discoveries shift the burden of guilt in new directions, for in retracing his ancestral line, the protagonist documents the century-old contribution of Algerian migrant workers to the French economy, the role of colonial troops in support of France during various wars, and the brutality with which French rule was imposed in Algeria. These reconstructed memories of the injustices suffered by Algerians at the hands of the French and of the substantial benefits, both economic and military, that have accrued to France from successive generations of colonial troops and migrant laborers implicitly serve to cut the ground from under the feet of those who argue that France should rid itself of its Algerian minority. If the country owes so much to past generations of Algerians, how can it now deny their descendants a place in France's future?

Conclusion

Shortly before the fortieth anniversary of 17 October, the national football teams of France and Algeria met to play each other for the first time at full international level. The match had been billed as an act of reconciliation, a friendly encounter, which, it was hoped, would help to heal old wounds. But jarring notes were sounded by young ethnic Algerians from the *banlieues*. During the opening ceremonies, they blew whistles of disdain when the "Marseillaise" was played and as each member of the French team—with the single and pointed exception of Zinedine Zidane—was named on the public-address system. In the seventy-sixth minute, with Algeria trailing by one goal to four, scores of youths brandishing Algerian flags brought the match to a halt by invading the pitch. Writing in *Le Monde* a few days later, Azouz Begag and Christian Delorme argued that this turn of events was rooted in a generational gap. Where Begag and Delorme, like others of their age, had looked to the match as a historic moment of reconciliation between old national enemies, the young pitch invaders had other preoccupations:

> From the outset, this friendly game had been made tense by a symbolic charge that was too heavy to bear. But let it not be forgotten what that charge meant to us, for we had lived through the Algerian War and its embers had been kept alive in our memory.
>
> We were the ones who wanted it to be a game of reconciliation. Not so the younger invaders of the Stade de France [the French national soccer stadium]. It was obvious that they didn't share our concerns, for these were not their problems. For them, the game was an opportunity for having a good time, at least up to the 76th minute, an opportunity to rekindle a sense of pride in their identity. On 6 October, they were no longer afraid of stating their Algerian origins, no longer ashamed to pronounce the word "Algerian," and the flag they waved in

> the middle of that sporting arena was that of their new-found sense of pride. (Begag and Delorme 2001)

It is undoubtedly the case that for this new, third generation of ethnic Algerians, born twenty years after independence, memories of empire are far more diffuse than for second-generation Algerians such as Begag, born during the death throes of the colonial system. Yet one cannot but be struck by the perhaps unconscious parallels between this defiant flag-waving display of Algerian identity in the Stade de France and the similar defiance with which Algerian migrants marched through the streets of Paris in October 1961.

An article in the same edition of *Le Monde* written by the Algerian ambassador to France, Mohamed Ghoualmi, illustrated how far the political agenda has moved on in the decades since 1961. In attempting to excuse those who had whistled disdainfully during the French national anthem, Ghoualmi asserted that they did not understand the historical symbolism of their behavior. Their whistles were not aimed against

> the France of Chirac, Jospin, Juppé or Séguin . . . —it would be impossible to cite every one of them—and all those responsible for seeking to facilitate their integration. . . .
>
> Their whistles were aimed against a minority of the French, but what a difficult minority, for it stands in their way when they go looking for a job or somewhere to live or when they are refused entry to a nightclub. Their whistles were aimed against the 30 percent unemployment rate they suffer. Their whistles were aimed against the "Get back to your country" that many of them have had thrown into their face at least once in their young lives. . . .
>
> So it goes without saying that their heartfelt cries went far beyond a football game rightly described as historic by a generation they don't understand or belong to, but whose inhibitions, mental hang-ups, and guilt complexes continue to weigh heavily upon them. (Ghoualmi 2001)

Ghoualmi's comments are striking not only because they reveal how far the Algerian authorities have now gone in accepting the idea of postcolonial minorities' being integrated into French society—a far cry from the stubborn nationalist rhetoric long maintained by the FLN—but also because they correctly identify the stubbornness with which racist stereotyping and old animosities inherited from the past are frustrating aspirations toward integration. Although the third generation now emerging among the Algerian minority is far removed in time from the colonial era, its future in France clearly remains heavily conditioned by the legacy of that period.

15 Derrida's Nostalgeria

LYNNE HUFFER

> Tu perçois du coup l'origine de mes souffrances, puisque cette langue les traverse de part en part, et le lieu de mes passions, de mes désirs, de mes prières, la vocation de mes espérances.[1]
>
> —Jacques Derrida, "Prière d'insérer," *Le monolinguisme de l'autre*

> Je souffrais de voir à tout moment confondues dans le récit de notre actualité, Nature et Histoire, et je voulais rassaisir dans l'exposition décorative de *ce-qui-va-de-soi,* l'abus idéologique qui, à mon sens, s'y trouve caché."[2]
>
> —Roland Barthes, *Mythologies*

WRITTEN DURING THE RUPTURE that was the twentieth century's "first" Algerian War,[3] Roland Barthes's *Mythologies* (1957) reminds us of the power of myths in shaping public perceptions of current events—"the account . . . of our contemporary circumstances." These perceptions of the present become over time the repository of myth we call cultural memory. Nowhere is this power to shape collective consciousness more visible than in the ongoing French elaboration of myths about Algeria, especially during moments of catastrophic violence. As Barthes persuasively demonstrated in "African Grammar," his study of the

1. "You can then perceive the origin of my sufferings, because this language cuts right through them, as well as the place of my passions, my desires, my prayers, the call of my hopes" (Derrida 1996a, translation mine). (Because there are also published translations of some works that I discuss or quote from in this chapter, and because I use some of these translations, I have clarified where translations are mine in all cases.)

2. "In the account given of our contemporary circumstances, I suffered at seeing Nature and History confused at every turn, and I wanted to track down, in the decorative display of *what-goes-without-saying,* the ideological abuse which, in my view, is hidden there" (Barthes 1972a, 11, translation modified; originally published in French [Barthes 1957, 9]).

3. In "Deuxième guerre Algérienne?" (1995, Second Algerian War?), Benjamin Stora argues that the bloody civil war in Algeria repeats, in its rhetoric and cultural representation, many of the themes of the 1954–62 Algerian War of Independence.

code words used by the French press to make the colonial army's atrocities during the Algerian struggle for independence more palatable to a French audience, myth is a linguistic edifice that naturalizes particular perceptions and political interests, converting ideology into truth. "I suffered," he writes in the preface, "at seeing Nature and History confused at every turn" (1972a, 11). The medium through which that mystification of ideology occurs, Barthes continues, is fundamentally linguistic. "Myth," he asserts, "is a language" (1972a, 11). Importantly, he exposes not only ideologies, but also the role cultural mythologies play in legitimating some languages and therefore some myths at the expense of others: while language forms the pictures that entire societies mistake for reality, it at the same time blurs the contours of other myths and thus other realities, ultimately occluding them altogether: "Colonization evaporates, swallowed up in the halo of an impotent lament" (1957, 138, translation mine).

Barthes's focus on myth as language establishes a context for reflecting on a present-day nostalgic French discourse about Algeria, which was colonized by the French in 1830 and given up with Algerian independence in 1962. This chapter explores nostalgic myth making as it appears in the highbrow discourse of the French intellectual by looking at the highly visible work of well-known writers such as Hélène Cixous and Jacques Derrida. Breaking their silence about their personal stories as Jewish *pieds-noirs* who, during their childhood years in the 1940s, experienced both the privilege of their Frenchness and, as Jews under Philippe Pétain, the trauma of their marginalization as non-French, both Derrida and Cixous recently published works that attempt to come to grips with their place in that vexed and contradictory Franco-Judeo-Algerian past. In "Pieds nus" (Bare Feet), a story published in the 1997 anthology *Une enfance algérienne* (An Algerian Childhood), and, more recently, in *Les rêveries de la femme sauvage: Scènes primitives* (2000, Dreams of a Wild Woman: Primal Scenes), Cixous evokes her Algerian childhood as a scene for the staging of family dramas and the difficult but happy commingling of French and Algerian lives. During the same period, Jacques Derrida made public for the first time his reflections on his own childhood in Algiers in "Circonfession" (1991), *Monolinguisme de l'autre* (1996a, *Monolinguism of the Other* [1998b]), and, most recently, in Safaa Fathy's film *D'Ailleurs, Derrida* (1999, Derrida's Elsewhere).[4] In this chapter, I focus on one work in particular, Derrida's *Monolinguism of the Other,* in order to look at the complex way in which the myth of Algeria interfaces with the equally powerful myth of the French intellectual.

4. Derrida has also discussed Algeria in recent interviews and public interventions. See "Parti pris pour l'Algérie" (1995); "Déclaration de J. Derrida" (2000); and his interview with Eribon, "Oui, mes livres sont politiques" (1996b).

In its evocation of Algeria as an experience of childhood, *Monolinguism of the Other* typifies a recent trend in French letters, where France's double shame—for the violence of its colonial practices and for its subsequent refusal to remember them publicly—is mitigated by the rendering of history through the child's innocent gaze. Like Albert Bensoussan's *Pour une poignée de dattes* (2001, For a Handful of Dates) or Jean Pélégri's *Ma mère l'Algérie* (1989, My Mother Algeria), the return of *Monolinguism of the Other* to childhood should be interpreted not only as the description of an individual experience, but also with a view to the more general cultural work it performs. With the rise of Islamic fundamentalism during the 1990s, Algeria came to represent murderous fanaticism and an Islamicist repression of difference that in the French cultural imaginary still threatens at every moment to spill over into France. In that context, these recent evocations of *pieds-noirs'* childhoods allow their innocent protagonists to lament the loss of a preindependence and preterrorist Algerian *métissage,* where a plurality of cultures and languages peacefully coexisted in the childhood world of play. Further, through the gaze of childhood, the violent rupture of the Algerian War is attenuated by the perception of the innocent witness who is caught in the conflict but in no way responsible for it. The lack of responsibility associated with the perspective of childhood provides a convenient lens through which France can gaze nostalgically toward colonial Algeria. Indeed, this innocent, *prepolitical* gaze allows France to romanticize the 130-year period of its colonial domination; in the persona of the child at play, the colonizer becomes, in the words of Alain Vircondelet, "almost 'Arab' " himself (1997, 241, translation mine).[5] Finally, this transformed image of a harmonious past allows France to express horror at Algeria's current violence without attending to the difficult moral and political question of France's historical relationship to the present state of affairs.

Unlike Cixous's *Une enfrance algérienne, Les rêveries de la femme sauvage,* or *Pour une poignée de dattes,* Derrida's *Monolinguism of the Other* is fundamentally a philosophical text. It is arguably most famous for its memorable evocation of what Derrida calls "my 'nostalgeria' " (1998b, 52), a neologism whose word play epitomizes Barthes's idea of myth as the culturally legitimated linguistic rendering of something, a place and a time—in this case Algeria in the 1940s.[6]

5. "Quand? Quel jour, pensait l'enfant tandis que le paquebot filait vers l'horizon et qu'Alger se dérobait au regard, à quel moment précis de son existence recluse avait-il compris qu'il était résolument de là-bas? Presque 'arabe' lui aussi?" (Vircondelet 1997, 241).

6. This postmodern mythologizing operation becomes all the more salient in view of the fact that, despite numerous critical assumptions to the contrary, Derrida did not coin the term *nostalgeria.* In fact, according to Philip Dine (1994), Montherlant first used the term *la nostalgérie* in his anticolonialist novel *La rose de sable* (The Sand Rose), written between 1930 and 1932 but not

In addition, however, "nostalgeria" in Derrida becomes even more important, for him, the linguistic rendering of a linguistic rendering—in other words, less a myth about Algeria than a myth about language.[7] In this self-reflective move, the nostalgic voice of Derrida's text is subjected to a rigorous, self-referential critique, doubling back on itself in order to ironize its own nostalgic longing.

This specifically Derridean reinvention of French "nostalgeria" provides a path through "Algeria" as a nostalgic myth by focusing on the relation between the loss of Algeria and the intellectual self whose subjectivity is bound up with that past and that loss. First, Derridean "nostalgeria" serves a key function in Derrida's particular autobiographical construction of himself as a French and, more important, Jewish intellectual; it is, in fact, central to what he calls elsewhere "an impossible autobiography."[8] Second, "nostalgeria" raises questions about nostalgia in general and in particular about the contradictory impulses of desire and shame in relation to a lost colonial past. Third, this nexus of issues about the self, nostalgia, and loss speaks to the problem of cultural memory as

---

published until the 1960s after French decolonization (see Montherlant 1982). Whether or not Derrida actually knew about the Montherlant reference is less important than the common contemporary assumption that "nostalgeria" is a specifically Derridean and therefore postmodern invention. Having slipped through the sieve of *political* memory during the same three decades as Derrida's silence regarding Algeria, "nostalgeria" can now be recuperated by postmodernism as a particular kind of *apolitical* mythology. For examples of false attribution, see Bennington and Derrida: "J. D. often speaks of his " 'nostalgeria' " (1991, 303, translation mine). Also see Ofrat: Derrida's "powerful links with the Algerian period of his life are illustrated in the term he coined: 'nostalgeria' " (2001, 11). In fact, as Philip Dine points out, "nostalgeria" is the constant theme of an entire body of French artistic production that dates back to at least 1899, when Louis Bertrand published *Le sang des races* (The Blood of the Races) (1994, 148). Also see Friedman, whose ethnographic interviewee also uses the term: " 'For my generation, our sentiment of exile lies at our very center . . . *la nostalgérie,*' he jokingly punned" (1988, xi). Also see Siblot 1985 and Stein 1992.

7. In addition to "Circonfession," *Monolinguism of the Other,* and *Derrida's Elsewhere,* Derrida in his later years spoke out in public forums regarding the question of Algeria. For example, he participated in a 2001 colloquium whose purpose was to bring to light the 1961 massacre of dozens of Algerians by the Paris police during a nonviolent demonstration, adding his name to a list of 2,940 signatories of a statement, "Pour que cesse l'oubli," and making his own individual public declaration. "En réparant l'injustice et en sauvant la mémoire," he declares, "il nous revient de faire oeuvre critique, analytique et politique" (Derrida 2000). On the 1961 massacre, see Einaudi 2001 and chapter 8 in this volume.

8. In Safaa Fathy's film *Derrida's Elsewhere* (1999), Derrida remarks on his own autobiographical project in "Circonfession" and *Monolinguism of the Other:* "I spoke of an impossible autobiography, in the classical sense of the term, because autobiography implies at least that the 'I' knows who he is, identifies himself before writing, or supposes a certain identity . . . Who ever met a 'me'? Not me."

the repository of myth. What forms of memory are recuperated in that process? What forms of memory are effaced? And finally, these questions about memory force us to ask about the histories that are and are not underwritten by "nostalgeria." Whose histories become part of cultural memory, and whose histories remain unspoken?

To be sure, it would be inappropriate to reduce metonymically the whole of *Monolinguism of the Other* to merely one of its parts: the term *nostalgeria*. Indeed, *Monolinguism* is many things: a meditation on the nature of language; a self-critical deconstruction of Derrida's own philosophical, linguistic, and psychological quest for origins; and an autobiographical exploration of the role of identity within the context of the larger political and historical forces through which countries are colonized, wars are waged, groups are disenfranchised, and populations are displaced. Reflecting on his childhood as an Algerian Jew under the Vichy regime, Derrida forces us to confront the complexity of those relationships that history and cultural studies all too easily reduce to the binary oppositions of colonizer and colonized, oppressor and victim, conqueror and conquered. Exposing the scars that mark Derrida's own experience of disenfranchisement when in 1940 Pétain reversed the 1870 Crémieux decrees and revoked the citizenship rights of all French Jews, *Monolinguism of the Other* unabashedly reveals Derrida's own contradictory status both as a marginalized subject and as one of the most celebrated philosophers of the twentieth century.

In that context, it can be argued that "nostalgeria" hardly suffices as a summation of all that is going on in Derrida's text. However, if "nostalgeria" is a myth and, following Barthes, "myth is a language," then there are valid reasons for focusing on "nostalgeria" in a book that, as the title suggests, is ultimately about language—the stuff of myths. As the chapter epigraph from Derrida reminds us, Derrida, like Barthes in 1957, too suffers from language: "the origin of my sufferings, because this language cuts right through them, as well as the place of my passions, my desires, my prayers, the call of my hopes." More specifically, Derrida suffers from the *French* language; in that perspective, *Monolinguism of the Other* is a book about French and Derrida's conflicted relationship to it. The confusion of this relationship is dramatized toward the middle of the book, where Derrida is penetrated and possessed by French. Historically situated a few years after the landing of the Allied forces in North Africa in November 1942, the scene unfolds as the story of a loss of innocence. During a historical moment when French literature flowered on Algerian soil, Derrida is deflowered by language: "In the still-sparkling wake of this strange moment of glory, I seemed to be harpooned by French philosophy and literature, the one and the other, the one or the other: wooden or metallic darts, a penetrating body of enviable, formidable, and inaccessible words even when they were entering me" (1998b, 50).

The contradictory violence and seduction of this act of penetration marks the historical complexity of Derrida's situation as a French Algerian Jew. French is at one and the same time the language of the colonizing group of which Derrida was a part and from which he benefited; the language of his parents and an entire Jewish community that had been brutally told it was no longer "French"; the language of Pétain and the Vichy regime that took away his citizenship; the language that he learned and perfected at school within a larger Arabic and Berber culture he was explicitly forbidden to know; the language that would later gain him entry to the École normale supérieure and launch his success as a French intellectual star. French, then, is for Derrida both his only language and at the same time a language he will never possess. French is both the vehicle of his life's work—the writing through which life reveals itself to him—and the obstacle that forever blocks him from true knowledge of life and self.

As recounted in *Monolinguism of the Other,* this evocative and disturbing narrative of Derrida's individual relationship to the French language powerfully speaks a certain personal truth about a particular lived experience. And yet, however moving his narrative might be, Derrida's personal truth cannot free him from the ideological function his discourse both masks and serves. Again, if "myth is a language," as Barthes puts it, then *Monolinguism of the Other* is a particularly seductive version of the quintessential deconstructive myth of language as trace, as *différance,* as an inaccessible archewriting.[9] But what differentiates *Monolinguism of the Other* from *De la grammatologie* (1967a, *Of Grammatology* [1974]) or from *L'écriture et la différence* (1967b, *Writing and Difference*) or from *Marges de la philosophie* (1972, *Margins of Philosophy*) is its articulation of deconstructive archewriting in the explicitly autobiographical and historical context of postcoloniality. For this reason, *Monolinguism of the Other* reveals more clearly than Derrida's other texts the political and ethical stakes of

9. *Trace, différance,* and *archewriting* are all terms that express, for Derrida, the infinite process of difference and deferral through which signification occurs. His invocation of the "origin" as writing deconstructs the illusory logic wherein writing has traditionally been conceived as coming *after* a more originary speech. As Derrida puts it in *Of Grammatology:* "The trace is in fact the absolute origin of sense in general. Which amounts to saying once again that there is no absolute origin of sense in general. The trace is the difference which opens appearance and signification" (1974, 65). This structure carries within it what Gayatri Chakravorty Spivak calls "the trace of a perennial alterity." "To this structure," Spivak continues, "Derrida gives the name 'writing' " (1974, xxxix). For a useful introduction to the philosophical logic behind Derridean archewriting, see Spivak 1974.

deconstruction or, as Barthes would put it, the ideological abuse that lies hidden there. Derrida himself would be the first to admit that "free play" is never entirely free; that he, like all subjects, is situated in a particular social, political, and historical setting.[10] As such, and like all subjects, he is engaged in the process of myth making. As Philip Dine reminds us, "not only colonial Algeria, but every society, makes ideological myths out of its history, both to provide justifications for its world-view, and to confer legitimacy upon its adopted system of economic, social and political relations" (1994, 150). In its evocation of "nostalgeria," *Monolinguism of the Other* rewrites and exposes the ideological myths that over the past three decades have so insistently been politically neutralized, even naturalized, as "deconstruction."[11]

How does "nostalgeria" reveal these myths? Derrida's admission of his own "nostalgeria" in *Monolinguism of the Other* occurs, not surprisingly, in the guise of myth, as a colorful inscription of language as trace. Presented by Derrida as his dream "to make something happen to this language" (1998b, 51) that had penetrated him, "nostalgeria" becomes an image of an indelible but unspeakable writing, the "ineffaceable archive" of an unnamable "event" of communication: "not necessarily an infant but a tattoo, a splendid form, concealed under garments in which blood mixes with ink to reveal all its colors to the sight" (1998b, 52). In the context of this meditation on loss—of Algeria, of the motherland, of a nonoriginary origin—this event of communication is the familiar and paradoxical Derridean articulation in language of the loss that will always be a never-quite-adequate language. Here, at the site of "nostalgeria," the inaccessible place of flesh, birth, and voice is both noted and negated by a writing where *physis* and *tekhne,* Nature and History, blood and ink, intermingle in the "splendid form" of a dazzling tattoo. As a cipher of loss, this phantasmatic tattoo constitutes the nostalgic image of a fullness of language that never was and never will be. Inverting

10. For Derrida's concept of "free play" *(le jeu),* see especially "La structure, le signe, et le jeu dans le discours des sciences humaines" (Derrida 1967c). For Derrida's responses to critical misunderstandings of the structure that frames "free play," see especially his *Limited Inc.* (1988).

11. This statement does not deny the myriad interpreters of Derrida who have raised questions about his politics. For example, Nancy Fraser asked in 1984 why a supposedly leftist Derrida "deliberately and dexterously avoided the subject of politics" (1984, 127). In another notorious example, Rosemary Jolly argues that Derrida's description of apartheid as "the ultimate racism in the world" in a 1985 article distracts his readers from their own complicity in European and American colonial policies. See Derrida's "Racism's Last Word" (1985) and Jolly's "Rehearsals of Liberation" (1995). For a critique of Derrida's politics with regard to Israel and the Palestinians, see Marrouchi 1997, 23–24.

his past victimization by French, the master language that literally penetrated his body, Derrida creates as a colorful inscription on the surface of the body a new, mythical language that can never be read or mastered. Having been penetrated by French in the 1940s, he reappropriates and transforms this invasive language, emerging, over half a century and dozens of books later, as the "nostalgerian" bearer of an inaccessible tattoo language impervious to the seductions of the French master. This tattoo is Derrida's dream of language: "the incarnate liturgy whose secret no one will betray . . . not even I who would, however, be in on the secret" (1998b, 52).

What is the significance of this corporeal and symbolic secret that cannot be spoken, not even by the one, Jacques Derrida, who in the moment of its seductive evocation reveals himself to be in on it, privy to that which, for the rest of us, remains "concealed under garments"? More pointedly, what is the relationship between this phantasmatic glimpse of a tattoo language in that seductive place where the clothing gapes[12] and Derrida's undisguised nostalgia for his own Algerian past? How are we to interpret his teasingly ironic and elliptical remark immediately following the evocation of the tattoo: "I must still dream about it, in my 'nostalgeria' " (1998b, 52)?

For all its transcendent aesthetic power, Derrida's "nostalgeria"—like all nostalgia—also has a structure and a history. However, in the case of Derrida's postmodern Algerian nostalgia, the structure and history of "nostalgeria" are literally inked over by Derridean language: "a splendid form" that confuses "Nature and History," the "decorative display" of the secret tattoo. If, like Barthes in the 1950s, we begin to demystify cultural myth, what ideologies lie hidden beneath the ink and blood of Derrida's tattoo writing? How might an exploration of nostalgia's philosophical, emotional, and political structure lay bare some of deconstruction's most fundamental ideological underpinnings in relation to the Algerian question?

In his analysis of Algerian nostalgia, Paul Siblot (1985) describes the nostalgic writings of postindependence *pied-noir* exiles in Freudian terms as a psychic response to trauma, where the writer's trauma is resolved through the aesthetic work of mourning. This common psychoanalytic understanding of nostalgia conflates a collective phenomenon with the individual's emotional and psychic reaction to traumatic loss. At the heart of this view of nostalgia's structure lies a search for origins—as home, mother, or the ground of Truth—that, paradoxically, is des-

12. As Roland Barthes famously put it in *The Pleasure of the Text,* "Is not the most erotic portion of a body *where the garment gapes?*" (1975, 9, emphasis in original).

tined to fail.[13] Indeed, nostalgia happens precisely because we cannot go home again; if we could go home, we would not feel nostalgic. Further, this repeated failure to go home—to unite with the lost other—also guarantees our existence as subjects of desire who will never be freed of our longing. Thus, as thinking subjects, we will forever yearn for a Truth, a home, or a mother we cannot have; as speaking subjects, we will always desire an unattainable fullness of language. No one knows this better than Derrida, whose most explicitly nostalgic book, *Monolinguism of the Other,* is tellingly subtitled *The Prosthesis of Origin.*[14]

A less familiar aspect of nostalgia is its history as a political concept. In a fascinating article on the political history of nostalgia, Kimberly Smith traces the genealogy of the term from its first use by a Swiss physician in 1688 to its familiar contemporary uses. Smith's analysis of nostalgia as a political concept is particularly useful for understanding the ideological underpinnings of Derridean "nostalgeria." Most important, Smith explores nostalgia as a concept that shapes political meanings within modernity: "Nostalgia," she writes, "figures prominently in struggles over the creation of collective memory precisely because it is a key concept in the political conflict over modernity—an important weapon in the debate over whose memories count and what kinds of desires and harms are politically relevant" (2000, 507). Specifically, she argues that "the concept of nostalgia is bounded by a loose consensus as to what constitutes the proper content of nostalgic longing. That consensus, and the many cracks in it, are significantly influenced by politics" (2000, 508). As she puts it, "it would seem strange to wax nostalgic for the years one spent in a concentration camp" (2000, 508). Thus, despite its modern association with individual loss and grief, nostalgia is a political phenomenon that is "socially constructed" (Smith 2000, 511).

Smith carefully traces the permutations of the meanings of *nostalgia* from the seventeenth- and eighteenth-century medicalized interpretation—its symptoms, first associated with the experience of Swiss mercenaries fighting in foreign countries, included "persistent thinking of home, melancholia, insomnia, anorexia, weakness, anxiety, smothering sensations, and fever"—to a more political valence in the nineteenth century as the distinctive "symptom of the social dislocation that was the hallmark of industrialization" (2000, 510, 511). Over the course of the nineteenth century, nostalgia evolved from a disease to an emotion,

13. See Davis 1979; Turner 1987; Stauth and Turner 1988; Shaw and Case 1989; and Huffer 1998.

14. As Jean-Luc Nancy puts it in *Derrida's Elsewhere,* this theme of prosthesis or "graft" *(la greffe)* lies at the heart of Derrida's work, marking "the heterogeneity at the heart of the ideal of a homogenous self" (Fathy 1999).

and by the second half of the twentieth century it had become not only an emotion but a philosophical principle: "a universal and ubiquitous phenomenon, common to all times and places, rooted in human nature and representative of the human condition" (2000, 514).

Smith's most important political insight regarding the term has to do with the often unacknowledged ideological work it performs. "Nostalgia," she writes, "is not simply a neutral description of a modern emotional quirk, but an ideologically charged construct. And its configuration . . . reflects long-standing debates about whose memories count, what kind of attachments and modes of life are valuable, and what kinds of harms are politically relevant" (2000, 515–16). However, with the advent of industrialization, nostalgia's ideological function was masked through its consignment to the realm of the private, the emotional, and the sentimental. Maurice Halbwachs, following the work of his teacher Henri Bergson, focuses on the importance of collective, non-nostalgic memory in its relation to political action, wherein nostalgia is relegated to the private, dreamlike, Proustian realm of an apolitical elite whose primary desire is to escape from society rather than to engage in it through action. In that Halbwachian context, nostalgia becomes what Smith calls "mere nostalgia" (2000, in the title of her article), a nonharmful if politically irrelevant emotion symbolized by Proust's madeleine, modernity's archetypal symbol of an aesthetic vehicle of remembrance completely divorced from politics.

So how are we to read Derrida's "nostalgeria" in the context of its structure and political history? On a first reading, it would seem that, like Halbwachs, Derrida marks his own nostalgia ("*my* 'nostalgeria' ") as part of a personal rather than collective fantasy; indeed, his nostalgia is like the secret tattoo, indelibly inscribed on the body, but invisible and unreadable to all but its bearer. This mark of the personal is even more striking in that, along with "Circonfession," *Monolinguism of the Other* constitutes a rare instance in Derrida's oeuvre where the personal pronoun *I* appears at all. However, just as Derrida's autobiographical "I" is subverted by its own undoing—his "autobiographical anamnesis" becomes "an entirely other anamnesis . . . an anamnesis of the entirely other" (1998b, 28, 60)—so too is his "nostalgeria" put into question in the very act of its evocation. Derrida's longing is not the crude nostalgic yearning of what Jean-Claude Vatin (1974) calls the "tear-jerker" films and novels of exiled *pieds-noirs* such as José Castano (1982) or Gabriel Conesa (1970) (see Dine 1994, 146–77), or even the more subtle desires of contemporary writers such as Bensoussan, Cixous, and Pélégri. Rather, through the careful diacritical marking of a "nostalgeria" ensconced within quotation marks, the Derridean "I" simultaneously reveals and puts into question his own emotional condition. Adopting the stance of an ambiguous but unmistakable ironic detachment, Derrida's nostalgia for the Algeria of his childhood expresses itself through the performative irony of a "nostalgeria" that is both claimed and disavowed, something merely glimpsed, like the tattoo, or easily laughed out of existence, like his earlier description of himself as "the last defender and illustrator of the French language (from here, I can hear the protests, from various sides: yes, yes, laugh away!)" (1998b, 47).

This ironic detachment, whether ludic ("laugh away!") or erotically phantasmatic ("concealed under garments"), has implications for any political reading one might offer of Derrida's "nostalgeria." Whether laughing or daring us to take a peek, Derrida conveys his message: we all know nostalgia is politically problematic from any but the most boorish right-wing perspective, and it is especially problematic in relation to a shamefully violent and oppressive colonial past. Thus, in separating himself from "nostalgeria" through the performative distancing of quotation, Derrida reminds us that he, the demystifier of origins par excellence, knows all about nostalgia's problems, whether those problems are articulated philosophically as a metaphysics of presence or politically as a colonialist longing for *algérianisme*.[15] His irony also suggests that he, a French Algerian Jew, does not fully occupy the subject position of the exiled colonizer. As he put it in an interview about the French schooling he received in Algeria, "The teachers, for the most part, came from the metropole. . . . A bit like the colonized, we had a rapport that was at once intimidated and *ironic* also. . . . Thus, there was a kind of *irony* with regard to this culture they taught us" (Derrida 1999–2000, 4, translation and emphasis mine).[16]

Nonetheless, the ironic detachment of Derrida's "nostalgeria" does not remove him entirely from the colonizer position, nor does it free him from the nostalgic ideological structures that *Monolinguism of the Other* and, indeed, his entire corpus claim to dismantle. If, like Smith, we read Derrida's ironic "nostalgeria" as part of a political history of nostalgia, the ideological stakes of "nostalgeria" become clear. "Nostalgeria" is not the nostalgia of an unrepentant colonizer bitter over his expulsion from Algeria after independence; rather, it derives its power as a seductively ambiguous aesthetic form, a splendid tattoo that

15. On *algérianisme,* see especially Dine, who explains how in the early decades of the twentieth century an attempt was made among some French *pieds-noirs* to assert their "aesthetic autonomy" by painting the picture of an Algerian *peuple neuf* as a "challenge to metropolitan cultural hegemony" (1994, 148).

16. In another interview, Derrida suggests that the Algerian Jews were among the colonized: "I belonged to a minority in a colonized country. The Jewish community in Algeria was there long before the French colonizers. So on the one hand, Algerian Jews belonged to the colonized people, and on the other they assimilated with the French" (1998a, 2).

in its ambiguity becomes another version of the classic Derridean trope of archewriting. Most significant, Derridean ironic repetition of the past in "nostalgeria" blurs the distinction between colonizer and colonized, thereby exposing ethical questions about the relationship between memory and the telling of the past we call history. What constitutes an ethical relation to the past? And how does our memory inform our present moral positions and political actions in the face of that past?

Because *Monolinguism of the Other* constitutes, in Derrida's words, both an "autobiographical anamnesis" and an "anamnesis of the other," one means of approaching these ethical questions is through a reading of the relation in the text between the self and its other, an "other" that appears variously as "you," as a friend, as the past, as language. This relation is dramatized, in one of its forms, as Derrida's friendship with Abdelkebir Khatibi in an important instance of what Adam Zachary Newton calls the "recursive, contingent, and interactive dramas of encounter and recognition" (1995, 12) that constitute "narrative ethics." Indeed, nowhere are the ethical stakes of "nostalgeria" more clearly revealed than in this staging of the intersubjective relation between Derrida and his Moroccan friend. Significantly, the scene of this encounter is a U.S. academic context, an international colloquium in Louisiana whose invited guests were, as Derrida puts it, "Francophones *belonging,* as we strangely say, to several nations, cultures and states" (1998b, 10). Derrida continues: "And all these problems *of identity,* as we so foolishly say nowadays. Among all the participants, there were two, Abdelkebir Khatibi and myself, who, besides an old friendship, meaning the blessing of so many other things from memory and the heart, also shared a destiny. They live in a certain 'state' as far as language and culture are concerned: they have a certain status" (1998b, 10). This "state" to which Khatibi and Derrida both *belong* and *do not belong,* which both does and does not constitute a shared *identity,* is their shared "Franco-Maghrebian status." This status, says Derrida, "is indeed 'my country' " (1998b, 10).

Although it is tempting here, for obvious linguistic and cultural reasons, to dismiss Derrida's claim of sameness with Khatibi, there are compelling reasons not to condemn it too quickly. First, Derrida is quite explicit in demonstrating his recognition of the ways in which identities are deployed for legitimation in certain postcolonial contexts. As he puts it in his self-mocking opening chapter of *Monolinguism,* "And now in order to stir us and win us to your cause, there you are, playing the card of the exile and immigrant worker, there you are, claiming, in French, that French has always been a foreign language to you!" (1998b, 5). Again, he uses irony here to put preemptively into question his own motivations in claiming a "Franco-Maghrebian" identity. Second, and even more important, rather than basking in the simplicity of a union and shared identity created within the borders of a secure Franco-Maghrebian "country" called Derrida-Khatibi, Derrida highlights the violent rupture of that hyphenated state:

> Still, assuming there were some historical unity of a France and a Maghreb, which is far from being certain, the "and" will never have been given, only promised or claimed. At bottom, that is what we must be talking about, what we are talking about without fail, even if we are doing it by omission. The silence of that hyphen does not pacify or appease anything, not a single torment, not a single torture. It will never silence their memory. It could even worsen the terror, the lesions, and the wounds. A hyphen is never enough to conceal protests, cries of anger or suffering, the noise of weapons, airplanes, and bombs. (1998b, 11)

This recognition of the "silence of that hyphen" between France and the Maghreb constitutes, in my view, Derrida's most explicit statement in the book about an ethical obligation to the "other": to his Maghrebian friend, to the past, to the writing of history that informs our perceptions of the present. In the hyphen that joins France and Algeria, where Derrida both "promises" and "claims" the *and* that joins him to Khatibi, the differences and the violences that both link and separate them—"protests, cries of anger or suffering, the noise of weapons, airplanes, and bombs"—are remembered and named. Alluding, perhaps, to an " 'official' French memory [that] is full of holes" (Stora 1995, 242, translation mine) and that participates in what Pierre Vidal-Naquet denounces as an "unforgivable silence" (in Stora 1995, 245, translation mine), this rare imagistic evocation of the Algerian War in *Monolinguism of the Other* affirms that the illusory hyphen of the Franco-Maghrebian union cannot conceal the ongoing Algerian struggle.

However, the ethical status of that hyphenated claim and promise is rendered ambiguous as Derrida moves farther back in his "nostalgeria," toward the secret tattoo that is archewriting. Through the introduction of another hyphen, further complicating the hyphenated identity he shares with Khatibi, he is pulled farther and farther toward a different space-time continuum, toward a different "other," and away from his Arab Algerian friend. This complication is, of course, his "Judeo-Franco-Maghrebian genealogy" (1998b, 71). This "genealogy," Derrida writes, "does not clarify everything, far from it. But could I explain anything without it, ever?" (1998b, 71–72). To be sure, the additional hyphen that marks Derrida's Jewish difference from his friend Khatibi functions on a number of different levels. It marks, importantly, the particularity of his experience as an Algerian Jew and specifically that other, unspeakable violence perpetrated against the Jewish people in the Holocaust. For Derrida, however, that Jewish difference also and more pronouncedly serves an entirely different function. Although the genealogy may "not clarify everything," it changes everything in relation to language and dramatically highlights his difference from Khatibi.

Thus, whereas Khatibi has a mother tongue (Arabic), Derrida claims to have none. This claim may seem somewhat surprising because Derrida was raised and schooled in French. Nonetheless, he says, French "is not my mother tongue" (1998b, 61). Playing on the classic *pied-noir* myth of dispossession,[17] this absence of a mother tongue allows Derrida to move beyond the ambiguity of an irony tied to his socio-political-historical location, to construct a "prosthesis of origin" as a Jewish archewriting that never was. Evoking "the poetic solemnity of the chant or prayer" (1998b, 41), his "nostalgeria" circles back beyond the lost "country" of "Franco-Maghrebian" or "Derrida-Khatibi" to the more ancient mother tongue of the Jewish people: "the sacred language, the language of prayer, which remains a language *proper* to the Jewish people" (1998b, 84, emphasis in original).[18] In this return to the origin of origins, to "a certain *sacrality* of the *root*" (1998a, 91, emphasis in original), Derrida bypasses Algeria altogether, replacing "Franco-Maghrebian" with the true mother tongue that cannot be replaced. To the one who has no mother tongue comes the irreducible mother tongue: as Derrida puts it in glossing Hannah Arendt, "the mother tongue cannot be replaced" (1998b, 87).

So what are the grounds for an ethical critique of Derrida, who, it might be argued, is simply marking and claiming a Jewish identity inscribed within a history of the repeated expropriation of the Jewish people? Indeed, if that were the case, there would be no reason to raise ethical questions at all. But Derrida's turn toward Judaism is not about historical specificity or an ethical obligation to remember the particularities of the other, whether that other is Khatibi, the past, or the Jewish people. Rather, it is part of a more general Derridean trajectory by

17. Dine explains this "theme of settler dispossession": "According to the myth, the characterizing feature of the lot of the first colonizers of Algeria was its injustice: dispossessed by the old continent, through no fault of their own, the early colonists were obliged to seek their salvation in a hostile Africa. It was this background of extreme poverty [*la misère*], rather than a desire for profit, which explained the European presence in Algeria" (1994, 150).

18. This description of sacred language appears in a long footnote where Derrida glosses Rosenzweig in order to situate the typical linguistic "expropriation" of the Franco-Maghrebian Jew. Derrida identifies three levels of loss: (1) "authentic" French; (2) Judeo-Spanish; and (3) "the sacred language, which, more often than not, where it was still used in prayer, was neither authentically nor widely taught, nor therefore understood, except in exceptional cases" (1998b, 84).

which historical specificity is ultimately rendered irrelevant through its mystification as poetic language.[19] Here, as elsewhere, Derrida moves away from history through a turn to the aesthetic: "the poetic solemnity of song or prayer." As Habermas puts it in his critique of Derridean archewriting, Derrida, in "the anonymous, history-making productivity of writing," "clings to the dizzying thought of a past that has never been present" (1987, 178–79). In this evocation of "the sacred language," we come face to face, once again, with the unreadable tattoo: the "incarnate archive of a liturgy whose secret no one will betray" (Derrida 1998b, 52). Although in *Monolinguism of the Other,* in particular in this autobiographical anamnesis of his Algerian past, Derrida appears to ground his critique of metaphysics in a concrete and personal history, that ground again slips away through the mystification of the "palpable social pathologies" (Habermas 1987, 181)—such as anti-Semitism, anti-Arab violence, or acts of torture by the French army—that we glimpse but soon forget. Derrida's endless quest for archewriting, appearing in *Monolinguism of the Other* as the Jewish "secret" that both precedes and hyphenates his "Franco-Maghrebian" identity, is the nostalgic search for, as Habermas puts it, "the authority of a no longer holy scripture, of a scripture that is in exile, wandering about, estranged from its own meaning, a scripture that testamentarily documents the absence of the holy" (1987, 181).[20]

In this sense, Derrida's "nostalgeria"—the tattoo liturgy of an "incarnate archive" whose secret can be known only by him—rearticulates the same logic that Habermas has famously critiqued as the mythical structure of Derrida's thought. Through the gaze of "nostalgeria," Algeria, Khatibi, and the Algerian Jews—the concrete social anchors that are country, friend, and community—become nothing more than anonymous place-holders for a sacred presence made palpable by its absolute absence. This is Derrida's true nostalgia: a desire to return to the purity of poetry, to the sacrality of the ineffable, to the irreplaceable mother who cannot be located in space or time.

How does this critique of Derrida's mystical "nostalgeria" elucidate the questions posed throughout this chapter? How does it feed the ongoing public con-

19. Derrida's reliance on aesthetic transcendence here is reminiscent of the early poststructuralism of *Tel Quel.* For a classic example of the poststructuralist myth of art as a vehicle of transcendence, see Kristeva 1974. For an ethical critique of the Kristevan model, see Huffer 1998, 73–95.

20. In *Derrida's Elsewhere,* Derrida glorifies this state of secrecy and alienation through his identification with the figure of the Marrano, a fourteenth century Spanish Jew who practiced his religion in secret after converting to Christianity to escape persecution. "It so happens," Derrida says, "that I find myself . . . in the situation of émigré or immigrant . . . a clandestine Marrano, invisible, without papers" (Fathy 1999).

sumption of that mythical object, the French intellectual? How can we understand this Derridean version of a return to Algeria as an ethical question about memory, history, and the politics of the present? And finally, how does "nostalgeria" become a question about the U.S. academy and, more generally, about globalization in the twenty-first century?

Drawing again on Benjamin Stora's theme of historical repetition, I argue that Derridean "nostalgeria" not only situates itself in a broader French moment of return to the past, but also repeats a relationship to politics that bears a striking resemblance to the discourse of French structuralism in the 1950s and 1960s. In many ways, Derrida still embodies what Barthes in 1963 called "structural man" (see Barthes 1972b). As Kristen Ross points out, in the context of the Algerian War and French decolonization "structural man was a disembodied creature, a set of mental processes" (1995, 160). Like "structural man," the post-structural Derrida "takes the real, decomposes it, then recomposes it in view of creating the general intelligibility underlying the object" (Ross 1995, 161). The structuralist object, in its poststructuralist turn, becomes culture in general, which, like an object, reveals an underlying "general intelligibility." The specificity of violent struggle and decolonization is reconfigured, through Derridean archewriting, as "an essential *coloniality* . . . of culture" founded on a "universal structure," "a type of originary 'alienation' that institutes every language as a language of the other" (Derrida 1998b, 24, 63, emphasis added). And although structuralism "slammed shut the Algeria chapter and relegated it to another temporality" (Ross 1995, 196), Derridean poststructuralism replays that relationship to politics in a different guise, claiming to uncover through the universality of archewriting the sources of that which we call *political:* "Such a reminder," Derrida writes, "permits one at once to analyze the historical phenomena of appropriation and to treat them *politically*" (1998a, 64, emphasis in original).[21] Although structuralism tended to avoid the colonial question altogether, poststructuralist "nostalgeria" redeploys the term *colonialism* in the name of the political, but reconfigures the political as an aesthetic structure. As an unreadable tattoo, as "yesterday's inaudible poem" (1998b, 67, translation modified), as a "*prior-to-the-first* language" (1998b, 61, emphasis in original), "nostalgerian" archewriting is the postmodern trope for a general concept of futurity that is the

21. In *Derrida's Elsewhere,* Derrida makes explicit the link between secrecy and a concept of the political as that which, paradoxically, resists politics. Again, the Marrano "evokes a culture of secrecy, . . .secrecy being that which resists politics, that which resists politicization, citizenship, transparency, phenomenality. Wherever we seek to destroy secrets there is a threat of totalitarianism" (Fathy 1999).

repetition of an Arcadian past—a promise, a "beyond"—that, like structuralism, moves away from geography, contingency, or political specificity: "beyond any cartography, and beyond any knowledge that can be taught" (1998b, 60).

This poststructuralist, postcolonial version of structural man is imperfect, incomplete, and marked with scars: "a trace, a specter, the phantomatic body, the phantom-member—palpable, painful, but hardly legible—of traces, marks, and scars" (1998b, 61). But even as the prosthetic replacement of a "man" that never was, postmodern man still lays claim, as a "universal Marrano,"[22] to the privileges of universalism, undoubtedly one of France's most enduring political and intellectual legacies. In the figure of the postmodern public intellectual, French universalism continues to hold sway by articulating politics as a mere condition of the enduring features of language.[23]

In the U.S. context where Derrida first gave the lecture that became *Monolinguism of the Other,* French poststructuralism's disavowal of its "own constitutive identity as a colonizer" (Ross 1995, 196) serves broader cultural and ideological interests as well. First, in the age of multiculturalism and postcolonial studies, Derrida's public return to his "Judeo-Franco-Maghrebian" origins gives him *both* the legitimacy of a "postcolonial subject" *and* the caché of classic French "purity" for those who still cling, however ashamedly, to the traditional image of France's "civilizing mission." His "nostalgeria" allows him and us to have it both ways: we can embrace the excluded subject who is *not* French *and* at the same time marvel at the mental pirouettes of this postmodern defender and illustrator of a French language spoken by humanism's universal man. Further, there are important reasons why this timely intellectual positioning should occur at this particular historical juncture. At a moment in the U.S. academy when "French theory" has increasingly been displaced by "cultural studies," "nostalgeria" might perhaps make Derrida relevant again as that age-old myth of the French intellectual reborn. As Jean-Philippe Mathy explains, although Derrida's star status has had greater longevity in the United States than in France, the recent "decline of the demand for French culture and society on American campuses" can in large part be attributed to a "growing impatience with the Eurocentric, elitist character of French theory" (2000, 11, 46), epitomized by the figure of Derrida. With "nostalgeria," the elitist Derrida myth can be conveniently rewritten as a subaltern myth about Derrida as a postcolonial subject.[24]

22. A phrase used by Derrida in the film *Derrida's Elsewhere* (Fathy 1999).

23. For a feminist analysis and critique of French universalism, see especially Schor 1995.

24. This image of Derrida as a postcolonial subject is reinforced by Safaa Fathy's 1999 film, where Derrida remarks: "I am a kind of colonial product, or postcolonial, if you prefer. . . . In a way,

Finally, Derrida's mystical "nostalgeria" can be situated within a more general contemporary opening toward Algeria on the part of many French intellectuals and writers, including not only the writings about childhood mentioned at the beginning of the chapter, but also a plethora of historical studies of the Algerian War.[25] Unfortunately, this opening conversation, in its Derridean form, deftly avoids ethical and political questions about both French and U.S. responsibility for the ongoing terror and misery that defines the lives of the vast majority of the Algerian people. Following a decade of insurgent and state-sponsored violence that has claimed more than one hundred thousand Algerian lives, Algeria also faces the threats of starvation and violence that are a direct result of extreme poverty. In that context, part of the more general "return" to Algeria by French intellectuals such as Derrida and Cixous is undoubtedly a disillusionment with what was once seen as the promise of Algeria following independence in 1962. To be fair, Derrida, along with many others, publicly took a stand and denounced the atrocities of Algeria's civil war during the 1990s, especially in his "Parti pris pour l'Algérie" (1995). And although his name is missing from the 1961 "Manifeste des 121" in support of the Algerian struggle for independence, he did add his signature to the 2001 petition "Le 17 octobre 1961: contre l'oubli" (17 October 1961: Against Forgetting), which condemns France's cover-up of its own atrocities during the "first" Algerian War.[26] However, these more overtly political interventions have not been translated from their original French context, nor have they been widely disseminated beyond their local Parisian audience. Rather, an increasingly global intellectual culture has been transfixed by a more personal and more familiar apolitical Derrida whose "nostalgeria" diverts our attention from questions of complicity, violence, the relationship of the West to the Muslim world, and, most ominously, the growing global economic and military domination by the United States. In hearing and retaining only what Derrida calls "the sentimental temptation" to speak his "painful love of Algeria" (1995, 236, translation mine), both Derrida's French and non-French interpreters perpetuate a hegemonic political story about "whose memories count, what kind of attach-

---

everything I do, everything I write, I try to think has a certain synchronous affinity with postcoloniality." Derrida's self-description is visually reinforced in this and other sequences in the film by the juxtaposition of shots of Derrida with shots of anonymous veiled women.

25. For example, in 2001 alone the following books appeared in France: Aussaresses 2001a, 2001b; Barrat and Barrat 2001; Branche 2001; and Hervo 2001a, 2001b. On the contemporary period, see Mary 2001.

26. The details of the 1961 massacre of dozens of Algerians by the Paris police remained hidden from the public for thirty-eight years. See "Déclaration de J. Derrida" (Derrida 2000).

ments and modes of life are valuable, and what kinds of harms are politically relevant" (Smith 2000, 515—16).

This story about a symbolic, economic, and political hegemony should not, however, lead us into an all too predictable ethical and political despair. If nostalgia "represents a set of politically charged claims about community, memory, and harm" (Smith 2000, 508), Derridean "nostalgeria" has much to teach us about the use of public memory in a global, twenty-first-century context. Specifically, through "nostalgeria" we can "track down," as Barthes would put it, "the ideological abuse" (1972a, 11) that lies hidden beneath deconstruction's glittering and seductive surface. For unlike the terms *archewriting* or *trace* or *différance,* the term *nostalgeria* invites us to ask ethical and political questions about the past precisely because it gestures toward the contingency of history. And yet as a cipher for the predictable mystification of language that is the hallmark of Derrida's thought, the term *nostalgeria* also participates in the construction of a postmodern myth about the world as language, thereby occluding ethics and politics in the moment of its evocation. Indeed, as a powerful figure of postmodernism itself, "nostalgeria" fulfills the task that Barthes ascribes to myth: "giving an historical intention a natural justification, and making contingency appear eternal" (1972a, 142). Our enchantment with this postmodern myth keeps us from seeing other realities in which we are nonetheless implicated. Occluded by the trauma of "nostalgeria" lies another kind of violence—less dramatic, perhaps, than the bombs and torture of the "first" and "second" Algerian wars, but just as deadly. This violence links the vast oil and gas reserves of the Sahara desert to the U.S. government's post–11 September courting of Algeria as a strategic partner in the "war on terrorism." In the guise of a commitment to the end of violence, the United States is now arming the Algerian military and taking steps to double the volume of Algero-American trade, increasing the wealth of Halliburton, Exxon-Mobil, ARCO, and Bechtel at the expense of the Algerian people.[27] These "postmodern" economic and military practices carried out in the name of freedom continue the French colonial project in a twenty-first-century American form. In that sense, "nostalgeria" reminds us not only that history repeats itself, but that in the consolidation of public memory through which history itself is constituted, we are ethically called to remember *another* Algerian memory of violence and resistance effaced by Derridean writing.

27. See Flanders 1998; Badis 2001; S. Malley 2001; Mundy 2001; and Bureau of Democracy, Human Rights, and Labor 2002.

16 Confronting the Past

The Memory Work of Second-Generation Algerians in France

RICHARD L. DERDERIAN

THE ALGERIAN WAR raises fundamental questions about the usefulness of working through the past. Are media reports about French crimes associated with the war a healthy sign of a nation grappling with some of the darker events in its history? Do democratic societies have an obligation to shed light on past actions and policies fundamentally at odds with their purported values? By fixating on stories about torture, murder, and rape committed by the French during the Algerian War, do we risk undermining the legitimacy of the nation? Should we heed the call of French historian Suzanne Citron for a memory perestroika in France (1991, 278), or should we remember what happened to the Soviet Union once the guardians of the past put down their arms?

France must resist the "temptations of national masochism," argued former minister and past presidential candidate Jean-Pierre Chevènement in 2000. We have an obligation to remember, explained Chevènement, but "memory must be impartial, showing the light as well as the shadows, revealing the heroes without obsessing about the villains—even though we know they existed." No country is perfect, and although "the republic certainly has room for improvement, its overall record is positive." We shouldn't forget that "France, no less than any other country, can't move forward into the future unless it has a reasonably positive image of itself" (Chevènement 2000).

Turning to France's Algerian community and commenting on the October 2001 incident at France Stadium, *Le Monde* journalist Philippe Bernard warned us that failing to offer a fuller accounting of the past might actually hinder the integration process. On 6 October 2001 at the France Stadium outside Paris, the Franco-Algerian youths who booed the "Marseillaise" and threw projectiles on to the field, forcing officials to call off the first ever soccer match between France and Algeria, were, in Bernard's opinion, acting out of a sense of alienation. In stark contrast with the earlier celebration of France's multicultural success story following the 1998 World Cup victory, the cancelation of the France-Algeria match demonstrates that many Franco-Algerian youth still have trouble identifying with the nation. The inclusion of these youths, Bernard argued, can only succeed if France's immigration history and the history of the Algerian War are integrated into its national history. "For *'beurs'* to become French requires shedding light on the colonial past and the Algerian War in particular, including the murkiest and most unsettling episodes" (2001).

Bernard was quick to add that history must also become more complex and plural. "More than just a simple 'memory' that only reinforces a victims-villains relationship, we need to run the risk of a history with many contradictions and perspectives." For Bernard, developing multiple viewpoints and challenging simplified accounts, or making history more complex, is the only way "to understand today why you can boo the Marseillaise and still, deep down, be French" (2001).[1]

By looking at the memory-charged cultural productions of second-generation Algerians in France, this chapter concurs with Bernard that working through the past is essential to the success of the integration process. The first part of the chapter underlines how the stories of the Algerian past, found in diverse initiatives ranging from theater and music to novels and television documentaries, are intended to restore a sense of dignity to Algerians in France. Telling stories about past injustices, sacrifices, and hardships conveys the basic humanity of an Algerian community too often cast in terms of a temporary labor force, an integration problem, or simply something to be ignored altogether. Confronting the past is a way of vanquishing shared sentiments of shame, humiliation, and anger, as well as of refusing to perpetuate the silence of their fathers and mothers. Rather than exploding in self-destructive forms of behavior, the memory work of second-generation Algerians can be understood as a constructive search for resolution of a past that continues to exert a powerful hold on the present.

The second part of the chapter questions the often-heard dichotomy of simplified memories and complex histories. It challenges the assertion made by historian Charles Maier (1993) that history is about understanding, whereas memory is too often inspired by the desire to relive past experiences of victimization. According to Maier, there is a "surfeit of memory" today that threatens the

1. *Beur* is the slang term used to designate second-generation North Africans. Once a self-designation invented by North African youth, it is now largely rejected for casting them in the kinds of simplified frameworks of understanding that Bernard seemed to be repudiating.

nation-state. Indicative of and contributing to a lack of faith in the future-oriented nature of nation-states, too many groups are bogged down in the politics of demanding respect and recognition by evoking past crimes and injustices. To the contrary, I suggest that the memory work of Algerians often sheds light on neglected events, offers new critical perspectives, and opens up the past to a greater degree of public scrutiny and debate.

Part I

Viewing Yamina Benguigui's television documentary *Mémoires d'immigrés* (1997b) might raise questions about the usefulness of dredging up the Algerian past. Based on several hundred interviews with first- and second-generation North Africans, Benguigui's two-and-a-half-hour production evokes many of the painful memories of immigrant experiences. Now retired workers struggle to rein in their emotions while recounting the memories of rejection, alienation, and solitude that followed their arrival in France. Immigrant wives recount the shock of arriving in France's *bidonvilles,* or shantytowns, and the strains endured by North African families living in a foreign culture. Their children relate their own bitter memories of being locked away for years in makeshift communities and supposedly temporary, prefabricated "transit cities" on the forgotten margins of France's urban centers.

Yet, for Benguigui, dredging up the past, especially one that is little known outside the North African community and not discussed enough inside it, has an inestimable therapeutic value. North Africans cannot have a future in France unless they become aware of their past, Benguigui explained in a recent interview I had with her (Benguigui 2001b). She acknowledged that these memories are difficult for her parents' generation. Many were silent about the past because of the feeling of shame for having left their country to work in France. For Benguigui, talking about their lives and transmitting these memories would vanquish the sentiment of shame. "I wanted to restore a sense of dignity to them," she exclaimed in another interview. "We are products of this history. There are more than three million North Africans in France. We are more than just numbers and statistics" (Benguigui 1997a).

Restoring a sense of dignity means informing viewers about the basic humanity of North African workers, women, and children. Emotionally charged personal accounts of the wrenching experience of leaving behind friends, family, and a familiar way of life are deliberately interspersed with expert commentaries by former French ambassadors, ministers, labor recruiters, and housing officials coolly elaborating on the technical challenges of successfully managing the immigrant community. In stark contrast with the Algerians' difficult memories of adjusting to life in a foreign country, French officials reflect on the expertise required to select workers with the appropriate psychological and physical qualifications, the need to find effective means of controlling North Africans after their arrival, and the task of educating families about modern households and French approaches to parenting. Benguigui employs this juxtaposition of the vivid human experiences of the North African community with the colorless managerial techniques of French administrators and officials throughout the documentary to remind viewers that North Africans are more than numbers and statistics.

Telling the stories of a lived past is a form of catharsis for the North African community that began with the first cultural productions by immigrant children in the mid-1970s. Challenging the perception of the North African community as being composed primarily of single male workers was the primary objective of the theater company Kahina (1976–82). Troupe founder Saliha Amara (1994) explained how she hoped to draw attention to the fact that the North African population also consisted of mothers, sons, and daughters. Kahina's first play, "Pour que les larmes de nos mères deviennent une légende" (1976, unpublished), recounts the story of Algerian women during and after the war for independence. Scenes of Algerian women captured and tortured by French authorities during the war are juxtaposed with revelations about the imposition of a strict family code after the war. Kahina's story of the sacrifices and treatment of Algerian women conveys both the Algerian government's failure to share the fruits of victory with half the population and daughters' refusal to perpetuate their mothers' status.

For singer turned novelist Mounsi, music and now novels provide a constructive outlet for understanding and expressing a sense of outrage about past and present injustices. In songs such as "Bâtard" from his album *Seconde génération* (1984), Mounsi reminds listeners that North African youths are products of an older history inextricably intertwined with that of France.

Paris, your racists have already forgotten
To refresh their memories,
Tell me, should we make them drink
The blood of the foreigners who died for France.

A succession of references to soldiers from the empire who died fighting for France, the 1958 coup in Algiers, the Nanterre shantytown, and the October 1961 massacre of Algerian protestors by French police in Paris compound the frustration caused by the absence of economic opportunities in the present and culminate in a call to fight back: "DELINQUENCY . . . REVOLT. . . . REVOLT . . . DELINQUENCY" (Mounsi 1984). DELINQUENCY AMONG NORTH AFRICAN YOUTH IN

THE PRESENT, MOUNSI EXPLAINED IN AN INTERVIEW I HAD WITH HIM, CANNOT BE UNDERSTOOD IN ISOLATION FROM THE COLONIAL AND IMMIGRANT PAST (Mounsi 1994).

In both Medhi Charef's *Le harki de Meriem* (1989) and Ahmed Kalaouaz's *Point kilometrique 190* (1986), racial crimes in the French present are clearly linked to an Algerian War that never seems to have ended. The main character in *Le harki de Meriem,* Azzedine, finds himself imprisoned for life in his status as a *harki*—an Algerian who fought in the French army during the Algerian War. Ostracized by his friends, relatives, and country as a traitor, he is doubly punished when his son Sélim suffers a violent death at the hands of a gang of French skinheads. For the remainder of the story, Azzedine struggles unsuccessfully to gain permission from unsympathetic Algerian authorities to bury his son in his native land.

In Ahmed Kalaouaz's *Point kilometrique 190,* it is the character H who falls victim to past hatreds. The story draws from the author's research into the real-life murder of Habib Grimzi, thrown to his death from the window of a moving train by French Foreign Legion recruits in 1983. Bloody scenes of French soldiers massacring villagers from Grimzi's birthplace during the Algerian War blur together with images of H's brutal death in the present. As in many other memory-charged narratives by second-generation North Africans, this intentional juxtaposition and confusion between the past and the present lead the reader to conclude that the Algerian War is a drama that still has no end in sight.

If memory never fades, Franco-Algerian cultural productions suggest that it does not because it is forever inscribed on the bodies of the people of North African descent. Certain physical features such as dark skin and curly black hair act as memory triggers for a French population still traumatized by the past. In *Le harki de Meriem,* it is the photo on Sélim's French passport that causes his attackers to fly into a fit of deadly rage. "See your face . . . you can't be French with a mug like that," exclaims one of the assailants just before plunging a knife into Sélim's stomach (Charef 1989, 33–34). In Nacer Kettane's *Le sourire de Brahim* (1985), the typical perpetrators of racial violence are described as former policemen or retired soldiers who, with the help of a little "trigger nostalgia," single out "tanned target[s] with curly black hair." "Petty bourgeois, crazy about sawed-off shotguns, nostalgic for the *ratonnades,* they take themselves for heroes" (132).[2]

Franco-Algerian protagonists sometimes strategically manipulate the physical characteristics that recall old hatreds, fears, and prejudices. In Mehdi Charef's first novel, *Le thé au harem d'Archi Ahmed* (1983), the main character, Madjid,

2. The *Petit Robert* defines *ratonnades* as punitive expeditions carried out by Europeans against North Africans.

perfects a pickpocketing strategy on the Paris metro by using French presumptions about his own guilt to deflect attention from Patrick, his French friend and accomplice. In Malik Chibane's film *Hexagone* (1994), the character Staff is able to overcome the romantic disinclinations of an attractive French woman by convincing her that he is really of Sicilian descent.

In other cases, North African youth try to erase what they themselves perceive as their debilitating physical markers. The character Farida in Ferrudja Kessas's *Beur's Story* (1989), cut off from the French friends and lifestyles she finds powerfully appealing, identifies her body as the source of her suffering. "She was filled with self-hate as she looked with horror in the mirror, slapping herself to try to destroy this face, just dark enough to remind her that her name was Farida and not Francine" (14). On a somewhat lighter note, the song "La Moda" (1984) by the 1980s group Carte de séjour (Green Card), features a North African who despite all his attention to fashion is unable to gain admission to French nightclubs. In a moment reminiscent of the Franco Brusati film *Bread and Chocolate,* he finally realizes that he has overlooked one thing: "next time, I can't forget to change my hair color."

Perhaps the most powerful memory associated with North African bodies is that of the massacre of 17 October 1961. Images of bodies floating under the bridges of the Seine are "enough to drive a kid mad," sings Mounsi in "Bâtard" (1984). Scenes of panic-stricken demonstrators desperately seeking shelter under cars and in apartment entranceways in a hopeless effort to flee the blows of police night sticks are painfully drawn out in Bourlem Guerdjou's film *Vivre au paradis* (1998). The nightmare of people jettisoned off the bridges of the Seine, black-and-white visions of lifeless bodies caught in the icy water below, and the horrified expression of French onlookers are the rush of images that mark the opening pages of Mehdi Lallaoui's most recent novel *Une nuit d'octobre* (2001b).

Yet Lallaoui stressed in a recent interview I had with him that evoking crimes in the French urban past and present is not inspired by a rejection of French society. No topic should be taboo, argued Lallaoui, whose long list of novels, illustrated histories, exhibitions, and documentary films address many of the darker episodes of France's Algerian past. Only by shedding light on past events is it possible to build a meaningful present and future. Returning to a theme raised earlier, Lallaoui stressed that providing a fuller accounting of the past offers a vital sense of justice and dignity to the Algerian community—the absence of which now complicates the integration process. "How can we tell young people today to pay their taxes and to stay out of trouble if there is no justice regarding the memories of the past?" For Lallaoui, a more honest and open treatment of the past does not lead to a rejection of the nation, but rather to a greater sense of self-respect that is invaluable to the successful integration of France's Algerian community (Lallaoui 2001a).

Part II

In my interview with him, Lallaoui was quick to challenge the notion that ethnic minorities outside the historical profession are unable to contribute to a fuller understanding of the past. He readily admitted that the past is personal and political. His own father participated in the demonstrations on 17 October 1961, an event that Lallaoui has chronicled on film and in fiction. However, he claimed that what motivates his work is not the politics of identity, but rather a search for a more complex treatment of the past. He pointed out that many of the events he has explored had previously been neglected. He surmised that his documentary on the repression of the Sétif uprising in 1945 was perhaps the first film on the subject. When he founded his association Au nom de la mémoire around 1990 to mark the thirtieth anniversary of 17 October 1961, he recalled that most people still had a hard time believing that Algerian demonstrators were or could ever have been massacred by French police in the heart of Paris (Lallaoui 2001a).

Lallaoui insisted that what he offers is not just additional work on neglected topics, but a vital corrective to traditional interpretations of past events. In the opening section of *Kabyles du Pacifique* (1994), he remarks, "the history of the insurrection of 1871 in Algeria has, until recently, been left to the sole appreciation of the victors of this revolt." He goes on to explain that what he provides is not a narrative more sympathetic to the losers, but a more critical reading of the sources left behind by the winners. In the case of the Kabyle insurrection, Lallaoui points out that historians have up to now relied far too much on sources like that of French commander Louis Rinn who were complicit in the events they recorded and distorted. By bringing a more critical reading to traditional sources and trying to uncover new ones through exhaustive archival research, Lallaoui argues that he has been able to root out many longstanding errors in the historical scholarship (1994, 15).

Characteristic of the memory work of other second-generation Algerians, Lallaoui takes great pride in bringing the past to the public. Over the past decade, he has spent countless hours interacting with diverse audiences and public institutions. For his film *Le silence du fleuve* (Lalloui and Denis 1991), on the events of 17 October 1961, he estimates having visited at least a hundred communities around France. He planned to visit several dozens towns for his illustrated volume on France's immigration history, *Un siècle d'immigration* (Lallaoui and Assouline 1996a, 1996b), and was working closely with the national education system on a CD-Rom version of the project (Lallaoui 2001a).

Similarly, theater companies such as Kahina, Ibn Khaldoun, and Chakchouka (1981) performed in scores of festivals, community centers, and open-air venues in the 1970s and 1980s. Performances were typically followed by debates that allowed audiences to challenge and enrich each performance with their own perspectives and experiences. Yamina Benguigui thought she set the record for public debates following the release of her documentary *Mémoires d'immigrés.* She estimates having participated in nearly four hundred debates over a period of two years (Benguigui 2001b).

In their efforts to make the past more public, Franco-Algerian cultural actors have demonstrated a willingness to confront the complexity of the past. As Philippe Bernard urged, this confrontation has required a readiness to move beyond simplistic depictions of the Algerian community as hapless victims of French oppression. Kahina's play "Pour que les larmes de nos mères deviennent une legende" (1976) underlines both the hypocrisy of Algerian Front de libération nationale (FLN) leaders who quickly forgot the sacrifices made by Algerian women during the war for independence and immigrant daughters' refusal to perpetuate the unequal status of their mothers in France. In Bourlem Guerdjou's *Vivre au paradis* (1998), it is quite clear that the main character Lakhdar has little sympathy and much resentment for the FLN money collectors who complicate his efforts to find a way out of the Nanterre shantytown for himself and his family. It is only the burden of guilt imposed by his wife and friends that finally convinces him to offer his assistance to the FLN and to participate in the fateful demonstration of 17 October 1961.

Being truthful, Lallaoui pointed out in an interview, means revealing facts that might be embarrassing to the Algerian community. He explained, for example, that many Algerian demonstrators did not willingly turn out on a cold and rainy Tuesday evening in October 1961, but were coerced to do so (Lallaoui 2001a). Although arguing that no topic should be taboo, Lallaoui also recognized that certain topics have yet to receive much attention. He noted that he is unaware of a single film on the Algerian nationalist leader Messali Hadj, one of the fathers of the Algerian independence movement who began his career within the ranks of France's North African immigrant community.

Conclusion

French historian Pierre Nora, in his introduction to *Realms of Memory* (1996c, the abridged English translation of *Les lieux de mémoire* [1992]), singles out ethnic minorities as the group chiefly responsible for the surge of memory work in France since the 1980s. If history has gone public in the form of memory, it is above all inspired by what Nora describes as the search for roots among ethnic minorities. Memory work has become obsessive today, Nora asserts; "practically every organized social group, and not just the intellectuals or educated, has followed the lead of ethnic minorities in seeking their roots and identities" (1996a, 10). What is at risk with the rise of memory work is the basic cohesion and solidarity of the nation no longer bound by a shared pride in a common past. Group histories and the archival impulse to store away more than it is possible to remember represent the centrifugal forces that threaten to tear apart French society.

In a recent interview I had with him, Nora reiterated his refusal to see private forms of memory work as anything other that what he described as a Balkanizing danger:

> The memory work and memory movements today are very dangerous instruments. Private memory for a long time functioned within a liberationist dynamic. This is now over for most, and it has since become a dynamic of self-enclosure, a lack of understanding of the other, alienation from one's own history, a means of legitimizing oneself, the loss of common ground, and very often a powerfully aggressive ethnic nationalism that sometimes even results in murder. All you need to do is to look at the role of memory in the Balkan wars. I'm very interested in memory from a historical point of view, but I'm wary of the sentimental power of particularist memories. I understand it, I see it, but I'm absolutely convinced of its dangers, its pettiness, and its false legitimacy. (Nora 2000)

The possibility, as cultural actors such as Lallaoui see it, that private citizens from the Algerian community can play a vital role in providing a fuller and more complex reading of the past seems unlikely to Nora. The main objective of *Les lieux de mémoire* was to rally the support of professional French historians to the rescue of the nation's now largely abandoned sites of collective memory. By encouraging historians to play a more assertive role in addressing the national past, Nora hoped to reduce the dangers of memory going public.

Yet *Les lieux de mémoire* is a glaring example of the need to open up research on the French past to those outside of academia. Although Nora's voluminous project took nearly a decade to complete, involved the collaboration of scores of France's most eminent scholars, and resulted in seven volumes and several thousands of pages, the story of the nation's imperial past is almost entirely absent in those volumes. Despite the fact that nearly an entire generation of French men did their military service in an Algerian War that precipitated the collapse of the Fourth Republic, not a single chapter is devoted to the war. For critics such as

Steven Englund (1992), *Les lieux de mémoire* is sadly undercut by an overriding nostalgia for a lost golden age of national pride—a time when people supposedly felt better about the nation. In my interview with Nora, he countered these charges by explaining that the absence of the Algerian War in the work was simply the result of time constraints and the lack of public interest in the topic at the time of the writing. He remarked that he began his career writing about the Algerian War and would certainly have included the topic if it had generated as much interest as it does today (Nora 2000).

But Lallaoui argued in 2001 that it is precisely because actors such as himself are personally implicated in the Algerian past that they are able to offer a more sustained treatment in their work. "It took forty years for articles to start appearing on the war," he remarked, "and it was only officially recognized as a war two years ago." Too often, he regretted, public interest in the past hinges on fleeting moments of media attention. He commented that his first novel, *Les beurs de la Seine,* on the life of ethnic minorities in the working-class suburbs, was inspired by the same sentiment that journalists only paid attention when there was some kind of drama (Lallaoui 2001a).

Rather than contributing to the breakup of France, the kind of memory perestroika called for by Citron is central to the process of integrating new members of French society. Time and again, second-generation North Africans engaged in diverse forms of memory work have stressed that recounting the complexity of their own experiences and that of their community afforded them an indispensable sense of dignity and justice. Telling their story was a therapeutic act that helped alleviate not only their own pain and suffering rooted in past experiences, but also the sense of humiliation and injustice suffered by their parents.

No doubt narratives of the past produced by the children of North African workers have their own lacunae—the neglect of Messali Hadj and the failure to address the violent conflict between rival Algerian nationalist organizations in France during the Algerian War are just a couple. But they also appear to respond to what Benjamin Stora describes as the most difficult legacy of the Algerian War: the challenge of moving beyond long-established, fixed group narratives of the past, or what he labels as cloistered memories. From victimized *pied-noir* narratives to stories of abandonment and betrayal by former officers, the Algerian past, according to Stora, has not so much been forgotten as locked into unchanging, almost mythical constructions (1997, 190–93). By assuming a much more public and confrontational approach to events such as the Algerian War, second-generation North Africans may help to achieve a broader consensus of memory rather than a further fragmentation of the past.

17 The Return of the Repressed

War, Trauma, Memory in Algeria and Beyond

DAVID PROCHASKA

Guerre d'Algérie

1970s

BACK FROM SOUTH ASIA, where I had gone to avoid being sent to Southeast Asia, I saw *La battaglia de Algeria* (The Battle of Algiers) directed by Gillo Pontecorvo (1966).[1] In San Francisco, in the Fillmore district, a bright sunny Saturday afternoon, on a double bill with Bunuel's *Belle du jour* (1967). From Catherine Deneuve to Ali la Pointe. After four hours, senses pummeled in the movie theater, I staggered out onto the street, shop fronts locked tight behind accordion-style metal gates drawn shut, liquor bottle broken glass littering the sidewalk. *Streetfighting Man. Goat's Head Soup. Got to Revolution.*

There and then, I knew that I had to write a Ph.D. dissertation on Algeria and that it could also be politically progressive, even radical. On Algeria, colonial Algeria, the story of colonialism in Algeria. And the more I read, the more I learned about what could be termed an "Algerian syndrome," analogous to a "Vichy syndrome," both defining moments of twentieth-century French history, both historical blind spots, freighted combinations of willed forgetfulness, collective denial, misremembering, and, first for Vichy and now increasingly for Algeria, the return of what has been repressed, occluded, ignored, put away. Imbued with Thompsonian social history from the bottom up, I began by asking, "Who/Whom?" I rapidly realized a disconnection between the paucity of historiography on the European settlers, the *pieds-noirs,* and the important historical role they had played. Where were the settlers in the literature? Answer: too big to be seen (Prochaska [1990] 2004). The title of Pierre Nora's 1961 book *Les français d'Algérie* was right down the alley; at first I feared he had beaten me to

1. This essay is a version of Prochaska 2003.

it.[2] Confirmation of the rightness of my thesis choice came on visiting Algeria in 1975. After viewing Pontecorvo's film, made in consultation with Algiers Front de libération nationale (FLN) leader Yacef Sâdi and numerous Algerian participants, as well as in solidarity with the Algerians, I *had* to stay in the lower Casbah just off the Place des Martyrs, the former Place du Gouvernement. A hole in the wall, the cheaper the better, Turkish-style toilet, dank, gray. From the Casbah, I went to the still-imposing French Gouvernement-Général building just above the spot where the 13 May 1958 army-settler demonstrations led to the fall of the French Fourth Republic, got my letter from the Conseil de la révolution authorizing unlimited access to the Algerian archives without a hitch, and then celebrated by eating lunch in a popular café run by *pieds-noirs* and frequented by Algerians.

1980s

Teaching at a midwestern university, I regularly screen *The Battle of Algiers;* I still say to my students, "This movie is gonna knock your socks off" (see analysis of the film in Mellen 1975; Ory 1990; Dine 1994, 1997). The opening sequence still rivets me—the army truck tailgates go down, and the soldiers jump out, all while the rhythmic, pounding soundtrack accelerates the tension (no light-pop Nina Rota soundtrack, this). Then blowing up Ali la Pointe and the other three.

> Captain (off): Make up your mind, Ali? Do you want us to wall you in, or do you prefer that we blow you to pieces? . . . Alright. So much the worse for you.
>
> *Ali's expression is still firm; his stare is dark and sullen.* (Solinas 1973, 9, emphasis original)

Afterward, the soundtrack slows, thickens, descends in tone, the film grinds to a halt as if a hole burned in the film stock; then we flash back to 1 November 1954, the outbreak of the revolution. The torture sequence still makes me want to look away. Even with the slow stately soundtrack, plaintive classical chords, the sequence seems interminable.

> *An Algerian is lying down on the table, his arms and ankles bound with belts . . .*
>
> Electrical wires wrenched from their outlets, a generator with crank, . . .the tops of the wires held between two prongs, the pliers applied to a naked body, the most sensitive parts. . . . Faucets, tubing, buckets, funnels, a mouth forced open, held open with a wooden wedge, tubing in the mouth, rags scattered around, water, a belly that is swelling. (Solinas 1973, 127, emphasis original)

2. Not based on original research and devoid of scholarly apparatus, Nora's remarkably insightful book resulted from his 1958–60 stint teaching at an Algerian lycée.

In an earlier scene, we have already seen the Casbah blocked off, Algerians checked for papers, one by one, and the tension mounts: Will the women carrying bombs be allowed through or caught? And the final scene—the Algerians cascading out of the Casbah, wave upon ju-juing wave, during the December 1960 demonstrations, irrepressible—still gives me chills as we recognize among the crowd those now dead.

When I teach the movie, it is in the course "From *The Battle of Algiers* to the Algerian Revolution." If the Algerians lost the battle of Algiers, I ask, then how did they win the Algerian Revolution according to the film? I point out similarities with Sergei Eisenstein's *Battleship Potemkin* (1925), how the part stands for the whole, the episode for the revolution. How the plot's structure revolves around escalating violence on both sides. How the point of view is certainly pro-Algerian, but how the film also shows Algerian terrorism, primarily the women bomb-carriers, and how some French figures, notably Colonel Mathieu, are rounded individuals, not one-dimensional cardboard characters. How Mathieu echoes the Cold War line that wants to distinguish a militant minority from a nationalist mass: "There are 80,000 Arabs in the Casbah. Are they all against us? We know they are not. In reality, it is only a small minority that dominates with terror and violence. This minority is our adversary and we must isolate and destroy it" (Solinas 1973, 85). How Mathieu challenges the assembled journalists on torture: "Should France remain in Algeria? If you answer 'yes,' then you must accept all the necessary consequences," including torture (Solinas 1973, 125).[3] How historically the battle of Algiers constituted an urban interlude in an otherwise primarily peasant-based revolutionary movement.

All this fits George W. Bush's view of terrorism to a T, which entails giving Ariel Sharon a free hand against the Palestinians. While the Israelis launched preemptive, offensive attacks in the name of "self-defense" on the Jenin refugee camp in June 2003 and Rafah in May 2004, the Americans invaded Iraq in March 2003 in a preemptive attack to prevent the use of weapons of mass destruction that we now know never existed. Israel regularly carries out "targeted assassinations," the euphemism for extrajudicial killings, which are in fact instances of state-conducted terrorism; in March 2004, the Israelis killed Hamas spiritual leader Sheik Ahmed Yassin, a paraplegic. During the 1982 Israeli invasion of Lebanon, Sharon was among those responsible for massacres in the Sabra and Chatilla refugee camps and was later judged a war criminal by some. Yesterday Lebanon, today the West Bank and Gaza Strip.

3. For two views, see H. Roberts 1997 and Shohat and Stam 1994, 251–55.

Sharon once told an interviewer that "he keeps Alistair Horne's book on Algeria, *A Savage War of Peace* (1977), on his night table" (Elon 2002). How can Sharon study French counterinsurgency techniques in Algeria, including torture, but miss the main point that the French lost? Sober and balanced, Horne clearly shows the folly of continuing to seek a military solution in a settler colonial situation against a nationalist movement when only a political solution is viable. Yet both Sharon and Bush practice the same approach to terrorism—namely, repression and more repression, apparently however much it takes. Both have made terrorism worse, making their nations more insecure and dangerous. Both pretend that suicide bombers and other militants can be distinguished and dealt with separately from the general Palestinian (and Iraqi) population—hence, in the Israeli case the misguided aim to "destroy the infrastructure of terrorism."[4] Thus continues the de facto Israeli colonial occupation of Palestine.

In my course, I introduce in addition Frantz Fanon and *The Wretched of the Earth* ([1961] 1968) and show how director Pontecorvo, working with screenwriter Pier-Nico Solinas and Algerian coproducer Yacef Saâdi, liberally drew on Fanon in his film. Fanon's Manichaean, all-or-nothing view of colonialism applies more accurately to settler colonies, where the stakes are higher, than to other colonial situations of direct and indirect rule. Pontecorvo simplifies Fanon's notion of violence by presenting an all-too-easy progression from Ali's petty street violence (for Fanon a direct consequence of the colonial situation) to revolutionary violence. Fanon's position on violence, usually considered a straightforward avowal of revolutionary violence as cleansing, purifying, and necessary, actually becomes much more ambivalent and ambiguous when the concluding case studies of *Wretched* are taken into account. Here Fanon clearly demonstrates the negative, deleterious effects of violence equally on torturer and tortured: "Both suffer lasting psychological damage. . . . Even in a just cause, we learn, violence is not liberating" (quoted in Burke 1976, 132). I point out that where Pontecorvo simplified Fanon, the FLN and Algeria largely forgot the Martinican writer after 1962. Yet Fanon was most prescient, first, in identifying the peasantry as the primary revolutionary class in struggles of decolonization, a position only very few commentators shared in 1961, and, second, in his especially harsh criticisms of the national bourgeoisie, of nationalist elites such as the FLN after independence (Burke 1976, 132–34).

The Battle of Algiers simplifies much to say much—and still packs a wallop;

4. In the Iraqi case, an estimated one hundred thousand Iraqis died as a result of violence in eighteen months after the March 2003 American invasion (Guterman 2005), along with many more to the present.

no wonder it was long banned in France. It remains an astonishing piece of movie making. Except that when I teach it now, instead of the "Algerian Revolution," I term it the "French-Algerian War," or *guerre d'Algérie* because things were not so revolutionarily straightforward (we knew that). Yes, *The Battle of Algiers* is a representation of Algeria and what went on there, but it is also a representation of its time, the 1960s, the time it was made, our time, my time. If we can historicize Marxism after 1989–91 in a way not possible before, then so, too, *The Battle of Algiers*. And in France, the key historical turning point is the so-called torture controversy that raged there during 1998–2002, especially in 2000–2001. To gauge how much the situation has changed, consider that in 1991 Benjamin Stora, the leading historian of contemporary Algeria, published *La gangrène et l'oubli* ([1991] 1998), in which he characterized the French attitude toward the French-Algerian War as *l'oubli,* forgetting, and that of the Algerians as *la gangrène,* the festering sore.[5] Today that is no longer the case. What the French still refer to as the *guerre d'Algérie* and especially torture have emerged front and center on the stage of political discussion.

The key events in the torture controversy can be briefly summarized. The 1997–98 trial of Maurice Papon found him guilty of complicity in the arrest and deportation of French Jews during the Second World War. Papon had the ignominy of having participated in both the Vichy regime and the French-Algerian War, in the latter as Paris prefect of police during the arrest and maltreatment of eleven thousand Algerians, including several dozen killed, in October 1961. His trial and conviction served thus as a hinge, which, on the one hand, put to rest the Vichy syndrome in postwar France and, on the other hand, simultaneously focused renewed attention on the Algerian syndrome. At the end of 1999, the French passed a law that for the first time acknowledged a war had been fought in Algeria, the *guerre d'Algérie,* rather than merely a series of events or military operations. In mid-2000, former FLN militant Louisette Ighilahriz gave an account of her torture in *Le Monde* (Beaugé 2000a). Two days later, on 22 June, the paper published interviews with generals Jacques Massu and Marcel Bigeard (Beaugé 2000b), the models (especially Bigeard) for Colonel Mathieu in *The Battle of Algiers*. Massu regretted using torture. "I am sorry, one could have done things differently" (quoted in Cohen 2001, 86).[6] In November 2000, General Paul Aussaresses also admitted to torture, but expressed no remorse; in January 2002 he was convicted for not repudiating war crimes. Meanwhile, in October

5. Stora has played an active role throughout this discussion. In addition to Stora 1991, see Stora 1997 and 1999.

6. See also Cohen 2002 and especially MacMaster 2002.

2000, a manifesto by twelve leading antitorture activists during the French-Algerian War, including Henri Alleg (see his preface to this book), Madeleine Rebérioux, Germaine Tillion, and Pierre Vidal-Naquet, called on France to acknowledge and condemn torture during the *guerre d'Algérie,* an appeal that served to open up the entire controversy. Of 1,700,000 French who fought in Algeria, an estimated 350,000 suffered and still suffer psychological trauma; many now spoke out (Beaugé 2000a). Finally, in December 2000 Raphaëlle Branche (2000, 2001) defended her doctoral thesis on torture during the French-Algerian War, a study based on French army archives.[7] A media event in its own right, this dissertation defense also drew attention to increasing access to the French historical archives.

The torture controversy in contemporary France at once vindicates and historicizes *The Battle of Algiers.* The latter because viewers can now watch the film from the 1960s French-Algerian War perspective, but also from the 1990s perspective of recent torture revelations. The former because it lets us consider Pontecorvo's work as one more early statement, along with others during the war itself, such as Henri Alleg's *La question* (1958), which presented and documented torture in a way now validated and massively reinforced by archivally based historical research.[8] On the one hand, we already knew much early on; on the other hand, we now know about torture in much greater detail, not only as a series of individual acts, but as a system sanctioned at the highest levels of the French government. But what about Algeria? Where is Algeria in all this discussion?

Quasi-Civil War in Algeria

1990s

One of the marvelous things about *The Battle of Algiers* is that it presents the Algerian—an Algerian—perspective on the war. Yet the Algerian attitude toward the war as *la gangrène* was already being overtaken by events in Algeria at the time Stora published his book—namely, the quasi-civil war that has raged there since. One way of comprehending opposition, first, to the FLN and, second, to an entrenched political-military elite is through Fanon's writings. Cases abound in which nationalist and anticolonial struggles unite large numbers of people in the run-up to independence, only to fall into relative disarray and disunity in the postindependence, postcolonial period. But who has been more prescient than

7. The outpouring of books and articles on the torture controversy in particular, but also on colonial Algeria more generally, has reached flood stage. *Le Monde* alone published six articles reviewing more than nine new books on 15 March 2002.

8. For other early statements, see Vergès and Arnaud 1957 and Vidal-Naquet 1989.

FLN-identified Fanon in warning about the potential dangers of the nationalist bourgeoisie, in clearly distinguishing the nationalist struggle from the necessity for ongoing, postindependence social revolution?

> It is absolutely necessary to oppose vigorously and definitively the birth of a national bourgeoisie and a privileged caste. . . . The bourgeoisie chooses the solution that seems to it the easiest, that of the single party. . . . The single party is the modern form of the dictatorship of the bourgeoisie, unmasked, unpainted, unscrupulous, and cynical. . . . The bourgeois leaders . . . imprison national consciousness in sterile formalism. . . . The national government, if it wants to be national, ought to govern by the people and for the people, for the outcasts and by the outcasts. ([1961] 1968, 200, 164–65, 204–5; see also Burke 1976, 133–34)

Political opposition in Algeria generally consists of different groups using different means to dislodge, or at a minimum to loosen the grip of, at first a single party, the *parti unique*—that is, the FLN—and, more recently, a dominant political-military elite, *le pouvoir,* "the power." Regarding torture specifically, the key question can be stated crudely as follows: Does the quasi-civil war, or what some in France call the "second Algerian war," in which Algerians employ torture against Algerians, invalidate the representation in *The Battle of Algiers* of the *guerre d'Algérie,* or what some term the "first Algerian war," in which the French employed torture against the Algerians?[9] Here I approach these issues by discussing a series of representations. To *The Battle of Algiers,* I initially counterpose Merzak Allouache's film *Bab el-Oued el-Houma* (1994, Bab el-Oued City), the latter constituting in many ways the antithesis of the former.

At first, *Bab el-Oued City* presents itself as a disquisition on daily life, *la vie quotidienne,* a "this is the way it is" essay on making one's way in contemporary Algeria that makes for a simultaneously kaleidoscopic and claustrophobic view of the working-class Bab el-Oued neighborhood of Algiers.[10] As befitting a series of character sketches, people not politics (let alone revolutionary politics) occupy center stage. Boualem, the main figure, works in a bakery. Feeling hedged in, tossing and turning on his bed mattress, vaguely oppressed by the Islamic exhortations broadcast from a loudspeaker on the rooftop, he rips out the speaker one day and throws it into the sea. Yamina, who lives in the same building, sees what Boualem did. Theirs is a relationship manqué; mutually attracted to each other,

9. On the use of these two terms in France, see Schalk 1999, 150 n. 7.

10. Bab el-Oued was the name of the city gate leading northwest out of Ottoman or Turkish Algiers (1529–1830) to what became during the colonial period the primarily working-class European Bab el-Oued quarter. See also Allouache's fictional version of the film (Allouache 1998).

they resort to subterfuge in order to meet. Yamina's letters to Boualem frame the film at beginning and end. She, too, feels frustrated and hemmed in. She spends her days mostly inside and on the rooftops, mostly with other women, although some of them smoke and many eschew veils. She wants to go out and get a job, but her older brother Saïd would never allow it. Saïd is the leader of the gang of neighborhood Islamists, Muslim fundamentalists; he doggedly pursues the speaker thief. Treating Yamina roughly, turning up the heat on Boualem, taking upon himself the religious cleansing of the quarter, Saïd is a militant and extremist in the making.

Several characters are portrayed against type, confounding our expectations, and making the film richer, more complex. Messaoud, who has washed up on the shores of Algiers from France without his French passport and joins Saïd's gang, is French not Algerian, despite his name, and speaks only French not Arabic. The imam of the local mosque is the antithesis of the stereotypical fiery, radical, Muslim preacher. Informed of the speaker theft, he points out that the mosque has fourteen others that are functioning just fine. His attempts to mediate the escalating vendetta against Boualem by Saïd are a failure, and he broadcasts his resignation with a warning on Aïd, the major Muslim holiday associated with remembrance and forgiveness. "Some people don't want peace. . . . Violence breeds violence. . . . There'll be no more peace in Bab el-Oued. . . . Because of petty matters, we are killing one another. . . . I tell you now it's the end of happiness here. . . . I want to warn you that you are responsible for what will happen in the future."[11]

Director Allouache sets these characters in motion at a specific historical moment. The story line begins with Boualem's theft of the mosque loudspeaker and culminates when he leaves on a ship bound for France in his literal expulsion from Bab el-Oued and Algeria by Saïd and his band of Islamists. The plot of *The Battle of Algiers* centers around escalating French and Algerian violence; the plot of *Bab el-Oued City* focuses on escalating tension, increasing polarization between secularists like Boualem and militant Islamists like Saïd. The film is set in the aftermath of the October 1988 riots, when the army responded to antigovernment demonstrators by deploying tanks and killing hundreds. By the end of the film, three years later, roughly 1991, the imam's prediction has come to pass, Saïd himself has been killed, and Yamina writes that "death prowls" Bab el-Oued.

In many respects, *Bab el-Oued City* stands *The Battle of Algiers* on its head. The latter, shot in black and white, is gray and gloomy; the former, shot in color, is sunny and bright; in it the women pass their days outside on their rooftops, the

11. The quotations from the film were copied from the English subtitles.

men swim and fish in the sea—how blue the Mediterranean is! In a nice historical twist, *Bab el-Oued City* is set in the former European working-class, *petit blanc* quarter of Algiers that also served as the headquarters of the settler terrorist Organisation armée secrète (OAS), made up of diehard supporters of *l'Algérie française.* Thirty years after the *pieds-noirs* have left, the former habitués of Le Milk Bar and other French sites of *Battle of Algiers* terrorist attacks have grown old and doddering, and Monsieur Paulo and his blind aunt return reeking of *nostalgérie,* nostalgia for French Algeria. Yamina's mother ushers them onto the rooftop and introduces them saying, "They're old neighbors." Paulo describes to his blind companion the view in a dithyramb that the old woman punctures by saying, "I smell such a [foul] odor," as the Algerian onlookers remark accurately to themselves, "He doesn't want to upset her." The Algerians regard the *pieds-noirs* as if they have come from another world, another time, and indeed they have. Mercilessly lampooned for their *nostalgérie,* the couple, no longer the colonial oppressor, serve as unsubtle comic relief to the gathering storm of 1990s Algeria. In *Bab el-Oued City,* with its *pieds-noirs* and other markers of the colonial past (the Catholic cemetery overgrown with weeds), we may not be beyond colonialism in the sense of having worked through or overcome it, but we are certainly in the period that comes after it.

In contrast to *The Battle of Algiers,* where everything is clear-cut and everyone transparent (even Colonel Mathieu in his own way), everyone in *Bab el-Oued City* is complicated, if not compromised, and everything is complex, if not utterly opaque. Messaoud, the good French Islamist, is caught out in the cemetery with an Algerian woman by a friend of Boualem. Boualem's baker boss, too, is compromised and forced to fire Boualem when Saïd's Islamist sidekick Rachid threatens him, "We have your file. With the French." Other relationships remain purposely opaque, such as that between Saïd and the BMW-driving men in suits who give him a gun.

Compromised individuals add up to a neighborhood, a society that has lost its way. This is literally the case in the scenes in which Yamina writes Boualem. After he leaves on the boat, she repeatedly asks his brother Kader and sister Hanifa his whereabouts, but either they do not know or they will not tell her, so that she has no idea even what country he lives in. So Yamina writes to Boualem, but instead of mailing the letters, she keeps them, waiting and hoping that he will return—but we (and she) know better.

It is a society that has lost its way, its sense of direction: the most telling example here is Ourdya, Boualem's friend. She smokes, she drinks; she already stays indoors and avoids people when we first see her with Boualem, who supplies her with wine and cigarettes. At their last meeting, she tells him her story. How as a student she had been in love with a fellow political radical, presumably in the 1970s. How they were imbued with "revolution, the Third World, Marxism." How they "mobilized" to build "a new country" with a group of "extremists." And how they were arrested, put in prison, and how she was confined in a cell for nine days, at the end of which time her father obtained her release. However, her lover "was not as lucky. He 'disappeared,' " most likely tortured and killed. As a result, her life collapsed, "everything went dark, I had no desire." "Then I met this," she gestures to a wine bottle. For her "dissolute" living, Saïd threatens her at gunpoint near the end of the film and tells her to leave in a week, or else.

What is the solution? What is the way out? The way out ultimately depends on one's idea of Algeria, on what is termed *algérienité,* "Algerianness," the nature or identity of Algeria as a country, a nation.[12] For the imam, the way out is resignation; for Boualem, Ourdya, and others, it is to leave. As Boualem's boat shoves off, we hear a *rai* song on the soundtrack. "I want to get out . . . I'm unhappy in my country." Most stay, however, making their way in Algeria: Yamina writes unmailed letters to Boualem.

How did we get from *The Battle of Algiers* to *Bab el-Oued City?* From Fanon on the 1960s national bourgeoisie and the *parti unique* to 1990s Algeria and quasi-civil war? To summarize a complex situation, we may say that forty years have passed since independence, but that the hopes engendered by freedom from France have gone unfulfilled. The FLN waged one of the most violent, protracted Third World wars of national liberation since 1945, yet once in power the organization steadily established one-party rule ultimately guaranteed by the army, first under Ahmed Ben Bella (1962–65) and then under Houari Boumedienne (1965–78). Economic development took the form of state capitalism; huge firms were created to exploit large oil and natural-gas reserves. By the 1980s, a new, postindependence generation had come of age, but economic development had not kept pace with population growth. By 1988, needed oil revenues had declined precipitously, the economy had gone into free fall, and riots broke out in Algiers in October. Hundreds of Algerians were killed when the army called out tanks. Initially, at least, political opposition took the form of Islamism, seemingly the only viable political discourse available to opponents of the secular FLN. Internal splits within the FLN and the army—now led by a high command different from the preceding generation that fought the 1954—62 revolution—had already occurred by 1988.

Reforms undertaken after 1988 amounted to too little too late. President

12. A conference, "Algeria: The Search for Identity," was organized by John Ruedy at Georgetown University, 12 March 2002.

Chadli Bendjedid (1979–92) called for elections in 1991. In the first round of voting, the Islamist party, the Front islamique du salut (FIS, Islamic Salvation Front), delivered a stunning defeat to the FLN. Chadli, who intended nonetheless to hold the scheduled second round of voting, was opposed by *le pouvoir,* the civilian and military elite, and forced to resign. *Le pouvoir,* also referred to as *les décideurs,* "the ones who decide," proceeded to cancel the scheduled elections over protests of the opposition parties, which now included the FLN, the FIS, and the predominantly Berber Front des forces socialistes (FFS, Socialist Forces Front); named Mohamed Boudiaf president; and cracked down on the Islamists as Algeria descended into quasi-civil war. In 1992, Boudiaf, one of the original leaders of the 1954 uprising that began the French-Algerian War, was assassinated, and Liamine Zéroual was named president (1994–98), then succeeded in turn by Abdelaziz Bouteflika (1999 to the present). Since 1992, the unofficial death toll has run perhaps as high as 150,000 owing to widespread violence, including torture and physical mutilation employed especially by the government and the militant Groupe islamique armée (GIA, Armed Islamist Group).[13] Although the violence has abated recently, no fundamental resolution has occurred between the government run by a shadowy military clique and a variety of Islamist, secular, and Berber opposition groups (Ruedy 1992; Stone 1997; Stora 2001; H. Roberts 2002).

Where do Allouache and *Bab el-Oued City* fit in here? Allouache is a secularist who shuttles back and forth between France and Algeria. Born in Algeria in 1944, he has made seven features between 1976 and 2001, including *Salut cousin* (1996). Set in both France and Algeria, they focus on daily life in the 1970s and the 1990s. Currently residing in France, he is part of a Frenchified Algerian intellectual and artistic elite.[14] Certain themes of *Bab el-Oued City* resonate with the work of another current French resident, writer Assia Djebar. *L'amour, la fantasia* ([1985] 1995a; translated into English as *Fantasia: An Algerian Cavalcade* in 1993), not to mention *Le blanc de l'Algérie* (1995b; translated as *Algerian White* [2000]), treats the entwined relations of French and Algerians; women, gender, and Algerian patriarchy; the strains of secularism both in the sense of secular tendencies and currents and in the sense of ongoing tensions and conflicts; and the impact of history and current events on individual lives, on how history does and does not get written.

Pontecorvo's film leads us to empathize with Ali la Pointe, Allouache's with

13. On the GIA, see Gacemi 1998. Thanks to Terry Burke and Fanny Colonna for this reference.

14. See, for background information, http://www.algeriades.com/news/article.php3?id_article=591.

Boualem. Boualem just wants to make his way, to live his life in Algeria. He espouses no worked-out political position, antigovernment or otherwise. In the end, Islamists expel him from Bab el-Oued, just as the FLN had expelled the two visiting *pieds-noirs,* also originally from Bab el-Oued, thirty years earlier. The main fault line in *Bab el-Oued City* increasingly pits Islamists against secularists, yet there is little if any explicit criticism of the government, of either the FLN or the army, which is perhaps understandable in a film shot in Algeria. *Bab el-Oued City* makes references to the 1988 riots, but not to the FLN's repressive role; there is nothing on the government quashing the 1991–92 elections and banning the FIS; nothing on the 1992 assassination of Boudiaf; nothing on the antigovernment Berber opposition generally; nothing on Berber Kabyle writer Tahar Djaout's 1993 murder by Islamists specifically. No, the motor driving *Bab el-Oued City* is instead escalating Islamist power; when Saïd gets a pistol, he ratchets up the fundamentalist opposition to a higher, deadlier level. In *The Battle of Algiers,* violence is represented as escalation by both French and Algerians; in *Bab el-Oued City* the Islamists become more and more threatening, but the government has not yet responded violently, repressively. Yet by the time the latter film was made, the political and military clique already had a much greater presence in the quasi-civil war that has riven Algeria since the 1990s than Allouache's film suggests.

Why is this so? The opacity of political power, for one thing; what can (and cannot) be said, for another. *Bab el-Oued City* already stages opacity, government opacity, quite clearly. Two men in suits driving a fancy black BMW meet with Saïd on several occasions; later they supply him with his gun. One is identified laconically in the film credits as "BMW man"; they are recognizably agents of *le pouvoir.* Behind the purposeful murkiness of the film swirls the de facto secrecy of the current Algerian regime. Behind the managed elections, behind the handpicked leaders, who comprises *le pouvoir, les décideurs?* Names surface, mostly of generals, but the internal power struggles are even less clear. Moreover, there is the general opacity of this quasi-civil war, the unanswered questions. In 1992, did Islamists or the ruling military clique kill Boudiaf? In the truly awful 1997 slaughters of the entire villages of Bentalha and Raïs outside Algiers, what do we make of repeated charges of government complicity (Yous 2000)? These and other aspects of contemporary Algerian political culture lead some in the opposition to term the regime *Stalinist,* its workings conjuring up the former Soviet Union and eastern Europe (Ahmed 2000).[15] For citizen onlookers in Algeria, politics at such times is reduced to a who/whom parlor game of sheer speculation.

15. Aït Ahmed is leader of the FFS.

More lethal, this milieu lets terrorism and torture thrive; behind the scenes are the "disappeared," now numbering in the thousands. Depressing thought: threats of Islamist terror only strengthen a violently repressive regime that has adroitly played the terrorist card with Western governments eager for Algerian oil.

It is against this background that we must consider the torture discussion in Algeria, one that runs parallel and in tandem with, yet differs from and appears more muted and timid than the one in France (Mouffok 2000; Stora 2002).[16] Whereas in France the discussion centers around the French torture of Algerians, in Algeria the controversy concerns Algerian violence, including torture, directed against fellow Algerians during both the *guerre d'Algérie* and the quasi-civil war. The political and intellectual stakes differ on either side of the Mediterranean. Politically, a discussion of torture today in Algeria directly implicates the current regime in a way that the torture controversy in France does not (even with the specter of Jean-Marie Le Pen's Front national). Intellectually, the stakes in recovering a previously occluded historical past in Algeria are even higher than in France, where it is about recovering a key episode in recent French history, because in the Maghreb it is ultimately a matter regarding the history of the Algerian nation in the past half-century, the history of Algerian nationalism, and the FLN's claim of embodying Algerian nationalism.

In Algeria, the discussion ultimately turns on the military and political elite's willingness to employ violence and torture to maintain power. It concerns the FLN's earlier use of terror and torture against Messali Hadj's nationalist Mouvement national algérien (MNA); against the *harkis,* Algerian collaborators of the French; and against dissident FLN members. It is also about personal testimonies of torture by the Algerian army today, such as that of Habib Souaïdia (2001). Against this backdrop, no wonder the silence of the Algerian government regarding the French torture controversy has been deafening. No wonder the focus has remained, even among the opposition, more on torture during the *guerre d'Algérie* than on the quasi-civil war.

Given such a patently authoritarian, undemocratic regime, it is easy to advocate democracy, civil liberties, and the like. Too easy, because against a tenacious, entrenched elite, straightforward calls for democracy must perforce have a certain unreality about them. In France, *l'oubli,* the earlier forgetting, has conduced, as a result of the torture controversy, to taking the first steps in working through the so-called Algeria syndrome or Algerian question. Currently, the operative metaphor in France is "turning the page" (with or without a question mark), moving beyond the French-Algerian conflict (Schalk 1998, 1999; Cohen 2002;

16. Mouffok is a journalist based in Algiers.

Hargreaves 2002). But turning the page on French-Algerian relations once again comes from and reflects the French perspective, not the Algerian. For Algeria, there is not resolution, but only continuing stalemate; not *la gangrène,* but an open wound requiring immediate attention.

In a series of political plays, Alek Baylee Toumi stages certain of these themes and in the process asks again, "Where is Algeria going?" "What is the nature of 'Algerianness'?" The main conceit of Toumi's trilogy of plays is to bring back to life during the second Algerian war a number of leading French figures involved in the first Algerian war: Jean-Paul Sartre (and Simone de Beauvoir) in *Madah-Sartre* (1996, 2003), Albert Camus in *Albert Camus: Entre la mère et l'injustice* (2004), and de Beauvoir in *De Beauvoir a beau voile* (under consideration).[17] Simultaneously, he stages the caught-in-the-crossfire plight of Algerian common folk through the character of a taxi driver; Toumi's driver is kith to Allouache's *Bab el-Oued* kin.

In *Madah-Sartre,* Sartre and de Beauvoir return to life in order to attend the funeral in Algeria of Berber Kabyle writer and poet Tahar Djaout, assassinated by Islamists in 1993. Afterward, however, they are kidnapped and interrogated by an Islamist group that Toumi dubs the Groupe international armé (Armed International Group [GIA]).[18] There are scenes in which de Beauvoir is interrogated separately by Islamist women, called *tchadorettes,* but the main focus lies on the dialogues between Sartre and Madah, an Islamist "converter of atheists" (Toumi [1996] 2003, 21).[19] Madah is a fictional representation of the real-life Anouar Haddad.

> 1991: Haddam elected to the Algerian National Assembly as a member of FIS. 1992: leaves Algeria when government cancels second round of elections. 1993: files for asylum while living in Washington, D.C. As leader of FIS in exile, allegedly recruits Algerians for CIA to fight in Afghanistan. 1996: request for asylum denied, taken into custody by U.S. government. U.S.-based human rights organizations charge he is involved in terrorist campaigns by FIS and [Groupe in-

17. According to Toumi, "Because of death threats, in order to protect my family in Algiers, my first plays *Madah-Sartre* and *Taxieur* were published under the pen name Baylee. Later, in 1998 I 'came out' and added my real last name Toumi" (e-mail to author, 5 June 2004). "Alek Baylee" is a play on words; when it is pronounced as one word, it becomes "al Kabyle," the Kabyle.

18. This GIA is not the Groupe islamique armée (GIA) named earlier.

19. *Tchadorettes* combines *bachelorette* and *tchador,* the latter Islamist garb imported from Iran and Afghanistan as opposed to the traditional Algerian *haik* or veil. The third play in Toumi's trilogy features de Beauvoir and prominently stages issues of gender and feminism. *Madah* is short for *Mad-d-Allah,* a term that suggests Islamic extremism.

> ternational armé] like those that targeted Khalida Messaoudi, Toumi's sister in Algeria. 1997: condemned to death in absentia by Algerian government. Held by U.S. on "secret evidence" charges by order of Attorney General Janet Reno. 2002: released from U.S. custody, U.S. refuses to extradite him to Algeria because believes life in danger. (Le Sueur 2002, 516 n. 16)

Toumi's play *Madah-Sartre* is filled with neologisms, puns, and other wordplay. In act 3, "Les intellos-juifs" ("Jewish intellectuals"): atheism ("that's forbidden"), womanizing ("God has given you that right"), drinking ("that is very, very bad") (Toumi [1996] 2003, 21). Going on the offensive, Sartre attacks Madah's either Islamist or government attitudes, criticizes Madah and his ilk for holding "the people hostage between the military hammer and the Islamist sword," and argues, against this forced choice, in favor of democracy, pointing out that Algerians have always been multilingual as well as multiethnic (89). The clincher comes, however, when Sartre reveals that God is female.

> Sartre: You see, God is a woman.
>
> Madah (howls): That's heresy.
>
> Sartre: Sorry to disappoint you. It's Satan who is a man . . .
>
> Madah (Forbidden. He nearly has a heart attack). (92)

Madah-Sartre proceeds simultaneously on another level, driving the streets of Algiers with the *taxieur* Hamid Lounar. Arguably the main character in the play, the taxi driver represents the Algerian man-on-the-street caught in the all too dangerous, no—man's-land between religious fanaticism and governmental repression. In staging Hamid's plight, Toumi goes considerably further than Allouache in evoking the Kafkaesque, absurdist, and violent atmosphere of Islamist-ruling elite strife in what is now mid-1990s Algeria. At a traffic checkpoint on the outskirts of the capital, plainclothes cops stop Hamid. After looking at his papers, one officer asks,

> What do you think of the government?
>
> Taxi driver: But, Mr. Police Officer, I don't think anything. I'm not political. I work. I have nine children to feed. I'm 50 years old. I am for nothing.
>
> Cop: For the FLN or for the FIS?
>
> Taxi driver: But me . . . I am for nobody.
>
> Cop: You are against religion. You are against God.
>
> Taxi driver: But no, I am not against . . .
>
> Cop: Then you work with the cops. You're a spy, an informer. . . . Talk. (11)

After more such exchanges, the cop says, "You're wicked. You refuse to talk," and slashes Hamid on the left cheek (12).

Hamid drives on but soon comes to another checkpoint, manned by policemen who look exactly like the first ones. Again he is asked to take sides.

> Cop: Choose your camp. Between your mother and justice, which do you choose?
>
> Taxi driver: I don't know. Justice.
>
> Cop: Whose justice? That of man or that of God?
>
> Taxi driver: I don't know. Yours, I'm sure it is the good one.
>
> Cop (showing his uniform): What is this getup?
>
> Taxi driver: That of a policeman.
>
> Cop: So, like that, you are for the officials of Security. You're wrong again. We are God's warriors. (13–14)

And the officer slashes him on the other cheek. Wounded and bleeding, like Algeria, Hamid spends the rest of the play trying fruitlessly to have his wounds attended to, also like Algeria. He's given the runaround from one medical clinic to another, from one friend of a friend to another, unable to find any help, and told to pay in foreign currency, to supply his own bandages and thread for sutures, to boot.

> I've had to run around without stopping, I've been tossed back and forth like a tennis ball. From one office to another. It's an endless game. I was told to ask for Tombéza. He knows everyone, but he wasn't there. Out of the office. I asked for Dergez. He no longer works there. Si Sliman? Exiled. Boudiman? Assassinated. I was told to bring foreign currency. Cotton bandages, thread. I can't take it anymore! (he starts crying again). (71)

What is the way out for the *taxieur?* For Algeria? To both Toumi and Allouache, both secularists, the only viable Algeria is a more tolerant, democratic, multiethnic, and multicultural one. For them and others, such as Djebar, *algérienité* is not singular, either secular or religious, but multiple, plural. Toumi has a Berber Kabyle background, and the political differences in his family mirror the differences in Algeria. His sister, Khalida Messaoudi (1998), a leading Algerian feminist, challenged the FIS in 1993 on Algerian television and received in return a *fatwa* for her death. Toumi is aware of the situation's complexity, of the political situation's evolution since the mid-1990s. In a more recent stand-alone play entitled *Taxieur* (2001), he spells out certain of the ambiguities, complexities, and difficulties. They include, internally, a divided opposition: "Sartre: I am for . . . the Algerian people . . . For a free and democratic Algeria, a plural Algeria. For the resisters, the representatives of civil society, journalists, and women.

The drama is that my friends are too divided" (Toumi 2001, 69, emphasis added). And externally, foreign duplicity: "Sartre: There is a civil society, and it is that that is being massacred. Internally, the Beast cuts throats, decapitates and lies. Externally, Beauty strangles economically. The West also has its Authorized Influence Groups [the Groupe international armée]" (70). The character of *le manipulateur* stands in for *le pouvoir:* wearing black clothes and sunglasses, he pulls strings from behind the play's curtain. Yet a certain disconnect remains between art (read: theater) and life (read: politics), which finds its echo in *Madah-Sartre* in the deus ex machina recourse to dead French personages in order to make clear the political stakes in Algeria today. Yes, the violence is currently in remission, but no fundamental resolution has been arrived at. "As for me," Toumi says, "I have no solution for the situation Algeria is living through" ([1996] 2003, 101).

Madah-Sartre, with its 1954–62 personages injected into the quasi-civil war present, brings us back to *The Battle of Algiers,* and it also connects via the taxi driver Hamid to the denizens of *Bab el-Oued City.* But we are by no means back to where we started. Granted, there is a "What have I wrought?" quality to Sartre's character in Toumi's play, as if to say, "I did not intend by my support of the FLN then for things to have worked out the way they have now." Yet it is far too teleological to draw a straight line from the "first Algerian war" to the "second Algerian war," for linking the violence of the two conflicts more tightly than they should be makes it too easy to draw the implication that "the Algerians did it then (to us), and they're doing it now (to each other)." Yet by substituting *guerre d'Algérie* and "quasi-civil war" for "first Algerian war" and "second Algerian war," respectively, I by no means wish to condone terrorism and torture then, certainly not by the French—which Massu disavows today and Aussaresses reaffirms—or by female Algerian bomb carriers. I simply want to recognize that Sartre and de Beauvoir acted in solidarity with the Ali la Pointes then, and that today they would be on the side of the Boualems and Yaminas and Hamids.

Epilogue

In France, *The Battle of Algiers* has gone from being viewed as reportage forty years ago to being considered history at the beginning of the twenty-first century.[20] In France and especially in the United States, reception has taken another twist, and the film is again current-event, real live-action news clips from the U.S.

20. A different version of these remarks was presented at a screening of *The Battle of Algiers* in conjunction with an international workshop, "Walls of Algiers," Getty Museum, Los Angeles, May 2004.

war in Iraq (Blumenfeld 2004; Hakem 2004b; Harbi 2004). Already in September 2002, two American officials invited producer Yacef Saâdi in France to come to the United States and talk about *The Battle of Algiers* (Hakem 2004a). Early in 2003 at least one American academic was invited to speak to military reservists, who completely missed the point about *The Battle of Algiers*. The academic commented that "[t]he reservists' supervisor told me he liked the film because it showed how the French had crushed the Algerian revolt—the opposite lesson from what I intended" (C. Smith 2004). Later, in September 2003, the Pentagon screened the film (without Saâdi), and the *New York Times* asked, "What does the Pentagon see in *The Battle of Algiers?*" (Kaufman 2003). The key question for visual culture, for reception, is: How can the Pentagon, how can the army, see in the film only a how-to manual of counterinsurgency techniques, including torture? How can it *not* see that the French won the battle of Algiers, yes, but lost the Algerian Revolution? How can it *not* see that French repression and torture powerfully contributed to defeat in the end?

The question of how different audiences view the same work differently is a fascinating intellectual and aesthetic one. But it has been completely preempted by what has occurred in Iraq since the March 2003 U.S. invasion, for now we know that already by September 2003 the United States was practicing torture. We may surmise that if *The Battle of Algiers* was not the direct inspiration for Pentagon policy, then certainly the Pentagon's wildly off-base reading of the film contributed to the policy of abrogating the Geneva Conventions.

The United States in Iraq is like *The Battle of Algiers* in at least five ways, and here it is necessary to be as precise as possible. First, so-called abuse is in fact torture as clearly defined by the Geneva Conventions: "any act by which severe pain or suffering, whether physical or mental, is intentionally inflicted on a person for such purposes as obtaining from him or a third person information or a confession" (quoted in Glanz 2004).[21] Second, in both Algeria and Iraq water torture

21. Still more explicit are guidelines set down by the Army Intelligence Center and Fort Huachuca in Arizona: "Soldiers cannot use any form of physical torture, including food deprivation, beating, infliction of pain through chemicals or bondage, or electric shock. Soldiers also may not use mental torture, such as mock executions, abnormal sleep deprivation or chemically induced psychosis" (Glanz 2004). However, whether even these explicit guidelines were followed is questionable, according to one academic referred to earlier: "all interrogators at Fort Huachuca are instructed in the Geneva Conventions and the laws forbidding physical or mental torture during interrogations. But the institution's manual also states that applications of some interrogation techniques 'may approach the line between lawful and unlawful actions.' Given this, it is not surprising that some interrogators in the field may cross that line if under pressure to acquire information—or

has been used "whereby a suspect is pushed underwater and made to think he will be drowned" (Barry, Hirsh, and Isikoff 2004). Third, like the French, the Americans refer to Iraqi "cells" and the "cellular" structure of resistance; both cite the same need to obtain information as the excuse for torture (Hersh 2004).[22] Fourth, torture in Iraq is not isolated but systemic, not the initiative of those lower down, but authorized in general and condoned in practice by those higher up (Danner 2004; Hersh 2004; Sontag 2004a, 2004b). A culture of torture has been created, including the taking of "trophy photos" (Beaugé 2004). Fifth, language, too, has been twisted and perverted (I purposely avoid saying "tortured") (Sontag 2004a, 2004b).[23] In France, the French-Algerian War was *les évenements* (the events) or *la guerre sans nom* (the war without a name). In Iraq, the reality is that the United States is practicing torture, not "abuse"; not "detainee abuse," but "prisoner torture." In conclusion, if the Geneva Conventions define what constitute war crimes, if torture by Americans in Iraq contravenes the Geneva Conventions and thereby constitutes war crimes, and if those who either condoned, created the climate for, or ordered such practices are guilty of war crimes, then George W. Bush and those around him are war criminals.

For such a book as this one on history, memory, and Algeria, a key issue concerns future memory: How will we write the history of the present? How will actions (and inactions) and events occurring (and the denial that they are occurring) be remembered and written about in the future when some see them in the present for what they plainly are? In France, it took nearly forty years for those who fought—including those who tortured—in Algeria to step forward, toward the end of their lives, to tell their stories, to unburden themselves of the past (Beaugé 2000a). For Americans in Iraq—and Americans in the United States—how long will it take to learn these truths? Will it happen now or only at some later date?

---

that they develop a sense of unrestricted power that their superiors may allow, or indeed encourage" (C. Smith 2004).

22. A "cellular" view of resistance or insurgency leads implicitly to a policy to kill or eradicate the "bad" cells. It fails completely to consider the degree to which the "bad" cells are supported by the surrounding cells, resulting in what the Pentagon euphemistically terms *collateral damage*—that is, the death and injury to the surrounding "cells," or civilians.

23. "To refuse to call what happened at Abu Chraib —and what has taken place elsewhere in Iraq and in Afghanistan and at Guantánamo Bay—by its true name, torture, is as outrageous as the refusal to call the Rwandan genocide a genocide" (Sontag 2004a, 25). I agree that torture in Iraq was systemic and extended to and included Afghanistan, Guantánamo Bay, and domestic U.S. prisons for that matter, but I am focusing here specifically on the parallels between Algeria and Iraq.

Acknowledgements

Thanks to Jim Barrett, Roger Benjamin, Eric Breitbart, Terry Burke, Omar Carlier, Zeynep Çelik, Julia Clancy-Smith, Fanny Colonna, Habiba Demming, Phil Dine, Hafid Gafaiti, Alec Hargreaves, Jane Kuntz, Jim Le Sueur, Patricia Lorcin, Neil MacMaster, Nabila Oulebsir, Dave Roediger, David Schalk, Charles D. Smith, and Alek Baylee Toumi.

Works Cited • Index

Works Cited

"40e anniversaire de la répression du 17 octobre 1961 sur fond de polémique." 2001. *Le Monde,* 17 Oct.

"1962–1992: 30 ans après." 1992. *Paris-Match* 2250 (9 July): 92–93.

"Le 17 octobre 1961, au fronton de l'histoire." 1991. *El Moudjahid,* 16 Oct.

Abbas, Ferhat. 1984. *L'indépendance confisquée, 1962–1978.* Paris: Flammarion.

Abbou, Selim. 1981. *L'identité culturelle: Relations inter-ethniques et problèmes d'acculturation.* Paris: Anthropos.

Abdallah, Mogniss H. 2000. " 'L'effet Zidane,' ou le rêve éveillé de l'intégration par le spor." *Hommes et migrations* 1226: 5–14.

Abitbol, Michel. 1985. "The Encounter Between French Jewry and the Jews of North Africa: Analysis of a Discourse (1830–1914)." In *The Jews in Modern France,* edited by Frances Malino and Bernard Wasserstein, 31–53. Hanover, N.H.: Univ. Press of New England.

Adas, Michael. 1989. *Machines as the Measure of Man: Science, Technology, and Ideologies of Western Dominance.* Ithaca, N.Y.: Cornell Univ.

Agence France presse. 2000. 9 Nov.

Ageron, Charles-Robert. 1968. *Les Algériens musulmans et la France.* 2 vols. Paris: Presses Univ. de France.

———. 1991. *Modern Algeria: A History from 1830 to the Present.* London: Hurst

———. 1993a. "Une histoire de la guerre d'Algérie est-elle possible en 1992?" In *La guerre d'Algérie dans l'enseignement en France et en Algérie,* 155–58. Paris: CNDP.

———. 1993b. "Pour une histoire critique de l'Algérie de 1830 à 1962." In *L'Algérie des Français,* edited by Charles-Robert Ageron, 8–13. Paris: Éditions du Seuil.

———. 1994. "Le drame des harkis en 1962." *Vingtième siècle* 42: 3–6.

———. 1995. "Les supplétifs algériens dans l'armée française pendant la guerre d'Algérie." *Vingtieme siècle* 48: 3–20.

———. 1996. "La décolonization au regard de la France." In *Histoire de la France coloniale,* vol. 3: *Le déclin 1931 à nos jours,* edited by Catherine Coquery-Vidrovitch and Charles-Robert Ageron, 281–386. Paris: Armand Colin.

———, ed. 1997. *La guerre d'Algérie et les Algériens 1954–1962.* Paris: Armand Colin.

———. 2000. "Le 'drame des harkis,' mémoire ou histoire?" *Vingtième siecle* 68: 3–15.

Agulhon, Maurice. 1983. *The Republican Experiment: 1848–1852.* Cambridge: Cambridge Univ. Press and Éditions de la Maison des sciences de l'homme.

———. 1991. "Intervention." In *De Gaulle et son siècle: T. 1 dans la mémoire des hommes et des peuples.* Institut Charles de Gaulle no. 177. Paris: La documentation française-plon.

Aït Ahmed, Hocine. 1983. *Mémoires d'un combatant.* Paris: Éditions Sylvie Messinger.

———. 2000. "La torture en Algérie, aujourd-hui comme hier." *Le Monde,* 14 Dec.

Akhbar (newspaper). 1850. 22 Oct.

Alger républicain (newspaper). 1954. Various editions, 9 Sept.–30 Oct.

Alia, Josette. 2002. "Le vrai visage de l'Islam français." *Le nouvel observateur* 1946 (21–27 Feb.): 4–10.

Alleg, Henri. 1958. *La question.* Paris: Minuit.

Allouache, Merzek. 1994. *Bab el-Oued el-Houma* (film). Algiers and Paris: Flashback Adiovisuel and La Sept Cinéma.

———. 1996. *Salut cousin* (film). Brussells: Artémis Productions.

———. 1998. *Bab el-Oued.* Translated by Angela M. Brewer. Boulder, Colo.: Lynne Rienner.

Altaras, Jacques-Isaac. 1842. "Rapport sur l'état moral et politique des Israélites de l'Algérie, et les moyens de l'améliorer." Reproduced in *Les juifs d'Algérie et la France: 1830–1855,* by Simon Schwarzfuchs, 67–201. Jerusalem: Institut Ben-Zvi.

Alzieu, Teddy. 2001. *Mémoire en images: Oran.* Joué-lès-Tours: Éditions Allan Sutton.

Amar, Marianne. 1987. *Nés pour courir: La Quatrième République face au sport.* Grenoble: P.U. de Grenoble.

Amara, Saliha. 1994. Interview by Richard Derderian. Aubervilliers, France, 25 July.

Amicale des Algériens en Europe. 1987. *17 octobre 1961: Mémoire d'une communauté.* Paris: Actualité de l'émigration.

Amman, Peter. 1975a. "The Paris Club Movement in 1848." In *Revolution and Reaction: 1848 and the Second French Republic,* edited by Roger Price, 13–28. New York: Barnes and Noble.

———. 1975b. *Revolution and Mass Democracy: The Paris Club Movement of 1848.* Princeton, N.J.: Princeton Univ. Press.

Anglade, Jean. 1976. *La vie quotidienne des immigrés en France de 1919 à nos jours.* Paris: Hachette.

Année politique, economique et sociale. 1962.

Apter, Emily. 1999. *Continental Drift: From National Characters to Virtual Subjects.* Chicago: Univ. of Chicago Press.

Arcady, Alexandre. 2000. *Là-bas mon pays* (film). Paris: Bac Films.

Archives Israélites (journal). 1840. Vol. 1.

———. 1843. Vol. 4.

———. 1844. Vol. 5.

———. 1846. Vol. 7.

———. 1848. Vol. 9.

Arnaud, Pierre, ed. 1987. *Les athlètes de la république: Gymnastique, sport et idéologie républicaine 1870–1914.* Toulouse: Privat.

Arnoulet, François. 1991. "Les problèmes de l'enseignement au début du protectorat français en Tunisie (1881–1900)." *Revue de L'Institut des belles lettres arabes* 54, no. 167: 31–62.

Assemblée nationale. 1999. *Rapport* no. 2005 (8 Dec.).

Association des oulémas. 1936. "Déclaration nette." In *L'Algérie des Français,* edited by Charles-Robert Ageron. Paris: Éditions du Seuil.

"Atteintes aux accords d'Evian." 1962. 26 Nov. MAA 540. Archives nationales, section outre-mer, Aix-en Provence, France.

Audisio, Gabriel. 1930. "A propos d'une concurrence touristique." *Terre d'Afrique illustrée* 139 (12 Jan.): 12.

Aussaresses, Paul. 2001a. *Pour la France: Services spéciaux, 1942–1954.* Paris: Rocher.

———. 2001b. *Services spéciaux: Algérie 1955–1957.* Paris: Perrin.

Aux soldats méconnus: Étrangers, immigrés, colonisés au service de la France (1914–1918 et 1939–1945). 1991. Special issue of *Hommes et migrations* 1148 (Nov.).

Azoulay, Paul. 1980. *La nostalgérie française.* Paris: Eric Baschet.

Bach-Hamba, Mohamed. [1918] 1991. *Le peuple algéro-tunisien et la France.* 2d ed. Carthage: Beit al-Hikma.

Badis, Abane. 2001. "Il n'y a pas que le terrorisme en Algérie." *Algeria Watch* 18. Available at: http://www.algeria-watch.de/farticle/inondations/badis.htm.

Baduel, Pierre-Robert. 1987. "De l'économie des corps aux strategies d'identités." In *Monde Arabe: Migrations et identities.* Special issue of *Revue de l'Occident musulman et de la Méditerranné* 43: 5–14.

Bal, Mieke. 1999. "Introduction." In *Acts of Memory: Cultural Recall in the Present,* edited by Mieke Bal, Jonathan Crewe, and Leo Spitzer, vii-xvii. Hanover, N.H.: Univ. Press of New England.

Balibar, Etienne. 1997. "Algérie, France: Une or deux nations?" *Lignes* 30: 7–22.

Barrat, Denise, and Robert Barrat. 2001. *Le livre blanc sur l'Algérie 1956.* Paris: L'Aube.

Barry, John, Michael Hirsh, and Michael Isikoff. 2004. "The Roots of Torture." *Newsweek* (24 May).

Barthes, Roland. 1957. *Mythologies.* Paris: Éditions du Seuil.

———. 1972a. *Mythologies.* Selected and translated by Annette Lavers. New York: Hill and Wang.

———. 1972b. "The Structuralist Activity." In *Critical Essays,* translated by Richard Howard, 213–20. Evanston, Ill.: Northwestern Univ. Press.

———. 1975. *The Pleasure of the Text.* Translated by Richard Miller. New York: Hill and Wang.

Bastien-Thiry, Jean. 1994. *Sa vie, ses écrits, témoignages.* La Celle St. Cloud, France: Cercle Jean Bastien-Thiry.

Batty, Peter. 1984. *La guerre d'Algérie* (film). Television production, Channel 4, London. DVD, Paramount, 2001.

Baylee, Alek. See Toumi, Alek Baylee.

Beaugé, Florence. 2000a. "350,000 anciens d'Algérie souffriraient de troubles psychiques liés à la guerre." *Le Monde,* 27 Dec.

———. 2000b. "Le general Massu exprime ses regrets pour la torture en Algérie." *Le Monde,* 22 June.

———. 2000c. "J'obtiens la justice par la vérité, je ne demandais rien d'autre." *Le Monde,* 25 June.

———. 2004. "L'Irak, au miroir des exactions commises pendant la guerre d'Algérie." *Le Monde,* 9 May.

Béclard to Bogo. 1854. 20 Oct. Série H, carton 64, dossier 755, armoire 6, Archives nationales de Tunisie, Tunis.

Bédarida, Catherine. 2001. "Devoir de mémoire, travaux d'auteurs." *Le Monde,* 16 Oct.

Begag, Azouz. 1986. *Le gone du Chaâba.* Paris: Éditions du Seuil.

———. 1989. *Béni ou le paradis privé.* Paris: Éditions du Seuil.

Begag, Azouz, and Christian Delorme. 2001. "Energumènes ou énerg-humaines?" *Le Monde,* 13 Oct.

Belghoul, Farida. 1988. Interview by Alec G. Hargreaves. France, 29 Sept.

Ben Achour, Mohamed El Aziz. 1989. *Catégories de la société tunisoise dans la deuxième moitié du XIXème siècle.* Tunis: Institut national d'archéologie et d'art.

Benaïcha, Brahim. 1992. *Vivre au paradis: D'une oasis à un bidonville.* Paris: Desclée de Brouwer.

Ben Ali, Saad, and René Pottier. 1933. *Aichouch la Djellabya, princesse saharienne.* Illustrated by R. Pottier. Paris: Oeuvres représentatives.

———. 1934. *La tente noire.* Illustrated by R. Pottier. Paris: Oeuvres représentatives.

Ben Chérif, Si Ahmed. 1920. *Ahmed ben Mostapha, goumier.* Paris: Payot.

Benguigui, Yamina. 1997a. "L'intégration des immigrés" (television program. On *Europe* (26 May).

———. 1997b. *Mémoires d'immigrés: L'héritage maghrébin.* Paris: Canal+ Éditions.

———. 2001a. *Inch'Allah dimanche* (film). Paris and Algiers: ARP Sélection and Baudits Long.

———. 2001b. Interview by Richard Derderian. Paris, 14 June.

Benhabilès, Chérif. 1914. *L'Algérie française vue par un indigène.* Algiers: Imprimerie Fontana frères.

Ben Ibrahim, Sliman, and Etienne Dinet. 1926. *Khadra, danseuse Ouled Naïl.* Illustrated by E. Dinet and Mohammed Racim. Paris: L'edition d'Art H. Piazza.

Bennabi, Malek. 1948. *Lebbeik, pèlerinage de pauvres.* Algiers: Algériennes en Nahdha.

Bennington, Geoffrey, and Jacques Derrida. 1991. *Jacques Derrida.* Paris: Éditions du Seuil.

Bennoune, Mahfoud. 2000. *Education, culture et développement en Algérie: Bilan et perspectives du système educatif.* Algiers: Marinoor-Enag.

Benoit, André Jean. 1996. *Sport colonial: Une histoire des exercices physiques dans les colonies de peuplement de l'océan Indien: La Réunion-Maurice, des origines à la Seconde Guerre Mondiale.* Paris: L'Harmattan.

Ben Oliel, Isaac, and Salomon Sarfati. 1848. Letter to [Emanuel Menahim] Nahon. 1 Feb. Carton 3U/1, folder "1847–1848." Centre des Srchives d'outre-mer, Aix-en-Provence, France.

Benrabah, Mohamed. 1995. "La langue perdue." *Esprit* 208: 35–47.

———. 1999. *Langue et pouvoir en Algérie: Histoire d'un traumatisme linguistique.* Paris: Éditions Séguier.

Bensoussan, Albert. 2001. *Pour une poignée de dattes.* Paris: Maurice Nadeau.

Benton, Lauren. 2002. *Law and Colonial Cultures: Legal Regimes in World History, 1400–1900.* Cambridge: Cambridge Univ. Press.

Berbrugger, Louis Adrien. 1843. *Algérie historique, pittoresque et monumentale: Recueil de vues, monuments, ceremonies, costumes . . . des habitants de l'Algérie.* 3 vols. Paris: J. Delahaye.

Bernard, Augustin. 1931. *L'Algérie.* Paris: H. Laurens.

Bernard, Philippe. 1991. "A Paris 'contre le racisme et l'oubli.' " *Le Monde,* 19 Oct.

———. 1992. "Guerre d'Algérie: La mémoire apaisée." *Le Monde,* 27 Feb.

———. 1998. "Selon le rapport Mandelkern, trente-deux personnes ont été tuées dans la nuit du 17 au 18 octobre 1961." *Le Monde,* 5 May.

———. 1999. "L'une des rares fois depuis le XIXe siècle ou la police a tiré sur des ouvriers à Paris." *Le Monde,* 15 Feb.

———. 2001. "Du match France-Algérie au 17 octobre 1961." *Le Monde,* 26 Oct.

———. 2002. "Memoire d'Algérie: Mémoire d'en France" *Le Monde,* 20 Mar.

Bernard, Philippe, and Christine Garin. 2001. "Le massacre du 17 octobre 1961 obtient un début de reconnaissance officielle." *Le Monde,* 16 Oct.

Berque, Jacques. 1970. *Le Maghreb entre deux guerres.* Paris: Éditions du Seuil.

Berstein, Serge. 2000. Interview by Jo McCormack. Paris, Feb.

Berstein, Serge, and Dominique Borne. 1996. "L'enseignement de l'histoire au lycée." *Vingtième siècle* 49 (Jan.-Mar.): 122–42.

Berstein, Serge, and Pierre Milza, eds. 1983–98 *Histoire terminales.* Paris: Hatier.

Bertrand, Louis. 1930. *D'Alger la romantique à Fès la mysterieuse.* Paris: Éditions des Portiques.

———. 1938. *Alger.* Paris: Sorlot.

Bhabha, Homi, ed. 1990. *Nation and Narration.* London: Routledge.

Biget, préfet de police d'Oran. 1962. Pour M. le Ministre (juin). 770346/08. Centre des Archives contemporaines, Archives nationales, Paris.

Blanchard, P. 2000. "Un musée pour la France coloniale." *Libération,* 17–18 June.

Bleys, Rudi C. 1996. *The Geography of Perversion: Male-to-Male Sexual Behavior Outside the West and the Ethnographic Imagination, 1750–1918.* London: Cassell.

Blumenfeld, Samuel. 2004. " 'La bataille d'Alger,' passion américaine." *Le Monde 2* (16–17 May): 34–37.

Bongie, Chris. 1991. *Exotic Memories: Literature, Colonialism, and the Fin-de-Siecle.* Stanford, Calif.: Stanford Univ. Press.

Borne, Dominique. 1989. "L'histoire du vingtième siècle au lycée: Le nouveau programme de terminale." *Vingtième siècle* 21 (Jan.-Mar.): 101–10.

Boualem, Bachaga. 1962. *Mon pays la France.* Paris: France-Empire.

Boudjedra, Rachid. 1992. *Le FIS de la haine.* Paris: Denoël.

Boulin, Robert. 1962. Secrétariat d'etat aux rapatriés. "Comité des affaires algériennes du Mercredi 23 Mai à 15h30. OBJET: Personnes rentrant d'Algérie." Ministère des affaires étrangeres, 39.

Bouzet, Ange-Dominique. 2001. "17 octobre 1961: À la mémoire des Algériens." *Libération,* 18 Oct.

———. 2001b. "Sur la vie de ma mère." *Libération,* 5 Dec.

Boym, Svetlana. 2001. *The Future of Nostalgia.* New York : Basic Books.

Branche, Raphaëlle. 2000. "L'armée et la torture pendant la guerre d'Algérie—les soldats, leurs chefs et les violences illégales." Thèse de doctorat d'histoire, Institut d'études politiques, Paris.

———. 2001. *La torture et l'armée pendant la guerre d'Algérie (1954–1962).* Paris: Gallimard.

Brown, L. Carl. 1974. *The Tunisia of Ahmad Bey, 1837–1855.* Princeton, N.J.: Princeton Univ. Press.

Brunet, Jean-Paul. 1999. *Police contre FLN: Le drame d'octobre 1961.* Paris: Flammarion.

Bureau of Democracy, Human Rights, and Labor. 2002. *Country Reports on Human Rights Practices—2001: Algeria.* Available at: http://www.algeria.watch.de/mrv/mrvrap/state_depart_2001.htm.

Burke, Edmund, III. 1976. "Frantz Fanon's *The Wretched of the Earth.*" *Daedalus* 105: 127–35.

Buzard, James. 1993. *The Beaten Track: European Tourism, Literature, and the Ways to Culture, 1800–1918.* Oxford: Clarendon Press.

Camou, Hélène. 2000. "La franc-maçonnerie en Tunisie à l'aube du protectorat." In *La Tunisie mosaïque: Diasporas, cosmopolitisme, archéologie de l'identité,* edited by Jacques Alexandropoulos and Patrick Cabanal, 357–67. Toulouse: Presses Univ. du Mirail.

Camus, Albert. 1939. *Noces.* Paris: Gallimard (Folio).

———. 1942. *L'etranger.* Paris: Gallimard (Folio).

———. 1947. *La peste.* Paris: Gallimard (Folio).

———. [1954] 1994a. *Noces suivi de l'eté.* Paris: Gallimard (Folio).

———. 1994b. *Le premier homme.* Paris: Gallimard.

Cardinal, Marie. 1975. *Les mots pour le dire.* Paris: Grasset et Fasquelle.

———. 1994. *Les pieds-noirs.* Paris: Place Furstemberg.

Carte de séjour. 1983. "La moda." In *Carte de séjour* (recording). Paris: n.p.

Castano, José. 1982. *Les larmes de la passion.* Paris: Robert Laffont.

Cavard, Col. 1962. Chef d'Etat-Major-2è Bureau; Corps d'armée d'Alger. "Bulletin Hebdomadaire de renseignement psychologique; n. 1540/RT/CAA/2.SC (semaine 16–22/5/62)." 1H/2549/ 2. Service historique de l'armée de terre, Vincennes, France.

Çelik, Zeynep. 1997. *Urban Forms and Colonial Confrontations: Algiers under French Rule.* Berkeley: Univ. of California Press.

"Le centenaire." 1929. *La voix indigène,* 7 Nov.

C'était les harkis (television program). 1963. On Colonne 5 sur 5, 7 June.

Chabrun, Laurent, Alexandre Lenoir, and Thomas Varela. 2001. "La plainte des harkis, est elle justifiée?" *L'Express* 2617 (30 Aug.): 12–15.

Chakchouka. 1981. "Fait divers." Unpublished play.

Chambre de commerce et d'industrie Marseille. 1838. 4 Sept. Série MQ 52, carton 79, Commerce International, Tunisie.

Chanony. 1853. *Mémoire d'un voyage en Algérie et retour par l'Espagne.* Paris: Charles Hingray.

Charef, Mehdi. 1983. *Le thé au harem d'Archi Ahmed.* Paris: Mercure de France.

———. 1989. *Le harki de Meriem.* Paris: Mercure de France.

Charles-Collomb. 1930a. "A l'orée du Centenaire de l'Algérie française" (editorial). *Evolution nord-africaine* 570 (1 Jan.): 1.

———. 1930b. Editorial. *Evolution nord-africaine* 587 (14 Mar.): 1.

Chatterjee, Partha. 1986. *Nationalist Thought and the Colonial World: A Derivative Discourse.* Delhi: Oxford Univ. Press.

Chejne, Anwar G. 1969. *The Arabic Language: Its Role in History.* Minneapolis: Univ. of Minnesota Press.

Chevalier, Louis. 1958. *Classes laborieuses et classes dangereuses à Paris.* Paris: Plon.

Chevènement, Jean-Pierre. 2000. "La corse au miroir de la France." *Le Monde,* 24 Nov.

Chibane, Malik. 1994. *Hexagone* (film). Pays, France: Alhambra Films.

Chollier, Antoine. 1929. *Alger et sa région.* Grenoble: B. Arthaud.

Chouraqui, André. 1952. *Marche vers l'Occident: Les juifs d'Afrique du Nord.* Paris: Presses Univ. de France.

Christelow, Allan. 1985. *Muslim Law Courts and the French Colonial State in Algeria.* Princeton, N.J.: Princeton Univ. Press.

Citron, Suzanne. 1991. *Le myth national: L'histoire de la France en question.* Paris: Découverte.

Cixous, Hélène. 1997. "Pieds nus." In *Une enfance algérienne,* edited by Leïla Sebbar, 55–66. Paris: Gallimard.

———. 2000. *Les rêveries de la femme sauvage: Scènes primitives.* Paris: Gallilée.

Clancy-Smith, Julia. 1994. *Rebel and Saint: Muslim Notables, Populist Protest, Colonial Encounters (Algeria and Tunisia, 1800–1904).* Berkeley: Univ. of California Press.

———. 1997. "The Maghrib and the Mediterranean World in the Nineteenth Century: Illicit Exchanges, Migrants, and Social Marginals." In *The Maghrib in Question: Essays in History and Historiography,* edited by Michel le Gall and Kenneth Perkins, 222–39. Austin: University of Texas Press.

———. 1998. "Islam, Gender, and Identities in the Making of French Algeria." In *Domesticating the Empire: Race, Gender, and Family Life in French and Dutch Colonialism,* edited by Julia Clancy-Smith and Frances Gouda, 154–74. Charlottesville: Univ. Press of Virginia.

———. 2000. "Gender in the City: The Medina of Tunis, 1850–1881." In *Africa's Urban Past,* edited by David Anderson and Richard Rathbone, 189–204. Oxford: Currey.

———. 2002. "Marginality and Migration: Europe's Social Outcasts in Pre-colonial Tunisia, c. 1830–1881." In *Outside in: On the Margins of the Modern Middle East,* edited by Eugene Rogan, 149–82. London: Tauris.

Clancy-Smith, Julia, and Frances Gouda, eds. 1998. *Domesticating the Empire: Race, Gender, and Family Life in French and Dutch Colonialism.* Charlottesville: Univ. Press of Virginia.

Le clin d'oeil. 1997. Dec., 110.

Le clin d'oeil. 1998. Feb., 111.

Club démocratique des fidèles (Jews of Paris). 1848. To Gouvernement provisionel de la République Française. 9 Apr. Carton F19 11015, Archives nationales, Paris.

Cluny. 1930a. "Alger-Paris-Alger." *La dépêche algérienne,* 4 Feb.

———. 1930b. "Alger-Paris-Alger." *La dépêche algérienne,* 19 Feb.

Cohen, Joseph. 1843. *De l'instruction publique parmi les Israélites algériens. Archives Israélites,* vol. 4.

Cohen, William B. 2001. "The Sudden Discovery of Torture—The Algerian War in French Discourse, 2000–2001." *French Politics and Society* 19, no. 3: 82–94.

———. 2002. "The Algerian War, the French State, and Official Memory." *Historical Reflections/Réflexions historiques* 28: 219–39.

Cohen Albert, Phyllis. 1977. *The Modernization of French Jewry: Consistory and Community in the Nineteenth Century.* Hanover, N.H.: Brandeis Univ. Press.

"La colonialisme, voilà le danger." 1933. *La voix du people,* 17 Nov.

Colonna, Fanny. 1975. *Les instituteurs algériens, 1883–1939.* Paris: Presses de la Fondation nationale des sciences politiques.

Colston, Marianne. 1822. *Journal of a Tour in France, Switzerland, and Italy during the Years 1819, 20, and 21.* Paris: A. and W. Galignani.

Combat. 1962. 23 May 1962.

Commandement supérieur des forces en Algérie (CSFA). 1962a. "Bulletin de Renseignements Mensuel—Mois de juin, n.2108/CSFA/EMI/2/OPE." 2ème Bureau/Etat-Major InterArmées/Commandement Supérieur des Forces en Algérie; signed by Col. Mangin. 1H/1428/1. Service historique de l'armée de terre, Vincennes, France.

———. 1962b. "Extraits du journal parlé 'Europe Midi' CSFA B2/EXT (19 March 1962)." 1H/1784 /2. Service historique de l'armée de terre, Vincennes, France.

———. 1962c. "Notes." 24 Aug. 1H 1397/D8. Service historique de l'armée de terre, Vincennes, France.

Commissaire civil de Mostaganem. 1848. To directeur des affaires civiles à Oran. 26 Jan.

Carton 3U/1, Folder "1847–1848." Centre des Archives d'outre-mer, Aix-en-Provence, France.

Conan, Eric. 1998. *Le procès Papon: Un journal d'audience.* Paris: Gallimard.

Conesa, Gabriel. 1970. *Bab-el-Oued: Notre paradis perdu.* Paris: Robert Laffont.

Conklin, Alice L. 1997. *A Mission to Civilize: The Republican Idea of Empire in France and West Africa, 1895–1930.* Stanford, Calif.: Stanford Univ. Press.

Connelly, Matthew. 2002. *A Diplomatic Revolution: Algeria's Fight for Independence and the Origins of the Post-Cold War Era.* Oxford: Oxford Univ. Press.

Conrad, Joseph. [1902] 1991. *Heart of Darkness: An Authorative Text, Backgrounds and Sources, Criticism.* Edited by Roger Kimbrough. New York: W. W. Norton.

Consistoire central des Israélites de France. 1836. To ministre de la guerre, 12 Dec. F19 11143. Archives nationales, Paris.

Consistoire Israélite de la circonscription de Paris. 1843. To ministre de justice et des cultes. 26 Oct. Carton F19 11030. Archives nationales, Paris.

Consistoire Israélite de la Province d'Oran. 1848. To directeur des affaires civiles à Oran. 11 Apr. Carton 3/U1, folder "1847–1848." Centre des Archives d'outre-mer, Aix-en-Provence, France.

Cooke, George Wingrove. 1860. *Conquest and Colonisation in North Africa: Being the Substance of a Series of Letters from Algeria Published in the "Times" and Now by Permission Collected with Introduction and Supplement Containing the Most Recent French and Other Information on Morocco.* Edinburgh: William Blackwood and Sons.

Cornette, Joël, and Jean-Noël Luc. 1985. "Bac-Génération 84: L'enseignement du temps présent en terminale." *Vingtième siècle* 6 (Apr.-June): 103–30.

Côte, Marc. 1988. *L'Algérie, ou l'espace retourné.* Paris: Flammarion.

Coubertin, Pierre de. [1912] 1992. *Essais de psychologie sportive.* Reprint. Grenoble: Jérôme Millon.

Courrière, Raymond. 1985. Installation du conseil d'admininistration. 11 Jan. Sécrétariat d'état auprès du Ministère des affaires sociales et de la solidarité nationale chargé des rapatriés. 870444/1. Archives nationales, Paris.

Courrière, Yves. 1972. *La guerre d'Algérie* (film). Paris: Éditions Montparnasse.

Cousin, Lt.-Colonel. 1962. 2ème Bureau, Etat-Major InterArmées, Commandement Supérieur des Forces en Algérie. "Bulletin Hebdomadaire de renseignements. Semaine du 19 au 25 mai 1962. N. 1558/CSFA/EMI/2/OPE." 1H/1437/1. Service historique de l'armée de terre, Vincennes, France.

Créhange, Alexandre Ben Baruch. 1848. *Des droits et des devoirs du citoyen, instruction tirée de l'histoire sainte, ou entretiens d'un maître d'école avec ses elèves.* N.p.: n.p.

Crenshaw Hutchinson, Martha. 1978. *Revolutionary Terrorism: The FLN in Algeria 1954–1962.* Stanford, Calif.: Hoover Institution Press.

Curtis, Sarah. 2002. " 'Men Like Us': Missionary Sisters and Race Relations in Post-revolutionary France." Paper presented at the Annual Conference of the Society for French Historical Studies, Toronto.

Daeninckx, Didier. 1983. *Meurtres pour mémoire*. Paris: Série Noire.

Danner, Mark. 2004. *Torture and Truth: America, Abu Ghraib, and the War on Terror*. New York: New York Review of Books.

Davis, Fred. 1979. *Yearning for Yesterday: A Sociology of Nostalgia*. New York: Free Press.

Debèche, Djamila. 1947. *Leïla, jeune fille d'Alger*. N.p.: n.p.

"Dégageant la signification économique des fêtes du Centenaire, le ministre du commerce nous dit." 1930. *l'Echo d'Alger*, 12 Jan.

De la Gorce, Paul-Marie. 1962. "Alger: L'histoire de la trêve." *France-Observateur* 631 (7 June): 6–10.

Delanoue, Gilbert. 1998. "L'Arabe en Egypte 1800–1940: Histoire et idéologie." In *Langues et pouvoir, de l'Afrique du Nord à l'Extreme-Orient*, edited by Salem Chaker, 41–60. Aix-en-Provence, France: Edisud.

Delarue, Jacques. 1992. "La malédiction des enfants des harkis." *Matériaux pour l'histoire de notre temps* 26: 29–36.

Delassus, A. 1919. *Métropole et colonies: La conquête morale des indigènes*. Algiers: Librairie pour tous.

Deleuze, Gilles, and Felix Guattari. 1980. *Mille plateaux*. Paris: Minuit.

Derrida, Jacques. 1967a. *De la grammatologie*. Paris: Minuit.

———. 1967b. *L'ecriture et la différence*. Paris: Éditions du Seuil.

———. 1967c. "La structure, le signe, et le jeu dans le discours des sciences humaines." In *L'ecriture et la différence*, 409–28. Paris: Éditions du Seuil.

———. 1972. *Marges de la philosophie*. Paris: Minuit.

———. 1974. *Of Grammatology*. Translated by Gayatri Chakravorty Spivak. Baltimore: Johns Hopkins Univ. Press.

———. 1985. "Racism's Last Word." Translated by Peggy Kamuf. *Critical Inquiry* 12: 290–99.

———. 1988. *Limited Inc*. Translated by Samuel Weber. Evanston, Ill.: Northwestern Univ. Press.

———. 1991. "Circonfession." In *Jacques Derrida*, by Geoffrey Bennington and Jacques Derrida. Paris: Éditions du Seuil.

———. 1995. "Parti pris pour l'Algérie." *Les temps modernes* 580: 233–41.

———. 1996a. *Monolinguisme de l'autre, ou la prothès de l'origine*. Paris: Gallilée.

———. 1996b. "Oui, mes livres sont politiques." *Le nouvel observateur* 1633: 60–62.

———. 1998a. "An Interview with Jacques Derrida." *Cardozo Life*. Available at: http://www.cardozo.net/life/fall1998/derrida/.

———. 1998b. *Monolinguism of the Other; or, Prosthesis of Origin*. Translated by Patrick Mensah. Stanford, Calif.: Stanford Univ. Press.

———. 1999–2000. "Conversation avec Jacques Derrida." Available at the Wled El Bahdja Web site: http://www.multimania.com/farabi/conversation.html.

———. 2000. "Déclaration de J. Derrida." *Colloque "17 et 18 octobre 1961: Massacres d'Algériens sur ordonnance?*" 21 Oct. Available at: http://www.algeria-watch.de/farticle/ colloque/17octobre4.html.

Despiques, Paul, and Jean Garoby. 1930. *Le chef d'oeuvre colonial de la France: L'Algérie.* Algiers: Baconnier.

Desprez, Charles. 1860. *L'hiver à Alger: Lettre d'un compère à sa commère.* Meaux, France: A. Carro.

———. 1863. *Alger l'été.* Alger: Éditions de L'amateur.

Dessaigne, Francine. 1964. "*Déracinés!*" Paris: Éditions du Fuseau.

———. 1988. *Bordj bou Arreridj: L'insurrection de 1871.* Versailles: Éditions de l'Atlantide.

———. 1996. *Journal d'une mère de famille pied-noir: Alger 1960–62.* Paris: Éditions Confrérie Dastille.

Deville-Dantu, Bernadette. 1992a. "Les activités physiques et sportives dans l'empire français: Instrument de colonisation, outil de subversion?" In *L'empire du sport: Les sports dans les anciennes colonies françaises,* edited by Daniel Hick, 61–68. Aix-en-Provence, France: AMAROM.

———. 1992b. "L'AOF pépinière d'athlètes: Révélation, illusions et désillusions." In *Jeux et sports dans l'histoire,* edited by the Comité des travaux historiques et scientifiques (CTHS), 255–70. Paris: Éditions du CTHS.

———. 1992c. "Les jeux d'outre-mer." In *L'empire du sport: Les sports dans les anciennes colonies françaises,* edited by Daniel Hick, 11–13. Aix-en-Provence, France: AMAROM.

———. 1992d. "La participation des sportifs indigènes à l'Exposition Coloniale Internationale de Paris: Polémique autour du rôle du sport aux colonies." *Sport et histoire* 2 (new series): 9–26.

———. 1992e. "Les premières tentatives d'encadrement des activités physiques et sportives de la jeuness en A.O.F. (1922–1936)." In *Les jeunes en Afrique,* vol 2: *La politique et la ville,* edited by Hélène D'Almeida-Topor, 448–62. Paris: L'Harmattan.

———. 1997. *Le sport en noir et blanc: Du sport colonial au sport africain dans les anciens territoires français d'Afrique occidentale, 1920–1965.* Paris: L'Harmattan.

Dine, Philip. 1992. "*La France du tiercé:* Horse-Racing and Popular Gambling since 1954." In *Popular Culture and Mass Communication in Twentieth-Century France,* edited by Rosemary Chapman and Nicholas Hewitt, 181–206. Lampeter: Edwin Mellen Press.

———. 1994. *Images of the Algerian War: French Fiction and Film, 1954–1992.* Oxford: Clarendon Press.

———. 1996a. "Un héroïsme problématique: Le sport, la littérature et la guerre d'Algérie." *Europe* 806–7: 177–85.

———. 1996b. "Sport, Imperial Expansion, and Colonial Consolidation: A Comparison of the French and British Experiences." In *Sport as Symbol, Symbols in Sport,* edited by Floris van der Merwe, 63–69. Sankt Augustin, Germany: Academia Verlag.

———. 1997. "Trois regards étrangers: *Les oliviers de justice* de James Blue, *La bataille d'Alger* de Gillo Pontecorvo, *Les centurions* de Mark Robson." In *La guerre d'Algérie à l'écran,* special issue of *CinémAction* 85: 80–86.

———. 1998. "Sport and the State in Contemporary France: From *La charte des sports* to Decentralisation." *Modern and Contemporary France* 6, no. 3: 301–11.

———. 2000. "Sport and Identity in the New France." In *Contemporary French Cultural Studies,* edited by William Kidd and Siân Reynolds, 165–78. London: Arnold.

Diop, Moustapha. 1990. "Regards croisés." *Hommes et migrations* 1135: 34–38.

Directeur des affaires civiles, Oran. 1848a. To commissaire civil de Mostaganem, 5 Feb. Carton 3U/1, folder "1847–1848." Centre des Archives d'outre-mer, Aix-en-Provence, France.

———. 1848b. To gouverneur général d'Algérie, 27 May. Carton F80 1631. Centre des Archives d'outre-mer, Aix-en-Provence, France.

———. 1848c. To [Emanuel Menahim] Nahon, 7 Apr. Carton 3/U1, folder "1847–1848." Centre des Archives d'outre-mer, Aix-en-Provence, France.

Djait, Hichem. 1985. *Europe and Islam: Cultures and Modernity.* Translated by Peter Heinegg. Berkeley: Univ. of California Press.

Djebar, Assia. 1980. *Femmes d'Alger dans leur appartement.* Paris: Des Femmes.

———. [1985] 1995a. *L'amour, la fantasia.* Paris: Albin Michel. Translated into English by Dorothy Blair as *Fantasia: An Algerian Cavalcade.* Portsmouth: Heinemann, 1985, 1993.

———. 1995b. *Le blanc de l'Algérie.* Paris: Albin Michel.

———. 2000. *Algerian White.* Translated by David Kelley and Marjolijn de Jager. New York: Seven Stories Press.

Donadey, Anne. 2001. "Anamnesis and National Reconciliation: Re-membering October 17, 1961." In *Immigrant Narratives in Contemporary France,* edited by Susan Ireland and Patrice Proulx, 47–56. London: Greenwood Press.

Donato, Marc. 1985. *L'émigration des Maltais en Algérie au XIXème siècle.* Montpellier, France: Éditions Africa Nostra.

Dornier, François. 2000. *Les Catholiques en Tunisie au fils des jours.* Tunis: l'Imprimerie Finzi.

Douzon, Henri J. 1986. "Les occasions perdues." In *La guerre d'Algérie,* vol. 1: *De l'Algérie des origines à l'insurrection,* edited by Henri Alleg, 287–596. Paris: Éditions Messidor.

Droit, Michel. 1982. "Pour l'honneur d'un capitaine." *Figaro Magazine* (2 Oct.).

Droz, Bernard, and Evelyne Lever. 1982. *Histoire de la guerre d'Algérie* Paris: Éditions du Seuil.

Dubois, Charles. 1861. *Alger en 1861.* Algiers: A. Bourget.

Duchesne, Edouard Adolphe. 1853. *De la prostitution dans la ville d'Alger depuis la conquête.* Paris: J-B Ballière.

Dumay, Jean-Michel. 1998. *Le procès de Maurice Papon.* Paris: Fayard.

Duranton-Crabol, Anne-Marie. 1995. *Le temps de l'OAS.* Paris: Éditions Complexe.

Durmelat, Sylvie. 2000. "Transmission and Mourning in *Mémoires d'immigrés, l'heritage Maghrebin:* Yasmina Benguigui as 'Memory Entrepreneuse.' " In *Women, Immigration, and Identities in France,* edited by Jane Freedman and Carrie Tarr, 171–88. Oxford: Berg.

Edmond, R. 1997. *Representing the South Pacific: Colonial Discourse from Cook to Gauguin.* Cambridge: Cambridge Univ. Press.

Edney, Matthew H. 1990. *Mapping an Empire: The Geographical Construction of British India, 1765–1843.* Chicago: Univ. of Chicago Press.

Einaudi, Jean-Luc. 1991. *La bataille de Paris: 17 octobre 1961.* Paris: Éditions du Seuil.

———. 2001. *Octobre 1961: Un massacre à Paris.* Paris: Fayard.

Einaudi, Jean-Luc, and Elie Kagan. 2001. *17 Octobre 1961.* Paris: Actes sud.

Elon, Amos. 2002. "No Exit." *New York Review of Books,* 23 May.

Emerit, Marcel. 1949. "L'esprit de 1848 en Algérie." In *La Révolution de 1848 en Algérie: Mélanges d'histoire,* edited by Marcel Emerit, 115–32. Paris: Éditions Larose.

Englund, Steven. 1992. "Ghost of the Nation Past." *Journal of Modern History* 64 (June): 299–320.

"Entre 30 et 200 morts: L'impossible bilan." 2001. *Le Monde,* 16 Oct.

"Entretien avec Omar Boudaoud (ONM): 'La désintégration de l'unité nationale est le plus grave danger.' " 1992. *El Watan,* 14 Oct.

Evans, Martin. 1997. *The Memory of Resistance: French Opposition to the Algerian War (1954–1962).* Oxford: Berg.

Faivre, Maurice. 1994. *Un village de harkis.* Paris: L'Harmattan.

———. 1995. *Les combattants musulmans de la guerre d'Algérie.* Paris: Harmattan.

———. 2000. *Les archives inédites de la politque algérienne, 1958–1962.* Paris: L'Harmattan.

Fanon, Frantz. [1961] 1963. *The Wretched of the Earth.* Translated by Constance Farrington. New York: Grove Press.

———. [1952] 1967. *Black Skin, White Masks.* Translated by Charles Lam Markmann. New York: Grove Press.

Fathy, Safaa. 1999. *D'Ailleurs, Derrida* (film). New York: Icarus Films.

Fellous, Sonia, ed. 2003. *Juifs et musulmans en Tunisie: Fraternité et déchirements.* Paris: Somogy.

Feraoun, Mouloud. 1962. *Journal.* Paris: Editions du Seuil. Translated into English by Mary Ellen Wolf and Claude Fouillade. Lincoln: University of Nebraska Press, 2000.

Ferdi, Saïd. 1981. *Un enfant dans la guerre.* Paris: Éditions du Seuil.

Ferguson, Charles A. 1959. "The Arabic Koine." *Language* 35: 616–30.

———. 1991. "Diglossia Revisited." *Southwest Journal of Linguistics* 10, no. 1: 214–34.

Ferrié, Jean-Noël, and Gilles Boetsch. 1992. "Du Berbère aux yeux clairs à la race eurafricaine." In *Le Maghreb, l'Europe et la France,* edited by K. Basfao, 191–207. Paris: CNRS.

Ferro, Marc. 1994. *Histoire des colonisations: Des conquêtes aux indépendances XIIIe-XXe siècle.* Paris: Éditions du Seuil.

Feydeau, Ernest. 1862. *Alger: Etude*. Paris: Michel Lévy.

Figaro (newspaper). 1962–2001. Various, 23 May 1962; 26 Sept. 2001.

Flanders, Laura. 1998. "Algeria Unexamined." *On the Issues: The Progressive Woman's Quarterly* 7, no. 2: 24–28.

Foucault, Michel. 1978. *The History of Sexuality.* Vol. 1: *An Introduction*. Translated by Robert Hurley. New York: Random House.

———. 1991. *Discipline and Punish: The Birth of the Prison*. Translated by A. Sheridan. Harmondsworth. U.K.: Penguin.

La France islamique. 1913. 27 Mar.

Fraser, Nancy. 1984. "The French Derrideans: Politicizing Deconstruction or Deconstructing the Political?" *New German Critique* 33: 127–54.

French consul. 1837. To Morali, Tunis, 28 June. Série H, carton 206, dossier 85, armoire 21. Archives nationales de Tunisie, Tunis.

———. 1851a. To bey, 25 Aug., Tunis. Cartons 483, 484, cours beylicale. Archives diplomatiques d'outre-mer de Nantes, Tunis.

———. 1851b. To Bishop de Rosalia, 2 Dec., Tunis. 1er versement, cours beylicale, carton 483. Archives diplomatiques d'outre-mer de Nantes, Tunis.

———. 1851c. To the consul of Sardinia, 15 Sept., Tunis. Carton 483, cours beylicale. Archives diplomatiques d'outre-mer de Nantes, Tunis.

———. 1855–56. To bey, 3 Aug. 1855 and 8 July 1856, Tunis. Carton 484. Archives diplomatiques d'outre-mer de Nantes, Tunis.

———. 1873. To Khayr al-Din, 6 Dec. Série H, carton 207, dossier 105. Archives nationales de Tunisie, Tunis.

———. 1876. To Khayr al-Din, 11 Dec. Série H, carton 68, dossier 813, armoire 7. Archives nationales de Tunisie, Tunis.

Friedman, Elizabeth. 1988. *Colonialism and After: An Algerian Jewish Community.* South Hadley, Mass.: Bergin and Harvey.

Fromentin, Eugène. [1858] 1887. *Sahara et Sahel*. Paris: E. Plon, Nourrit et Cie.

Fussell, Paul. 1975. *The Great War and Modern Memory.* Oxford: Oxford Univ. Press.

Gacemi, Baya. 1998. *Moi, Nadia, femme d'un emir du GIA*. Paris: Éditions du Seuil.

Gacon, Stéphane. 1995. "Histoire d'une amnistie—l'amnistie de la guerre d'Algérie." In *Traces de la guerre d'Algérie: 40 ans de turbulence dans la vie politique française*, edited by Serge Wolikow, 15–34. Dijon: Éditions Univ. de Dijon.

———. 2000. "L'amnistie et la république en France: De la commune à la guerre d'Algérie." Thèse doctorat d'histoire, Institut d'études politiques.

Garcia, Alexander. 2001. "Entre 30 et 200 morts: L'impossible bilan." *Le Monde*, 16 Oct.

Gaspard, Françoise. 1995. *A Small City in France*. Translated by Arthur Goldhammer. Cambridge, Mass.: Harvard Univ. Press.

Gastau, Yvan. 2000. *L'immigration et l'opinion en France sous la Ve République*. Paris: Éditions du Seuil.

Gauthier, L. 1906. "La question indigène en Algérie." *Bulletin de la société de géographie de l'Afrique du Nord* 11, no. 11: 210–40.

Gautier, Théophile. [1845] 1973. *Voyage pittoresque en Algérie (1845).* Edited by Madeleine Cottin. Geneva: Librairie Droz.

Gay-Lescot, Jean-Louis. 1991. *Sport et éducation sous Vichy, 1940–1944.* Lyon: Presses Univ. de Lyon.

———. 1992. "Propagande par le sport: Vichy." In *L'empire du sport: Les sports dans les anciennes colonies françaises,* edited by Daniel Hick, 56–58. Aix-en-Provence, France: AMAROM.

Génériques. 1999. *Les etrangers en France: Guide des archives publiques et privées, xixe-xxe siècles.* 3 vols. Paris: Génériques, Direction des Archives de France.

Genestout, Lt-Col. 1962. "Bulletin de renseignement hebdomadaire. Semaine du 15 au 22 avril 1962. n. 1.394 CAC/2/INT-S." 1H/2836/1. Service historique de l'armée de terre, Vincennes, France.

Gerland, B. 2001. *Ma guerre d'Algérie.* Villeurbanne, France: Éditions Golias.

Ghoualmi, Mohamed. 2001. "France-Algérie: Match révélateur." *Le Monde,* 13 Oct.

Gildea, Robert. 2000. "The Resistance Myth, the Pétainist Myth, and Other Voices." In *Remembering and Representing the Experience of War in Twentieth-Century France: Committing to Memory,* edited by Debra Kelly, 27–48. Studies in French Civilization, vol. 20. Lewiston, N.Y.: Edwin Mellen Press.

Glanz, James. 2004. "Torture Is Often a Temptation and Almost Never Works." *New York Times,* 9 May.

Glissant, Edouard. 1981. *Le discours antillais.* Paris: Éditions du Seuil.

———. 1989. *Caribbean Discourse.* Translated by Michael Dash. Charlottesville: Univ. Press of Virginia.

Golsan, Richard J., ed. 1996. *Memory, the Holocaust, and French Justice.* Hanover, N.H.: Univ. of New England Press.

———, ed. 2000. *The Papon Affair: Memory and Justice on Trial.* New York: Routledge.

Gouvernement général civil de l'Algérie. 1876. Correspondence with the ministre de l'intérieur in Paris, 18 Apr., 23 May, and 26 May. F 80 1816. Centre des Archives d'outre-mer, Aix-en-Provence, Algérie.

Gouvernement général de l'Algérie. 1954. *Exposé de la situation générale de l'Algérie en 1953.* Algiers: Gouvernement général de l'Algérie.

Gouverneur général d'Algérie. 1848a. To directeur général des affaires civiles à Oran. 22 Feb. Carton 3U/1, folder "1847–1848." Centre des Archives d'outre-mer, Aix-en Provence, France.

———. 1848b. To directeur général des affaires civiles à Oran. 16 Aug. Carton 3U/1, folder "1847–1848." Centre des Archives d'outre mer, Aix-en-Provence.

Gramsci, Antonio. [1949] 1996. *Prison Notebooks.* New York: Columbia Univ. Press.

"Grandes fêtes sahariennes." 1930. *Afrique du Nord illustrée,* 3 May.

Grandguillaume, Gilbert. 1983. *Arabisation et politique linguistique au Maghreb.* Paris: Éditions Maisonneuve et Larose.

———. 1990. "Language and Legitimacy in the Maghreb." In *Language Policy and Political Development,* edited by Brian Weinstein, 150–66. Mahwah, N.J.: Ablex.

———. 1991. "Les aléas de l'arabisation." In *L'etat du Maghreb,* 399–402. Paris: Découverte.

Grant, James. 1844. *Paris and Its People.* London: Saunders and Otley.

Greffou, Malika Boudalia. 1989. *L'école algérienne de Ibn Badis à Pavlov.* Algiers: Laphomic.

Guerdjou, Bourlem. 1998. *Vivre au paradis* (film). Paris: Arte Video.

Guérin, Victor. 1895. *La France catholique en Tuisie, à Malte et en Tripolitaine.* Tours, France: Alfred Mame.

Guibert, N. 2000. "L'école fait face à une montée des revendications identitaires des élèves." *Le Monde,* 15 Apr.

Guilhaume, Jean-François. 1992. *Les mythes fondateurs de l'Algérie française.* Paris: L'Harmattan.

Guterman, Lila. 2005. "Researchers Who Rushed into Print a Study of Iraqi Civilian Deaths Now Wonder Why It Was Ignored." *Chronicle of Higher Education,* 27 Jan.

Habermas, Jürgen. 1987. "Beyond a Temporalized Philosophy of Origins: Jacques Derrida's Critique of Phonocentrism." In *The Philosophical Discourse of Modernity: Twelve Lectures,* translated by Frederick G. Lawrence, 161–84. Cambridge, Mass.: MIT Press.

Hadj Hamou, Abdelkader. 1925. *Zohra, la femme du mineur.* Paris: n.p.

Hakem, Tewfik. 2004a. "Populaire jusqu'au Pentagone, toujours sulfureux en France." *Le Monde,* 13 May.

———. 2004b. "Yacef Saâdi, commandant et producteur." *Le Monde,* 13 May.

Halbwachs, Maurice. [1925] 1975. *Les cadres sociaux de la mémoire.* 3d ed. La Haye: Mouton. Issued in English as *On Collective Memory.* Translated by Lewis A. Coser. Chicago: Univ. of Chicago Press, 1992.

Hamel, L. 1890. "De la naturalisation des indigènes musulmans en Algérie." *La revue algérienne et tunisienne de législation et de jurisprudence.* Reprinted under the same title. Algiers: Jourdan.

Hamoumou, Mohand. 1993. *Et ils sont devenus harkis.* Paris: Fayard.

Harbi, Mohamed. [1980] 1993. *Le FLN, mirage et réalité.* Paris: Éditions Jeune Afrique; reprint, Algiers: ENAL.

———. 2004. "*La bataille d'Alger* de Gillo Pontecorvo." *Le monde diplomatique* (May).

Hargreaves, Alec G. 1989. "Resistance and Identity in Beur Narratives." *Modern Fiction Studies* 35, no. 1: 87–102.

———. 2002. "Introduction: France and Algeria, 1962–2002: Turning the Page?" *Modern and Contemporary France* 10: 445–47.

Hargreaves, Alec G., and Michael J. Heffernan, eds. 1993. *French and Algerian Identities from Colonial Times to the Present: A Century of Interaction.* Lewiston, N.Y.: Edwin Mellen Press.

Haroun, Ali. 1986. *La 7e wilaya: La guerre du FLN en France, 1954–1962.* Paris: Éditions du Seuil.

H. C. de Paris. 1962. "Nos lecteurs écrivent. Pourquoi cet exode?" *France-Observateur* 629 (24 May): 2.

Henry, Jean-Robert. 1987. "La norme et l'imaginaire: La construction de l'altérité en droit colonial algérien." *Procès* 18.

———. 1993. "Introduction." In *French and Algerian Identities from Colonial Times to the Present: A Century of Interaction,* edited by Alec G. Hargreaves and Michael J. Heffernan, 1–20. Lewiston, N.Y.: Edwin Mellen Press.

Hersh, Seymour M. 2004. *Chain of Command: The Road from 9/11 to Abu Ghraib.* New York: Harper Collins.

Hervo, Monique. 2001a. *Chroniques du bidonville: Nanterre en guerre d'Algérie.* Paris: Éditions du Seuil.

———. 2001b. *La folie et la guerre d'Algérie 1956.* Paris: Éditions du Seuil.

Herzberg, Nathaniel. 1999. "Trente-cinq ans de mensonge official sur les crimes policiers de 1961." *Le Monde,* 13 Aug.

Heurgon, Marc. 1994. *Histoire du PSU. 1. La fondation et la guerre d'Algérie 1958–62.* Paris: Découverte.

Hick, Daniel, ed. 1992. *L'empire du sport: Les sports dans les anciennes colonies françaises.* Aix-en-Provence, France: AMAROM.

Higonnet, Margaret, ed. 1987. *Behind the Lines: Gender and the Two World Wars.* New Haven, Conn.: Yale Univ. Press.

Hodgkin, Katherine, and Susannah Radstone, eds. 2003. *Contested Pasts: The Politics of Memory.* New York: Routledge.

Holt, Richard. 1981. *Sport and Society in Modern France.* London: Macmillan.

Horne, Alistair. [1977] 1978. *A Savage War of Peace: Algeria, 1954–1962.* London: Macmillan; reprint, New York: Viking.

Houari, Leïla. 1985. *Zeida de nulle part.* Paris: L'Harmattan.

Huffer, Lynne. 1998. *Maternal Pasts, Feminist Futures: Nostalgia, Ethics, and the Question of Difference.* Stanford, Calif.: Stanford Univ. Press.

Humanité. 2001. Various, 29 Aug., 26 and 29 Sept.

Hureau, Joëlle. 1987. *La mémoire des pieds-noirs.* Paris: Olivier Orban.

Hutin, P. 1933. *La doctrine de l'association des indigènes et des Français en Algérie.* Paris: F. Loviton.

Hyam, Ronald. 1990. *Empire and Sexuality: The British Experience.* Manchester: Manchester Univ. Press.

"Il n'y a pas assez de Français" (editorial). 1962. *Paris-Match* 681 (28 Apr.): 7.

Imache, Tassadit. 1989. *Une fille sans histoire.* Paris: Calmann-Lévy.

"Inauguration à Paris d'un monument à la mémoire des victimes civiles et militaires tombées en Afrique du Nord de 1952 à 1962." 1996. Available at: MACROBUTTON HtmlResAnchor at http://www.elysee.fr/cgi-bin/auracom/aurweb.

Inglis, Fred. 1977. *The Name of the Game: Sport and Society.* London: Heinemann.

Jarnoux, Maurice. 1962. Photo in *Paris-Match* 686: 1.

Jessop, Thomas. 1928. *Journal d'un voyage à Paris en septembre-octobre 1820*. Edited by F. C. W. Hiley. Paris: Honoré Champion.

Jews of Mostaganem. 1848. Petition to gouverneur général d'Algerie Duc d'Aumale. 18 Feb. Carton 3U/1, folder "Batiments Civils-Mostaganem." Centre des Archives d'outre-mer, Aix-en-Provence, France.

Jews of Oran. 1848. Petition to Général Cavaignac, gouverneur général d'Algérie. 1 Apr. Carton 3U/1, folder "1847–1848." Centre des Archives d'outre-mer, Aix-en-Provence, France.

Jolly, Rosemary. 1995. "Rehearsals of Liberation: Contemporary Postcolonial Discourse and the New South Africa." *PMLA* 110, no. 1: 17–29.

Joly, Danièle. 1991. *The French Communist Party and the Algerian War*. New York: St. Martin's Press.

Jordi, Jean-Jacques. 1993. *De l'exode à l'exil: Rapatriés et pieds-noirs en France. L'exemple marseillais*. Paris: L'Harmattan.

———. 1995. *1962: L'arrivée des pieds-noirs*. Paris: Autrement.

———. 2002. "Les pieds-noirs: Constructions identitaires et reinvention des origins." *Hommes et migrations* 1236: 14–25.

Jordi, Jean-Jacques, and Mohand Hamoumou. 1999. *Les harkis: Une mémoire enfouie*. Paris: Autrement.

Jordi, Jean-Jacques, and Emile Temime, eds. 1996. *Marseille et le choc des décolonisations*. Aix-en-Provence, France: Edisud.

Journal de l'Union nationale des anciens combatants. 1990. Vol. 13 (Jan.).

Journal official de la République Française. 1962. Various volumes.

"Journée de l'émigration: Le peuple solidaire avec la communauté émigrée." 1989. *Révolution africaine* 1338 (27 Oct.): 18.

"Journée nationale de l'émigration, par-delà le symbole." 1990. *Actualité de l'émigration* 207 (17 Oct.): 21.

Joutard, P. 1995. "L'enseignement de l'histoire." In *L'histoire et le métier d'historien en France 1945–1995*, edited by Francois Bedarida, 45–56. Paris: Éditions de la Maison des sciences de l'homme.

Juchereau de Saint-Denys, Comte de. 1934. *Le miracle des sables*. Paris: Eugène Figuière.

Judt, Tony. 1992. *Past Imperfect: French Intellectuals 1944–56*. Berkeley: Univ. of California Press.

Julien, Charles-André. 1961. "Introduction." In *Les Français d'Algérie*, by Pierre Nora, 7–35. Paris: Julliard.

———. 1964. *Histoire de l'Algérie contemporaine: Conquète et les debuts de la colonisation (1827–1871)*. Paris: Presses Univ. de France.

Kaberseli, Ahmed. 1996. *Requiem pour un massacre*. Paris: Éditions Publibook.

Kahina. 1976. "Pour que les larmes de nos mères deviennent une légende." Unpublished play.

Kajman, M. 1992. "L'Algérie de la deuxième mémoire: Des historiens encombrés." *Le Monde*, 17 Mar.

Kalaouaz, Ahmed. 1986. *Point kilométrique 190.* Paris: L'Harmattan.

Kaplan, Harvey A. 1987. "The Psychopathology of Nostalgia." *Psychoanalytical Review* 74, no. 4: 465–86.

Kara, Bouzid. 1984a. "Entretien avec Bouzid Kara: 'Après la phase gentille de la Marche confronter la réalité sur le terrain. . . . ' Propos recueillis par Malika Boutahra et Mogniss H. Abdallah." *IM'média magazine* 1 (autumn): 9–11.

———. 1984b. *La marche.* Paris: Sindbad.

Kaufman, Michael T. 2003. "What Does the Pentagon See in *Battle of Algiers?*" *New York Times,* 7 Sept.

Kazdaghli, Habib, ed. 1993. *Mémoire de femmes: Tunisiennes dans la vie publique, 1920–1960.* Tunis: Édition Média Com.

Kenbib, Mohammed. 1996. *Les protégés: Contribution à l'histoire contemporaine du Maroc.* Rabat: Publications de la Faculté des lettres et des sciences humaines.

Kennedy, Dane. 1990. "The Perils of the Midday Sun: Climatic Anxieties in the Colonial Tropics." In *Imperialism and the Natural World,* edited by John M. MacKenzie, 118–40. Manchester: Univ. of Manchester Press.

Kepel, Gilles. 1987. *Les banlieues de l'Islam: Naissance d'une religion en France.* Paris: Éditions du Seuil.

Kessas, Ferrudja. 1989. *Beur's Story.* Paris: L'Harmattan.

Kettane, Nacer. 1985. *Le sourire de Brahim.* Paris: Denoël.

Khalfa, Boualem, Henry Alleg, and Abdelhamid Benzine. 1987. *La grande aventure d'Alger républicain.* Paris: Éditions Messidor.

Khatibi, Abdelkebir. 1971. *La mémoire tatouée.* Paris: Les lettres nouvelles.

———. 1983. *Amour bilingue.* Paris: Fata Morgana.

Khodja, Chukri. 1929. *El euldj, captif de Barbaresques.* Prix Littéraire de la Sociéte des Artistes Africains. Arras: INSAP.

———. [1928] 1992. *Mamoun, l'ébauche d'un ideal.* Paris: Éditions Radot; reprint, Algiers: OPU.

Koch, Capt. 1962a. Commandant de la Compagnie de Gendarmerie d'Oran. "Annexe à joindre au rapport n. 555/4 du juin 1962. REF: Note d'orientation n. 2826/CGA/2B/5 du 28 mai Oran." 1H/3086/1. Service historique de l'armée de terre, Vincennes, France.

———. 1962b. Commandant de la Compagnie de Gendarmerie d'Oran. "Rapport . . . sur les événements survenus pendant la periode du 16 juin au 31 juin [*sic,* should read "May"] 1962. n. 555/4." Oran. 1H/3086/1. Service historique de l'armée de terre, Vincennes, France.

Kristeva, Julia. 1974. *La révolution du langage poétique.* Paris: Éditions du Seuil.

Kundera, Milan. 1980. *The Book of Laughter and Forgetting.* New York: Knopf.

Lacheraf, Mostefa. 1963. "L'avenir de la culture algérienne." *Les temps modernes* 19, no. 209: 720–45.

———. 1964. "Réflexions sociologiques sur le nationalisme et la culture en Algérie." *Les temps modernes* 19, no. 214: 1629–660.

Lacouture, Jean. 2001. "13 Sept. 1991: Un massacre honteux pour la France et pour l'Algérie." *Télérama: Libération* (30 Aug.).

Lallaoui, Mehdi. [1981] 1986. *Les beurs de Seine.* Paris: Arcantère.

———. 1989. *20 ans d'affiches antiracistes.* Paris: Association black, blanc, beur.

———. 1993. *Du bidonville aux HLM.* Paris: Syros and Au nom de la mémoire.

———. 1994. *Kabyles du Pacifique.* Bezons, France: Au nom de la mémoire.

———. 1995. *Kabyles du Pacifique* (film). Bezons, France: Au nom de la mémoire.

———. [1995] 1998. *La colline aux oliviers.* Paris: Éditions alternatives, SEDAG.

———. 2001a. Interview by Richard Derderian. Paris, 19 June.

———. 2001b. *Une nuit d'octobre: Roman.* Paris: Éditions alternatives.

Lallaoui, Mehdi, and David Assouline. 1996a. *Un siècle d'immigrations en France.* Vol. 1: *De la mine au champ de bataille, 1851–1918.* Paris: Syros and Au nom de la mémoire.

———. 1996b. *Un siècle d'immigrations en France.* Vol. 2: *De l'usine au maquis, 1920–1945.* Paris: Syros and Au nom de la mémoire.

———. 1997. *Un siècle d'immigrations en France.* Vol. 3: *De 1945 à nos jours.* Paris: Syros and Au nom de la mémoire.

———, eds. 2001. *A propos d'octobre 1961: Etat des connaissances.* Bezons, France: Au nom de la mémoire.

Lallaoui, Mehdi, and Agnès Denis. 1991. *Le silence du fleuve* (film). Bezons, France: Au nom de la mémoire.

Lallaoui, Mehdi, and Bernard Langlois. 1995. *Les massacres de Sétif* (film). Bezons, France: Au nom de la mémoire.

Lallemand, Charles. 1890. *Tunis et ses environs.* Paris: Maison Quantin.

Lanfranchi, Pierre. 1994. "Mekloufi, un footballeur français dans la guerre d'Algérie." *Actes de la recherche en sciences sociales* 103: 70.

Lanfranchi, Pierre, and Alfred Wahl. 1996. "The Immigrant as Hero: Kopa, Mekloufi, and French Football." In *European Heroes: Myth, Identity, Sport,* edited by Richard Holt, J. A. Mangan, and Pierre Lanfranchi, 114–27. London: Frank Cass.

Laraoui, Abdallah. 1995. *L'histoire du Maghreb: Un essai de synthèse.* Casablanca: Centre culturel arabe.

Larguèche, Abdelhamid. 1999. *Les ombres de la ville: Pauvres, marginaux et minoritaires à Tunis (XVIIIème et XIXème siècles).* Tunis: Centre de publication univ.

Lazreg, Marnia. 1984. "The Reproduction of Colonial Ideology: The Case of the Kabyle Berbers." *Arab Studies Quarterly* 5, no. 4: 380–95.

Le Cour Grandmaison, Olivier. 2001. *Le 17 octobre 1961: Un crime d'etat à Paris.* Paris: La Dispute.

Lenzini, José. 1987. *L'Algérie de Camus.* Aix-en-Provence, France: Edisud.

Le Sueur, James. 2001. *Uncivil War: Intellectuals and Identity Politics during the Decolonization of Algeria.* Philadelphia: Univ. of Pennsylvania Press.

———. 2002. "Ghost Walking in Algiers? Why Alek Baylee Toumi Resurrected Sartre and de Beauvoir." *Modern and Contemporary France* 10: 507–17.

Leune, Jean. 1930. *Le miracle algérien.* Paris: Berger-Levrault.

Levine, Michel. 1985. *Les ratonnades d'octobre: Un meurtre collectif à Paris en 1961.* Paris: Ramsay.

Lewes, Darby. 1993. "Nudes from Nowhere: Pornography, Empire, and Utopia." *Utopian Studies* 4, no. 2: 66–73.

Liauzu, Claude. 1999. "Le 17 octobre 1961: Guerres de mémoires, archives réservées, et questions d'histoire." *Cahiers d'histoire immédiate* 15 (spring): 24.

Lionnet, Françoise. 1998. "Immigration, Poster Art, and Transgressive Citizenship: France, 1968–1988." In *Borders, Exiles, Diasporas,* edited by Elazar Barkan and Marie-Denise Shelton, 197–216. Stanford, Calif.: Stanford Univ. Press.

Le livre blanc de l'armée française en Algérie. 2001. Paris: Éditions contretemps.

Lorcin, Patricia M. E. [1995] 1999a. *Imperial Identities: Stereotyping Race and Prejudice in Colonial Algeria.* New York: St. Martin's Press; reprint, London: I. B. Tauris.

———. 1999b. "Imperialism, Colonial Identity, and Race in Algeria, 1830–1870: The Role of the French Medical Corps." *Isis* 90: 653–79.

———. 2002. "Rome and France in Africa: Recovering Colonial Algeria's Latin Past." *French Historical Studies* 25, 2: 295–329.

Lowe, Lisa. 1991. *Critical Terrains: French and British Orientalisms.* Ithaca, N.Y.: Cornell Univ. Press.

"La Lutte en terre ennemie." 1993. *El Moudjahid,* 17 Oct.

Machuel, M. Louis. 1885. *Rapport adressé à M. le Ministre Résident de la République Française à Tunis.* Tunis: Borrel.

———. 1889. *L'enseignement public dans la régence de Tunis.* Paris: Imprimerie nationale.

MacMaster, Neil. 1993. "Patterns of Emigration, 1905–1954: 'Kabyles' and 'Arabs.' " In *French and Algerian Identities from Colonial Times to the Present,* edited by Alec G. Hargreaves and Michael J. Heffernan, 21–38. Lewiston, N.Y.: Edwin Mellen Press.

———. 1997. *Colonial Migrants and Racism: Algerians in France, 1900–1962.* New York: St. Martin's Press.

———. 2002. "The Torture Controversy (1998–2002): Towards a 'New History' of the Algerian War?" *Modern and Contemporary France* 10: 449–59.

Maier, Charles S. 1993. "A Surfeit of Memory? Reflections on History, Melancholy, and Denial." *History and Memory* 5, no. 2: 136–51.

Mailhé, Germaine. 1995. *Déportation en Nouvelle-Calédonie des communards et des révoltés de la Grande Kabylie: 1872–1876.* Paris: L'Harmattan.

Makaci, M. 1936. *La faillite de la naturalisation individuelle en Algérie.* Mostaganem, Algeria: Impr. de l'Aïn Sefra.

Malley, Robert. 1996. *The Call from Algeria: Third Worldism, Revolution, and the Turn to Islam.* Berkeley: Univ. of California Press.

Malley, Simon. 2001. "Pourquoi Washington se rapproche d'Alger?" *Le nouvel Afrique Asie.* Available at: http://www.algeriawatch.de/farticle/analyse/washington_alger.htm.

Mangan, J. A., ed. 1992. *The Cultural Bond: Sport, Empire, Society.* London: Frank Cass.

Marchaut, C. 1999. "Cela me fait mal au coeur qu'on oublie ça" (interview). *Hommes et migrations* 1219 (May-June): 62.

Marion, George. 1991. "La commémoration de la 'ratonnade' du 17 octobre 1961 à Alger, un recueillement douloureux." *Le Monde,* 19 Oct.

Marmier, Xavier. 1847. *Lettres sur l'Algérie.* Paris: A. Bertrand.

Marrouchi, Mustapha. 1997. "Decolonizing the Terrain of Western Theoretical Productions." *College Literature* 24, no. 2: 1–34.

Marseille, J., ed. 1998. *Histoire terminales.* Paris: Nathan.

Martin, Claude. 1936. *Les Israélites Algériens de 1830 à 1902.* Paris: Herakles.

———. 1963. *Histoire de l'Algérie francaise, 1830–1962.* Paris: Éditions des 4 fils Aymon.

Martin, Phyllis M. 1991. "Colonialism, Youth, and Football in French Equatorial Africa." *International Journal of the History of Sport* 8, no. 1: 56–71.

Marty, Paul. 1948. "Les Algériens à Tunis." *Revenue de l'Institut des belles lettres arabes* 11: 301–32.

Marx, Karl. 1926. *The 18th Brumaire of Louis Bonaparte.* Translated by Edean Paul and Cedar Paul. New York: International.

Mary, Jean-Paul. 2001. *Sur l'Algérie.* Paris: Nil.

Mathy, Jean-Philippe. 2000. *French Resistance: The French-American Culture Wars.* Minneapolis: Univ. of Minnesota Press.

McClintock, Anne. 1995. *Imperial Leather: Race, Gender, and Sexuality in the Colonial Conquest.* New York: Routledge.

McDougall, James. 2002. " 'Soi-même' come 'un autre': Les histories coloniales d'Ahmad Tawfiq al'Madani (1899–1983)." In *Débats intellectuals au Moyen-Orient dans l'entre-deux-guerres,* special issue of *Revue des mondes musulmans et de la Méditerranné* 95–98: 95–110.

Meddeb, Abdelwahab. 1995. "L'interruption généalogique." *Esprit* 208: 74–82.

Mélia, Jean. 1930a. "L'humiliante platitude." *La presse libre,* 2 Feb.

———. 1930b. "Une lettre de M. Jean Mélia à M. André Tardieu. L'oeuvre néfaste du Commissariat général du Centenaire de l'Algérie." *La presse libre,* 11 Jan.

———. 1930c. "L'oeuvre néfaste: La plus dangereuse erreur du Commissariat général du centenaire." *La presse libre,* 4 Mar.

Méliani, Abd-el-Aziz. 1993. *La France honteuse-le drame des harkis.* Paris: Perrin.

———. 1995. Interview on TF 1 Television. 21 Sept.

Mellen, Joan. 1975. *Film Guide to* The Battle of Algiers. Bloomington: Indiana Univ. Press.

Melman, Billie. 1998. *Borderlines: Genders and Identities in War and Peace 1870–1930.* New York: Routledge.

Melnik, Constanin. 1988. *Mille jours à Matignon: Raisons d'état sous de Gaulle, guerre d'Algérie 1959–1962.* Paris: Bernard Grasset.

"La mémoire des Français a été selective." 1991. *El Watan,* 17 Oct.

Mémoire et enseignement de la guerre d'Algérie: Actes du colloque, 13–14 mars 1992, Paris. 1993. Paris: Institut du monde arabe and Ligue de l'enseignement.

Messaoudi, Alain. 1996. "Du vulgarisateur à l'expert: Louis Machuel et Léon Bercher, deux savants orientalists au service de la France (1883–1955)." In *Astrolabe 1. Actes du Congrès de l'Afemam-Eurames,* Aix-en—Provence, France.

Messaoudi, Khalida. 1998. *Unbowed: An Algerian Woman Confronts Islamic Fundamentalism.* Translated by Anne C. Vila. Philadelphia: Univ. of Pennsylvania Press.

Messud, Claire. 1999. *The Last Life: A Novel.* New York: Harcourt, Brace.

Miller, C. L. 1993. "Nationalism as Resistance." *Yale French Studies* 82: 62–100.

Mimoun, Alain. 2000. "Alain Mimoun: Tout pour la France!" Interview by Karim Belal. *Hommes et migrations* 1226: 44–49.

Ministre de la guerre. 1839. To ministre de justice et des cultes. 6 Nov. F 19 11143. Archives nationales, Paris.

["M. Jean Leune"] (editorial). 1930. *Annales africaines* (15 Feb.): 4.

Moatassime, Ahmed. 1992. *Arabisation et langue francaise au Maghreb: Un aspect sociolinguistique des dilemmes du développement.* Paris: Presses Univ. de France.

———. 1996. "Islam, arabization et francophonie: Une interface possible à l'interrogation 'Algérie-France-Islam'?" *Confluences en Méditerrannée* 19: n.p.

Le Monde. 1962–2001. Various: 24 May, 13 Nov. 1962; 20 June 1963; 4 July 1973; 18 July 1995; 18–19 June, 16–17 July 2000; 8 Feb., 29 Aug., 31 Aug., 26 Sept. 2001.

Monicat, Bénédicte. 1996. *Itinéraires de l'écriture au féminin: Voyageuses du 19e siècle.* Amsterdam: Rodopi.

Montherlant, Henry de. 1982. *Romans et oeuvres de fiction non-théâtrales.* Paris: Gallimard.

Moss, Jane. 1999. "Postmodernizing the Salem Witchcraze: Maryse Condé's *I, Tituba, Black Witch of Salem.*" *Colby Quarterley* 35, no. 1 (Mar.): 5–17.

Mosse, George. 1990. *Fallen Soldiers: Reshaping the Memory of the World Wars.* Oxford: Oxford Univ. Press.

Mouffok, Ghania. 2000. "Une amnésie suicidaire: Mémoire meurtrie de la société algérienne." *Le monde diplomatique* (June).

Mounsi. 1984. "Bâtard." In *Seconde génération* (recording). Paris: Éditions Labrador.

———. 1994. Interview by Richard Derderian. Paris, 4 Jan.

Muller, Laurent. 1998. "Le travail de la mémoire au sein des familles de français musulmans rapatriés en Alsace." 2 vols. Thèse de doctorat, Université de Strasbourg.

———. 1999. *Le silence des harkis.* Paris: L'Harmattan.

Mundy, Jacob. 2001. "The Algerian Connection." *Eat the State* 21. Available at: http://www.algeria-watch.de/farticle/connection.htm.

Nahon, Emanuel Menahim. 1848a. To directeur des affaires civiles, 4 Feb. Carton 3U/1, folder "1847–1848." Centre des Archives d'outre-mer, Aix-en-Provence, France.

———. 1848b. To directeur des affaires civiles, 29 Mar. Carton 3/U1, folder "1847–1848." Centre des Archives d'outre-mer, Aix-en-Provence, France.

———. 1848c. To directeur des affaires civiles, 22 May. Carton 3/U1, folder "1847–1848." Centre des Archives d'outre-mer, Aix-en-Provence, France.

Nandy, Ashis. 1983. *The Intimate Enemy: Loss and Recovery of Self under Colonialism.* Delhi: Oxford Univ. Press.

Nation (newspaper). 1962. 23 May.

Naylor, Phillip C. 2000. *France and Algeria: A History of Decolonization and Transformation.* Gainesville: Univ. Press of Florida.

Newton, Adam Zachary. 1995. *Narrative Ethics.* Cambridge, Mass.: Harvard Univ. Press.

Nochlin, Linda. 1989. *The Politics of Vision: Essays on Nineteenth-Century Art and Society.* New York: Harper and Row.

Noirfontaine, Pauline de. 1856. *Algérie: Un regard écrit.* Le Havre: Imprimerie Alph. Lemale.

Noiriel, Gérard. 1988. *Le creuset français: Histoire de l'immigration, XIXe-XXe siècle.* Paris: Éditions du Seuil.

Nora, Pierre. 1961. *Les Français d'Algérie.* Paris: Julliard.

———. 1989. "Between Memory and History: *Les lieux de memoire.*" *Representations* 26 (spring): 7–25.

———, ed. 1992. *Les lieux de mémoire.* 3 vols. Paris: Gallimard.

———. 1996a. "Between Memory and History." In *Realms of Memory: Rethinking the French Past,* edited by Pierre Nora and translated by Arthur Goldhammer, 1–23. New York: Columbia Univ. Press.

———. 1996b. "From *Lieux de mémoire* to *Realms of Memory.*" In *Realms of Memory: Rethinking the French Past,* edited by Pierre Nora and translated by Arthur Goldhammer, x-xxiv. New York: Columbia Univ. Press.

———, ed. 1996c. *Realms of Memory: Rethinking the French Past.* Translated by Arthur Goldhammer. New York: Columbia Univ. Press.

———. 2000. Interview by Richard Derderian. Paris, 7 Dec.

Norindr, Panivong. 1996. *Phantasmatic Indochina: French Colonial Ideology in Architecture, Film, and Literature.* Durham, N.C.: Duke Univ. Press.

Nouschi, André. 1995. *L'Algérie amère, 1914–1994.* Paris: Éditions de la Maison des sciences de l'homme.

"Octobre à Paris." 1988. *Actualité de l'émigration* 147 (Oct.): 40–41.

O'Donnell, Hugh, and Neil Blain. 1999. "Performing the Carmagnole: Negotiating French National Identity during France 98." *Journal of European Area Studies* 7, no. 2: 211–25.

Ofrat, Gideon. 2001. *The Jewish Derrida.* Syracuse, N.Y.: Syracuse Univ. Press.

Organisation armée sécrète (OAS) Zone III. 1962. "Texte de l'émission réalisée sur les ondes de la TV le 16/6." 1H/3167/1. Service historique de l'armée de terre, Vincennes, France.

Ory, Pascal. 1990. "L'Algérie fait écran." In *La guerre d'Algérie et les Français,* edited by Jean-Pierre Rioux, 572–81. Paris: Fayard.

Ould Cheikh, Mohammed. [1936] 1985. *Myriem dans les palmes.* Oran, Algeria: Plaza; reprint, Algiers: OPU.

Pancrazi, Noël. 1995. *Madame Arnoul.* Paris: Gallimard.

Papon, Maurice. 1988. *Les chevaux du pouvoir: Le préfet de police du Général de Gaulle ouvre ses dossiers 1958–1967.* Paris: Plon.

Parat, for Biget, préfet de police d'Oran. 1962. "Note à l'attention de M. le Ministre, le 21 mai." 770346/08. Centre de Archives contemporaines, Archives nationales, Aix-en-Provence, France.

Pedersen, Susan. 1993. *Family Policy and the Origins of the Welfare State: Britain and France, 1914–45.* London: Cambridge Univ. Press.

Péju, Paulette. 1961a. *Les harkis à Paris.* Paris: François Maspero.

———. 1961b. *Ratonnades à Paris.* Paris: François Maspero.

Pélégri, Jean. 1989. *Ma mère l'Algérie.* Algiers: Laphomic; Arles, France: Actes sud.

Pereira, Acacio. 1999. "Des témoins évoquent un carnage lors de la manifestation du 17 octobre 1961." *Le Monde,* 13 Feb.

Pervillé, Guy. 1984. *Les étudiants Algériens de l'Université francaise, 1880–1962: Populisme et nationalisme ches le etudiants et intellectuals musulmans Algériens de formation française.* Paris: CNRS.

———. 1986. Untitled speech given at Les Agoras Méditerranéennes, Marseilles, 26–29 Oct. 1983. *Historiens et géographes* 308 (Mar.): 887–924.

———. 1995. "Manifestation du 17 octobre 1961." *Dictionnaire historique de la vie politique française au xxe siècle,* edited by Jean-François Sirinelli, 622–24. Paris: Presses Univ. de France.

———. 1999. "La tragédie des Harkis: Qui est responsable?" *Histoire* 231: 64–67.

Pervillé, Guy, and P. Fournier. 1986. "La guerre d'Algérie dans les manuels scolaires de terminale." *Historiens et géographes* 308 (Mar.): 893–98.

Peyrefitte, Alain. 1994. *C'était de Gaulle.* Paris: Fayard.

Peyrot, J. 1990. "Aux chocs de la vie." *Historiens et géographes* 328 (July-Aug.): 9–13.

Pfister, Christian. 2002. *Am Tag Danach; Zur Bewaltigung von Naturkatastrophen in der Schweiz 1500–2000.* Bern: Haupt.

Piesse, Louis. 1862. *Itinéraire historique et descriptif de l'Algérie, comprenant le Tell et le Sahara (Collection des guides-Joanne.* Paris: L. Hachette.

Planel, Anne-Marie. 2000. "De la nation à la colonie: La communauté française de Tunisie au XIXème siècle d'aprés les archives civiles et notariées du consulat général de France à Tunis." 3 vols. Doctorat d'état, École des hautes etudes en sciences sociales, Paris.

"Plus qu'un symbole." 1991. *El Moudjahid,* 17 Oct.

"La polémique enfle sur la commémoration du 17 octobre 1961." 2001. *Le Monde,* 15 Oct.

Poniatowska, Elena. 1995. *Nothing, Nobody: The Voices of the Mexico City Earthquake.* Translated by Aurora Camacho de Schmidt and Arthur Schmidt. Philadelphia: Temple Univ. Press.

Pratt, Mary Louise. 1992. *Imperial Eyes: Travel Writing and Transculturation.* London: Routledge.

Prax, Lt. 1847. "Le commerce de Tunis avec l'intérieur de l'Afrique." F80 1697, Centre des Archives d'outre-mer, Aix-en-Provence, France.

"La première fête du Centenaire de l'Algérie à Paris." 1930. *Afrique du Nord illustrée,* 3 May.

Presse et mémoire: France des étrangers, Frances des libertés. 1990. Paris: Mémoire générique and Éditions ouvrières.

"Problèmes posés par les harkis au moment du cessez-feu." 1961. 14 Dec. 1 H 1397/D8. Service historique de l'armée de terre, Vincennes, France.

Le procès de Maurice Papon 8 octobre 1997–8 janvier 1998. 1998. 2 vols. Paris: Albin Michel.

Prochaska, David. 2003. "That Was Then, This is Now: *The Battle of Algiers* and After." *Radical History Review* 85: 133–49.

———. [1990] 2004. *Making Algeria French: Colonialism in Bône, 1870–1920.* Cambridge: Cambridge Univ. Press.

"Prospectus." 1845. *La France algérienne,* 19 Feb.

"Prospectus." 1855. *Bulletin de l'Algérie.*

Pyenson, Lewis. 1993. *Civilizing Mission: Exact Sciences and French Overseas Expansion, 1830–1940.* Baltimore: Johns Hopkins Univ. Press.

"La question indigène: Electeurs et eligibles." 1919. *L'echo d'Alger,* 16 Feb.

"La question indigène: Heur statut personnel." 1919. *L'echo d'Alger,* 16 Mar.

Quotidien d'Oran (newspaper). 2001. 4 Oct.

Radio program. 1981. 880163/2. Archives nationales, Paris.

Radstone, Susannah, ed. 2000. *Memory and Methodology.* New York: Berg.

Randau, Robert. 1929. "La littérature coloniale, hier et aujourd'hui." *Revue des deux mondes* (15 July): 416–34.

"Rapport pour la création d'un centre national de l'histoire et des cultures de l'immigration." 2001. *Migrance* 19: 4.

Rauch, André. 1992. *Boxe, violence du XXème siècle.* Paris: Aubier.

Redon, J. Robert de. 1930. "Les sportifs algérois grossièrement insultés." *Echo des sports nord-africains* (2 Oct.): 1.

Renan, Ernest. [1882] 1999. "What Is a Nation?" In *Nation and Narration,* edited by Homi Bhabha, 8–22. London: Routledge.

Report by secrétariat d'état aux rapatriés. 1984. 21 June. 870444/10. Archives nationales, Paris.

Reseignements généraux (RG). 1962a. Direction centrale des Renseignements généraux; Dir. Gén. de la Police nationale; Ministère de l'intérieur. "Sommaire générale. 9 April 196." 800280. Article 216: 2. Centre des Archives contemporaines, Archives nationales, Paris.

———. 1962b. Direction centrale des Renseignements généraux; Dir. Gén. de la Police nationale; Ministère de l'intérieur. "Sommaire Générale. 18 April 1962." 800280. Article 216: 1. Centre des Archives contemporaines, Archives nationales, Paris.

———. 1962c. Direction centrale des Renseignements généraux; Dir. Gén. de la Police nationale; Ministère de l'intérieur. "Sommaire Générale (Paris, 27 June 1962)." 800280. Article 218. Centre des Archives contemporaines, Archives nationales, Paris.

———. 1963. Direction générale de la sûreté nationale; Ministère de l'intérieur. "Bibliographie de la guerre d'Algerie." *Bulletin de documentation de la direction des Renseignements generaux* 84. F/7/15581. Archives nationales, Paris.

"Résolution du Conseil National de l'O.N.M." 1991. *Horizons,* 17 Oct.

Ricoeur, Paul. 2000. *La mémoire, l'histoire et l'oubli.* Paris: Éditions du Seuil.

Ridha, Rachid. 1922. *La faillite morale de la politique occidentale en Orient.* N.p: n.p.

Rioux, Jean-Pierre, ed. 1990. *La guerre d'Algérie et les Français.* Paris: Fayard.

———. 1995. "Trous de mémoire.' *Télérama hors série* 90.

———. 1996. "A quoi servent les cours d'histoire?' *L'histoire* 202 (Sept.): 49–50.

———. 2000. Interview by Jo McCormack. France, Feb.

Roberts, Hugh. 1997. "The Image of the French Army in the Cinematic Representation of the Algerian War: The Revolutionary Politics of *The Battle of Algiers.*" *Journal of Algerian Studies* 2: 90–99.

———. 2002. *Commanding Disorder: Military Power and Informal Politics in Algeria.* London: I. B. Tauris.

Roberts, Stephen H. 1929. *The History of French Colonial Policy, 1870–1925.* London: P. S. King and Son.

Ross, Kristen. 1995. *Fast Cars, Clean Bodies: Decolonization and the Reordering of French Culture.* Cambridge, Mass.: MIT Press.

Roüan, Brigitte. 1992. *Outre-mer* (film). Paris: Canal+.

Roussel, Eric. 1999. "Quand la guerre d'Algérie se faisait à Paris." *Figaro,* 18 Nov.

Rousso, Henry. 1990. *Le syndrome de Vichy.* Paris: Éditions du Seuil.

———. [1991] 1994. *The Vichy Syndrome: History and Memory in France since 1944.* Translated by Arthur Goldhammer. Cambridge, Mass.: Harvard Univ. Press.

Roux, Michel. 1990. "Le poids de l'histoire." *Hommes et migrations* 1135: 21–27.

———. 1991. *Les harkis, les oubliés de l'histoire.* Paris: Découverte.

Rozet, Georges. 1911. *La défense et illustration de la race française.* Paris: F. Alcan.

Ruedy, John. 1992. *Modern Algeria: The Origins and Development of a Nation.* Bloomington: Univ. of Indiana Press.

Said, Edward W. 1978. *Orientalism.* New York: Random House.

Sarte, Jean Paul. [1963] 1991. Preface to *The Wretched of the Earth,* by Frantz Fanon, translated by Constance Farrington, 7–31. Paris: Présence Africaine; reprint, Paris: Éditions Gallimard.

Sayad, Abdelmalek. 1975. "El Ghorba: Le mécanisme de reproduction de l'émigration." *Actes de la recherche en sciences sociales* 2 (Mar.): 50–66.

———. 1977. "Les trois 'âges' de l'émigration algérienne en France." *Actes de la recherche en sciences sociales* 5 (June): 59–79.

Schalk, David L. 1998. "*Reflections d'outre-mer* on French Colonialism." *Journal of European Studies* 28, nos. 1–2: 5–24.

———. 1999. "Has France's Marrying Her Century Cured the Algerian Syndrome?" *Historical Reflections/Réflexions historiques* 2, no. 1: 149–64.

Schor, Naomi. 1995. "French Feminism Is a Universalism." *Differences: A Journal of Feminist Cultural Studies* 7, no. 1: 15–46.

Schwarzfuchs, Simon. 1980. "Colonialisme français et colonialisme juif en Algérie (1830–1845)." In *Judaisme d'Afrique du Nord aux XIXe-XXe siècles,* edited by Michel Abitbol. Jerusalem: Institut Ben-Zvi.

———. 1981. *Les juifs d'Algérie et la France: 1830–1855.* Jerusalem: Institut Ben-Zvi.

Schwebel to Raffo. 1836. Tunis, 13 Sept. Série H, carton 206, dossier 84, armoire 21, Archives nationales de Tunisie, Tunis.

Sebag, Paul. 1991. *Histoire des juifs de Tunisie: Des origines à nos jours.* Paris: L'Harmattan.

———. 1998. *Tunis: Histoire d'une ville.* Paris: L'Harmattan.

Sebbar, Leïla. 1982. *Shérazade, brune, frisée, les yeux verts.* Paris: Stock.

———. 1999. *La Seine était rouge.* Paris: Thierry Magnier.

Sénanès, Amram. 1848. To directeur des affaires civiles. 29 Mar. Carton 3/U1, folder "1847–1848." Centre des Archives d'outre-mer, Aix-en-Provence, France.

Serafino, Col. 1962. Etat-Major 2è Bureau; General de division Ducornau, Région Territoriale et Corps d'Armée de Constantine. "Bulletin de renseignement hebdomadaire. Semaine du 1 au 8 avril 1962. n. 618 CAC/2/INT-S." 1H/2836/3. Service historique de l'armée de Terre, Vincennes, France.

Servier, André. 1923. *L'Islam et la psychologie du musulman.* Preface by L. Bertrand. Paris: Challamel.

"La seule garanté" (editorial). 1962. *Paris-Match* 673 (3 Mar.): 27.

Shaw, Christopher, and Malcolm Chase, eds. 1989. *The Imagined Past.* Manchester: Manchester Univ. Press.

Shepard, Todd. 2002. "Inventing Decolonization: The End of French Algeria and the Remaking of France." Ph.D. diss., Rutgers Univ.

Sherman, Daniel. 2000. "The Arts and Sciences of Colonialism." *French Historical Studies* 23, no. 4 (fall): 707–39.

Shohat, Ella, and Robert Stam. 1994. *Unthinking Eurocentrism: Multiculturalism and the Media.* New York: Routledge.

Siblot, Paul. 1985. "Retours à 'l'Algérie heureuse' ou les mille et un détours de la nostalgie." In *Le Maghreb dans l'imaginaire français: La colonie, le désert, l'exil,* edited by Jean-Robert Henry, 151–64. Saint-étienne, France: Edisud.

Sicard, Christian. 1998. *La Kabylie en feu: Algérie, 1871.* Paris: Actes sud.

Sinha, Mrinalini. 1995. *Colonial Masculinity: The "Manly Englishman" and the*

"Effeminate Bengali" in the Late Nineteenth Century. Manchester: Manchester Univ. Press.

Sivan, Emmanuel. 1976. *Communisme et nationalisme en Algérie 1920–1962.* Paris: Fondation nationale des sciences politiques.

———. 1979. "Colonialism and Popular Culture in Algeria." *Journal of Contemporary History* 14, no. 1: 21–53.

Smith, Charles D. 2004. "What Instructing US Military Interrogators Taught Me." *Daily Star (Beirut),* 11 May.

Smith, Kimberly. 2000. "Mere Nostalgia: Notes on a Progressive Paratheory." *Rhetoric and Public Affairs* 3, no. 4: 505–27.

Solinas, Pier-Nico, ed. 1973. *Gillo Pontecorvo's* The Battle of Algiers. New York: Scribners.

Sontag, Susan. 2004a. "Regarding the Torture of Others." *New York Times Magazine* (23 May): 24–29, 42.

———. 2004b. "What Have We Done?" *The Guardian,* 24 May.

Souaïdia, Habib. 2001. *La sale guerre: Le témoignage d'un ancien officier des forces spéciales de l'armée algérienne.* Paris: Découverte.

Spicer, Nick. 2002. Interview. *Morning Edition,* National Public Radio, 26 Apr.

Spivak, Gayatri Chakravorty. 1974. Preface to *Of Grammatology* by Jacques Derrida, translated by Gayatri Chakravorty Spivak, ix-xc. Baltimore: Johns Hopkins Univ. Press.

Stauth, Georg, and Bryan Turner. 1988. "Nostalgia, Postmodernism, and the Critique of Mass Culture." *Theory, Culture, and Society* 5: 509–26.

Stein, Sylviane. 1992. "Soirs de 'nostalgérie.' " *L'Express* 31: 34–35.

Stoler, Ann Laura. 1995. *Race and the Education of Desire.* Durham, N.C.: Duke Univ. Press.

Stone, Martin. 1997. *The Agony of Algeria.* New York: Columbia Univ. Press.

Stora, Benjamin. 1986. "Faiblesse paysanne du Mouvement nationaliste algérien avant 1954." *Vingtième siècle* 12: 59–72.

———. 1989. *Les sources du nationalisme Algérien.* Paris: L'Harmattan.

———. 1991. *Histoire de l'Algérie coloniale (1830–1954).* Paris: Découverte.

———. 1992a. *Les années algériennes* (film). Paris: France 2.

———. 1992b. *Ils venaient d'Algérie: L'immigration algérienne en France.* Paris: Fayard.

———. 1992c. "Indochine, Algérie, autorisations de retour." *Libération,* 30 Apr.–1 May.

———. 1993. "Immigrants and Political Activists: Algerian Activists in France, 1945–1954." In *French and Algerian Identities from Colonial Times to the Present,* edited by Alec G. Hargreaves and Michael J. Heffernan, 39–75. Lewiston, N.Y.: Edwin Mellen Press.

———. 1994. "La guerre d'Algérie quarante ans après: Connaissances et reconnaissance." *Modern and Contemporary France* 2: 131–39.

———. 1995. "Deuxième guerre algérienne? Les habits anciens des combattants." *Les temps modernes* 580: 242–61.

———. 1997. *Imaginaires de guerre: Algérie-Viêt-nam, en France et aux Etats-Unis.* Paris: Découverte.

———. [1991] 1998. *La gangrène et l'oubli: La mémoire de la guerre d'Algérie.* Paris: Découverte.

———. 1999. *Le transfert d'une mémoire: De "l'Algérie française" au racisme anti-arabe.* Paris: Découverte.

———. 2001. *Algeria, 1830–2000: A Short History.* Translated by Jane Marie Todd. Ithaca, N.Y.: Cornell Univ. Press.

———. 2002. "Algérie: Les retours de la mémoire de la guerre d'indépendance." *Modern and Contemporary France* 10: 461–73.

["Succès du centenaire"] (editorial). 1930. *Presse libre,* 7 May.

Talbott, John. 1980. *The War Without a Name, France in Algeria 1954–1962.* London: Faber and Faber.

Tapiéro, Norbet. 1978. *Manuel d'Arabe algérien moderne.* 2d ed. Paris: Librairie C. Klisksieck.

Tavernier, Bernard, and Patrick Rotman. 1992. *La guerre sans nom* (film). Paris: Canal+.

Temine, Émile. 1987. "La migration européenne en Algérie au XIXe siècle: Migration organisée ou migration tolérée?" *Revue de l'Occident musulman et de la Méditerrannée* 43: 31–45.

Ternisien, X. 2000. "Le Haut conseil à l'intégration (HCI) dresse un état des lieux de l'Islam en France." *Le monde hebdomadaire* (23 Dec.): 10.

Thibaudat, Jean-Pierre. 2001. "Deux gardiens de la mémoire au placard." *Libération,* 1 June.

Thobie, Jacques. 1991. *La France coloniale de 1870 à 1914.* Paris: Armand Colin.

Thomas, Martin. 2000. *The French North African Crisis: Colonial Breakdown and Anglo-French Relations 1945–1962.* London: MacMillan.

Tocqueville, Alexis de. 2001. *Writings on Empire and Slavery.* Edited and translated by Jennifer Pitts. Baltimore: Johns Hopkins Univ. Press.

Toumi, Alek Baylee. 2001. *Taxieur: La libération miracu(ri/)euse de J P Sartre.* In *Nouveau théâtre algérien,* 5–75. Paris: Marsa.

———. [1996] 2003. *Madah-Sartre: Le kidnapping, jugement et conver(sa)s/tion de Jean-Paul Sartre et de Simone de Beauvoir mis en scène par les islamistes du Groupe international armé. Algérie littérature/action* 6 (Dec.): 5–96.

———. 2004. *Albert Camus: Entre la mère et l'injustice.* In *Albert Camus et les écritures algériens: Quelles traces?* edited by Collque Lourmarin, 143–78. Aix-en-Provence, France: Éditions Edisud.

———. 2005. *De Beauvoir a beau voile.* Paris: Marsa.

Tristan, Anne. 1991. *Le silence du fleuve.* Paris: Au nom de la mémoire.

Tuquoi, Jean Pierre. 2000. "A Verdun, l'hommage d'un président aux Algériens morts pour la France." *Le Monde,* 18 June.

Turner, Bryan. 1987. "A Note on Nostalgia." *Theory, Culture, and Society* 4: 147–56.

Univers Israélite (journal). 1843–44. Vol. 1.

———. 1844–45. Vol. 1.

Urry, John. 1990. *The Tourist Gaze: Leisure and Travel in Contemporary Societies.* London: Sage.

Vaincre l'oubli (television program). 1985. 880163/1. Archives nationales, Paris.

Vallory, Louise [Louise Mesnier]. 1863. *A l'aventure en Algérie.* Paris: J. Hetzel.

Vassel, E. 1909. "Un précurseur, l'abbé Bourgade." *Revue tunisienne* 20: 107–15.

Vatin, Jean-Claude. 1974. *L'Algérie politique: Histoire et société.* Paris: Armand Colin.

Verdès-Leroux, Jeannine. 2001. *Les Français d'Algérie de 1830 à aujourd'hui: Une page d'histoire déchirée.* Paris: Fayard.

Vergès, Jacques, and Georges Arnaud. 1957. *Pour Djemila Bouhired.* Paris: Minuit.

La Vérité. 1848. 17 Apr.

Versteegh, Kees. 1997. *The Arabic Language.* Edinburgh: Edinburgh Univ. Press.

Vidal-Naquet, Pierre. 1989. *L'affaire Audin (1957–1978).* Paris: Minuit.

La vie ouvrière (Algerian newspaper). 1954. Various editions, 14 Sept.–18 Oct., 23–29 Nov.

Viet, Vincent. 1998. *La France immigrée.* Paris: Fayard.

Vircondelet, Alain. 1997. "Le retour des sources." In *Une enfance algérienne,* edited by Leïla Sebbar, 229–43. Paris: Gallimard.

La voix du peuple 1933–34. Various, 17 Nov. 1933, 12 Jan. 1934.

Weiland, Baruch. 1837. To ministre des religions. 28 Nov. F19 11015, Archives nationales, Paris.

Windler, Christian. 2002. *La diplomatie comme expérience de l'autre: Consuls français au Maghreb (1700–1840).* Geneva: Droz.

Wood, Richard. 1866. British consul to French consul, Duchene de Bellecourt, 23 Aug. Carton 382, Archives diplomatiques d'outre-mer de Nantes.

Woodhull, Winnifred. 1993. *Transfigurations of the Maghreb: Feminism, Decolonization, and Literatures.* Minneapolis: Univ. of Minnesota Press.

Wright, Gwendolyn. 1991. *The Politics of Design in French Colonial Urbanism.* Chicago: Univ. of Chicago Press.

Yacono, Xavier. 1982. "Les pertes algériennes de 1954 à 1962." *Revue de l'Occident musulman et de la Mediterranée* 34, no. 2: 119–34.

Yous, Nesroulah. 2000. *Qui a tué à Bentalha?* Paris: Découverte.

Yushmanov, N. V. 1961. *The Struggle of the Arabic Language.* Washington, D.C.: Center for Applied Linguists, Modern Language Association.

Zappi, S. 2001. "M. Chirac exprime 'la reconnaissance de la nation' aux combattants harkis." *Le Monde,* 27 Sept.

Zehar, Aïssa. 1942. *Hind à l'ame pure ou l'histoire d'une mere.* Algiers: Baconnier.

Zenati, Rabah. 1930. Editorial. *La voix indigène,* 17 July.
——— [as Hassan]. 1938a. *Comment périra l'Algérie française.* Constantine, Algeria: Éditions Attali.
———. 1938b. *Le problème algérien vu par un indigène.* Paris: Publications du Comité de l'Afrique française.
Zenati, Rabah, and Akli Zenati. 1945. *Bou-el-Nouar, le jeune Algérien.* Algiers: Maison de livres.
Zimra, Clarisse. 1995. "Disorienting the Subject in Djebar's *L'amour la fantasia.*" *Yale French Studies* 87: 149–70.

Index